God's Surprising Way

The Path to Lasting Joy, Healing, and Love

The One who dwells in the High and Holy place is also the One who is pleased to dwell with the contrite and humble! This is our God! He is the God who mystifies us. In the book, "*God's Surprising Way*", Jeyran Main gives us a clear and powerful reminder of God's wisdom that confounds the wisdom of this world. His ways are often counterintuitive to ours. Humility produces greatness, weakness produces strength and death brings life! This book is a much-needed reminder that the Kingdom of our God is an upside-down Kingdom and that we can once again find great joy and delight in God's surprising ways!

- Rick Dressler, Sr. Pastor Maple City Baptist Church

"God's Surprising Way" is an inspiring journey into the upside-down kingdom of God — a book that reveals how true power is made known through humility, service, and love. I hope every reader not only gains from its deep insight but also, through small steps of humility and service, experiences God's joy and love in daily life — the very path I consider the most precious message of this book.

- Amir Hassanpour, Pastor Standing in Christ

I've enjoyed what I've read so far more than I anticipated. You have fresh eyes for things I've taken for granted.

- Dan Christiaans, Pastor Maple City Baptist Church

Jeyran Main is an outstanding author with devout faith. Her book God's Surprising Way is a delight to read. Even as a layperson, she writes like a biblical scholar, infusing her book with many useful Scriptural references and quotes by the Church Fathers along with medieval, Reformation, and modern theologians. This book demonstrates the value of practical theology. I highly recommend it.

- Rev. Dr. Victor Lujetic, BA, MDiv, DMin, PhD, Retired Baptist Pastor, Canadian Baptists of Ontario and Quebec

God's Surprising Way

The Path to Lasting Joy, Healing, and Love

Jeyran Main

Review Tales Publishing & Editing Services

God's Surprising Way: The Path to Lasting Joy, Healing, and Love
© 2026 by Jeyran Main

All rights reserved. No part of this book may be reproduced, stored in a retrieval system, or transmitted in any form or by any means—electronic, mechanical, photocopying, recording, scanning, or otherwise—except for brief quotations used in critical reviews, articles, or devotional studies, without the prior written permission of the publisher.
Published in the United States of America by Review Tales Publishing & Editing Services. This book may be purchased in bulk for educational, business, fundraising, or promotional use. For information, please email:
Jeyran.main@gmail.com
All Scripture quotations in this book, unless otherwise noted, are taken from the New King James Version (NKJV).

ISBN (Hardcover): 978-1-988680-84-2
ISBN (Paperback): 978-1-988680-86-6
ISBN (Digital): 978-1-988680-85-9

The information in this book is intended for devotional, inspirational, and educational purposes only.
Printed in the United States of America

To Zakaria, Elijah, and Amina

Your laughter, wonder, and love remind me each day that God's surprising way is already alive in the simplest moments.
May this book be a reflection of the healing, joy, and lasting love you inspire in me, and a reminder that the path of Christ is never without beauty, hope, and transformation.

"For the Lord reverses the ways of the world, lifting the lowly and humbling the proud."

—Inspired by Luke 1:52

Contents

Contents XIII

Preface XVII

Acknowledgement XXI

Introduction XXIII

Chapter One: The Last Will Be First, And The First Will Be Last 1
- CONFRONTING Human Expectations 7
- Healing In God's Reversals 17
- Love As The Fruit Of Being Last 22
- Biblical Anchors 27
- Theological Witnesses 31
- Living The Reversal Today 36

Chapter Two: The Gentle Heart Of Jesus 45
- The Reversal Of Power 45
- Old Testament Roots 50
- Gentleness In The Life Of Christ 55
- Healing Through Gentleness 60
- Joy In Gentleness 65
- Love Expressed In Gentleness 69
- Theological Voices 74
- Practicing Gentleness Today 80

Chapter Three: I Am 89
- The Reversal Revealed 89
- God's Name In The Old Testament 95
- Jesus' "I Am" Sayings 101
- The Paradox Of The Eternal Word In Flesh 108
- Healing Through The Presence Of "I Am" 113

    Joy In The God Who Is 118
    Love As The Overflow Of "I Am" 124
    Living With The "I Am" Today.. 129

Chapter Four: Because He Is – I Am 137

    The Reversal Of Identity 137
    Identity In Christ.. 142
    Christ The Ground Of Our Being 147
    Freedom From Performance And Comparison 154
    Joy In Belonging To Christ.. 157
    Love Flowing From Identity 162
    Biblical Anchors... 167
    Living As Children Of God 172

Chapter Five: What We Are Called To Do 181

    Following Jesus In Practice 187
    Healing In Obedience.. 196
    Joy In God's Mission 202
    Love As The Fruit Of Vocation 207
    Theological Insights 212
    Living Out Our Calling Today 217

Chapter Six: Living In Surprise 229

    Joy In The Surprising Ways Of God 238
    Love Flourishing In Surprising Contexts 249
    Biblical Anchors Of Surprise... 255
    Theological Reflections... 260
    Living In Surprise Daily.. 266

Chapter Seven: The Power Of The Cross...................................... 277

    Biblical Witness To The Cross 283
    Healing Through The Cross 288
    Joy In The Cross 294
    Love Demonstrated In Sacrifice.. 299
    Theological Reflections... 305
    Living The Cross Today 310

Chapter Eight: The Spirit Of Work In Us 325
- Biblical Work Of The Spirit 330
- Healing Through The Spirit 336
- Joy In Spirit-Filled Living 342
- Love Expressed Through The Spirit 348
- Theological Reflections 353
- Living Spirit-Filled Lives Today 359

Chapter Nine: The Coming Kingdom 373
- Biblical Promises Of The Kingdom 379
- Joy In Anticipation 385
- Healing In Kingdom Perspective 391
- Theological Reflections 401
- Living Kingdom Values Today 406

Chapter Ten: Living As People Of The Great Surprise 421
- The Reversal In Daily Life 421
- Embracing Christ's Example 427
- Joy In Everyday Discipleship 433
- Healing Through Kingdom Living 438
- Healing Wounds Through Forgiveness And Patience 442
- Love As The Defining Mark 444
- Biblical Anchors 450
- Theological Reflections 456
- Practicing The Great Surprise Today 463

References/Bibliography 471

Preface

Christianity is almost entirely a story of reversal. The Kingdom of God unfolds not in the steps or patterns of human power, prestige, or achievement, but in ways that reverse expectations. From the very beginning of the gospel story, with Jesus' birth in a stable, His cruel death on a cross, and His triumphant resurrection from the tomb, God chose the weak, the hidden, and the foolish to reveal His glory. The story of salvation is a story of surprise—a story that defies human logic, yet holds out the hope of eternity.

When Jesus walked the earth, those who listened to Him were often shocked by His teachings. "The last will be first, and the first last" (Matt. 20:16). "Blessed are the poor in spirit" (Matt. 5:3). "Whoever desires to become great among you, let him be your servant" (Matt. 20:26). Each declaration seemed to turn the world upside down. Yet in the wisdom of God, it was not upside down, it was right side up—the way that creation was intended to be. To Israel, God chose those considered unworthy—those ignored, those sidelined by history, those diminished by hardship—for honour, for blessing, for purpose in God's plan.

This book was inspired by the desire to explore these surprising ways of God. Many have explored the great reversals of the gospel—eternally a source of existential wonder. Martin Luther introduced the "theology of the cross," establishing the premise that God's most profound revelation of Himself occurs in suffering and weakness (Luther 1520, 36). Thomas à Kempis called Christians to quiet service, reminding us that spiritual greatness is measured by humility (à Kempis 1425, 88). Henri Nouwen called the church to embrace the "downward mobility" of Christ. True spiritual authority flows not from awing others, but from surrendering to God (Nouwen 1981, 61). These voices from across the centuries reaffirm the upside-down kingdom of God, which does not align with worldly expectations but does provide for life, joy, and love.

These divine reversals are not only theological abstractions; they are eminently practical. How does the good news of these surprises impact our lives now? How do we, as contemporary followers of Jesus, live from the joy, healing, and love derived from the kingdom? The kingdom of God not only engages our intellect (as crucial as that is), but it also transforms our affections and relationships, and ultimately, our decisions each day. The way of Jesus, opposite the natural inclination of our flesh, is a place of true flourishing. This flourishing stands in stark contrast to a world system that seeks to seduce minds through competition, power, and control but offers a different path built around humility, service, and extravagant love.

Think about Joseph. His brothers betrayed him and sold him into slavery. Nevertheless, God's plan has unfolded in ways that have inverted expectation: "You intended it for evil, but God intended it for good" (Gen. 50:20). The last - Joseph in the pit - has become first, as he rules over Egypt, saving nations from famine. Similarly, David, the least likely son of Jesse, was secretly anointed to become Israel's greatest king (1 Sam. 16:11-13). Even the shepherds at Christ's birth, the lowliest and most disenfranchised, were the first to receive the angelic announcement of the Messiah (Luke 2:8-12). These accounts remind us that God's methods of selection, blessing, and honor often jolt us from our expectations.

In the chapters that follow, we will consider the contradictory nature of faith as understood in the Christian tradition. We will see greatness found through servanthood, gentleness exemplifying true power, identity expressed not through self-assertion but through our union with Christ, and ultimate victory often found in apparent defeat. We will take the time to listen closely to Scripture and walk alongside the voices of saints and scholars from the past, including Augustine, Aquinas, Luther, Calvin, Edwards, Owen, Stott, Bonhoeffer, Wright, and Nouwen. Their great thoughts can shed light on the surprising ways of God, so we can hear the word with fresh ears and apply it vitally in our own lives.

However, what is presented to you is a series of abstractions with which to engage. Each chapter is meant to be lived. Humility can heal pride, envy, and the desire for comparison. Gentleness can mend broken relationships and foster reconciliation. The cross can liberate us from guilt and shame, while the invisible work of the Spirit can fill our ordinary days with great joy. The promise of the coming kingdom can keep our lives anchored in hope, even as the world around us shuffles on in instability, confusion, or injustice.

Living in the upside-down kingdom is often challenging. Following Jesus pushes us to rethink our assumptions, to reorder our values, even to let go of what we hold tightly - control, recognition, self-sufficiency - and to let God give us the things that He loves to provide us with: joy that cannot be taken, healing that touches our deepest places, and love that can overflow to others. The decisions we make each day become the means by which God's reversal can shine through: granting forgiveness to enemies, putting the overlooked in a place of importance, serving in quiet ways, and trusting Him with outcomes beyond our control.

So, I invite you to read not just with your mind, but with your whole being. Approach each chapter with an open mind to God's Spirit. Allow the Scriptures to speak. Allow the wisdom of the church to inspire, provoke, and stretch you. And, above all, allow Jesus Himself - the Great Surprise - to invite you into the life of the kingdom. God's ways are not what we expect, but they are invariably better than anything we could ever conceive.

It is with this hope that this book shows you the upside-down kingdom to be the true reality. May it bring you long-lasting joy, healing, and love in and through Christ. And may you find, as so many others have, that God's surprising way is truly the only way to life.

—Jeyran Main

Family Day, 2025

Acknowledgement

This book would not have been possible without the love, encouragement, and support of so many faithful people who have walked with me on my journey.

To my friends, whose presence has been a constant source of inspiration and joy—thank you for the meaningful conversations, Bible studies, and countless moments of fellowship that shaped my understanding and lifted me more times than I can count.

I am especially grateful to Effie, whose patience, wisdom, and guidance have been unwavering. Whenever I was unsure or needed clarity, she reminded me of what truly matters and gently pointed me toward hope. Her kindness and support have left a lasting mark on both my life and this book.

I also wish to acknowledge the guidance and encouragement of Pastor Dan, Pastor Rick, Pastor Andrew, and the Maple City Baptist Church community. Your teaching, example, and dedication have deeply influenced my reflections, and your generosity of spirit has been a steady reminder of what it means to live faithfully.

I am also indebted to the many writers and scholars whose work has illuminated my understanding. J.I. Packer, John MacArthur, Dane Ortlund, and so many others inspired me with their clarity and devotion. Their words stirred reflection, prayer, and deeper devotion, becoming building blocks for these chapters.

To my family, who nurtured me with love and example—your encouragement has given me the strength to persevere, and I am deeply grateful.

Finally, I give thanks for the One whose love is the source of all healing, joy, and peace. It is my hope that every page of this book reflects even a glimpse of that lasting love.

To all of you, I offer my deepest gratitude.

Introduction

The Upside-Down Kingdom

Christianity begins with surprise! From the moment the Word became flesh, God has been showing us that His ways are not our ways. He made incarnate the Savior, not in a palace but in a stable. He was welcomed by shepherds first, the lowly, marginalized outcasts of society (Luke 2:8–12). Jesus continued to reverse our expectations throughout his life. He taught everyone that the last would be first, and the first last (Matthew 20:16), that the meek would inherit the earth (Matthew 5:5), and that greatness was about servanthood, not privilege or authority (Matthew 20:26–27). Everywhere he went, the crowds were astonished—they were forced to recalibrate their understanding of power, privilege, and God's blessing.

This reversibility, what some have called the upside-down kingdom, is key to understanding the surprising way of God. Where we see strength, control, and recognition, He delights in lifting the humble, exalting the meek, and blessing the poor in spirit. This is what Augustine means when he observes, "In the wisdom of God, they are overturned, and what seemed to be less is more weighty than it seemed in the world" (Augustine 1998, 54). This is often the counterfactual logic of the kingdom: surrender as a means of power, weakness as a source of strength, and service as a path to greatness.

The scriptures are replete with examples of reversibility. Joseph is sold into slavery by his brothers, and ultimately rules nations and saves them from famine (Genesis 50:20). David, the youngest and least regarded son of Jesse, becomes the greatest king of Israel (1 Samuel 16:11–13). The disciples, though zealously devoted to Jesus, have to learn that glory comes through humility, self-denial, and love for others (Mark 10:42–45). Jesus Himself modelled the supreme example; the Son of God, made majesty incarnate, suffers and dies, allowing defeat to become eternal victory.

Inviting us into the upside-down kingdom is more than a theological concept; it also shapes how we perceive our lives today. Our human assumptions—about success, happiness, and significance—are misguided. While learning to honour God's surprising way, we see that consideration for a fleeting bit of favour from others gives way to joy, that surrender to God's will yields health, and that loving others sacrificially through humble service changes relationships.

The upside-down kingdom is an invitation to see the world through God's eyes—a way to fulfill what Jesus says; a way where "the last are first," the "lowly are received" and "the hidden thing of love and service" is of eternal weight. The Paradox of Joy, Healing, and Love

In the upside-down kingdom, joy, healing, and love often appear to be contrary to human expectations. True joy is not the product of achievement, recognition, or comfort; healing is not always immediate; and love is rarely transactional. Instead, the Christian life invites believers into a paradox: the more we surrender, serve, and humble ourselves, the more these blessings flow into our lives.

Jesus captures this dynamic in the Beatitudes, declaring, "Blessed are those who mourn, for they shall be comforted" (Matthew 5:4) and "Blessed are the meek, for they shall inherit the earth" (Matthew 5:5). At first glance, these promises seem upside down: mourning is not usually associated with comfort, and meekness rarely leads to inheritance. Yet Christ reframes human experience by grounding joy, healing, and love in God's character and purposes. By letting go of pride and self-reliance, believers open themselves to God's transformative presence (Augustine 1998, 72).

The parables of Jesus illustrate these principles. In the story of the lost sheep, the shepherd rejoices over the one found, highlighting that God's joy is relational and restorative (Luke 15:4–7). Similarly, the parable of the prodigal son demonstrates that love often precedes merit: the father restores the wayward son, celebrating his return rather than condemning his failings (Luke 15:11–32). These narratives show that God's approach subverts human expectations, creating spaces where joy, healing, and love coexist with brokenness and humility (Nouwen 1981, 52).

Historical theologians have reflected on this paradox. Augustine notes that "joy is the reflection of God's eternal delight within the soul, not the applause of men" (Augustine 1998, 72). Bonhoeffer emphasizes that discipleship requires surrender: joy and peace emerge not in controlling life, but in trusting God even amid suffering (Bonhoeffer 1959, 112). Nouwen extends the idea into relational terms: when we embrace vulnerability and minister from our wounds, healing flows both inwardly and outwardly (Nouwen 1981, 52). Together, these voices remind us that the kingdom's blessings are cultivated in hearts surrendered to God's reversal of worldly values.

Practically, living this paradox involves embracing small, intentional acts of faithfulness. Choosing to forgive a persistent offense, offering service without recognition, or loving those society deems unworthy cultivates resilient joy, deep healing, and love that endures. Paul exhorts, "Be kindly affectionate to one another with brotherly love, in honor giving preference to one another" (Romans 12:10). When we act according to God's upside-down principles, we participate in the tangible expression of the kingdom, where the last are lifted, the humble are exalted, and the surrendered heart is filled with grace (Packer 1973, 215).

The story of Joseph illustrates the paradox of God's kingdom. Betrayed, imprisoned, and overlooked, Joseph experienced pain and injustice, yet God's providence turned his suffering into a means of salvation for many (Genesis 50:20; Owen 1677, 121). Similarly, David, overlooked as the youngest son, was raised to kingship according to God's plan (1 Samuel 16:11–13). In both cases, joy and love were inseparable from humility and trust, while healing emerged through God's providence.

The paradox of joy, healing, and love challenges human intuition but aligns with divine order. Living these truths requires surrender, humility, and attentiveness to God's ways. Each act of humility or service becomes a conduit for divine joy, a channel for healing, and an expression of love, reflecting the radical, surprising ways of God's kingdom in everyday life.

Historical and Theological Perspectives

Over human history, God's unexpected manner of "being" has intrigued theologians, scholars, and spiritual advisors, and all have shown how the paradox of the upside-down kingdom abounds. From the earliest church fathers to the present day, a common motif has been evident: God continually lifts the lowly, strengthens the weak, and displays glory through the lowly and the foolish, as measured by the world. The historical and theological events serve to foster a deeper understanding of the divine nature of reversal and its important daily implications for us all.

Augustine of Hippo writes that human calculus is often bewildered by divine logic: "It is evident that the providential ordering of the Father often works in reverse of our anticipations, and at no point more conspicuously than in the matters of the world. The foolish and the wise are often but one degree apart, yet when God observes humility, and works through oxen, beggars, a mound of gold, or a loaf of bread, we soon arise to find a door opened into the divine" (Augustine 1998, 54). Augustine's pondering on lowly humility, ordination, and grace expresses the uniquely Christian conviction that joy, relief, and love "cultivate" not worldly successes and positional power, but rather God's fostering in creating a flourishing planet. Origen also makes the point that often, the deeper meaning of Scripture emerges from its paradoxes, teaching us that the human life of prayer and spirituality is intensified through the paradoxes that appear contrary to the work of the human mind (Origen 1994, 73). In these earliest of voices, we can already recognize the pattern: the kingdom of God subverts the human ambition and arrogance implicit in reason and rationale found in nature and experience.

In the medieval era, Thomas Aquinas demonstrates how reason and revelation converge to reveal God's revelation. In *Summa Theologica*, he asserts that authentic power refers to power exercised in accordance with God's ordering of things, not for self-gain or advantage, and that true greatness comes from humility and virtue (Aquinas [1274] 1947, II–II, q. 162). Bonaventure likewise reflects on Christ's humility as the model for spiritual elevation. That joy and true alteration come through surrendering to God's will (Bonaventure [1268] 1978, 45). These authors remind us that God's wisdom often does not seem reasonable: the meek shall inherit the earth (Matthew 5:5), the last shall be first (Matthew 20:16), and strength is made perfect in weakness (2 Corinthians 12:9).

The Reformation put renewed emphasis on God's surprising ways. Martin Luther's *Theology of the Cross* reminds us that God reveals His glory most perfectly in suffering and humility, thereby displacing human expectations of power and success (Luther [1520] 1957, 27). John Calvin states that God regards the humble, and that prominence and privilege in the world are no assurance of stature with God (Calvin [1559] 1960, 112). John Owen, as a representative of Puritan reflections, illustrates the ongoing human struggle to internalize such reversals; the believer must cultivate humility by resisting the desire for prominence and by aspiring to serve and obey (Owen [1677] 1965, 205).

Theologians today continue this conversation. Dietrich Bonhoeffer reminds us that for discipleship to be effective, it requires costly grace — a surrender of self-interest and obedience to God's inversion of logic (Bonhoeffer 1959, 117). Henri Nouwen suggests that we can cultivate the "downward mobility of the spirit," allowing joy, healing, and love to emerge through attentiveness and care for others (Nouwen 1981, 52). N. T. Wright offers a perspective to contemporary readers that the kingdom of God is not only real, but it also radically transforms any who embraces the unexpected realities of God; he challenges believers to live countercultural lives according to Christ's priorities (Wright 1996, 143). These authors converge on a common point: apprehending God's unexpected way is a theological and practical enterprise that informs our actions, relational claims, and pursuits of the fruit of the Spirit within our contexts.

As we look at the contributions of Augustine, Aquinas, Luther, Calvin, Owen, Bonhoeffer, Nouwen, and Wright, we see that there is continuity across time: God continually chooses the humble, takes our human measures of greatness and inverts them, and invites followers to embody a kingdom that does not follow instinct. The historical and theological testimony assures us that we can reflect on and apply this, substantiating that obedience to God's will actualizes joy, healing for the broken, and love that emanates from us to others, in both individual and communal contexts alike.

Practical Implications for the Believer

The upside-down kingdom is not an abstract theological dissertation, but a concrete phenomenon that is to be seen in every area of a believer's life. It takes an embodied form in the believer's life through an understanding of God's reversals—those who are last become first, the humble are exalted, service defines greatness, and so on. The believer learns to embody these truths through the events of life. Relationships, work, prayer, and service all engage the believer to be agents of the upside-down kingdom in immediate contexts. Joseph's life, for example, is a vivid representation: objectified by his brothers, sold into slavery, and unjustly imprisoned, he maintained faith in the providential care of God's complex ways and lived out his encounter with God in the integrity of whatever situation he was in (Gen. 39:1–23). This faith, patience, and humility positioned Joseph to save nations ultimately; it is in obeying God's reversals that we see the lasting impact of God's blessing. David's trajectory from shepherd to king was also a commitment to dependence on God, a sense of responsibility regarding ownership, and a heart inclined towards God's priorities (1 Sam. 16:11–13). These moments in the history of belief provide the necessary data and framework for engaging with kingdom principles today.

In contemporary life, acting in ways that bring joy, healing, and love through obedience to God's upside-down way requires intention. Intentionally choosing to speak with patience instead of irritation in family life, offering forgiveness to those who have caused painful hurt, or serving others rather than seeking acknowledgement at work, all engage in upside-down ways. The early church offers additional guidance; believers shared resources, cared for the marginalized (the poor, widows, orphans, etc.), and sought communal flourishing over individual gain (Acts 2:44–47). In each sequential scenario, the priorities of God's way were clear: humility, mercy, and selfless love. Stott claims the Sermon on the Mount is not merely a set of broader ethical ideals; it is a course of moral and practical obedience (Stott 1994, 68).

For a believer to align their life with God's will, reflection and prayer are also essential tools for living in God's way. In prayer, the believer surrenders their will to God's ways, engaging with the Holy Spirit through the pain of any wounds and seeking God's direction for their actions. As Bonhoeffer observes, discipleship is active obedience, not merely speculative knowledge, and surrendering self-interest is fundamental to moving in God's way (Bonhoeffer 1959, 117). Obedience brings joy as a result of being in harmony with God's purpose, healing as relational and personal wounds are reconciled, and love when actions are offered outwardly without expectation of return.

Moreover, witnessing practical service that is inverted from worldly systems of value confirms the existence of God's kingdom. Nearly invisible acts of generosity, mentoring, and encouragement may not seem much; however, they carry lasting weight in God's economy. Lewis notes that God's grace often subverts human expectations, and engaging with that grace through service gifts the believer an opportunity to exemplify the extravagant generosity of God (Lewis 1943, 76). Even in small gestures—offering remaining time or energy to be a listening ear to a friend who is struggling, helping a neighbor, or mentoring a younger colleague—these become tangible expressions of the kingdom.

Ultimately, practical obedience not only brings about transformation in the individual but also in the local community. As a believer demonstrates joy, healing relationships, and love, God's priorities permeate and transform the relational complexities of homes, schools, and congregations. As a believer lives, embraces, and engages in God's upside-down ways daily, the upside-down kingdom is internalized, spiritual growth occurs, and the power of humility, service, and sacrificial love is evident in a world still entangled by worldly expectations of success.

Encountering God Today

Experiencing God in the present day compels us to acknowledge that His upside-down kingdom continues to confound and transform lives. Contemporary believers often assume that spiritual growth will happen in a recognizable sequence. In reality, God often chooses to speak and act in ways that surprise us, in ways that are hidden in humble acts, and actions of surrendered, sacrificial weakness in our lives. During these times, we personally and collectively experience His reversals as He works in us and about us to shape our hearts, priorities, and relationships. With this in mind, we recall Scripture's encouragement, "Come to Me, all you who labor and are heavy laden, and I will give you rest" (Matt. 11:28). This invitation is astounding in its gentleness and radicalism: God summons us to a life of self-neglect, where He gives rest, renewal, and transformation.

Spiritual disciplines provide visible means by which we can embrace God and the shock of His purposes in our daily lives. Prayer is one example of allowing God to break in on us; it is more than a ritual; it is a channel where surrendering control, humility, and allowing our desires to attune to God's will and purposes are made possible (Stott 1994, 68). Service is an example of living out the reversal: we choose to meet the needs of others, which, by God's upside-down logic, elevates their situation to ours, where greatness is measured by love, not status (Bonhoeffer 1959, 117). Generosity, in terms of time, resources, or encouragement, allows God's grace to flow visibly and shape explanations that blessing is a product of obedience and trust, not merit (Packer 1973, 215).

Living together as the people of God amplifies/ intensifies these encounters. The early church was characterized by mutual assistance, a shared pool of resources, and sacrificial concern, which highlighted the relational context in which God operates through His kingdom (Acts 2:44–47). The same is true in our churches, workplaces, and neighborhoods today: empathy, careful listening, and honoring other people create spaces where God's reversals can be experienced and displayed. As John Chrysostom states, "Our faithfulness is measured by how we love others, especially those least likely to love us in return" (Chrysostom [ca. 390] 1986, 202).

Experiencing God also involves engagement with suffering and unforeseen grace as formative. The joy, healing, and love that Jesus expresses and embodies in earthly life will be most clearly present in our lives when we are vulnerable. In suffering, believers are invited to relinquish control, wait upon the Lord, and then do whatever is done as Jesus would have, which stands as an invitation to each new person (Wright 2012, 98). Henri Nouwen observed: "The place for our spiritual maturity is often hidden in the fullness of ordinary faithfulness - because that is the place where the heart is quietest and most open to hearing God's voice" (Nouwen 1981, 52).

Encounters with God today can be as mundane and intentional as carving out time for reflection and prayer, engaging in youth work or quieter acts of service, offering forgiveness where a relationship is in distress, or practicing humility in the midst of conflict. Each of these actions aligns us with the upside-down kingdom of God and creates experiential knowledge of his love. In the disciplines of surrender, attentiveness, and generosity, joy is created, wounds of relationship are healed, and love flows again. We show that the reversals of the kingdom are not ideas but realities.

Discipleship is a vibrant engagement with a God whose wisdom is always higher (Isa. 55:8–9). Engaging with God today involves being open enough to be surprised, patient enough to endure suffering, and engaged enough to serve and commit. Engaging in the spiritual disciplines of the church, in faithful relationships, and surrendering to God's providence continues in the encounter with the living reality of the upside-down kingdom. In that encounter, joy is deepened, healing is realized, and love is seen and made transformable—because the heart of God we experience grows in a world often guided by logic instead of revelation.

Closing Invitation

As we end this introduction, I encourage you to approach the following pages with an expectant heart and a willing spirit. The upside-down kingdom of God challenges our assumptions about success, strength, and importance, calling for humility in our relationships, generosity with our gifts, and faithful service despite being overlooked. The way of Jesus does not conform to earthly metrics but rather cultivates enduring joy, wholeness, and love (Ps. 16:11; Matt. 11:28–30).

Living this way asks for attentiveness and intentionality. Augustine teaches that human hearts are restless until they rest in God, and this rest is often found in surrender rather than control (Augustine 1998, 23). Bonhoeffer asserts that discipleship entails dying to oneself so that one may live in Christ (Bonhoeffer 1959, 117). Our daily practices, whether praying, listening, being silent in service, or forgiving, become the patterns through which God's grace forms us.

This book serves as much as an invitation as it does a challenge. When you read it, I invite you to do so with an open mind to God's Spirit and guidance—inviting Scripture and the voices of saints and scholars to help unfold your path. May the wisdom of God's people through the centuries inspire your steps, but most importantly, may the life of Christ invite you into His surprising ways. The upside-down kingdom of God is not a future reality, but something to be lived into today. Receive it with joy, pursue it with tenacity, and witness it through love.

Overview of the Book

In this book, we invite the reader to travel throughout the divine or upside-down kingdom of God and explore how divine reversals create spaces of joy, healing, and love in everyday life. Each chapter explores a paradox of the gospel, demonstrating how God's actions disrupt human expectations and ultimately lead to profound spiritual transformation. Chapter One provides a foundation for the upside-down kingdom of God through Jesus' life and teachings on its values. The Beatitudes (Matt. 5:3) embody the upside-down nature of God's kingdom, as does servant leadership (Matt. 20:26) and obedient humility. Each of these teaches and encourages readers toward humility and trust. The following chapters show a few practical implications for daily living (in examples of community life, work, and relationships) by demonstrating how humility, service, generosity, and sacrificial love can play out for the reader. The examples of Joseph's perseverance (Gen. 50:20), David's faithful action (1 Sam. 16:11–13), and the early church's communal life of prayer, worship, and devotion (Acts 2:42–47) in Scripture served as examples of "acceptable" manifestations of the values of God's kingdom. The writings and theological musings of past theologians are also included, such as Augustine on humility (Augustine 1998, 54), Luther on the theology of the cross via a life of humble service (Luther [1520] 1957, 27), Bonhoeffer's costly discipleship (Bonhoeffer 1959, 117), and Nouwen on compassion (Nouwen 1981, 52). These examples are helpful for modern-day applications through the various lenses and spirits of change throughout the ages.

Finally, the prompts provide an opportunity to act, reflect, and examine Scripture. In this way, we hope readers will take the time to explore and consider the surprises God has in store for us through our ordinary days and humble obedience, which cultivates spiritual growth. Each chapter concludes with prompts designed to foster joy, encourage healing, and inspire love in ways that provide a conceptual bridge between a theological understanding of the divine kingdom and practical action. This is an essential goal of this book, as we aim to shape a transformation of context and understanding, and a change in character and praxis so that we may begin to demonstrate the values of God's kingdom with joy, humility in service, and trust (John 13:34–35; Col. 3:12–14).

Chapter 1

The Last Will Be First, and the First Will Be Last

The Reversal Announced

The kingdom of God represents a drastic reversal in human expectations. The world values power, wealth, and influence. Yet, Christ declares true greatness to be found in humility, servanthood, and self-denial. Jesus declared, "Whoever desires to become great among you, let him be your servant; and whoever desires to be first among you, let him be your slave" (Matt. 20:26–27). This is disrupting human assumptions: life, joy, and fulfillment as found in surrender, not accumulation; obedience rather than self-assertion.

The biblical story has, again and again, proclaimed this reversal. The prophets declared God's ways alongside human hubris, culminating in the incarnation, wherein the Son of God became humble for the sake of redeeming the world (Phil. 2:5–8). Augustine once reflected on the tension between human ambition and divine vocation, noting that humanity is defined by a restless longing—a desire that can only be met by God, not through self (Augustine 1998, 67). John Calvin noted that God's call was both gracious and authoritative, and it covenanted believers to a vocation that challenged social hierarchies (Calvin 1559, 431).

This ongoing reversal requires discernment and the courage to act. It means repeatedly choosing God's purposes over socially acceptable measures of success. Let us consider the disciples, who threw down their nets and left their way of life to follow Christ (Matt. 4:18–20), as they chose to obey. In a somewhat paradoxical way, the disciples found a more profound and more enduring life as they relinquished worldly security and acclaim. This pattern appears repeatedly in the Scriptures.

Significantly, reversal also forms how we live our ordinary, day-to-day lives. In upholding good ethics, professional interactions, and relationships, we embody the values of the kingdom within the world. As J. I. Packer observed, when we are obedient to God's call, we receive the gift of joy, peace, and integrity, rather than God's substitutes for worldly convenience that offer only momentary satisfaction (Packer 1973, 215). Henri Nouwen reminds us that even in small, ordinary acts—such as attentively listening, quietly serving another, and heartfully forgiving—when lived as a response to God's upside-down kingdom, these are acts grounded in God's love and authority (Nouwen 1981, 47).

Here, we see that the directed conversion is both an ongoing lived reality and a theological assertion. It confronts human ambition, liberates one from a self-serving endeavor, and entices participation in God's redemptive purposes. Hear the ongoing call of the kingdom: we discover our lives not in upholding the self, but in the surrender, servanthood, and joyful obedience to the other.

The Kingdom Turned Upside Down

Jesus' proclamation of the kingdom of God often radically reverses human expectations of power and privilege. While human kingdoms rely heavily on force, hierarchical structure, and a push to dominate, Jesus' kingdom is defined by humility, service, and radical grace (Matt. 20:25–28). Most of what is considered "last" in human terms becomes "first" (Col. 3:11), showing that in God's economy, God's power reveals itself not through coercion, but through radical love and self-giving. This radical reversal becomes a foundation for understanding the gentle heart of Christ.

The Gospels provide constant examples of this reversal. For example, in Luke 14:7–11, Jesus observes as guests attempt to secure the places of honour at the feast and instructs them to take the lowest seat, so that God may exalt them. This teaching provokes cultural categories, specifically that only the least ambitious and least powerful earn a place in the kingdom of heaven. Wright reminds us that Jesus' kingdom, which was proximate to them, is supplied by God's initiative and mercy and not by human merit (Wright 1996, 142).

Another example of this radical inversion is the story of the vineyard workers, where the labourers hired last receive the same wages as the labourers employed first (Matt. 20:1–16), leaving Jesus' audience scandalized because they were operating with logic and fairness that made sense to them. Here, Jesus demonstrates that our expectations cannot confine God's abundance and goodness, but instead flow freely, often disrupting the human ordering of social status and hierarchy (Carson 1991, 110).

Further attention to this theme can be found among the patristic writers. Augustine noted God's kingdom raises the humble and brings down the proud, placing divine order contrary to human ordering (Augustine 1998, 215), and witnessed that the paradox of power through meekness and servanthood has facilitated humility and patient endurance for Jesus' followers.

Practically, reframing the notion of humanity's inclination to take power and authority over others in light of Jesus' gentle teaching also allows believers to leverage the way they approach relationships, leadership, and their spiritual formation. For the believer, this construct prompts a commitment to forming live relationships that replace domination with gentleness. It also allows the believer to reframe success not in terms of power and status, but also in terms of faithfulness and obedience. For the Christ-follower who has embodied and internalized the truth of God's upside-down kingdom, they understand that true power is expressed in radical love, nurture, and serving the needs of others above their own preferences, inclinations, and assumptions (Matt. 11:29).

"The Last Will Be First": Jesus' Radical Claim

Jesus's radical assertion, "So the last will be first, and the first last" (Matt. 20:16), upends typical ideas of merit, reward, and God's favor. This assertion challenges pride, entitlement, and hierarchical views of the world by demonstrating God's sovereignty in granting grace. The "first" in worldly terms—the haves (wealth, status, prestige, etc.)—are not guaranteed God's favor, and the "last" (the humble, the marginalized, and those who have gone overlooked) are given priority in God's kingdom.

Historically, the principle of divine inversion has deep roots in the prophetic tradition (Horsley 2011). Isaiah declares that God raises the lowly and brings down the proud (Isa. 57:15). Jesus exemplifies this pattern and shows that God's values often contradict those of the society in which we live. Jesus associated Himself with the vulnerable and the marginalized, indignantly asserting that true authority in the kingdom of God would be manifested through humble service and gentleness (John 13:12–17).

Theologically, N. T. Wright notes that Jesus's assertion is about more than reward; it is also about identity and vocation. Those who live in humble obedience are also part of God's reign now and in the eschaton (Wright 2012, 88). John Calvin similarly notes that grace is unmerited and bestowed according to God's wisdom, not man's works (Calvin 1559, 112).

Practically, believers live against the grain. Success is set off in a different light. Being faithful, humble, and loving shapes how preeminence is determined in the eyes of God. In faith communities, the principle of divine inversion makes sense of serving collaboratively, equitably, and with concern for the marginalized. Nouwen gestures toward the practical implications of defining the "last" as "first" when he highlights how this enables us to imagine empathetic responses and dismantle patterns of domination (Nouwen 1994, 73).

By opting to embrace this inversion in their lives, Christians exemplify the humility and gentleness befitting Christ. The glory lies in the fact that God's power is made perfect in human weakness (2 Cor. 12:9). Inversion reframes our personal ambitions and our relationships with one another, inviting reflection on our motives, priorities, and attitudes. The claim is radical, unsettling, and transformative; it offers a vision of authority rooted in love, rather than other coercive endeavors.

The Vineyard Parable and the Scandal of Grace

The vineyard parable (Matt. 20:1–16) illustrates the scandalous nature of God's grace. There are laborers hired at different times of the day, and yet they all receive the same pay. Those who are accustomed to proportionality in rewards are shocked by this story, as we have an innate desire for all rewards to be fair. We want everything that comes to us to be commensurate with the time and effort we invest. The parable grapples with various notions, including fairness, merit, and entitlement. It ultimately presents us with God's grace that is free, sovereign, extravagant, and unexpected.

Jesus constantly pushes the boundaries of what is expected in his parables to draw out spiritual truths, and this parable is doing just that. In this story, those who think they deserve the greatest reward, the "first," are humbled. Those who worked the least (the "last") are celebrated for receiving generous grace from the owner (Matt. 20:13–15). As Bonhoeffer suggests, the stories Jesus told can attack our self-righteousness and cause us to think differently about God's mercy and generosity (Bonhoeffer 1959, 102).

Ultimately, the parable theologically emphasizes a relational economy of faith rather than a merit economy. J. I. Packer notes that God rewards with His wisdom, not according to human calculations of effort (Packer 1973, 198). Augustine relates God's generosity to humility, admitting that we are unworthy, which builds a sense of gratitude and enables believers to become dependent on God and ready to be used by Him (Augustine 1998, 144).

The scandal of grace also represents an ethical model. It challenges the church to participate in God's generous economy by incorporating the lesson of Jesus' parable into the community's daily life. Fairness, in human terms, is no longer important; now the focus shifts toward love, compassion, and reconciliation for all involved in these shared, gracious experiences, without attempting to compare or compete with one another. Nouwen reminds us that we should not become agitated when people receive God-like grace, and we are called to extend kindness even when that kindness is not deserved (Nouwen 1981, 67).

Practically, the parable challenges believers to reflect on our attitudes toward privilege, reward, and service. Leaders, teachers, and parents are called to remember that success in God's kingdom is not primarily about achievement or recognition, but rather about faithfulness, humility, and service. A parable like this one can disrupt the entitlement we hold and create a posture of gratitude and agape love in return.

The vineyard parable describes this new way of being people, which ultimately reflects the reversal brought by the arrival of Christ's kingdom and the voice of the glorious gospel. The grace that comes from God is far beyond anything we might measure. Generosity often trumps merit, and God's wisdom will continue to perplex our worldly logic. Accepting this makes room for gentleness and humility while inviting us to adopt a posture of service to others rather than asserting ownership over them (Matt. 11:29).

Confronting Human Expectations

Jesus' declaration that "the last will be first, and the first will be last" (Matt. 20:16) pushed against not only the cultural default of his time, but also the inner assumptions of his own disciples. In a culture that values honor, wealth, and power above all else, this claim overturned traditional ideas of worth and reward. True greatness, he argued, is not public prominence or power, but is rather humility, participation in selfless services, and aligning oneself with God's will. As John Chrysostom points out, "the road to glory lies in the road to self-denial; the humble are exalted and the proud are humbled, because the measure of God's kingdom is unlike the world" (Chrysostom c. 347–407, 202, trans. Kennedy).

Jesus lived out the counter-intuition of this claim both through teaching and acting. He associated with those who were entirely forgotten around him, and those who were known only as tax collectors and sinners. He put these persons together, with the poor, at the centre, so that his example would show that God's heart is inclusion, not exclusion. Thus he lived the enactment of this central rule of the kingdom of heaven. The rich young ruler illustrates the tensions between the world's ambition and kingdom obedience (Matt. 19:16–22), calling for a greater surrender of possessions, power, and pride, even though God's standard of greatness is entirely relational and spiritual, not material and hierarchical. Augustine strengthens this observation, arguing that "He exalts the humble and humbles the arrogant so that all may see that true honour lies in virtue, not in the esteem of this world" (Augustine 1998, 102).

Matthew 20:1–16 illustrates this strangeness regarding God's justice, in that those who worked in the vineyard for one hour received the same payment as those who worked for twelve hours. The hourly wage of the vineyard labourers represents God's generosity and sovereignty, inviting us into a substantive reevaluation of what "fair" means. According to Bonhoeffer, to follow Christ is to experience radical obedience and to embrace God's upside-down logic in everyday life (Bonhoeffer 1959, 117). Being able to live out this impulse in one's own life changes relationships at home and at work, as well as one's interactions in community life with others. The quest for status turns to serving, recognition becomes humility, and competition becomes care.

Jesus' radical claim calls us to respond with trust, consideration, and imitation. Believers must come together to resist predictable realities and embrace the great paradox of the last being first. The great expectation of God's kingdom is that we are invited not only to share God's work but also to begin to share its reality: a life of intangible joy, spiritual restoration, and love shown in humble service.

Greatness Redefined in God's Eyes

Jesus redefines greatness as often as he is confronted with the concept, and always questions the cultural constructs of power, authority, and influence. In the kingdom of God, greatness is not measured by success, power, privilege, pedigree, or followership but by humility, service, and obedient action (Matt. 23:11–12). Part of the upside-down reality of God's evaluation of greatness is how human priorities emphasize achievement, mastery, and "getting it done." The paradox of what it means to serve selflessly in the way of Jesus reflects the heart of Christ by exemplifying the non-hierarchical and real spiritual significance derived from love and faithfulness.

This theme of humility and servant-mindedness as an alternative way of being is exemplified at various points in Scripture. When Moses receives his calling (Exod. 3:1–12), and when Christ puts on the apron of a servant

(John 13:12–17), we see an authority that is buttressed by humility. N.T. Wright writes extensively about how the teachings of Jesus consistently challenged the hierarchical assumptions of culture, and challenged followers to adopt a countercultural posture (Wright 1996, 214). The lessons of greatness in the kingdom teach us that status is not the point, but a responsibility towards the good of others.

The patristic writers contribute to this theological view. Augustine notes that humility enables the believer who exercises a faithful response to being in a state of grace with God to embrace God's wisdom in conforming character and action (Augustine 1998, 182). Origen echoes this value of humility by telling us that greatness in God's economy manifests itself as obedience and gentleness, rather than coercion and domination (Origen 1994, 59). This turning upside-down reorders spiritual formation, making space for the heart to consider the good of God and one's neighbor, rather than selfish interest.

While believers may become selfless servants of God in their lives with family, work, and community responsibilities, acts of care, attention, and sacrifice cultivate a demeanor of quiet dignity and true greatness. Awareness of God's redefinition of significance alters our personal ambitions and moral decision-making, and this reordering directs our energy towards acts of fidelity and service rather than personal promotion. Believers allow this vision of the upside-down kingdom to reshape our lives; most importantly, our experience of spiritual freedom in submitted relationships (Matt. 11:29).

The Struggle of the Disciples with Ambition

Jesus redefines greatness as often as he is confronted with the concept, and always questions the cultural constructs of power, authority, and influence. In the kingdom of God, greatness is not measured by success, power, privilege, pedigree, or followership but by humility, service, and obedient action (Matt. 23:11–12). Part of the upside-down reality of God's evaluation of greatness is how human priorities emphasize achievement, mastery, and "getting it done." The paradox of what it means to serve selflessly in the way of Jesus reflects the heart of Christ by exemplifying the non-hierarchical and real spiritual significance derived from love and faithfulness.

This theme of humility and servant-mindedness as an alternative way of being is exemplified at various points in Scripture. When Moses receives his calling (Exod. 3:1–12), and when Christ puts on the apron of a servant (John 13:12–17), we see an authority that is buttressed by humility. N.T. Wright writes extensively about how the teachings of Jesus consistently challenged the hierarchical assumptions of culture, and challenged followers to adopt a countercultural posture (Wright 1996, 214). The lessons of greatness in the kingdom teach us that status is not the point, but a responsibility towards the good of others.

The patristic writers contribute to this theological view. Augustine notes that humility enables the believer who exercises a faithful response to being in grace with God to embrace God's wisdom in conforming character and action (Augustine 1998, 182). Origen echoes this value of humility by telling us that greatness in God's economy manifests itself as obedience and gentleness, rather than coercion and domination (Origen 1994, 59). This turning upside-down reorders spiritual formation, making space for the heart to consider the good of God and one's neighbor, rather than selfish interest.

While believers may become selfless servants of God in their lives with family, work, and community responsibilities, acts of care, attention, and sacrifice cultivate a demeanor of quiet dignity and true greatness. Awareness of God's redefinition of significance alters our personal ambitions and moral decision-making, and this reordering directs our energy towards acts of fidelity and service rather than personal promotion. Believers allow this vision of the upside-down kingdom to reshape our lives; most importantly, our experience of spiritual freedom in submitted relationships (Matt. 11:29).

Pride, Power, and the Illusion of Control

Pride and the pursuit of power and control lead to an illusion of control, which masks our dependence on God's wisdom and God's ways. Throughout the story of God in the Scriptures, human attempts to control and manipulate reality are always placed in tension with God's gentle and sovereign guidance. Jesus repeatedly helped his followers deconstruct their reliance on self-control and encouraged them to trust in God's provision and direction (Proverbs 3:5–6; Matthew 6:25–34). The kingdom of God inverts cultural expectations about power and control, where the objective is not to confront or dominate, but rather to surrender, obey, and have faith.

The Old Testament shows examples of how pride leads to downfall. King Saul disobeyed God, which was a form of power (1 Samuel 15:1–23), and the pride of Babylon (Isaiah 14:12–15) that believed itself sovereign and powerful led to destruction. In contrast, David and the prophets did the will of God, even when it was impossible or in the midst of persecution, which was God's will for them. Brueggemann observes that the foundational stories of defeat and success expose biblical assumptions about the perfection of divine power in the context of human weakness (Brueggemann 1994, 76).

Theologically, Owen asserts that pride is blinding and inhibits the previously discussed transformative work of the Spirit in spiritual growth (Owen 1677, 58). It is the opposite for humility; it contributes to a desire for gentleness, seasons our patience, and opens our hearts to be filled with grace. As Nouwen notes, God's restorative and relational work on earth requires relinquishing the illusion of control (Nouwen 1981, 84).

Practically, humility leads to an honest examination of ourselves, confession, and intentional development of humility to confront pride. However, this requires a willingness to recognize our limits, to relinquish our authority for the sake of others, and a commitment to prioritizing others' needs over our own as we point to Christ's gentleness. This will allow us to be people of peace with relational integrity; hence, knowing our freedom from the illusion of control allows us to be blessed through greater gentleness as we depend on God's sovereignty rather than our calculations (Matthew 11:29–30).

Humility as the Path to Joy

In the upside-down Kingdom of God, humility, as we know, is not viewed as weakness but rather as the ultimate gateway to authentic joy. Jesus constantly demonstrated that greatness does not rest in one's status or fame among men. However, in his humility to serve others, Jesus displayed this quantitatively and qualitatively through many examples, including — and importantly —his washing of the feet of his disciples (John 13:4–5), and his invitation to see the poor as important, especially the marginalized and outcast. The Beatitudes reiterate the theme of wealth through humility: "Blessed are the poor in spirit, for theirs is the kingdom of heaven" (Matthew 5:3). Perhaps it is not self-promotion, but obedience that brings Godly great joy to exist in us, thus exposing the paradox touching the world's natural living inclination.

The disciples struggled to comprehend His upside-down Kingdom. James and John were looking for the highest reward, desirous to be in the first-class seats in his kingdom (Mark 10:35–37). Jesus' response clearly reveals the nature of these deals: "But many who are first will be last, and the last first" (Mark 10:31). At this tension, human ambition comes into direct contrast with the wisdom of God. To be humble is to act with the conscious removal of personal ambition, recognizing the impetus for

God's value to determine relationally and spiritually rather than by the world's standards of hierarchical or material (Augustine 1998, 102).

Joy from service exists tangibly through small acts of equity and faithfulness. Daily acts of faithfulness and obedience, being sensitive to others, being patient under trial, giving generously without the return of kindness, are all expressions of the paradoxical existence of exaltation of God. As Augustine said, through an act of self-realization, climbing the ladder of humility requires not feeling dependent on God, but seeking His will ahead of my own and seeing others as higher than myself (Augustine 1998, 87). Each step towards humility generates some peace within, allowing a Christian to relinquish envy or comparisons found in the secular world.

This is a true transformation of relationships and community. With humility guiding all actions, conflict fades, collaboration flourishes, and love takes shape. Lewis describes the experience of serving joy without ego and without visibility as aligning oneself with the heart of God, thereby creating freedom in one's spirit (Lewis 1960, 42). It is reasonable and regular to think that pursuing humility is a mere ethical experience; however, it is more restorative than it is ethical; it creates a joy beyond situation, exemplifies and mirrors the heart of Christ, and prepares a believer for the ultimate reversal we noted above for eternal recognition in the kingdom that God values and serves.

Joy in Serving Rather than Being Served

Jesus Himself constantly reveals that true joy and satisfaction come from serving others, not from putting one's own interests first or seeking personal validation. In the kingdom of God, greatness is measured through humility, and considering the needs of others before your own (Mark 10:43–45). This is contrary to worldly assumptions that see significance and satisfaction derived from position and influence. So, not as a weight, but service becomes a channel for spiritual joy, and our hearts are matched with Christ's self-giving love.

As we have seen, the Scripture is replete with examples of this principle. Jesus washing the disciples' feet (John 13:1–17) embodies humility; he exemplifies humble service, showing that genuine leadership is informed by sacrificial care. Notice how the moment models joy out of an act of love and obedience, as opposed to an act of validation. It is worth noting that, as N.T. Wright reminds us that such a moment demonstrates the nature of the kingdom is flipping societal norms upside down (Wright 1996, 221).

The Church Fathers confirm this insight. John Chrysostom writes that serving others is nurture for the soul, healing pride and creating communion with God and neighbor (Chrysostom c. 347–407, 152). Henri Nouwen notes that the attitude of service shifts the heart, allowing believers to experience joy in God's gifts rather than human approval (Nouwen 1981, 87).

Practically, it also means engaging in small service opportunities that believers can do in their daily lives—caring for the vulnerable, nurturing youth, and illustrating faith patiently all act as opportunities to practice Christ's humility. All joy through service stems from redirecting the heart towards God's purpose, moving away from self-serving striving while creating connections with one another. Where joy is found through service, the quiet, nourishing recognition in the soul is a joy that comes from participating in God's blessing through an act of obedience out of love, inviting God's own gentle, meek presence (Matthew 11:29–30).

The Paradox of Exaltation Through Lowliness

Scripture consistently portrays a paradox: the lowly are exalted and the proud are brought low (Matt. 23:12; Luke 14:11). Lowliness, properly embraced, can be a channel of divine honour and spiritual satisfaction. The paradox will not support our common conclusion that achievement, advancement, or prevalence by force make us worthy; on the contrary, it teaches that we are lifted by submission to the will of God. Jesus exemplifies the truth of this paradox throughout his ministry. As fully God, he exhibited lowliness, served others, and suffered (Phil. 2:5–8). His exaltation upon the Cross teaches us that the proper display of power and honour is always the result of obedience completed through self-emptying, not violent coercion or worldly ambition. Edwards claims that humility (the lowly disposition) invites reliance upon God, and joy whereby we glimpse the glory of being obedient (Edwards 1746, 64).

Reflections from the Patristic authors draw out the implications of the paradox. Augustine describes the ladder of humility as a means of spiritual ascent. To ascend spiritually is to make oneself small (Augustine 1998, 215). The lowly are dependent upon God, do not need to promote themselves, and can serve others. In this way, our character is transformed, we grow spiritually, and we are being made ready for the eternal joy of life with God (Matt. 7:7–11).

As a matter of spiritual practice, Christians can embody the paradox of Jesus' humility through prioritizing God's kingdom over their own ambitions, exhibiting patience towards one another, and embracing unglamorous moments of quiet service. Knowing that exaltation does not derive from human striving or progressing at others' expense gives rest, liberating the soul from envy, anxiety, and pride. As we align ourselves with God's timetable and provision, we can cultivate a humble spirit like Jesus, which will produce characteristics of deep joy, peace, and resilience reflective of Jesus' humble leadership (Matt. 11:29).

Augustine on the Ladder of Humility

Augustine of Hippo offers a profound understanding of the path of ascent, which begins with humility. In the Confessions and City of God, he proclaims that humility is a disposition and a practice central to communion with God. Augustine insists that pride prohibits the way of grace; humility opens up the soul to know God. Humility is the beginning of love, desire, affection, and action toward God's will.

Augustine's teachings are well-grounded in Scripture. James reminds us to "humble yourself in the sight of the Lord, and He will lift you up" (James 4:10). Additionally, Jesus blesses and shows rest in meekness and lowliness (Matt. 11:29; Luke 1:52). It may also be prudent to view all of this as a metaphor of a ladder. Humility is mythically developed over time through practices of self-examination, confession, service, and hope in God's mercy as one ascends or descends the ladder, ultimately reaching spiritual maturity.

Besides viewing a metaphor of a ladder of humility, Augustine also points to various practical dimensions of humility. Humility means relying on God rather than self-reliance, acknowledging oneself as lesser than others, and being receptive to learning. In pastoral experience, such as counseling and mentoring, humility allows for receptive space and gentle comportment, similar to Christ, toward the least of these. Dietrich Bonhoeffer remarks that a disposition of humility not only enables one to obey God's will (Bonhoeffer 1959, 142) but also forms the basis for authentic fellowship and integrity with others, as well as deep abiding joy.

Theologically, humility reconciles human weakness with divine power. Not only does humility draw upon the notion that believers are not self-sufficient, but it also recognizes that believers are sustained by God's power alone, which enhances the believer's hope to practice their vocation in mission to the world and ultimately experience a sense of clarity and peace. Augustine states that wisdom, heaven, and humanity are mediated through humility, as any virtue is enacted as a function of humility. Therefore, moral discernment, prayer, and moral action toward the good occur through and in humility (Augustine 1998, 228).

The contemporary application of this ladder of humility encourages believers to act patiently in correction, gently in their demeanor, and to begin slowly with the little things, practicing humility personally through their self-care. The way of humility is not the way of pride. However, when one continually chooses to engage in obedience, it places one on the way of the meek. It brings about large spaces of the divine economy formed by the character of Christ, and the invincible joy of God, without counting on worldly recognition (Matt. 5:5).

Healing in God's Reversals

In the upside-down kingdom, healing is intimately tied to God's reversal of the world's expectations. There is a great deal of value in the world that comes with successful achievement, influence, and recognition. However, God reverses that reality, valuing restoration, wholeness, and relationships that flourish. When we relinquish self-interest and become humbled, we are liberated from the burdens of comparison, envy, and striving driven by our esteem. Jesus' ministry exemplified this, as he healed the blind, the lame, and the outcasts, and did not just heal physical maladies, but also restored their dignity, purpose, and inclusion (Matt. 9:27–31; Luke 14:13–14).

Healing in God's kingdom attends to the internal wounds caused by human ambition and rejection. Augustine again points out that "God's grace touches the heart before it reforms the hands; only the healed heart can act rightly" (Augustine 1998, 77). In reversing the power structure of the world, God opens up room for those pushed aside to thrive and for the weary to rest (Matt. 11:28–30). In the parable of the laborers in the vineyard (Matt. 20:1–16), divine justice is restorative because the latecomers received the same wage as the first workers, not resentfully begrudging it. Instead, all workers rejoiced in God's justice and equity.

The act of healing is never limited to individuals. Within communities, God's reversal facilitates reconciliation and peace, ultimately erasing envy, resentment, and rivalry. Nouwen reflects that "true healing takes place when, in fact, we are willing to appropriate God's embrace and that of each other, so that woundedness can be turned into compassion" (Nouwen 1981, 45). In a ministry of this nature, believers are encouraged to actively practice forgiveness, generosity, and patient care in their daily lives.

Thus, God's reversals are at once ethical and therapeutic. Healing occurs when humility supplants pride, service supplants self-interest, and trust supplants power and control. The last first is not simply a doctrinal idea but a legitimate pathway towards emotional, relational, and spiritual healing. Believers discover that the presence of the kingdom of God, with all its upside-downness and paradoxes of divine justice, produces communal flourishing and inner peace, unveiling a God whose strength is found in weakness and whose mercy can transform every aspect of life.

Freedom from Envy and Comparison

Presently, consider the most crippling hindrance to spiritual rest, which is envy, defined as the insidious comparison of ourselves to others. Take, for example, the way Jesus routinely addressed such tendencies in his students, reminding them that the kingdom of God operates according to different principles than the corner store (Matt. 20:1–16). Where envy breeds discontent and division, the grace of God invites the believer into a life of gratitude, contentment, and trust in the Lord's provision.

The vineyard story can help us understand this. The unfairness of equal wages for unequal hours was enough for the human mind to grapple with, but it also revealed the generosity of God. The simplicity of our subjective experience—God blesses when and where he wishes—gives rise to a freedom from resentment (Matt. 20:15). John Stott observed that seeing

God's sovereignty in ascribed provision extinguishes envy and fuels joyful humility (Stott 1994, 78).

Embracing examples of biblical heroes can reveal how this pattern works. Defending himself against critique, Moses contended with the vigilant discontent that all our hearts share, holding fast to his principle in God's appointed time (Num. 11:1–35). David patiently met Saul's envy (1 Sam. 18:6–11), and Paul learned to exist satisfied in all conditions (1 Cor. 4:7; Phil. 4:11–13). Moreover, Nouwen reminds us that knowing we are beloved with a unique calling, all our neighbors' happy gifts can be a source of joy, which releases our internal discontent (Nouwen 1981, 101).

Practical application may involve being active in gratitude, setting aside time for prayerful discernment, and cheering others' successes as gifts and blessings of God's wisdom are displayed in manifold ways. When we stop feeling the need to measure ourselves against others, we experience the gentle way that Christ's embrace liberates us, not because we consider ourselves better than others, but because we are loved (Matt. 11:29–30). Sacred maturity develops as we learn to rejoice in the goodness of God and find rest within the imbalances imposed upon us.

Rest for the Weary Striver

Jesus himself invites those encumbered by striving and self-imposed pressure: "Come to Me, all you who labor and are heavy laden, and I will give you rest" (Matt. 11:28). The weary from the driving forces of ambition, expectation, or having to manage outcomes into a predetermined course are invited into the gentle embrace of Christ. Rest is a space to be and exist in, with the confidence that comes from surrendering and trusting the Self.

Origen noted that divine rest sharply contrasts with the futility of self-reliance. Instead of weariness, rest nourishes a renewed and refreshing engagement with God's intended rhythm through patience or waiting

(Origen 1994, 112). From the interaction of Jesus and the disciples, we see that authentic leadership does not depend on ceaseless activity or an empty guiding that disengages from engagement. The truth we all have to face is that human effort alone cannot sustain us spiritually. Bonhoeffer offers an insightful lens for discerning the restorative qualities of following Jesus, asserting that "human obedience-in-gentleness therefore lifts unceasing fatigue to an abiding strength" (Bonhoeffer 1959, 137).

That unfortunate moment of realization for the weary striver is to move toward activity that is not striving; the blessed movement of intentionally choosing to meditate, cultivate prayerful practices, observe Sabbath, and dwell in the promises of God. Once they know and accept their limits and lean into God's provision, they will find they no longer navigate their anxiety over a preoccupation with performance. N.T. Wright reminds us that rest in the biblical sense is not a disengaged passivity, but rather participation in God's mission. In trust, it involves realignment through engagement, which promotes strength and clarity (Wright 1996, 198).

Enacting this posture of rest will be practical in our personal, relational, and vocational lives. When there is intentionality and clarity in our activities, nurturance and care for whatever we do, and patience is built into the fabric of our interactions, the compulsion to produce or force does not take hold. The believer who rests begins to resemble Christ: in a gentleness that acknowledges their authority and allows God's Spirit to breathe and move freely within and through the soul. Rest nurtures inward peace, gives faith and trust capacity to grow, and prepares the heart to serve; it testifies to the kingdom in gentleness, as gentleness persists over striving (Matt. 11:29).

Healing the Wounds of Rejection through God's Welcome

Rejection can cut deeply into one's spiritual and emotional well-being; nevertheless, Jesus' ministry represents radical inclusion and compassionate welcome. Jesus' ministry includes the excluded, the rejected, the despised, the socially marginalized, teaching us that we can heal wounds relationally with gentleness (Luke 15:1–7). God's welcome restores our dignity and trust, highlighting the transforming power of His love.

Patristic theology could not be more centred on this restorative embrace. Chrysostom contends that Jesus' encounters with sinners and the socially vulnerable raised them through relational, healing gentleness; thus, Jesus does not treat those who are rejected and marginalized from society with condemnation, but instead, he welcomes, encourages, and restores them (Chrysostom c. 347–407, 129). Augustine emphasizes that God's love surpasses human offense, and that God can reconcile Himself to us through love, thereby granting us inner peace (Augustine 1998, 219).

The examples from scripture could not be more illustrative: the woman caught in adultery received forgiveness rather than condemnation (John 8:1–11); Zacchaeus, the despised social outcast, received joy and transformation when Jesus intentionally welcomed him (Luke 19:1–10). Nouwen writes that whenever people experience encounters like the ones described above, they are clinging to the tender heart of Christ, who calls them out of their exclusion and into spiritual belonging (Nouwen 1994, 53).

At a practical level, believers can extend healing through little acts of inclusion, listening, and gentle encouragement. Situating beliefs in communities that preserve compassion—not condemnation—allows individuals to receive restorative care from God. Those who experience acceptance from Christ receive skills from God to respond to others in the same manner, creating cycles of relational healing.

Pain from rejection takes time, intentionality, and reliance on God's Spirit. When believers embrace God's welcome, they find a place of refuge for their wounded hearts and learn to harness the healing gentleness God provides in their day-to-day encounters, thereby demonstrating God's welcome as a spiritual practice. This means that Christ's gentleness is not passive, but a transformative action, leading to a template for abundant living in love alongside others, for believers and non-believers in a fractured world (Matt. 11:28–30).

Love as the Fruit of Being Last

In God's backward kingdom, humility is the fertile soil, and love is the fruit of embracing humility together. The void created by relinquishing ambition, status, and self-promotion enables love to grow and flourish— by acting in service, exercising patience, and being attentive to others' needs. Christ is our example. Christ was Lord. He washed the disciples' feet (John 13:1–17) and demonstrated that greatness and sacrificial love are indistinguishable. The act of washing was more than symbolic; it acted in the world and changed everything by demonstrating that love is itself cultivated by tangible, tactile, and often unseen acts of service.

This dynamic is reiterated throughout Paul's letters. In Romans 12:10, Paul writes to the body of believers, "Love one another with brotherly affection; outdo one another in showing honor," emphasizing that love, born of humility, grows through mutual care for one another. A humble preference for one another assures Christ-followers that they are participating in a reversal of worldly value systems, where self-promotion is replaced by generosity, jealousy is replaced by gratitude, and self-interest is replaced by compassion. John Owen refers to the love of the upside-down kingdom as self-disciplined love, stating that it arises when we have killed the sinful desires of the self, allowing God's grace to be operational within the believer (Owen 1677, 212).

In the upside-down kingdom, love embraces and restores relationships. Love mends the wounds of pride, competition, and bitterness and reconciles relationships in families, churches, and communities. Henri

Nouwen reminds us that love takes a downward mobility: "To love is to lower yourself. To enter the neighborhood of other people's needs without making any conditions or expectations to give something back to you" (Nouwen 1994, 33). In this way, God's people proclaim and live out His kingdom, making the unseen reality of God's love tangible.

Thus, the last will become the first, and love cannot be separated from humility. Humility is not simply normative or pragmatic; it is the soil where love grows. When followers of Christ embrace their last-place status, they are free to act with God-like generosity. Care, mercy, and service converge in the emotion of joy that is restorative. God prompts a healing and loving response to the horror of self-serving reversal through the lives of his people, so that God's reversal is not a mere doctrinal abstraction, but a possibility lived out in the lives of his people, enabling them to begin living in a way that is transformative and countercultural.

Servant Leadership in the Example of Christ

Jesus' model of leadership is contrary to cultural expectations. Society often tries to define power in terms of control, but Christ defines greatness in terms of how real greatness is revealed in service, humility, and self-sacrifice (Mark 10:42–45). Servant leadership turns the human assumptions on their head and places the interest and well-being of others above self-interest.

While the Gospels offer numerous examples, Jesus' washing of the disciples' feet at the Last Supper (John 13:1–17) is a clear case of humble service that focuses on elevating others and lowering self. As Augustine states, Christ's humility is designed to reflect God's right ordering, reminding us that exercising power primarily for one's own gain is contrary to God's purposes (Augustine 1998, 245). Thus, we see that spiritual authority should never be divorced from gentleness; in other words, a leader who serves manifests God's restorative work in human relations.

There is a long and rich heritage of Patristic reflections on this insight. John Chrysostom proclaimed that those leaders who promote their own self-importance ultimately do damage to their followers. In contrast, a Christ-like humility promotes the trustworthy, growth, and flourishing of all through the service (Chrysostom c. 347–407, 203). The church's tradition also reminds us of the paradox that the last shall be first, but they become first because of their path of service that takes the form of gentleness.

Practically, servant leadership is an intentional posture. It entails listening, authentically responding, making conscious room for others' needs, and opening oneself up to accountability. In all of this, believers wage an internal war against pride and self-promotion, recognizing that they have been entrusted with divine authority to nurture, defend, and empower others. N.T. Wright further asserts that as believers model Jesus' examples of servant leadership, they create communities characterized by trust, respect, and mutual submission (Wright 1996, 213).

As believers take seriously in their own lives the importance of modeling Jesus' example of leadership, they will discover that influence is recognized and appreciated through relational care, patience, and encouragement, rather than through coercive measures of power. Servant leadership is not a technique or strategy; it is a spiritual discipline that reflects the character of God in human relations by showing the world what it means to be a servant leader, while at the same time cultivating humility, peace, and emotional joy in their hearts (Matt. 23:11–12).

Paul's Vision of "Preferring One Another"

Repeatedly, Paul reminds the Church to live in an alternative community, living in a manner that honors others before ourselves. In Philippians 2:3-4, Paul writes, "let each esteem others better than themselves," and to "look out not only for his own interests, but also for the interests of others." This is not just a feel-good, ethical way to live, but the essence of gentleness, which is a way of being in community shaped by humility and characterized by love, respect, and unity.

Jonathan Edwards reminds us that this all requires an investment of our affections and desires to be in alignment with God's purposes above ourselves (Edwards 1746, 92). In a community characterized by gentleness, there is cooperation, reconciliation, and mutual encouragement. The apostolic vision is tethered to a relational and theological vision; when we serve others, we walk in a manner consistent with Christ, who prioritizes others above himself.

Examples abound. When tensions arose in the early Church, as described in Acts 6:1-7, the Church responded to its situation by appointing deacons to oversee the daily needs of the community. While the entire book could be written on the implications of deacon ministry here, it might be more appropriate to view "preferring one another" as prioritizing the needs of the community, actively performing acts of gentle service to one another, reducing problems, and enabling the community to grow spiritually into maturity. Augustine notes how this paradigm transforms articulate expression into imitative choices guided by love. Specifically, he outlines how the soul or entire being becomes attuned to divine love and manifests as a manifestation of God's grace (Augustine 1998, 272).

As with any teaching, the challenge is not so much the act of humility as it is combating our natural tendencies toward pride and competition. Bonhoeffer observes that the practice of humility requires us to be intentionally aware of others' needs, and attentiveness will require both spiritual discipline and practical patience (Bonhoeffer 1959, 145). Living into this ethic will require frequent reflection on oneself, the practice of prayer, and doing kind deeds of gentleness, not with the intent of being noticed or returned.

When we live into Paul's vision of putting others first, we build communities characterized by joy, trust, and resilience, which mirror the gentle leadership of Christ. In preferring others, we can create spaces for unity and environments where God can bring about spiritual gifts. Suppose we love others from a humble heart. In that case, every relationship can undergo a fundamental change, and grace ultimately glorifies God in the ordinariness of our lives (Rom. 12:10).

Love Made Visible in Small, Hidden Acts

Christ's teaching is that true love is often unnoticeable, at least on the surface, because love is best demonstrated in subtle, humble manners that often go unnoticed. Luke 21:1–4 shows us this widow's offering, small and humble and yet deeply sacrificial. The offering represents values aligned with God's intention, not separated from it. It therefore illuminates how God's love is intent-based and obedience-based rather than visibility- or recognition-based.

C.S. Lewis notes how the regular forms of love—gentle words, patient listening, thoughtful service—reveal the Kingdom in the public square, at least much of the time, but they escape notice for all kinds of reasons (Lewis 1960, 98). In fact, these unnoticeable acts of gentleness form gentleness in all. The whole self grows in sensitivity to the Spirit and the needs of others.

We can see similar reflections in the lenses of the patristic authors. Gregory of Nyssa notes that works of humility, at times almost imperceptible acts of service, provide a vehicle for growth in the life of faith and create a soul gradually shaped toward the nature of Christ's gentleness (Gregory of Nyssa c. 335–395, 76). Bonaventure posits that although small and seemingly insignificant, repeated acts of mercy establish a rhythm of holiness that provides structure to the community and establishes lasting relationships (Bonaventure 1268, 54).

From a theological perspective, hidden acts of love require a critique of the cultural meanings of visibility and recognition. The gentleness that is absent from needing applause seeks the well-being of others and the glorification of God, in contrast to self-promotion (1 Cor. 13:4–7). Henri Nouwen captures the essence of "growing the kingdom without anyone noticing," noting that these kinds of expressions transform us and others, creating an upward spiral of grace that is invisible (Nouwen 1994, 112).

Formally, we invite believers to seize everyday moments of opportunity: offer courage, serve without notice, and respond gently to needs, large or small. Indeed, each of these actions, although they seem small, results in some small spiritual development within them, and therefore, one hopes, in communal well-being. We begin to see that gentleness has been manifested as a lived, experiential reality, or a literal reality, such as Christ's quiet love in ordinary life (Matt. 10:42).

Biblical Anchors

The teachings of Jesus are rooted in Scripture, and the values of God's upside-down kingdom are continued throughout the biblical witness. The Beatitudes, for example, are an excellent example of a manifesto for humans' changed expectations by declaring, "Blessed are the poor in spirit, for theirs is the kingdom of heaven" (Matt. 5:3). Each Beatitude declares a turning of distortions of the world: true life is marked by humility, meekness, and a thirst for righteousness—not riches, power, and public recognition. As John Stott notes, "The Beatitudes call Christians to a counterculture which rejects the world's standards of success and reflects God's priorities of love and justice" (Stott 1994, 45).

Mary's song in Luke 1:52–53 illustrates her reflections: she praises God for scattering the proud and lifting the lowly, meaning God's reversal is cosmic, not moral. Augustine noted it as well, stating, "God exalts the humble, not because he is partial, but reveals the depth of love and mercy of God" (Augustine 1998, 223). Her reflections reveal the proximity and connections between God's reversals and human experience: the humble are raised up, which simultaneously means they are honored as part of God's redemptive plan.

Philippians 2:5–11 is another good anchor. The narrative of Christ's descent to human weakness to find His exaltation reflects the principle that greatness is not to be found in pride, power, and worldly glory, but in obedience and humility. For Paul, this was the mindset of believers: worldly notions of downward mobility are actually an advancement to spiritual heights. Nouwen captures this perfectly: "To take the lowest place, as Christ did, is to enter fully into the mystery of God's love and power" (Nouwen 1981, 88).

Through these biblical anchors, we can see the way for believers is being opened: humility, service, and love are not optional virtues; they are the life that grounds upside-down living in the kingdom of God. Engaging with the texts in the Bible allows for pause, reflection, and obedience in the pursuit of God's transformative justice, revealing joy, healing, and love to believers who are faithful in the example of Christ.

Beatitudes as a Manifesto of the Reversal

When the Beatitudes (Matt. 5:3–12) declared the poor in spirit, the meek, and the persecuted blessed, Jesus engaged in a radical reorientation of human assumptions. The Beatitudes are not simply moral teachings; they proclaim God's kingdom values, which differ significantly. Humility, gentleness, and dependence on God's grace are true greatness. As a kind of manifesto, Jesus's words contradict and challenge cultural expectations, specifically the associations of power with status and force (Matt. 5:5–6).

Thomas Aquinas, regarding meekness, has shown that this dispositional quality mediates strength to be exerted reasonably, combined with justice, charity, and not violence (Aquinas 1274, II-II, Q.123, Art. 4). In the

Beatitudes, spiritual poverty is accompanied by divine promise and reveals God's economy values reliance upon God beyond self-sufficiency in both blessedness and shame. Furthermore, Augustine states a property of the meek: they reflect a soul consentive with God's will, disinterested, and delighting in the Spirit rather than in one's reputation (Augustine 1998, 210).

In practice, when we put the Beatitudes into practice, we will need to adopt a countercultural stance of humility, mercy, and vulnerability, which can become the pathway to spiritual maturity. For Bonhoeffer, Christian discipleship is understood as active participation in God's reversal; strength manifests as patience or gentleness, and authority as service (Bonhoeffer 1959, 88).

Biblical examples also illustrate this point. Moses, whom Numbers 12:3 proclaims is the meekest of men, mediates God's charactered power through humility. David, that property of being God's anointed king, emerged on the verge of vengeance (1 Sam. 24:4–7) and modeled for us what the meek are blessed to be. The Beatitudes are descriptive and prescriptive; they describe a spiritually responsive heart and invite believers into Jesus's similar lifestyle of gentle perseverance.

Mary's Song: God Exalting the Lowly

Mary's Magnificat (Luke 1:46–55) celebrates God's unchanging disposition towards the humble and marginalized. In this canticle to God, Mary sings, "he has filled the hungry with good things, and the rich he has sent away empty" (Luke 1:53). Mary's song captures divine reversal, showing us a relationship between human humility and God's exaltation, one that shows in God's kingdom that the gentle and meek are favored.

Origen interprets the Magnificat allegorically, suggesting that God will exalt the spiritually humble and humble the proud (Origen 1994, 112). This behavior aligns with the ethics shared in the Beatitudes, in which human faithful responses to the grace of God are characterized by praise, surrender, and joyful submission. John Chrysostom emphasizes Mary's example—her acknowledging her own lowliness and the strength of God places before the Church that the meek are in God's presence (Chrysostom 1998 [c. 347–407], 214).

Mary's song not only serves to honor God but also invites believers to consider their own low status a priority before God, thereby developing a posture of gratitude, surrender, and trust. Dietrich Bonhoeffer argues that such a humble acknowledgment of God's sovereignty fosters spiritual endurance, predisposing the heart to give oneself in service and witness (Bonhoeffer 1959, 99).

Furthermore, Mary's example provides a helpful challenge for the Church to imagine God's grace in validating and valorizing the contributions of the overlooked and marginalized. In this economy of God, influence and blessing do not flow from exertion or wealth but from the disposition of obedience, faith, and receptivity to the spiritual work of God. By lifting the lowly, God illustrates through redemptive work that gentleness and humility are vital components in His action and plan (Luke 1:52–53).

Philippians 2: Christ's Descent and God's Exaltation

Philippians 2:5–11 exemplifies the kenosis of Christ: His voluntary humility to such a degree of death on a cross is a paradigm for Christian living. "He humbled Himself and became obedient to the point of death, even the death of the cross" (Phil. 2:8). This great descent is an imposition of gentleness—the ultimate display of power being given up for the sake of redemption of others.

Jonathan Edwards notes that Christ's humility serves as an ethical example and a divine mystery, revealing that God's Son could take on human weakness and show that true exaltation follows surrender, not force (Edwards 1746, 118). Augustine, like Edwards, interprets this humility as an analogy to what Christ bids the believer to model with the gentle force of the Spirit in day-to-day living, allowing God to use the seemingly insignificant actions of service and obedience to accomplish His work through them (Augustine 1998, 230).

The application for practice takes place broadly in both personal and communal contexts. In the calling of Christians as leaders, parents, and those in ministry, there is an expectation to practice self-emptying love, prioritizing the needs of others over one's own, with no coercive or dominating compulsion. N.T. Wright adds that followers of Christ subvert the definition of worldly success by establishing the pattern that greatness is bound to humility and service (Wright 1996, 202).

Christ's obedience is met with exaltation from God: "Therefore God also has highly exalted Him and given Him the name which is above every name" (Phil. 2:9). This theological reversal narrates the goodness of humility and gentleness and the consequential mark of spiritual authority. The believer who employs Christ-like humility enters into God's restorative work and is invited into a life rhythm of service that glorifies God and blesses others.

Theological Witnesses

Over the centuries, church leaders and spiritual authors have affirmed that, while a mystery, God's kingdom is constantly upending human expectation, exalting the downtrodden and abasing the proud. Martin Luther, in his own theology of the cross, contends that divine power, worth, and glory come exclusively from Christ's on-the-cross self-emptying: "the cross alone is our theology; the foolishness of God is the power that saves the world" (Luther 1520, 43). Luther's insight resonates with the idea introduced by Jesus that the first will be last, because the divine kingdom/reality rejects every human measure for success.

John Calvin bears witness to the preference for what is low (this is true with his concept of the royal priesthood of all believers) by stating in the *Institutes of the Christian Religion* that God "confuses the wisdom of the proud, he yolks the meek with a homely blessing, and thus glory is poured back into His sovereign grace" (Calvin 1559, 267). Calvin's theological insight helpfully supports the upside-down realities of the kingdom: human merit, status, or achievement always take a back row to humility and God-dependence. Calvin's emphasis on grace offers a pivot point for considering how believers might engage in a life cultivating joy and love, not by capitulating to the world's proper priorities, but by moving from the world's preoccupations to God's priorities.

Henri Nouwen makes this wisdom more practical and personal. In *The Wounded Healer*, Nouwen argues that people who open themselves to vulnerable and downwardly mobile spaces, as Jesus did, are joining God's redeeming work in the world (Nouwen 1981, 56). Just as the disciples learned to serve, believers, even today, can discover that real influence and leadership demand not authority over others, but simply the presence and care of others. Nouwen's pastoral and personal observations reflect Jesus' insistence that the last shall be first (Matt. 19:30), which is to love others, especially those who are left behind.

The last several centuries of church theological messengers converge on a single point: God's kingdom originates from spiritual wisdom that exceeds human expectation. When believers engage authentically with their theological messengers, they receive both support and a framework for embodying the reversal in their everyday lives. Whether from Luther's cross-oriented reflections, Calvin's theological explication of grace, or Nouwen's pastoral reflections, the message is consistently that those who choose to experience God's kingdom will do so through humility, service, and love. The beauty of each of the engaged reflections about God's kingdom offers encouragement to believers that they can choose to experience lowering themselves, forgiving their enemies, lifting the marginalized, and dropping ambition to live into the upside-down values of Jesus.

Luther and the Theology of the Cross

The theology of the cross that Martin Luther developed suggests that the gentleness and humility of genuine love (in its wholeness) are understood as God's inherent power. In memory of Paul's words in 1 Corinthians 1:25, we will resist the temptation to boast, assuming God works outside the world's framework of glory and might. In fact, the cross reminds us that as the foolishness of God is better than human wisdom and God's weakness stronger than human strength, God's true power likely operates behind our earthly edifices of power, authority, and wisdom (1 Cor. 1:25). Christ is, indeed, Jewish meekness in surrender, poised in sacrificial love. In this reversal, a genuine will to authority manifests as an exercise of authority in love and surrender, rather than domination.

Luther asserts that believers are called to engage in God's work with humility and suffering, rather than through means that embody secular authority, compulsion, violence, or achievement (Luther 1520, 44). The cross becomes a cruciform, liminal model for everyday life, as Christ's gentleness but power operates in obscurity, performing the deepest spiritual formation. Formally and pastorally, this invites Christians to enact their leadership, teaching, and love in ways that are patient and gently corrective—not coercive or harsh.

Additionally, Luther's emphasis on justification through faith reminds us that gentleness is not a moralism, but arises from a heart that thrives in grace. A faith that trusts God more than oneself, in this model, results in Christian agency participating in the reversal of human expectations, in which we mirror Christ's humble dispositions of thought, speech, and action (Luther 1520, 67). Because of the theology of the cross, human influence operates in reverse; greatness is defined by service, and strength implies restrained power.

The cross does not represent a merely historical happening, but a way of life: in unknowing, in ideal ethics and spiritual formation. When you are meek before Pilate, the Sanhedrin, and the crowd that is shouting for your execution, this is restraint. It indicates that gentleness can offer no offense or shaking, in order to disarm hostility and offer the possibility of repentance (Luke 23:9–12). Luther's insights challenge contemporary believers to understand meekness, which cultivates vulnerability as a channel of God's transformative power in humility, extending to relationships, leadership, and worship.

Calvin on God's Preference for the Humble

According to John Calvin, God exalts the humble while humbling the proud (1 Pet. 5:5; Matt. 23:12). Calvin takes the position in the *Institutes of the Christian Religion* that the governance of God over the world indicates God's preference for gentleness and humility, rather than force or human aspiration (Calvin 1559, I.15.5). The humble freely embrace God's purposes for them, having hearts open to grace, contemplation, and spiritual discernment.

Calvin read biblical stories—such as David's restraint in sparing Saul (1 Sam. 24:6), as well as the birth of Christ as humble (Luke 2:7)—as tangible examples of God's preference for meekness. When God lifts the humble, he subverts our positional elevation or favor. The point is that spiritual authority comes from obedience and humility, not from force or position. Calvin calls believers to adopt this position of reigning in our leadership, community, and personal life (Calvin 1559, II.2.8).

Incorporating this Trinitarian preference toward the humble into our devotional practice requires self-examination, gentleness in communication, and leading through servanthood. Paul's exhortation to "clothe yourselves with humility" (Col. 3:12) echoes Calvin's conviction that meekness is the only proper response to our relationship and submission to God's sovereignty. As Calvin explains, spiritual development and social authority are inseparable from Christlike gentleness; humility is both a morally liable action and a theological truth.

The different behavioral applications are ripe, especially in educational environments, ministry spaces, and family life. The humble whom God exalts call us to contain our restraining attitudes or force upon others, to listen attentively to the other, and correct compassionately. This leads to reconciliation and a grace-filled, empowered spiritual community, rather than a coercive and oppressive one. Calvin's understanding of his theology establishes a direct connection to Scripture and lived experiences, weaving together a framework for understanding gentleness as a divine strategy for addressing human frailty.

Nouwen and the Call to Downward Mobility

Henri Nouwen's framework for spiritual formation emphasizes a mode of experiencing "downward mobility" as a "Christlike" power. Nouwen suggests that true influence is exercised in presence, listening, and service—not in domination or striving (Nouwen 1994, 72). When we choose to descend into the experience of the marginal, lonely, and suffering, we are identifying with the humility of Christ as we engage in empathetic connections and change relationships.

Nouwen points to the life of Christ and how he constantly associated with the lowly, cared for the broken without exercising authority, and invited trust through his gentle or soft proposal of hope (Matt. 9:36; Luke 19:10). The relationality of power that took the shape of vulnerability is in complete opposition to the world system of power and success, where influence is judged by control and visibility. Nouwen describes this self-emptying or downward mobility as a continuous and deep spiritual discipline, one that limits our ambition and advances solely by meeting others' needs (Nouwen 1994, 88).

The theological connection between this self-emptying is echoed in Paul's suggestion to take on the humility of Christ (Phil. 2:3–8) and Augustine's notion that God honors the humble disposition while simultaneously reducing the pride of the proud (Augustine 1998, 245). Embracing the posture of downward mobility means the believer participates in the redemptive economy through which service becomes strength, and gentleness is another word for spiritual authority.

Nouwen's vision practically challenges contemporary believers in leadership, family life, and ministry to value listening, patience, and nurturing care with deep empathy for others, as well as humble service, rather than a continuation or reciprocity of assertive ambition or helping. Gentleness can promote, but it is not passivity; instead, it is a robust, Christlike engagement with, for, and on behalf of others that influences restoration, reconciliation, and trust.

The call to downward mobility represents a shift in human expectations, where spiritual depth and influence are nourished in place of humility, empathy, and sacrificial service to and for others, as God often prefers the meek or gentle of heart. Nouwen's perspective offers both a theological foundation and practical guidance on how to embody the gentleness of Christ's authority in our daily lives.

Living the Reversal Today

Embracing the upside-down way of God's kingdom is not just an idea; it is also practical and honest. Disciples must intentionally live out God's call for humility in their daily lives and deliberately choose to prioritize other-oriented actions and the expectation of service, mercy, and love, not recognition, privilege, or advantage. Jesus teaches, "Whoever exalts himself will be humbled and he who humbles himself will be exalted" (Matt. 23:12), and calls his followers to reorient their ascriptions from worldly acclaim to God's purpose. This calling encompasses all aspects of life—home, work, church, and community—where self-giving options compete against self-serving alternatives.

Practicing humility means beginning with small steps. Dietrich Bonhoeffer firmly believes that to be a disciple requires living into God's upside-down moral "order" through decisions—especially decisions made in daily, small choices. When we take up the call to follow Christ, we surrender "my way" to the way of Christ and offer ourselves as servants to our friends and family. To those who live on the margins—this is the economy of grace (Bonhoeffer 1959, 121). John Stott also reminds Christians how to live humbly, based on Jesus' teaching of the Beatitudes and the way that Jesus lived, "to honour others, to favour the weak and their needs, and to stoop and to wash others' feet rather than to seek worldly power" (Stott 1994, 89).

Joy is a natural outcome of this way of life. When believers surrender to no longer competing for recognition, they will find joy and contentment in their obedience. They will be free to serve and to embrace others, and their personal satisfaction will come from God's favour, not praise from fellow humans (Phil. 2:3–4). Healing arises from humility when envy, bitterness, and resentment are replaced with empathy, reconciliation, and gratitude. Communities living God's way of thinking selflessly experience honour and restore justice, with a glued compacted-ness that is the ultimate goal of the upside-down kingdom (1 Cor. 12:25–26).

Finally, love is the hallmark of God's people. Moreover, love is lived out in serving the overlooked, supporting the weak, and outwardly signalling our inner humble reality. Living upside-down discipleship opens doors to demonstrate Christ and give witness to a world primarily filled with self-interest, entitlement, and ambition. Practicing humility, service, and sacrificial love in their mundane and ordinary decisions creates daily opportunities for kingdom exchange, and as Jesus taught, the last shall be first and the first shall be last.

Practicing Humility in Daily Life

Humility is the bedrock of the upside-down kingdom, and it is most powerfully evident in our ordinary and everyday choices and interactions. The Scriptures often call believers to humility: "God resists the proud, but gives grace to the humble" (James 4:6). Daily acts of humility are not merely a passive act of humbling oneself; they are an active alignment of the heart and actions of the believer with God's agenda and desires. True humility understands and recognizes that any abilities, successes, or ventures are gifts entrusted by God, not trophies of our self-promotion.

Augustine proposes humility starts with knowing oneself and realizing one's dependence on God (Augustine 1998, 121). In the practice of daily life, self-knowledge and dependence on God resemble two ears and one mouth; that is, listening twice as much as we speak. Humility looks and feels like serving others, quietly and anonymously, so that we attend to the needs of others as well as our own. Assume, as Henri Nouwen writes, that our humanity is fundamentally relational; humility allows us to honor all we encounter and creates spaces for love and authentic community (Nouwen 1994, 46).

The Scripture provides models of humility and offers everyday, real-life examples. Jesus washing the disciples' feet (John 13:4–17) is an example fleshed out in humble washing, by turning a simple act into an example of a servant leader. In the same letter, Paul challenges believers to "count others more significant than yourselves," which challenges the Christian priority of self in self-promotion, to care for whom is in view (Phil. 2:3). The humble life is not about humility in terms of self-deprecation; it is about choosing to glorify God, instead of trying to win hearts for oneself.

Daily acts of humility are about joy and resilience. The believer lives into the freedom that comes with surrendering to a concern for control, and lives in a manner free from envy, anxiety, or rivalry. Bonhoeffer recognizes that humility is the only way to follow Christ faithfully in ordinary life, and to make the ordinary tasks acts of devotion rather than mere vocations (Bonhoeffer 1959, 88). Being humble at work, at home, and in your community can be as simple as listening, encouraging quietly, or providing support to fellow workers without making a fuss.

Therefore, humility in daily life is both assimilative and transformative. Humility changes relationships, reconciles communities, and opens the heart to God's blessings and giftedness. Practical acts of humility create conditions for joy, love, and realms of spiritual richness that reveal God's upside-down kingdom. We are reminded that the essential principles upon which Jesus' Kingdom is built are practiced most deliberately and spiritedly in the mundane and typically unremarkable mini-experiences.

Choosing Service over Self-Promotion

In the Kingdom Upside-Down, someone is not great because they have status or are known; they are great because they are willing to serve. This is the conviction that Jesus lived by: he came "not to be served, but to serve, and to give his life as a ransom for many" (Matt. 20:28). In this way, service is the active demonstration of humility and allows believers a tangible way to embody the inversion he revealed.

Living in service instead of self-serving requires intentionality. Every day, there are countless ways to serve the needs of others: offering to help a colleague with a project without seeking recognition, being present to listen to a friend in distress, or offering a kind word without expecting notice. Each choice, no matter how insignificant, flows from the believer's alignment with the values of the upside-down kingdom. John Stott reminds us that in the Christian ethic, action to serve others can be selfless, demonstrating God's love, and this both transforms the giver and the receiver (Stott 1994, 63).

The New Testament also bears witness to the power of service. The parable of the Good Samaritan (Luke 10:30–37) illustrates how service transcends social boundaries, prejudice, and convenience. Such service is never transactional and is also never reciprocal or required to be recognized; it is a model of Christ's self-giving love. Paul commanded the church to "through love, serve one another" (Gal. 5:13), demonstrating that a particular person's common good is always greater than their particular good.

In a theological frame, service forms character and spiritual maturity. C.S. Lewis argued that love is active; expressing love requires action, and love must be embodied. There is no love without action (Lewis 1960, 82). Bonhoeffer suggests that discipleship is the synthesis of courage and action for others, particularly when that action remains unnoticed (Bonhoeffer 1959, 91). In this way, service is simultaneously obedient and formative: not only is it a basic act of obedience, but it is also forming one's own heart to mirror his radical humility and generosity.

Choosing service creates joy, and it renews relationships. When believers choose to receive a summons to live into service and reject self-promotion that separates them from one another, they can be freed from envy, jealousy, ambition, and pride, and reintegrate beauty into their daily relationships. This is a theological kingdom logic, too: our world still operates with the logic that our influence and significance are drawn from a selfish ambition, rather than through service to others. The way to long-term significance and legacy is through a form of service to others. In fact, every small act of service—often an anonymous act of service—becomes a compost of God's grace and also demonstrates to the world that the first of God's people are the people who choose to take the last place.

Healing Communities Through Mutual Honor

God's upside-down kingdom is not only about the individual; it is about the communities that God's people are called to embody, communities of mutual honor, care, and restoration. The upside-downness that Jesus proclaims redefines greatness personally, but it also changes relationships and creates environments for the practice of humility, forgiveness, and encouragement. In a world of competition and comparison, this act of self-valuation to honor others is a countercultural response to God's call to prioritize community over self-inflation. The apostle Paul sums up this reversal well when he says, "Bear one another's burdens, and so fulfill the law of Christ" (Gal. 6:2). And bear one another's burdens is the essence of this communal reversal: the invitation to participate with God in his restorative work.

The early church reflected this notion in Acts 2:44–47, where believers shared their possessions, helped one another, and created a community while respecting their diversity. Henri Nouwen has noted that communities of mutual honor reflect the kingdom of God on earth: "Christian fellowship is not based on seeking power or acceptance but on nurturing life, healing, and belonging" (Nouwen 1994, 38). By reflecting mutual honor, the people of God bore witness to God's alternative logic in the world: where the low are lifted, and the strong learn to serve.

In addition, mutual honor involves recognizing and valuing each person's gifts, struggles, and contributions. In doing so, Paul exhorts, "Be kindly affectionate to one another with brotherly love, in honor giving preference to one another" (Rom. 12:10). For Paul, love within the community is relational, active, and practical. Mutual honor acts as a form of healing for those who have been hurt by rejection, jealousy, and exclusion along a journey of graced acceptance. As Bonhoeffer explains, discipleship within a transformative community involves humility and effort to hear and set aside self-interest: "The disciples who were living in community were to try to meet the needs of those around them and thus be obedient to God; they were to lay down their own desires and selfishness and reign as agents of reconciliation into God's kingdom" (Bonhoeffer 1959, 123).

In practice, creating communities of mutual honor continues to involve active listening, forgiving freely, and celebrating others' growth together. Both leaders and members are called to humility and charity, to patience and generosity, recognizing and honoring one another so that relationships reflect the upside-down way of the invitation of Christ's kingdom. For believers who aspire to mutual honor, together with churches and small groups, to be delighted as sites of healing, nurturing, and encouragement, is to experience a taste of the complete restoration of the kingdom to come, where the last are truly first. The first is to learn to serve, to love, and to bring joy and healing to all.

Love as the Mark of God's Upside-Down People

In God's kingdom, love is the hallmark of those who embrace the reversal. While the world measures greatness in terms of status, wealth, or power, the upside-down ethic that Christ champions elevates love to be the accurate metric of life lived in obedience to God. Jesus commands us, "A new commandment I give to you, that you love one another; as I have loved you, that you also love one another" (John 13:34). Jesus did not call for an emotion here, but rather a demonstrable expression of kingdom value. This love is sacrificial, humble, and relational, thus painting the very character of God.

The early church modeled this through practical means. Believers are described in Acts 4:32–35 as unrestricted in sharing and caring for one another's possessions and needs; they did not consider anything their own, and no one was in need. Their communal care, rooted in love, illustrates an active and selfless commitment to the well-being of others. In a discussion of the Greek word *agape*, John Stott emphasizes that love, expressed in humility and service, can and does transform people and their communities into places of grace, reconciliation, and encouragement (Stott 1994, 61).

Paul provides additional guidance on *agape*, elaborating on Christian love and faithfulness: preferring one another in honor (Rom. 12:10) and bearing one another's burdens (Gal. 6:2). Agape in this setting is associated with transformation that heals relational rifts, provides refuge for the rejected, and fosters unity of purpose. Henri Nouwen observes that true Christian love reaches out to the weak, the outcast, and those forgotten; the kingdom of God is revealed through the love of God enacted by His people (Nouwen 1981, 42).

Living the life of Christian faith with love as the guiding principle takes effort, manifesting in patience, listening, encouragement, and kindness—essentially a myriad of gifts and skills mostly unnoticed by a world fixated on loss and judgment, but recognized by a God who notices. When believers live out of love, rather than an agenda, they embody the upside-down kingdom, celebrating God for exalting the humble and glorifying those who serve, unnoticed and faithful.

Chapter 2

The Gentle Heart of Jesus

The Reversal of Power

In the teaching of Jesus, power is not the power to oppress but ignobility and gentleness. Jesus describes himself as being "gentle and lowly in heart" (Matt. 11:29). This proclamation turned conventional notions of authority and influence on its head. The world often associates power with coercion, authority, and visibility; Christ's model for us is strength exercised through service, patience, and restraint. In God's upside-down kingdom, those who are weak for righteousness' sake will be exalted, while those who are strong according to the world will be humbled (Matt. 20:26–27). Augustine captures this divine inversion when he observes that "the power of God lies in gentleness. The strong are not more powerful by virtue of their domination. They are strong by virtue of their service" (Augustine 1998, 132).

Jesus' own life reflects this. He reached out to those on the margins of society. He invited tax collectors to a feast. He healed people without insisting they owe him gratitude or recompense (Luke 19:1–10). Jesus had authority and power, but his strength was not coercive. As it moved from authority to compassion, Jesus did not need to insist (and he rarely did) that others render him honor or recognition. Chrysostom explains, "The Lord's gentleness is the best evidence of power. For he has subdued our souls without violence. He has providence, able to turn people's hearts" (Chrysostom 202, trans. Kennedy). Gentleness directly disrupts and explicitly challenges the human quest for worldly power, because it demonstrates that authentic leadership is not hierarchical, but relational and sacrificial.

This call to gentleness is not limited to Jesus alone; discipleship calls for followers to enter into the same way of living. Bonhoeffer describes discipleship as accepting an upside-down ethic: "to learn to yield, in love, where the world insists on assertion, and to bear weakness, where the world claims advantage" (Bonhoeffer 1959, 64). Packer clarifies that such gentleness is not passivity but "an active pursuit that is rooted in obedience, courage, and faith in God's providence" (Packer 1973, 88). Seen through this understanding, gentleness becomes a form of spiritual authority in communal identity for congregational living, service, and belonging; an authority that is transformative, reconciliatory, and reflective of the presence of Christ wherever chaos and pride prevail.

By redefining power in terms of gentleness, Jesus provides a concrete framework for life in God's kingdom: servants are leaders, the strong are gentle, and the influential serve in authority through love. Moreover, this inversion calls every believer to "be the humble, gentle, courageous, and trusting person," recognizing that the way of gentleness brings strength and honor from God.

Strength Perfected in Gentleness

From the very beginning of His ministry, it was clear that Jesus' power was never based on might or force, but one that was gentle. In Matthew's Gospel, we read how Jesus invites the weary and burdened to come to him for rest: "Take My yoke upon you, and learn from Me, for I am gentle and lowly in heart, and you will find rest for your souls" (Matt. 11:29). The invitation is juxtaposed against the idea of leadership as understood in first-century Judea, where authority might was imposed through coercive relationships, intimidation, or status. Jesus shows what true power looks like, one perfected in gentleness, for gentleness is strength under control.

Some ample biblical witnesses serve as exemplars of this particular expression of strength. Moses, noted to be "very meek, more than all people who were on the face of the earth" (Num. 12:3), never led Israel with human might but instead with trust and humility in God. Equally, the Servant of Isaiah models quiet endurance and self-restraint and demonstrates this apparent paradox inherent in God's Spirit at work in human weakness (Isa. 42:1–4; 53:7). Augustine contrasts Christ's humility as something different from weakness, but as the highest form of authority: "For it is by becoming humble that He raises the human race" (Augustine 1998, 121).

The idea of strength in gentleness is illustrated repeatedly across the Gospels. In his ministry among the marginalized, children, and sinners, Jesus' power was revealed through the lens of love rather than intimidation (Mark 10:14; Luke 7:36–50). John Chrysostom's notion of Christ's gentleness as a sort of obedient strength reveals that gentleness can be a power, as it can change people's hearts without coercion: "the gentleness of Christ is stronger than all the outward might, for it bends the soul without breaking it" (Chrysostom 202, trans. Kennedy).

In practice, to model this kind of gentleness, believers will posture themselves toward restraint, patience, and attentiveness to the needs of others. This strength requires believers to rely on God's Spirit to guide them in proper action and in how they exercise authority, regardless of whether at home, at work, or in the community. Gentleness can transform relationships, reveal God's character, and embody the paradox of the kingdom, where the strongest relinquish their self-interest and, in most instances, the most powerful act is one of gentleness.

"Gentle and Lowly": Jesus' Self-Description

Jesus' self-identification as "gentle and lowly in heart" (Matt. 11:29) offers profound insight into the authority and heart of his mission. Unlike worldly authorities, who often exercise power through coercion or domination, Jesus' power is seen in his humility, restraint, and compassionate presence among humanity. Moreover, this self-description cuts across the grain of cultural markers of leadership, while simultaneously calling believers to a disposition of trust, surrender, and relational connectivity. As Augustine wrote, "True strength is not identified with raw force... but is found in the gentle, still, and reverent obedience of mind and heart that is attuned to the will of God" (Augustine 1998, 215).

The gentle heart of Jesus is likewise demonstrative of the relational nature of divine authority. Jesus models gentleness in relation to others as he welcomes children (Mark 10:14), tenderly addresses the repentant, sinful woman (Luke 7:44–47), and invites the weary with rest-giving words (Matt. 11:28–30). Within this, Jesus is not reacting in weakness, but revealing that God's authority is not externally imposed on humanity but, like Christ, is internalized and flows from an alignment with divine love. Chrysostom explains that Christ's meekness is not a sign of weakness but a sovereign restraint, intended to bring others to repentance and restoration (Chrysostom 202, trans. Kennedy).

Jesus' gentleness also speaks to the human desire to feel secure or safe in the relationships of life. By describing himself as "lowly in heart," Jesus' self-identification draws upon the themes of vulnerability, marginalization, guilt, and shame. According to theologians like Nouwen, an encounter with Christ's lowly heart leads to a deeper experience of restoration with God, since feelings of anxiety, fear, and defensiveness are met with patient understanding rather than condemnation (Nouwen 1981, 58).

Practically speaking, the call to follow the gentle and lowly Christ challenges the believer to embody humility, patience, and grace in all encounters, in every moment of life. Our words, choices, and responses become physical manifestations of God's tender authority. While our culture outspokenly cherishes aggression, self-assertion, and control, Jesus' way of living is countercultural, thus providing the beginnings of community life where healing, trust, and love can flourish.

The World's Hunger for Force vs. God's Call to Meekness

In general, the power of human society is often identified with force, domination, and coercion, which compel the will of another. Whether it is a political leader, corporate leader, or organized crime figure, the ethos of human power values aggression and control as signs of strength. However, the Christ event and a Christian ethos supersede these beliefs, replacing them with more substantial and weaker ones, because the kingdom of God operates differently. Authority is made manifest not through coercion or oppression, but through gentleness, humility, and self-sacrificial love. After all, Jesus says, "Take My yoke upon you, and learn from Me, for I am gentle and lowly in heart" (Matt. 11:29). The "yoke" is representative of partnership with God, where we are invited to partner with God's ways and to reject the world's example of power.

The tension between worldly oppression and kingdom meekness reflects the life of Christ in vivid detail. While all look for military messiahs and kings who demand and exert their political and militaristic values, Jesus confronts injustice and oppression with nonviolence. He turned over the tables of the money changers (Matt. 21:12–13) not using sheer force, but as an expression of measured moral resistance, embodying righteous zeal and strength in a moment of total moral restraint. John Calvin describes God's power as expressed in humility and meekness, demonstrating that God transforms the hearts of people, not through coercion, but rather by willfully changing (Calvin 1559, 432).

This meekness can also be manifested through pastoral relationships. Those who follow Christ are invited to deny their own temptation to dominate, criticize, or manipulate. Augustine reminds us that meekness is not a passive action, but rather a disciplined strength, where the desires of the soul are aligned with the will of God, inviting each person to exercise influence toward restoration patiently (Augustine 1998, 87). As Henri Nouwen reminds us, when we adopt a meek posture, we develop reconciliation, trust, and a caring community to contest the fear, hostility, and competition of a force-driven world (Nouwen 1981, 102).

Hearing and accepting God's call to meekness is an intentional process. Believers learn to moderate ambition, overcome rage, and practice servanthood rather than self-vindication. As believers walk in meekness, they reflect the gentle heart of Jesus, providing testimony against cultural presumptions, healing relationships, and authentic authority over spirits that is rooted in love rather than fear.

Old Testament Roots

The gentle heart of Jesus is embedded in the Old Testament, wherein God frequently elevates a meek, patient, and suffering obedience over worldly power. In Isaiah 53, Isaiah refers to the Suffering Servant: a leader who does not gain strength and authority through conquest and repression, but rather through patience and suffering in acts of love. "He was oppressed and He was afflicted, yet He opened not His mouth; He was led as a lamb to the slaughter" (Isa. 53:7). The Servant's example illustrates that true authority is demonstrated through placing trust in God, patient restraint when provoked, and being committed to God's purposes even when suffering. Early theologians recognized that this was a prefiguration of Christ and believed that God's power often works through apparent weakness and otherwise visible normative vistas to bring about redemption (Origen 1994, 112).

Despite being anointed king, David offers many instances throughout the Old Testament of regular acts of gentle strength. In 1 Samuel 24, he refrains from vengeance against Saul, even though he was allowed to act and was anointed to take the throne. In this way, David's self-restraint demonstrated God's wise timing in place of hostility during dangerous circumstances because moral strength was evident in acting with self-control instead of impulse (Chrysostom 1986, 145). The life of David illustrates that obedience to God's initiated call, rather than just impulsively claiming authority, brings forth longevity in spiritual fruitfulness and relational outcomes.

The psalm speaks similarly when it calls for meekness and trust. "The meek shall inherit the earth, and shall delight themselves in the abundance of peace" (Ps. 37:11). Jesus echoes this entirely in the Beatitudes, joining the Old Testament wisdom with the New Testament promise of God's coming and ultimate Kingdom (Matt. 5:5). The promise is that as people voluntarily give up their self-seeking, self-glorifying struggles for power and allow patience and humility to cultivate trust in God's timing, they will receive God's long-sought promise of reward.

The fullness of these images from the Old Testament brings clarity to Jesus's teaching on gentleness. From the patient suffering of the Servant of Isaiah, to David's measured restraint, to the psalmist's exhortation for meekness, there is continuity throughout the Scriptures in humble strength and good reliance upon God. Christ's followers are asked to adopt the same disposition of loving grace, an intention of glory for God, and to pace themselves, venturing their ambitions, and above all, to trust God's timing over their own immediate aspirations.

In this manner, the gentle heart of Jesus is both anchored in and fulfilled by God's redemptive intent seen from the beginning of the record of Scripture.

The Suffering Servant of Isaiah

Isaiah 53's prophecy of the Suffering Servant offers a profound insight into the gentleness of God's heart and His Messiah. Here we find a figure described as "despised and rejected by men, a Man of sorrows and acquainted with grief" (Isa. 53:3) who provides leadership characterized not by overpowering force, but by sacrificial emptiness and humbleness. It is not in coercion, violence, and domination like worldly rulers display; however, the power of this servant is in fulfillment of God's will through submission, compassion, and suffering. He fulfills God's redemptive will through an existence of quiet obedience, and in the process shows us strength that is bled over with gentleness. This example repudiates any notion of authority as an act of brutality; God's ultimate victory in human history is entrusted to a Man who suffers at the hands of an opposed world that refuses to acknowledge God's hand (Bonhoeffer 1959, 92).

Not only does the ministry of the servant exemplify God's agency in humanity's suffering, but it also provides for a pastoral witness. For in His suffering, as He bears the sins and griefs of others, the servant demonstrates an aspect of power in relationship and amelioration—power through healing, not dominating; power through lifting, not crushing; and power through restoration, not shame. Augustine recognizes the paradox inherent in suffering by saying: "it is in the humble of the Cross that true greatness is revealed; what is weak in the eyes of the world, God has exalted" (Augustine 1998, 102). The servant's example of silence and endurance serves as an embodiment for believers to summon the strength to refrain from responding with a self-centered perspective of power and control over others, but rather to exhibit patience, understanding, care, and reconciliation.

There are parallels between Isaiah's vision and Jesus' own ministry, particularly in his encounter and engagement with the poor and marginalized, as well as those who are suffering. Matthew's summary of

Jesus' heart makes a connection between our servant description and a call to "gentleness and lowly of heart" (Matt. 11:29)—both are aspects of strength that are quiet, sacrificial, and empowering. Moreover, this linkage furthers God's unified course. It is the aforementioned aim of God not to perfect power in force, but to reveal strength in humble service. By discerning the obedience of servanthood, we have a possible spiritual template for leadership, ministry, and relationships—a power fraught with love, patience, and endurance for the good of others (Nouwen 1981, 44).

David's Restraint as a Model of Gentle Strength

David's characteristics offer a nuanced perspective on gentleness in power, suggesting that strength is often exhibited in the form of restraint. Even though David was the anointed king of Israel, he continually sought to practice patience instead of retaliation, especially as it pertained to Saul, whom David was aware had his life in jeopardy (1 Sam. 24:4–7). David demonstrated restraint by sparing Saul's life, showing a level of control over reactive, impulsive aggression. Ultimately, David wisely prioritized obedience to God and moral rightness over political expedience. Chrysostom comments, "The wise ruler fears not merely the enemy [without], but the passions [within]; to restrain [one's] wrath is as a king to imitate the Lord" (Chrysostom, c. 347–407, 152).

David's restraint is not weakness by any means; his restraint is illustrated as purposeful and deliberate strength when he controls his urges to retaliate and entrusts vengeance to God. David exemplifies gentleness that not only does not succumb to evil, but he also displays gentleness in directing power toward Godly ends. David demonstrates the ability of a king to assume power through gentleness that does not result in coercion, but rather shows humility, patience, and care for those who are vulnerable. Brueggemann suggests that David's measured response in moments of pressure is the same response encouraged by God in 1 Pet. 2:15. It is a response characteristic of God: "True authority is exercised not through domination, but through faithful covenantal obedience" (Brueggemann 1994, 63).

In addition, David's gentle posture is reflective of the spiritual fruit of gentleness. David's choices rewarded God and the community with his patience regarding God's timing, rather than with his own ambition. Today's readers can observe in David the intersection of leadership and personal conduct; gentleness under pressure can be an example of God's wisdom with the potential to elicit trust and respect rather than fear. David's restraint foreshadows the gentleness of Christ, as noted in 1 Pet. 2:23, which states of Christ, "when He was reviled, He did not revile in return; when He suffered, He did not threaten." God's people are instructed to live according to the spirit in which David exemplifies this (Packer 1973, 118).

The Meek Shall Inherit the Earth

The promise that "the meek shall inherit the earth" (Ps. 37:11; Matt. 5:5) highlights a countercultural principle: divine reward flows to those who embrace humility rather than aggressive self-assertion. Meekness, often mistaken for weakness, is in fact a profound spiritual strength. It represents the alignment of the heart with God's will, a deliberate choice to trust God's justice and timing rather than seizing control through human effort. Aquinas affirms, "Meekness is the tempering of strength with reason and charity; it is neither slothful nor timid, but ordered by virtue" (Aquinas 1274, II-II, q.123, a.2).

Psalm 37 reinforces this principle, contrasting the fleeting success of the wicked with the enduring inheritance of the humble. The psalmist exhorts believers to "Rest in the Lord, and wait patiently for Him" (Ps. 37:7), emphasizing that meekness is active trust, not passive resignation. Matthew 5:5 echoes this ethic in Jesus' Sermon on the Mount: meekness is blessed because it opens the heart to God's kingdom, granting spiritual and relational flourishing. Nouwen reflects that meekness enables Christians to participate in God's restorative work, promoting peace and reconciliation without resorting to domination (Nouwen 1994, 68).

Meekness also serves as a corrective to human ambition. In a world that prizes aggression and self-promotion, those who practice humility reveal the upside-down nature of God's kingdom. Through meekness, believers gain clarity in decision-making, cultivate patience in relationships, and mirror Christ's gentle strength. By embracing the divine paradox—that yielding to God leads to true inheritance—followers experience both inner peace and outward influence that aligns with God's purposes, demonstrating that the path of gentleness is not weakness but the very essence of spiritual power (Bonhoeffer 1959, 103).

Gentleness in the Life of Christ

The life of Jesus reveals gentleness, not as weakness, but rather as the most necessary demonstration of divine power. In Matt. 19:14, when interacting with children, He exposes societal notions about power, importance, and significance: "But Jesus said, 'Let the little children come to Me, and do not forbid them; for of such is the kingdom of heaven.'" In welcoming the vulnerable, Christ lifts those who have been put down by society and exhibits a strength that prioritizes an ethos of otherness over self-interest. As Chrysostom observes, Jesus' attention to the powerless is the heart of God's kingdom—leadership exemplified in humility and service as opposed to power (Chrysostom 1986, 203).

Jesus' gentleness also welcomes the broken and weary. Jesus approaches the sinner, the grieving, and the burdened without crushing the "bruised reed" while still calling them to transformation (Matt. 12:20). As Augustine teaches, such a measured response demonstrates God's perfect timing and patience, recognizing that growth flourishes most gently rather than violently (Augustine 1998, 198). When Jesus heals the blind, lepers, and paralytics, He consistently chooses restoration over judgment and mercy, which strengthens souls without dependence.

Even in the shadow of the cross, Christ, as the Lamb, models gentleness. He fulfills the prophecy in Isaiah by not resisting unjust suffering (Isa. 53:7). The gospels recount Jesus' silence before his accusers and his prayer for forgiveness over those who crucified him (Luke 23:34). Origen writes that Christ's meekness and endurance model what gentleness looks like in practice; the paradox of meekness is power, and power is submitting and serving with authentic love and self-sacrifice, as opposed to force (Origen 1994, 128).

Jesus' examples teach that gentleness is not a passive aesthetic, but rather an active strength. Jesus' welcome of the vulnerable, restoration of the broken, and his submission to suffering represent a kingdom logic that values humility over power, mercy over strength, and sacrificial love over self-interest. Disciples of Christ are invited to share this gentleness so that we might embody it in our own relationships, leadership, and service, allowing the heart of God to transform human interaction.

Welcoming Children and the Vulnerable

The biblical account of Jesus' interactions with children clearly illustrates the gentleness of divine power. When the disciples reprimanded those who were bringing their children to Jesus, he said, "Let the children come to me, and do not hinder them, for to such belongs the kingdom of heaven" (Matt. 19:14). In this action, Jesus subverts all human prejudices that value worthiness based on a person's rank, power, or intellectual status. Jesus honors the vulnerable, those who are powerless and dependent on anointed action, demonstrating that gentleness is not weakness or a lack of effectiveness, but a conscious decision to honor God's image in all people who are in some way incapable. Chrysostom further supports this understanding of welcoming the weak as divine grace: "By ... [being]

tender toward the least in the world, we imitate Christ in looking on those whom the entire world holds in contempt" (Chrysostom 1986, 88).

This action exemplifies pastoral care and relational care. These children are weak in terms of the community's understanding. They are brought to the center of the kingdom, simulating the overturning of God's kingdom. Likewise, those adults who are weak due to illness, poverty, or social standing find gentleness in Jesus, with actions that focus on restoration rather than condemnation. Nouwen suggests that providing this kind of care is an act of intention; it is strength under control, serving rather than being served (Nouwen 1981, 52). In a contemporary context, this has relevance for parents, leaders, and teachers as they approach those entrusted to them relationally, with patience, kindness, empathy, and respect, affirming their worth as reflections of God's image.

Theologically, the welcome of the vulnerable within a community relationship not only echoes God's covenantal concern for the weak (Ps. 68:5), but it also echoes Christ's active gentleness, not merely passive gentleness; it is not passive, neutral, or complacent. Christ's gentleness acts, intervenes, to bless, protect, and restore. The manner in which gentleness is acted out is relational and incarnational; it is literature that engages with the embodiment of human need, demonstrated without domination or coercion. For the believer, this posture in action also serves as the foundation for cultivating humility, obedience, and Christlikeness. By embracing the lowly, followers participate in God's way of inviting love that heals, belonging that restores, and presence that acknowledges worth. Furthermore, without a doubt, this is a truly remarkable strength, exemplified by gentle humility (Augustine 1998, 204).

Restoring the Broken without Crushing the Bruised Reed

Christ's ministry exemplified a slow and restorative approach to anyone who is spiritually, emotionally, or socially broken. In Matthew 12:20, the author applies the prophecy of Isaiah to Jesus, saying: "A bruised reed He will not break, and smoking flax He will not quench." The imagery suggests a gentle approach—God's way is not through crushing or destroying weakness, but through compassionate and restorative support. The bruised reed represents those afflicted by sin, oppression, or failure. Gentle treatment of the broken is standing next to the weak while orienting toward growth—reflecting divine patience and mercy.

Augustine notes that gentleness in correction or leadership is a receptacle of grace: "If you treat the weak with harshness, you quench the spirit; if you treat them with gentleness, you nourish it" (Augustine 1998, 312). This principle of leadership stands in great contrast to the worldly practices that often lean toward punishment, domination, and shaming for conformity. Jesus' approach provides healing for relational and spiritual wounds through the strength of relationship—without inciting shame or fear—which invites only repentance. Nouwen reminds us of the sorting that occurs when bringing tactful, gentle, courageous love and correction, in order to enter another's vulnerability without trying to control them (Nouwen 1981, 67).

When it comes down to practice, leaders, parents, mentors, or anyone called to a relationship of being a helper or guide must enact even more patience, listen deeply, and then encourage emotional or physical movement in the right direction. The delicacy of kairos, or sacred time, exists when strength and softness can be wielded such that the person in need is not harmed in any way, but instead they can take strength from it to flourish.

As followers of Christ, we can imitate that leadership posture by finding meekness. Our power can reflect Jesus' gentleness and compassion. That power may be able to heal and nurture, rather than intimidate, control, or even destroy.

The Silent Lamb before His Shearers

Jesus demonstrates the ultimate model of gentleness in His obedience to suffering, especially in the Passion. Isaiah 53:7 describes the Messiah: "He was oppressed, and he was afflicted, yet he opened not his mouth; like a lamb that is led to the slaughter, and like a sheep that before its shearers is silent, so he opened not his mouth." The silence of the lamb is not an absence of response, but silence that is born of self-control, humility, and trust. Bonhoeffer points out that the silence of Jesus is a paradoxical strength: "As we see Christ's silence before injustice and rejection to be the most poignant declaration of His power as living in love, we place love in its full perfection" (Bonhoeffer 1959, 114).

The image of the silence of the lamb stands in harsh contrast to preconceived worldly notions of resistance and retribution. Where humans often embody power through indignation, hostility, or retaliation, Jesus' gentleness embodies divine authority through submission and obedient service. Jesus' silence can signify trust and courage, as well as dignity, offering an incarnate relationship with strength balanced not by power, but by the might of endurance in the name of redemption. Noted Augustine states, "The lowliness of Christ is the power of God, which elevates the poor while confounding the proud" (Augustine 1998, 198).

From a theological standpoint, the silent lamb conveys the world's paradox to believers in the power of the kingdom: suffering while enduring service without resisting is a truly profound display of the authority of love, which exudes the transformative effect wrought by patience. In terms of its pastoral application, this example offers a similar challenge for Christians when confronting conflict, injustice, strife, or hardship. Rather than retaliate with severity, Christians ought to respond with suitable gentleness of principle and without resentful arrows for their choices. Justice yields a higher process of reconciliation and the way of love, which can augment the spiritual journey of the Christian, often bringing out in fuller effect the tenderness of Christ's gentleness in our daily life (Packer 1973, 145).

Healing through Gentleness

Jesus' gentleness offers profound healing for our wounded hearts and broken souls, freeing us from the harshness, rejection, and abuse that can cause us harm. Throughout the Scriptures, we receive a restorative power from Him that is in stark contrast to the abrasive methods the world tries to impose—it is often much harsher in its attempts at correction and control. Matthew 11:28–29 states, "Come to Me, all you who labor and are heavy laden, and I will give you rest. Take My yoke upon you and learn from Me, for I am gentle and lowly in heart, and you will find rest for your souls." This invitation reminds us that real healing begins in the arms of Christ, who offers the invitation to experience gentleness, embracing brokenness rather than condemnation.

The wounds from harshness, words, or unjust treatment and judgment of self can leave deep scars. However, the gentle way of Christ, rather than the harshness (or even simply the "not gentle" way), restores us instead of wounding us further. Augustine noted, "Indeed, if you are to ponder these things adequately, you must consider this: God has evidently acted patiently and kindly towards the whole human race, and this is a mark of love, since even in allowing something to progress he offers it the 'gift' of developing, although it is unable to cultivate itself" (Augustine 1998, 214). Similarly, John Chrysostom observed, "And well may the Lord be patient and endure their weaknesses in silence; for if he appeared to make no demands, it will be like punishing them in advance with reproach. Instead of reproaching them, he displays gentleness. He discloses the nature of their sin while he is refusing condemnation, so they may perceive guilt and repent from guilt, not shame, because…" (Chrysostom 1986, 207). In these moments, we perceive gentleness as a conduit of spiritual healing, as it offers the soul a glimpse of God's mercy and grace.

Jesus's patience is a comfort to the anxious and weary. When we can endure human frailty, we can listen earnestly and forgive, creating a space for homecoming and the restoration of heart and mind (Isa. 40:29–31). Origen emphasized that this patient engagement fulfills God's will, whereby humanity reconciles itself fully to Him. In God's kind action of renewing the soul from emotional and spiritual wounds, he approaches them tenderly to receive the homecoming they can experience (Origen 1994, 131).

Believers are called to respond with gentle ministry. By being patient, empathetic, and tender with others in relationships, we can be instruments of God's healing work and ministry for those who bear the scars of a harsh world. In this way, the disciple will become a vehicle to pass on Christ's gentleness to others who are broken and help them experience the rest our God has made available to us for our renewal.

Healing Wounds of Harshness and Abuse

Every facet of the human experience is filled with wounds, either by what others do to us or to themselves: rejection, harsh words, and abuse are but a few ways Christ's way is painful. Christ's ministry gives shape to a mode of restoration that is not characterized by venom, but rather by gentleness and relational affection. With respect to all, Jesus meets with those who are disregarded or dehumanized and offers them acts of compassion, dignity, and wholeness (Matt. 9:35–36; Luke 4:18). Christ deals with them differently than the world does today—with coercion, judgment, or burying one's pain without hope of healing. Through careful interactions with people in these situations, practitioners can begin to help one another learn restoration, as spiritual and emotional healing often begins with patience, presence, active listening, and genuine engagement.

As Origen pointed out, the Spirit of Christ enables Christians to approach each other's wounds even as they are healing, so that we can help them along the way and allow them to take their time with their pain (Origen 1994, 77). John Chrysostom reminds us of the importance of gentleness in caring for others; we must be tender while also communicating truth so that the heart can change without being defensive (Chrysostom 1986, 205). The mercy and tender care Jesus has shown to the community represent the contours of pastoral ministry and care for individuals, and the very orientations of restoration are relational and spiritual.

The usual manner of healing has its own pace, just as Christ took His time with the disciples responding to their mistakes. He did not rush coercively to correct their learning over their misunderstanding, nor scorn them for being misguided. Instead, he patiently corrected both their errors and encouraged their response, much like he is recorded doing with Peter (Matt. 18:21–22). In practical terms, for Christians, that means listening without being harsh and creating space for confession, reconciliation, and emotional recovery. Bonhoeffer concluded this section by observing that gentleness is not weakness; being strong in love in situations of deep suffering takes courage, and it must not be exploitative (Bonhoeffer 1959, 134).

Christ's mode of healing is comprehensive in its application to both spiritual and emotional harm. To participate in this healing means emulating Christ's gentleness, sustaining togetherness, and prioritizing others' restoration over retribution for what was done to them. This involves reconsidering one's behavior as a way of understanding and learning a relational model of forgiveness, thereby renewing personal dignity. Communities could become places where wounded and vulnerable people feel safe and spiritually renewed simply because they have the heart of Jesus in a world of cruelty and harshness.

The Balm of Christ's Patience

Christ's patience is a source of comfort to the weary and burdened. In a culture that demands immediacy and measurability, Christ offers a decidedly countercultural way of being and becoming. Suppose the way patience manifests in Christ's relationship with the disciples, crowds, and outcasts exhibits a gentleness that leads to spiritual growth, rather than a coercion to immediate obedience (Luke 8:40–42, 49–56). In that case, it illustrates the deliberate pace of life, a pastoral cadence that cultivates lasting change. Patience is not just an attitude; it is a trustworthy disposition that allows for the process of repentance. Origen suggests that Christ's patience is the outpouring of His love; it gives space for individuals to consider, repent, and then undertake the developmental task of growing without the pressures of erudition (Origen 1994, 77). The disciples' repeated misunderstandings of the ministry never caused Christ to erupt in anger, but were always met with calm instruction; patient instruction leads to understanding and resilience in the face of spiritual dangers. John Chrysostom notes that patience facilitates the holistic development of moral formation and emotional healing, respecting the learner and avoiding immediate reactions to correct (Chrysostom 1986, 205).

For contemporary followers of Christ, imitating the patience of Christ entails a deepening of listening, withholding immediate judgment, and creating spaces for relational ministry, parenting, or community involvement. Bonhoeffer describes patience as something other than passivity; in patience, we wait as courageous acts of love, waiting decidedly but trusting in God's timing and not humanity's urgency (Bonhoeffer 1959, 134). Christlike patience is not intended only to be a transformable characteristic in daily life contexts; it can soften hearts, create a practice of reflection, and allow grace to flourish.

By participating in this patient love, Christians fulfill the gentle heart of Jesus, which emphasizes that spiritual and emotional healing is developed, not made. If patience is a habitual response, it becomes a means for restoration, a channel for the transformative work of the Spirit, and a reflection of Christ's tender deferment.

Finding Rest for Our Souls in His Tender Care

Jesus calls those who are weary and burdened with life to come and rest in His gentle care (Matt. 11:28–30). This rest involves more than physical rest; it is a spiritual renewal that restores the heart, mind, and soul. By resting, Christ contradicts the demands of the world to constantly achieve and be self-reliant; here, trust in God and surrender to God's guidance are the models.

Bonhoeffer recognizes that the restful care of Christ supplants human striving with God's strength, allowing believers to experience both freedom and renewal (Bonhoeffer 1959, 134). This rest is not a "thing," but relational, arising from listening to Christ's voice and the willingness to dwell in Him. Augustine speaks to the power of this spiritual rest as it aligns the soul with God's order and creates a peace that is not based upon circumstance (Augustine 1998, 215).

Practically, participating in Christ's rest means adopting patterns of reflection, prayer, and trust, allowing God's tender care to shape the response to the pressures of the day. Origen describes rest and sustaining the soul as strengthening the soul's ability to endure events without becoming bitter or agitated (Origen 1994, 82). In restful moments, Christians need to surrender their lives; that is, give God their struggles in surrender, which then gives the believer a gentle patience and gentleness of character that is always present in Christ.

Rest shows up personally and collectively; those who accept the gentle care of Christ find renewal for themselves and contribute to spaces of gentleness and renewal, which then bear witness to God's character for others. Through this invitation, Christ exemplifies that true strength is not about dominating others or rushing to get things done, but about a nourishing and restorative love that touches the hearts of individuals and communities.

Joy in Gentleness

Christ's gentleness offers an alternative route to true joy that transcends worldly definitions of success and control. Joy emerges when believers relinquish their instinct for defensiveness and surrender their strength to God's strength, rather than striving for their own strength. As Matthew 11:29–30 reveals, "Take My yoke upon you and learn from Me, for I am gentle and lowly in heart, and you will find rest for your souls. For My yoke is easy and My burden is light." This rest is Christ's gentleness, free from the relentless burden we feel to demonstrate ourselves and constantly engage our fears in the continuous cycle of self-protection. Augustine thoughtfully notes this quiet strength in writing that human delight is found not in accolades, but in the stillness and gentleness of God's presence (Augustine 1998, 219). Joy emerges when a believer can relinquish the need to dominate, manipulate, and defend their own position while trusting the loving sovereignty of Christ. That inner security opens the soul to engage in life with gratitude, humility, and a hopeful outlook.

Gentleness also fosters relational joy: we can experience it when our response is one of patience, tenderness, and care. As Christ's meekness and compassion demonstrate, John Chrysostom observed that true strength is applied quietly and fosters harmony and mutual respect rather than fear or intimidation (Chrysostom 1986, 210). When we adopt this posture, believers develop joy that extends beyond an emotional response, but also as an outgrowth of our connection to God's presence and the fruit of living in His character.

Working, applicable means that in every interaction where we are to pause before reacting, we should offer forgiveness before judging or offering our accolades, or we should offer trust before seeking control. In resting under God's gentle leadership, Christians develop a source of joy beyond the circumstances that will sustain them through trials and minimize fear and anxiety while producing moments of what we believe to be "normal" into opportunities for greater delight (Ps. 16:11). True joy is not the pursuit of happiness, but the response of contentment in an everlasting deep reality of security, love, and patience of the gentle Christ.

Freedom from the Burden of Defensiveness

Defensiveness is a human reaction that occurs when our ego, pride, or self-identity is threatened. However, Jesus provides a model of a different path: exhibiting strength in gentleness by offering no defensive aggression when challenged, accused, or misunderstood (Matt. 26:57–68). In Jesus' example, the believer encounters incredible freedom to engage in a relationship without having to protect their identity. This freedom creates peace within, reconciliation with others, and ultimately spiritual growth (Chrysostom c. 347–407, 105).

Defensiveness can sometimes manifest as hasty, angry retorts, ill-tempered words, or withdrawal. The world often regards assertive or confrontational responses as a sign of strength, confusing them with resistance. Nevertheless, Christ completely changes this idea. He absorbs the insult and offense imposed on Him. He waits patiently for understanding and restoration (Luke 23:34). The believer who follows His model learns to entirely discard the task of constant self-defense, instead relying on God for justice or vindication at a time different from what they might have initially anticipated.

Augustine remarks that, with humility, a believer's heart may rise above self-justification, thus allowing an avenue for inner joy and interpersonal peace (Augustine 1998, 187). Once disengaged from defensiveness, the believer may recognize that gentleness arises within as a spiritual discipline rather than more passive management. Moreover, in the practice of gentleness, believers experience freedom from being further confronted, both externally and internally, by pride's tyrannical reign.

This method has the power to transform communities, workplaces, and families. Non-defensive stances foster dialogical encounter, welcome relational and cooperative reconciliation, and reduce emotional burdens. Freeing ourselves from defensiveness encourages an authentic engagement with Christ-like humility, which opens our lives to the incarnation of Christ and the possibility of His Spirit working in and through us. The invitation to disengage from defensive postures is not a call into passivity but to relational strength characterized by courage, gentleness, and trust.

Joy in Trusting the Lord's Strength, Not Our Own

The life of a Christian is often characterized by a constant striving for goals. Striving, in this case, can mean striving to know the outcome, striving to be approved, striving for some degree of success based on the strength of one's human actions. Jesus beckons us to a different way in: his strength, not our own (Phil. 4:13). Joy arises, not from self-sufficiency, but from trust in God's providence, power, and presence.

Repeatedly, Scripture tells of God's power being made perfect in weakness (2 Cor. 12:9–10). By relying on God, we exchange our anxious striving for God's peace and contentment in the Spirit. Packer elaborates, "Joy is itself activated when we willingly surrender our 'self-sufficiency,' adopting a position of dependence on the wisdom and strength of God," because this trust promotes a disposition that allows believers to encounter trials with a peaceful assurance that every moment of obedience, service, and love is carried by the power of God (Packer 1973, 215).

Striving to do things ourselves will only lead to exhaustion, frustration, and disappointment. Conversely, trusting God produces the opposite outcomes of resilience, detachment from fear, and joy in the midst of life's engagement. Even in suffering, joy prevails and can endure because it, unlike circumstances or the success of human performance, is rooted in the unchanging character and power of God (Wright 1996, 142).

The trust by which we rely on God's power (versus our own) also reshapes the nature of interpersonal relationships. When leaders, parents, or friends depend on God more than their own capabilities, they are better models of reliance and confident faith, inspiring others to do the same. Trust grows as a relational and spiritual contagion that promotes gentleness, patience, and cooperation. Trusting God, as a reliance upon His strength, expands the possibilities of transformative change, allowing the believer to discover what might best be described as empowerment rather than defeat. At the same time, paradoxical joy is sourced in humility and God's grace.

Augustine on the Quiet Strength of Christ

Augustine of Hippo emphasizes Christ's paradox of strength, which is quiet, unassuming, and present in humility, rather than in force (Augustine 1998, 212). True and ultimate strength is not defined by coercion and oppression but rather by gentleness and patient endurance. Jesus' authority is rooted in his perfect obedience to the Father, his steadfast love, and his willingness to serve, even to the point of death on a cross (Phil. 2:5–8).

This quiet strength invites believers to reimagine power and influence in their lives. Whereas earthly ideas of success often lead to domination and visibility, Christ models a lasting impact through humble service and self-emptying love. Augustine observes that hearts attuned to God's movements recognize this strength not as weakness but as the ultimate expression of God's authority (Augustine 1998, 214).

In practice, Christ's example of quiet strength encourages us to refrain from attempts to dominate relationships, conversations, and outcomes. It suggests patience in teaching, forgiveness in the face of offense, and restraint in judgment. Believers experience true power in every transformation that comes from reflecting the gentleness of God through the eradication of selfishness, anger, and guilt in their own inner lives. As a result, we experience joy, peace, and greater freedom to act in love as an extension of God's character, rather than out of a desire for our own self-demonstration of power.

This model of strength re-creates communities. Leaders who embody quiet strength cultivate bonds of trust, collaboration, and respect. Families who adopt this attitude of strength create environments where children flourish in safety and confidence, encouraged to develop their spiritual formation. Believers who live as models of quiet strength develop their spiritual resilience through submission to God's call, the courage to obey, and joy in realizing that God prevents self-driven ambition from overriding His divine guidance.

Lastly, Augustine reminds us that Christ's power is most fully seen in his humility, patience, and gentleness of endurance. All of these expressions of strength as a quiet presence are open and readily available to those who follow Jesus (Augustine 1998, 215).

Love Expressed in Gentleness

Love, expressed through Christlike gentleness, becomes penetrating and invasive as it upends worldly assumptions of domination and coercion. Paul urges believers to "put on tender mercies, kindness, humility, meekness, longsuffering" (Col. 3:12), viewing gentleness not as weakness, but as an ethical expression of God's love in human relationships. In humility, love acts unobtrusively, without seeking its own, as the apostle describes: "love is not proud, does not behave rudely, does not seek its own, is not provoked, does not think evil" (1 Cor. 13:4–7). The love of God, as expressed to us by Christ, involves understanding and respecting boundaries, embracing growth, and fulfilling our responsibilities to others when acting in love.

Calvin observes that gentleness, as seen in the church, is a gift of the Holy Spirit, but it is also a practical requirement for governing the body, since the Spirit works within the church, the body of Christ (Calvin 1559, 472). As Christians cultivate meekness, they participate in God's reconciling work among the faith community, establishing peace and reconciliation. Love expressed in gentleness becomes a means of reconciliation, encouragement to the weary, and restraint amid human harshness. It demonstrates that followers of Christ bear His likeness, who "did not strike or cry out, nor did anyone hear His voice in the streets" (Isa. 42:2), enacting divine authority in restraint and care.

Practically, love is patient in listening, measured in response, and sacrificial in service. Love recognizes conflict as an opportunity to discover understanding, frustration as a space for compassionate action, and power as ultimately service. Henri Nouwen notes that whenever Christians act in meek love, whenever their actions witness to the presence of Jesus, their ministries become arenas where God extends grace to others in ordinary life; such love reflects the gentle heart of Jesus and is enduring, patient, humble, and produces not only spiritual and human growth but relational unity (Nouwen 1994, 52).

If believers embrace gentleness as the medium of love and the basis for their response to the world, they will embody an alternative cultural norm. Ordinary engagement within community, family, workplace, and institutions will reveal God's kingdom to others.

Paul's Command to Clothe Ourselves with Gentleness

In Colossians 3:12, Paul appeals to believers to "put on tender mercies, kindness, humility, meekness, longsuffering" (Col. 3:12). Clothing metaphors reinforce Paul's idea that gentleness is not simply a surface-level quality; instead, it is an intentional disposition woven into our lives each day. Garments cover and protect the body, just as gentleness offers shaping and controlling elements in relationships, helping to avoid the harshness of spirit and self-seeking. Therefore, gentleness provides for a position or disposition of love rather than sentimentality, where love is faithfully and actively engaged.

Augustine argues that love expressed gently sustains the work of community life. Suppose believers exhibit measured patience and restrained speech. In that case, it reflects the character of Christ and encourages the formation of reconciliation and respect (Augustine 1998, 215). This notion aligns with Paul's pastoral desire for unity among the churches. It prevents aggression or pride from worsening already tenuous communal situations. Thus, gentleness is both a protective action and an instrument of love.

Paul's exhortation resonates with examples within the biblical narrative. A gentle love marks Jesus' interactions with the marginalized—children, lepers, and sinners. Jesus' love gently tempers authority to demonstrate and communicate the Gospel (Matt. 19:14; Luke 7:36–50). In contrast, Jesus' gentle love, even when confronted with opposition, such as from the Pharisees, models restraint in truth-telling without being alarmingly coercive. Textual scholarship has observed that Paul drew on Jesus as a model, teaching the church that their gentleness was a sign of grace and reflected God's character (Nouwen 1981, 102).

Clinging to gentleness is a summit that engages our inner life as we are intentional about our inward and outward lives. Prayer, reflection, and habitual mindfulness may form one's temperament in alignment with God's purpose. As Packer observed, fragments of spiritual growth produce a gentler, more conditioned heart, one where one can respond to offense rather than lash out (Packer 1973, 147). Thus, Paul's exhortation should be taken as both a theological and practical verse: firm, disciplined, loving action that will change one's relationships and conform to the spirit of Christ.

Love that Does Not Force Its Way (1 Corinthians 13)

In 1 Corinthians 13, Paul says love "is not irritable or resentful; it does not rejoice at wrongdoing, but rejoices with the truth" (1 Cor. 13:4–6). Paul explains that love is active and engaged, but also non-invasive. Implicitly, love takes on God's character of possessing power through restraint and gentleness. The authorship of the chapel in this manner honors the work by preserving freedom in others while seeking their good. Love that fights for what is good and right may be aggressive, but it is an imitation of worldly power. Christ-like love is distinguished from this by its enactment through humility and patience, slow and deliberate.

C.S. Lewis notes that the opposite of love—imposing moralism or domination—occurs when love is absent from gentleness (Lewis 1960, 88). Paul challenges the reader to embody love that honors the other's dignity while maintaining conviction, illustrating that any successful spiritual exuberance grows out of example, not compulsion. Many of the complications the early church and early Christians had, rooted in disagreements and factions, demonstrate the cost and complexities of not living out love that honors the freedom of others.

There are also biblical examples that illustrate this concretely. Jesus' teaching to the crowds (Matt. 5–7) and His mercy toward sinners (Luke 19:1–10) demonstrate His care for others without reducing them to props; instead, He seeks to help them find their rightful place in the created order. Nouwen observes that love that honors others and invites their participation is expansive and generous. In contrast, coercive love excludes and restricts (Nouwen 1994, 57). This type of gentleness is the medium through which love can have a sustained, intentional impact in the Spirit of the God we aim to emulate.

In practical terms, agenting love in the form of meekness means we need to be continually aware of our limits, the importance of patience, listening, and understanding other perspectives. Love, as expressed through meekness, requires layered reflection and resolution, as well as a humility that allows us or enables us to seek God over human expectations and impulses. It rejects ways of prioritizing results and worldly power as means for accomplishing goals. It acknowledges our limited role and time stake in humans, determined by long-term relationships and spiritual flourishing.

Calvin on the Spirit of Meekness in the Church

John Calvin describes meekness as being central to the health of the church, stating it is "the temper of spirit which restrains the inclination to assert personal rights, while at the same time making accurate judgments about the character, or actions of other people for the good of others in consideration of humility" (Calvin 1559, 326). Meekness tempers authority, and tempering authority is critical because it takes the form of oversight, and leaders should exercise oversight with care rather than coercion. A brief theological reflection on 2 Corinthians 10:1 aligns with Calvin's position that spiritual power is most effective when it is accompanied by gentleness.

Calvin associates meekness with obedience to God's law and imitating Christ. Pastors and elders are to model humility and restraint in a way that allows the congregation to flourish through guidance that is both effective and non-intimidating. Likewise, the laity are to respond with respect and patience in a manner that fosters an environment that nurtures spirituality in a reciprocal relationship (Calvin 1559, 328).

History shows that when churches are absent from meekness, conflict and division follow. Calvin cautions against the arrogant assertion of self and encourages a love-filled leadership that imitates Christ. Origen notes that gentleness, while not denying truth, has a proper care for human weakness as a reflection of divine wisdom (Origen 1994, 45). Such balancing acts eliminate alienation whilst keeping theological elements intact.

In a modern context, Calvin's tenet encourages leaders and supporters alike to practice humility. Thoughtful prayer, accountability, and intentional restraint are essential components for both leaders and congregants to exhibit a spirit of leadership that is also gentle. The church can become a place of value when meekness is openly encouraged, where love can be practiced, modeled, and multiplied into a life of health and sustainable community.

Theological Voices

Gently, the theological virtue of gentleness has been rendered. Used by various thinkers for contemplation and recognition of the nuanced realities of human life, gentleness has countless interpretations and practical implications for Christian life. For Thomas Aquinas, strength is never about domination, but always about restraint, moderation, and purposeful love. Importantly, in his work on the *Summa Theologica*, he places gentleness within the cardinal virtue of temperance. He describes gentleness as the correct moderation of anger and/or assertive power, according to reason and charity (Aquinas 1947, II-II, q. 137, art. 1). For Aquinas, a gentle person would exert influence and authority without coercion, able to move others toward what is good and maintaining self-control—a kind of power—in a moral-ordered way that promotes spiritual goodness.

In a Puritan context, Jonathan Edwards articulated gentleness, considering the fulfillment of raw affections in the human heart when directed toward God and others. He wrote, "Christian affections flow from a sincere and cordial love to God and to our neighbour." Christian affections are thus both empathetic and temperate; gentleness restrains pride, impatience, and harshness (Edwards 1746, 213). Edwards describes how the inward transformation of the heart is manifested outwardly in continued humility, patience, and tender care (Edwards' depiction of meekness is seen in Christ's example). He goes on to argue that it is the cultivation of affections aligned with God's love that "will be the great benefit to a person" in their spiritual growth and in bearing witness to relational connections with others. Edwards suggests that the close presence of Christlike gentleness in a believer's story may not be context-specific or confined, but instead lived out in all areas, contexts, and relationships of life.

Henri Nouwen's modern interpretation of gentleness complements that of Thomas Aquinas, Edwards, and others, effectively equating gentleness with a form of Christ-like power, accessible through vulnerability and an open heart. A tender heart is not weak, but strong and with great courage, a heart that seeks connection, sustains relationships, engages and speaks to the marginalized, and endures the hardships of ministry without bitterness (Nouwen 1981, 64). Nouwen's understanding of gentleness is dynamic, engaging, healing, and reconciliatory. Nouwen asserts that gentleness communicates God and God's love, providing a method by which God's presence in ministry can be enacted in ways that sheer authority cannot.

These theological voices imply that gentleness is not passivity or politeness; true gentleness is a restrained, Spirit-led expression of strength —a kind of Christ-like power, both in the person displaying it and in the person receiving it. That Aquinas, Edwards, and Nouwen each assert that gentleness is nothing less than divine love made visible through a human heart is remarkable, as it illustrates how gentleness is central to the character and witness of the believer. Understanding gentleness in this manner elevates the concept. It transforms gentleness into a theological and practical principle that enables the mission of God's kingdom to be enacted through the modest and unglamorous acts of quiet service, patience, and compassion offered to every one of us.

Aquinas on Gentleness as Moderated Strength

Thomas Aquinas characterizes gentleness in the *Summa Theologica* as a moral virtue that moderates natural forces, such as anger and harshness, thereby aligning human power, passion, and strength with God's intended purpose for humans (Aquinas 1274, II-II, Q.137, Art. 3). Gentleness is difficult to distinguish in a cultural context that claims power is an act of dominance or aggression over others. For Aquinas, one exercises strength from within and under the influence of reason and love. A morally virtuous person draws energy from their emotions and channels it into a constructive or positive purpose, embracing God's moral order. This idea resonates with Proverbs 15:1: "A soft answer turns away wrath." Anger leads to results that create more anger; therefore, one should exercise restraint with modulated responses. Gentleness models God's character and can help mitigate conflict when engaging in issues.

Throughout his earthly ministry, Christ expressed a modest and moderate strength. He responds to the challenge and intimidation of others in thoughtful, reflective ways—instead of losing control of his emotions—when responding to challenges from the Pharisees, crowds, and his disciples (Matt. 11:29). As Augustine explains, God's patience allows us space to repent and learn what it means to be a spiritual influence and a son of His (Augustine 1998, 128). Therefore, gentleness must not be assumed to imply passivity. Rather, gentleness is the expression of control that guides and encourages behavioral transformation. Aquinas' admonition about gentleness invites followers of Christ to pursue the practice deliberately, restraining impulses or urges to retaliate, choosing unreasonable wisdom, and honoring others through reconciliation rather than gratifying oneself to escape a situation or allowing anger to consume us.

Gentleness must be elaborated upon because it applies daily, specifically through gentle speech, gentle engagement via active listening, and gentle correction (Matt. 7:1–5). When in a position of leadership—whether within the church, family, or workplace—Aquinas' understanding of gentleness as a moral virtue encourages the exercise of influence through moral integrity and authority, rather than control. Gentleness is also a pathway to spiritual maturity; it encourages trust, fosters reflection through reading and meditating on the Word, and aligns the actions of believers with God's redemptive purposes (Packer 1973, 215). Living out gentleness through the example of Christ and setting aside our desire to respond as we wish allows believers to learn that true strength is often quiet yet powerful and transformative in the lives of other believers, both spiritually and relationally. Therefore, to make a practical assessment of gentleness, Aquinas redefines it as disciplined, active strength behaved in a morally sound way; a submissive and professed strength is countercultural to standard norms of power and is committed to serving God and others above oneself.

Edwards on True Christian Affections

Jonathan Edwards views the alignment of the heart with God's glory as an essential element of genuine Christian affection (Edwards 1746, 212). For Edwards, gentleness flows from the heart's disposition, as a gentle person responds to provocation or hardship not with agitation, resentment, or disdain, but with patience, goodness, and love because their affections are ordered toward God's glory. He noticed this in the ministry of Christ, who repeatedly responded with gentleness toward children, the disadvantaged, and sinners who repented (Luke 18:15–17). Edwards notes that Christ placed the welfare of others before his own desires. This act of self-denial is evidence of the creative power of affections, guided by inner moral compasses.

Edwards pointed out that unchecked passions cause relational conflict and spiritual disarray, and that whoever has their will under the dominion of new desires or emotions will have little or no influence on judgment.

Alternatively, affections ordered rightly toward God produce inner peace, relational peace, and faithful service to others. Gentleness is, then, a discipline that intentionally measures theological understanding with personal virtue. Gentleness requires both contemplation and practice: we listen, we restrain our instinct to react, and we respond by promoting reconciliation when we would otherwise prefer dominance or control (Bonhoeffer 1959, 134).

Theologically, Edwards connects gentleness to a broader understanding of settled sanctification, emphasizing the goal of becoming imitators of Christ. As the believer's heart conforms to Christ's character, gentleness begins to permeate thinking, speech, and action. Scriptural instruction supports Edwards, as in Colossians 3:12, where Paul instructs believers to "clothe yourselves with compassion, kindness, humility, gentleness, and patience." The gentleness Paul holds in view is both a gift, as a work of Christ in the life of their souls, and an ongoing moral responsibility of obedience to be cultivated nobly. Embedded in Edwards' reflections on gentleness, believers in the community are encouraged to reflect honestly about what motivates their inner hearts, as they seek to demonstrate outward gentleness that stems from deep love, ultimately producing joyfulness, trust, and relational restoration in every relationship within their lives together.

Nouwen: The Tender Heart as Christlike Power

According to Henri Nouwen, a tender heart is the defining quality of a mature person of faith and of Christlike leadership (Nouwen 1981, 89). In a culture where power is often equated with control, influence, or domination over people, Nouwen argues that real power is always exercised through presence, compassion, and empathy. Christ's ministry exemplifies this paradox: his authority and influence were evident in his gentle, vulnerable approach, where he engaged with everyone at the level they found themselves, rather than relying on fear and coercion (Matt.

11:29; Luke 8:40–42). Having a tender heart does not connote weakness; rather, it indicates that one is intentional and disciplined, aligned with God's purposes.

Nouwen refers to a concept of "downward mobility" in leadership as an example of humility, patience, and service as the seeds of lasting spiritual impact. This demonstrated Christ's gracious movement into the lives of broken individuals, which encompassed a healthy sense of care, relational restraint, and engagement without the need to impose worldly authoritative force. A tender-hearted leader is someone who creates a healthy space for healing, reflection, and spiritual growth (1 Cor. 13:4–7). Gentle leadership becomes an active form of power that fosters community growth and builds trust.

Theologically, Nouwen's reflections also disclose challenges for the present understanding of meaning, success, and leadership. Real, lasting spiritual influence and transformation are rooted in a gentle and empathetic presence that acts with intention. The biblical corroborations are plentiful: the way in which, even in the face of resistance, Christ responded with calmness; how he embraced, listened to, and encouraged the most vulnerable; the restraint and patience he communicated with his disciples and followers demonstrate this kind of tender-hearted authority (Luke 19:1–10). For practical application, Christians are called to embody this model by exercising empathy in everyday interactions, responding to conflict with love and patience, and fostering relational well-being and trust among fellow believers, rather than relying on power and control. When viewed through this lens, gentleness becomes a spiritual discipline as well as a type of divine power that allows individuals to lead, heal, and love in alignment with the way of Christ.

Practicing Gentleness Today

Living out gentleness in our world today requires operating with a level of intention and reconsideration, as gentle living runs counter to both our culture and our own instincts. Gentleness starts with our spoken words and tone. Speech is infused with the power to build up or injure (Prov. 15:1). In practicing gentleness we begin to choose softer words; we deliberate about when and how to respond, and we listen longer than we want in order to give a spirit of gentleness (Gal. 6:1) a chance to drive our response (Col. 3:12). This is not weakness but disciplined restraint, emulating Jesus' response to those who were troubled, anxious, and marginalized (Matt. 11:29). Gentleness theologically is a fruit of the Spirit (Gal. 5:22–23), nurtured as believers abide in Christ and the shape of His character transforms how we live and act.

As we think about parenting and leadership, it is one thing to talk about gentleness, but gentleness is often expressed as tender authority. As leaders and parents, we influence others not with heavy-handed threats or explicit coercions. Instead, we sit in our position of leadership and parental authority, offering patient guidance and relational presence. A gentle leader is aware and mindful of the dignity of other people. Gentleness encourages trust, shared leadership, mutual growth in morality, and collaboration (Stott 1994, 88). We gain a comprehensive vantage point of this when we examine how Jesus led and defined interactions with His disciples (Mark 10:14–16) and children.

In times of conflict or disagreement, gentleness is essential; hardness often escalates tensions. The soft or humble approach opens up space for discussion and reconciles differences. Proverbs 15:1 captures this picture as a soft answer turns away wrath. In terms of conflict, gentleness feels like humility, a willingness to actively listen, to give more importance to someone else's voice and presence, and to seek restoration over being right. Practically, it may mean apologizing, calming a heated argument, or maintaining silence to prevent significant damage.

Lastly, gentleness generates relational healing. Acts of kindness in life-giving ways, such as listening with grace and restraint, and caring for others, can relieve the pressures of broken ties. This is similar to God's restorative work in the human heart. It takes time and care to nurture gentleness, to cultivate a domain and a discipline that alters both the giver and the receiver (Nouwen 1981, 73). If being gentle is woven through our daily lives—in spoken words, parenting, leaders who soften authority, engaging in reconciliatory processes, and enhancing relationships—we reflect Christlikeness and concern while participating in God's mission for the kingdom. Woven through a sustained and deliberate pursuit of gentleness, joy, peace, and love flourish. We experience the transforming power of the Spirit-led life.

Gentleness in Our Words and Tone

Words hold incredible power. They can be life-giving and encouraging or hurtful and deflating. The Bible reminds us frequently to subscribe to responsible speech: "A soft answer turns away wrath, but a harsh word stirs up anger" (Prov. 15:1). To exercise gentle communication involves much more than steering clear of harshness; it reflects the character of Jesus, and the love of God (Col. 4:6). Those who offer gentleness in their speech invite dialogue, understanding, and spiritual development. Leaving behind gentleness creates a space for defensiveness and hurt.

John Chrysostom speaks to the pastor's duty to do all that is possible to exercise faith in the souls of those he interacts with; the authority in the pastor's tone of voice (gentleness or harshness) may either open souls to a faith relationship with God or frighten them off, presumably through intimidation (Chrysostom c. 347–407, 202). Augustine links gentleness to the heart's condition; a humble, loving heart will speak words of comfort and instruction, not of destruction (Augustine 1998, 124). Henri Nouwen elaborates that the way we speak is not merely human communication; we spiritually mark one another. Gentleness is the embodied patience of God, acting towards relationship as nurture (Nouwen 1981, 47).

Gentleness, as I mentioned, is also identified with listening attentively. As a rule of thumb, Paul addresses the believer's communication: "Let your speech always be gracious, seasoned with salt" (Col. 4:6). Speech should be deliberate, timely, and responsive primarily to the needs of the listener. This means, as a rule of thumb, the speaker often slows down before responding, chooses language conducive to establishing understanding, and refrains from uttering reactions and inflammatory speech. In the ministry context, or in the workplace, gentle words are often grounded in authority, not fear, but in love.

In reflection, gentle words are a reminder that they are conditioned on prayerful dependence on God. Choosing to seek God's guidance in our speech is a means of self-control and alignment that is distinct from the Spirit's gentle nudging (Packer 1973, 215). Over time, our gentle speech will evolve into spiritual habits in the world that reflect the Christ we wish to embody, promote reconciliation and orientations of humility, and encourage enduring relationships.

Parenting and Leading with Tender Authority

Gentleness is not weakness but rather a disciplined, measured authority that takes its strength from love. Jesus' model of leadership expressed strength and power while also demonstrating tender care. When believers follow Jesus' example, they are called to guide, not force, lead, not dominate (Matt. 20:25–28). Regarding parenting, leadership, and teaching, tender authority fosters trust and respect rather than fear and rebellion. When children, congregants, and followers receive discipline in a tender way marked by patience, understanding, and moral absoluteness, they flourish.

In his writings on authority, Augustine notes that proper authority is expressed in service to others while conforming to God's will and purpose (Augustine 1998, 317). According to Henri Nouwen, Jesus' style of leadership reveals to us that strength is most effective in weakness and vulnerability (Nouwen 1994, 59). In practical terms, we can also think of wielding tender authority as directing, not dominating, teaching, not compelling, and listening, not unilaterally deciding.

The Bible abounds in examples of leaders using gentleness. Moses led with meekness; even when the people sinned against God, he prayed for them (Exod. 32:11–14). The Apostle Paul exhorts believers among the churches to shepherd "not because you must, but because you are willing, as God wants you to be; not greedy for money, but eager to serve; not lording it over those entrusted to you, but being examples to the flock" (1 Pet. 5:2–3). What Paul emphasizes in this exhortation to fellow church leaders is that authority should be relational and accountable. Similarly, followers of Christ (both public and private) can follow Christ to create spaces of relative safety, fostering authentic learning, growth, and transformation.

Gentle leadership requires immense self-knowledge and submission to God's Spirit. As leaders, we need to balance discipline with encouragement in both content and tone, particularly when exercising authority and restraining those who lead (Packer 1973, 221). However, over time, tender authority becomes relational discipleship, leading and requiring those being led to internalize Christian values, develop spiritual maturity, and learn to discern right from wrong.

Gentleness in Conflict and Disagreement

Conflict is a regular part of life, but gentleness gives us a different lens through which to view it. Jesus emphasizes reconciliation rather than victory: "Blessed are the peacemakers, for they shall be called sons of God" (Matt. 5:9). Gentleness tempers our propensity toward anger, defensiveness, and aggression, and paves the way towards resolution based in truth and love (Eph. 4:2–3).

As Origen points out, gentleness "changes hard hearts into soft ones and allows disagreement to lead toward a more profound discussion of reality" (Origen 1994, 112). Augustine expresses a similar sentiment, saying that "by the involvement of humility and patience, the disagreements do not elevate into rage and violently distort the truth" (Augustine 1998, 215). As believers embody gentleness, we embody God's desire for patience and mercy, and act as agents of restoration instead of retaliation.

Gentleness, in application, can manifest as listening before responding, choosing words that encourage rather than wound, and acknowledging our own frailty and fallibility. In Scripture, Paul provides an example of this approach as he conducted himself before engaging verbally in any disputes, specifically concerning individuals (Gal. 6:1). Henri Nouwen points out that gentleness in the face of conflict is rooted in humility. Humility is more open to nurturing and valuing our relationships than preserving our opinions about who is right or wrong (Nouwen 1981, 91).

Gentleness also incorporates discernment (when to speak, when not to speak, when to let someone else mediate). Gentleness is also active and courageous—it is not passive, nor does it allow others to avoid conflict; gentleness embodies strength that is under self-control. With time and gentleness as an approach to resolving disagreements, trust is fostered, reconciliation is nurtured, and spiritual maturity is cultivated.

Healing Relationships Through Soft Answers

Gentleness is not weakness but rather a deep strength that creates space for reconciliation and healing. As Proverbs provides insight: "A soft answer turns away wrath, but a harsh word stirs up anger" (Prov. 15:1). It reflects a wisdom that we often overlook in our angry lives, which is that sometimes the way we say something matters as much as what we say—in other words, it is the manner we respond with gentleness that holds power to contain hostility, uphold people's dignity, and allow space for restoring fellowship. James, too, counsels Christians to "let every person be quick to hear, slow to speak, slow to anger" (James 1:19), reminding us that the practice of discipline, patience, and listening creates peace.

The church fathers understood the healing nature of gentleness toward others. Augustine noted that the work of reconciliation does not begin with self-righteousness, but instead starts in humility and love, as pride divides and gentleness unites (Augustine 1998, 98). The church father John Chrysostom likewise remarks on the power of gentle words to restore people by healing spiritual and emotional wounds, recognizing that words spoken in kindness are restorative (Chrysostom c. 347–407, 202). This teaching resonates with Paul's exhortation to all believers to let their speech always be "with grace, as though seasoned with salt" (Col. 4:6), so that we reveal Christ at the heart of our most intimate conversations, even ones we struggle with.

Gentleness is more than just a human strategy; it is participation with the very way that Christ exercises His generosity, compassion, and gentleness with His people. Henri Nouwen reminds us that gentle words reflect the heart of Jesus as we help nurture others toward maturity, without coercing them or shaming them (Nouwen 1994, 67). We see Jesus engage with Peter to restore him after the threefold rejection of Him. Instead of scolding him, Jesus asked Peter three times, "Do you love Me?" (John 21:15–17). This gentle inquiry led to healing, literally restoring Peter to his calling, while demonstrating that grace is all the more powerful when it is tied with a measure of truth.

For believers today, passing on soft answers through the way we engage with others in our circles means choosing humility over retaliation, compassion over defensiveness, and patience over harshness. It means listening intentionally, empathizing, and having the courage and Spirit to employ ways to de-escalate conflict in a Christlike love. When enacted, this gentleness becomes a visible manifestation of the kingdom, with the potential to transform our homes, churches, and communities into spaces of restoration and reconciliation. At the end of the day, soft answers reveal the surprising way of God, where grace thrives, peace conquers hostility, and love rebuilds what anger seeks to tear apart.

Gentleness as the Fruit of the Spirit

Gentleness is not only a personal choice, but also a gift of the Spirit (Gal. 5:22–23) that grows in a person's life when they are yielded to God. While it is a manner of being, gentleness is also a manner of doing, since as believers yield to the Spirit, gentleness will develop and be expressed in the way a given believer speaks, acts, and interacts with others. Gentleness adapts well to anger (the Christian virtue, not the sin). It works for the benefit of others while lacking orientational coercion. In the space between anger and going too far is gentleness, which may be described as strength controlled, articulated through concern and consideration.

C.S. Lewis observed that gentle behavioral patterns reflect a person's maturity and development of self-restraint, empathy, and humility (Lewis 1960, 87). Paul regularly couples gentleness alongside love, humility, and effectiveness as a witness, as gentleness manifests itself as part of the believer's spiritual life (Phil. 4:5). Augustine said that gentleness emanates from a heart yielded to a person's will such that the person expresses God-like patience in a God-like manner (Augustine 1998, 140).

Gentleness, as a work of the Spirit, taken together, is relational; it encourages peace, cooperation, and reconciliation. Nouwen stated that gentle behavior is God doing God-like work, which invites a person into the relational, human experience of God's divine love (Nouwen 1981, 101). Through times of prayer, reflection, and ultimately reliance on the

Spirit, believers share a personal character that shows the presence of Christ's gentleness with increasing intentionality.

Practically speaking, this means responding to provocation with calmness, being approachable and healthy in the authority of service, and being steady in nurturing relationships. As believers practice the process of gentleness over time, they begin to be transformed into persons of gentleness. Their practice strengthens communities, and in turn, may encourage the world to look credibly to and through God's kingdom.

Chapter 3

I Am

The Reversal Revealed

The announcement of God's reversal in Jesus profoundly challenges our most fundamental values that shape our perspectives on power, authority, and identity. He makes this revolutionary declaration in John 8:58, "I Am," and He does so not only by attaching Himself to the eternal existence that we identify with being God, but also by claiming the prerogative to define reality itself. This claim upended the people's understanding of lineage, time, and ultimately authority. Jesus reveals that, rather than competing for glory, life, and identity as descendants of Abraham, it is union with God that is determinative (Wright 1996, 412). The vehemence of their reaction, to pick up stones and seek to throw them at Him, tells us something about the scandal of divine claims that profoundly contradict expectations based on human-oriented, earthly metrics (France 2007, 325). Human beings tend to think about power in terms of hierarchy, influence, and population size. We struggle to receive a God whose power is expressed in humility, grace, and patience.

This reversal is tethered to the continuity of God's name, specifically God's name revealed in the burning bush to Moses: I AM WHO I AM (Exod. 3:14). The name "I Am" ties God's identity not to conquest or oppression but to God's faithful presence, liberation, and covenant faithfulness. Jesus, in Galilee, expressed the same self-disclosure of God and demonstrated that the kingdom of God operates in terms of authority based on relational fidelity rather than oppressive domination (Carson 1991, 245). By linking His revelation of God in the Exodus to the ministry He carried out, Christ not only asserts that God's salvific plan will continue in history to operate, but it will operate according to these standards—that is, in mercy rather than might and in servant leaders rather than leaders deemed powerful in political economies recognized by humans.

The most significant theological implication of this reversal is our own assumptions about our work and pursuits. The pursuit of honor, position, and control stands in contrast to discipleship to a Christ who holds the prerogative of divinity, yet knelt to wash feet, healed the marginalized, and bore the cross (Packer 1973, 215). To accept this as genuine Christianity involves humility, surrender to God, and having the courage to see power as transformative, as the love of God turning over injustice and restoring dignity for others (as defined by God). In this sense, the scandal of the crowd is a reflection of our own asynchronous human resistance to God's upside-down kingdom. It may encourage believers most to accept the Christological paradox that the eternal "I Am" resides most in meekness, mercy, and sacrificial service.

"Before Abraham Was, I Am"

In John 8:58, Jesus demonstrates his profound identity as "I Am" and then continues to challenge the foundation of the Jewish audience, which obviously understood the divine nature of this identity. Jesus' power to make this claim now opens to us a breathtaking theological wonder of the incarnation of Christ, along with the eternal God of Israel. This declaration clearly invokes God's self-revelation to Moses in Exodus 3:14 at the burning bush—"I AM WHO I AM." In using this divine title/name, Jesus claims his preexistence and unity with the Father, but he also challenges the contemporary ideas of messiahship and authority (Wright 1996, 112).

The "I Am" claim is more than about claiming an identity of loss or presentation. This profession has both relational and ethical implications based on its source and object. By using God's name in the title "I Am," Jesus implicates the people in identifying him with the life-giving source; he is the faithful, covenant-keeping God, the One who exists in absolute authority and ultimate command over his creation, and who inherently possesses eternal life and existence. The unity of Jesus Christ's authority with the name of God lives in contrast to worldly power, which is supported by dominion, coercion, or any human claim to achievement. Jesus' authority is God-like in its absolute state (Carson 1991, 248). These thoughts drive believers into the sheer radical reality of this identification of Jesus as being both extremely humble and majestic—a carpenter from Nazareth who perfectly shares in the essence and will of God.

The implications theologically are multi-layered. In the first instance, the statement is significant as bearing witness to Christ's eternal Word (John 1:1–3), position as being present in creation, and engaged in God's mission. The implications are also paradoxically illustrated in divine self-revelation, where God's glory is represented in servanthood and humility, contesting worldly notions of worth that establish value through merit and strength (France 2007, 183). Lastly, it moves the reader and believer toward relational trust, reverence, and obedience, both toward the One who sustains all things and also to follow the One who invites only gentle love.

Furthermore, it establishes more than a covenantal relationship, but a prophetic connection between the Old and New Testaments, as the God of Israel, who mediated to Moses the self-existent I AM, subsists entirely in Jesus Christ and fulfills the covenant promises (Augustine 1998, 123).

From a concrete understanding of trust, this acknowledgment of the I AM God "in Christ," is also an expression of what former believers now question—too a belief in the complexities of both security, hope, and purpose; trusting in Christ rests in an eternal and transcendent God who is not affected by or exists in temporal conditions of the present human/commanded situation.

In saying I AM, Jesus begins to artistically express a new way to respond to and live in this divine covenant reality, calling every person within earshot to not only know this identity but respond to it with faith that is both incomparably reverent and active—to respond with faith that trusts the eternal Word who lives under his redeemingly gentle authority (Packer 1973, 215).

Shock and Outrage: Why the Crowd Took Up Stones

The reaction of the Jewish audience to Jesus' statement, "Before Abraham was, I Am" (John 8:58), reveals not only their theological depth but also the radical nature of his claim. John tells us clearly why the audience wanted to stone him, because they considered his statement blasphemous, as he had associated himself with God's revealed name at Sinai (Exod. 3:14). For a first-century Jew, the name I AM implied a covenantal relationship with God, implying self-existence, unchanging, and moral authority. His assertion, using the name "I am," was not made casually. He was deliberately associating himself with the eternal, self-existent God (Bauckham 2008, 67).

We might also think that the criminal outrage of the crowd highlights the tension present in divine revelation: we tend to resist when the transcendent seeks to break into and disrupt the everyday. By claiming the divine name, Jesus shatters their expectations of an earthly, temporal messianic figure and simultaneously exposes their spiritual blindness to the values of cultural norms in relation to covenantal fidelity. Theologically speaking, the crowds' stoning of Jesus exemplifies the cost of God's revelation; truth often upsets others, is misunderstood, and even violently resisted (Carson 1991, 252). However, again, the crowd and the disciples alike are invited to contemplate the paradox that God's ultimate authority is not exhibited through violent means or coercive measures, but through self-revelation and sacrificial love in humility (Lewis 1943, 118).

This moment did not go unnoticed by the early church commentators. Origen, for example, noted that the crowd's decision to stone Jesus was not to display their disbelief. Instead, their response was profound resistance to God breaking into the finite world through the divine Word (Origen 1994, 45). Likewise, Chrysostom closely relates misunderstanding Christ's own identity to danger and emphasizes that divine truth often astounds while simultaneously provoking fear (Chrysostom c. 347–407, 202).

Practically, this episode signals to modern-day believers that following Jesus might threaten what they or others had thought was the acceptable way to be Christian. Faith in the I AM requires unique courage, discernment, and humility to yield to God's revelation, rather than others' approval. Furthermore, understanding why the audience reacted with such violent contempt provides further illumination of Jesus the person and the cost of following Christ, whose gentle yet absolute claim calls forth obedience, trust, and awe-inspiring reverence (Stott 1994, 57).

From Burning Bush to Galilee: The Continuity of God's Name

We encounter a strong phrase, "For I say unto you, Before Abraham was, I am" (John 8:58), when we understand a connection to God's self-disclosure at the burning bush, "I AM WHO I AM" (Exod. 3:14). The burning bush alongside "I Am" allows us to see a continuity between the witnesses of the Old and New Testaments, where the God of historic Israel is understood to be the eternal self-existing God. The Lord, who created a covenant with Abraham and revealed Himself to Moses, does not remain silent; He enters human history as a human being, as the person Jesus Christ. When Jesus asserts that "I Am," he directly identifies himself and human history with the liberator and sustainer: in one sense, making the transcendent eminently present to real people at Galilee (Wright 1996, 421).

There are many theological entanglements at work: first, he recognizes the oneness of God's redemptive work; the God who initiated a covenant with Abraham and then revealed himself to Moses is here fully present in the servant Messiah. Secondly, it expands our human preconceptions around God's accessibility; God, unlike a distant sovereign, is a relational and personal presence in Jesus Christ (Packer 1973, 215). The early Christian writings portray the "I Am" as both a name and an action, representing God's very being acting in history. Augustine (1998, 134) points out that Jesus bears the divine name not to assume unjustified authority over its differentiations, but rather to serve as the most significant expression of humility, allowing creation to enter its presence without surrendering its transcendent self.

Covenantal continuity has instructional ramifications for Scripture. Typology and echoes of covenantal teaching are God's way of pointing and helping His people to recognize the Hebrew Scriptures in light of anticipating the Messiah, following the same standard patterns and rhythms of divine revelation. Bonhoeffer (1959, 78) reminds us that possibilities of continuity require being able to identify Christ's identity through Scripture, for ultimately possessing a grounded theology that allows for (1) historical, and (2) spiritual awareness of who we are, and what God is doing in the present moment. Origen (1994, 112) considers the continuity of the burning bush made manifest in Jesus' claim of "I Am" as a definitive connection that shapes how we teach and think about God's pattern with humanity: "in the midst of the everyday, God acts directly. God is resisting the ordinary by making it holy every time God meets us."

Covenantal continuity is also pragmatic. Believers who understand this type of continuity recognize the importance of approaching Christ with the conviction that He is, indeed, the eternal God who walks with us in this space, and as such, can respond to Christ with reverence and gratitude. Identifying the connection with "I Am" creates a deeper context for our spiritual encounters when we recognize the divine alongside the human, and experience both awe and comfort, remembering that the God who liberated the people of Israel continues to save and to lead, and also dwells with His people. Jesus' "I Am" is not a rupture, but the continuance of God's ever-faithful manifestation of Himself: He, through Christ, links us, little ones, between His glory and our humanness, and inspires trust and worshipful obedience (Stott 1994, 63).

God's Name in the Old Testament

The appearance of God's name in the Old Testament is a deep theological and practical creator of meaning. In Exodus 3:14, God reveals to Moses, "I Am Who I Am," with Moses as the sole recipient of a self-revelation that is a statement of God's existence from the beginning. This was not simply a label but a statement of being: God exists from God's own existence and is uncreated; God is without time, situation, or circumstance (Augustine 1998, 72). God's identity is the source and ground of all reality. Everything we know about God's acts in history flows from God's character as the unchanging I AM (Gregory of Nyssa 1995, 116; Calvin 1990, 156). In revealing the name to Moses at the burning bush, God provided both an understanding of transcendence and immanence: the fact that God transcends creation while intimately knowing human suffering, and here, coming to deliver God's people (Chrysostom 1986, 45).

God's self-existence reveals God's sovereignty in ways that the rulers of this world are unable to do. Wealth, bloodline, or coercive action can create leaders of the world's nations, but for God, God's sovereignty rests entirely within God's own self. Sovereignty is relational, and God's sovereignty operates based on covenantal faithfulness first received in Israel. God's sovereign acts are known within the relational qualities of deliverance, judgment, and mercy (James 1980, 36). Therefore, God's use of the divine name acknowledges that, for the Israelites, the community of faith would only trust, obey, and worship the I AM who alone depended on no other being or situation (Gregory of Nyssa 1995, 128). With God grounding identity and authority purely on God's intentions for life and being with God's people, all people are called to live by faith, dependency, reverence, and moral action based on God's intention for all (Dunning 1991, 123).

The holiness of God's name evokes wonder, shaping the liturgical, ethical, and social life of Israel and the people of God. Leviticus and Deuteronomy repeatedly emphasize that God's name is holy and that the people must respect this holiness through their speech, actions, and rituals (Packer 1973, 46). The awe that shaped the holiness of God's name was a fear, but it was a settled, reverent state of awe, accompanied by a clear understanding that God's presence transforms ordinary reality. To invoke God's name is to enter into a relationship within God's covenant, trusting, recognizing, and relying on God's power and righteousness in living out God's redemptive purpose.

The Old Testament presents God's name as a layered revelation, representing a declaration of self-existence and claiming sovereign authority endowed by this name. It also highlights God's holy presence as worthy of reverence and awe, inspiring obedience. These Old Testament realities are meant to enthrall and prepare the way for the richer and fuller revelation of God found in Christ, whose life and ministry demonstrate the loving, faithful, and transforming eternal character contained in the I AM (Wright 1996, 207).

"I Am Who I Am" (Exodus 3:14)

When God reveals His nature to Moses at the burning bush, He begins His declaration of His name, "I Am Who I Am" (Exod. 3:14). The meaning of this is both remarkably complex and pointedly simple. It expresses that God, the One who exists as God in life and action, is an eternal, self-existent, and unchanging being. In Hebrew, the verb *hayah* conveys a continuous sense, referring to being, presence, and existence. This reminds us that God is not dependent on creation, time, or circumstance. God is the ground of all reality; God's being is the foundation for all other being; God is the One upon whom all living things depend (Brueggemann 1994, 23).

The name of God is a clear turning point in revelation. Moses was to bring Israel out of bondage, so he needed certainty that the God commissioning him was sovereign, trustworthy, and dependable. God's identification as "I Am Who I Am" provides precisely that. God's being does not shift with human doubt or political conditions; God's being is forever constant, permanent, eternal, and absolute in the sense that it is only a reference point for reality.

The early church and the fathers understood both the mystery and the assurance of this claim of God. Origen noted that God revealing Himself as this name in Exodus 3:14 carries both the invitation to wonder and worship and the assurance of His presence for believers always (Origen 1994, 45). To name God as "I Am" is to name God's essence as ineffable, incomprehensible, while offering comfort in the embracing of an intimate, constant, and never "departing" God. Likewise, Augustine reflects on Exodus 3:14 as "a call into loving obedience," which calls the faithful to recognize that God alone is Himself life, and a signature that provides a guarantee of God's covenant faithfulness (Augustine 1998, 92).

This phrase appears repeatedly throughout Scripture. The worship and theology of Israel often centered on God's eternal presence as the defining feature of their identity and mission. The prophets would often call the people to repentance and hope by reasoning with them that God being, always, is unchanging (Mal. 3:6). Once again, in the New Testament, as John writes that Jesus proclaims, "Before Abraham was, I Am" (John 8:58), Moses draws a straight line from this declaration to the infinite God who revealed Himself to Moses and Israel at Sinai.

Today, Exodus 3:14 calls believers to bear witness with awe, wonder, and intimacy. God reminds us, in relationship with Him, that no matter how human lust and need try to domesticate God, He will always remain God, and His essence always surpasses comprehension. At the same time, God reminds us of His compassion and faithfulness (Lam. 3:22) to provide unbroken consistency; He is not contingent nor incidental to human existence; He is therefore the unchanging source of life. For one to know God as "I Am" is to live dependent on Him, and therein rests assurance that His purposes endure as well as every promise where there is never failure.

God's Self-Existence and Sovereignty

Central to the sovereignty of God is His self-existence. Unlike human kings, whose power is vulnerable and subject to armies, wealth, and circumstance, God's sovereignty is based on His very existence. The Lord reveals in Exodus 3:14 that He is "I Am Who I Am," indicating that His authority stems from His own being, not from external sources. This speaks to the reality that God is beyond time, change, and limit. Therefore, He is a king who rules supremely and invincibly.

John Calvin argues that God's sovereignty arises from God's self-existence rather than from arbitrary decree. God sovereignly orders His creation in counsel with His eternal wisdom and glory (Calvin 1559, 112). Consequently, obeying God is more than submitting to might; it is trusting in the One whose very being ensures that His disposition toward justice, wisdom, and goodness is guaranteed. In biblical storylines, from the covenantal promise to Abraham (Gen. 12:1–3) to Isaiah's vision of the exalted Lord (Isa. 6:1–5), God's sovereignty is established through His speech and actions, inspiring reverence, awe, and reliance.

Thomas Aquinas adds metaphysical depth to this reality by teaching that God's aseity—or existence in and of Himself—means that He is the necessary ground for all created being (Aquinas 1274, I.3.3). Every other mode of existence (for example, the trees or the office where I write) must rely on something else's existence. God is the only being that exists necessarily and eternally. This theological affirmation formed part of Israel's worship, where the people always publicly acknowledged that their law, their land, and even their very lives were ultimately gifts from the One who alone has being in Himself (Ps. 90:2).

In our current moment, contemporary voices like N. T. Wright remind us that God is self-existent, but self-existence is not an abstract philosophical idea; rather, it is a reality revealed through God's covenantal faithfulness and redemptive history. In either case, God acts for His people, whether in the liberation of Israel from Egypt or the resurrection of Jesus from death (Wright 1996, 47). God's sovereignty is both transcendent and simultaneously relational; it evokes awe that reflects His majesty while also bringing comfort as we relate to and experience God's nearness.

For the believer today, reflecting on God's self-existence and sovereignty is an exercise in practicality. It draws us away from relying exclusively on ourselves and places us in reliance upon God. It reminds us that the foundations for all our existence do not rest on ourselves, space, or circumstance, but instead upon the eternal and self-existent Lord who reigns with wisdom, power, and love.

The Holy Name and Israel's Awe

The revelation of God's name in Scripture is a significant catalyst for awe and reverence throughout Israel's history. God tells Moses in Exodus 3:15, "The Lord God of your fathers... has sent me to you," linking God's sovereign, self-existent identity with the God of the covenant of Abraham, Isaac, and Jacob. This name is more than an identity marker; it reveals God's trustworthiness and reliability. Gregory of Nyssa notes that God's name conveys both greatness and nearness, demonstrating that God is transcendent yet intimately present (Gregory of Nyssa 2001, 66).

This recognition is evident in Israel's worship, prayers, and obedience. The Lord's name inspired reverence, shaping blessing, covenant, and sacrificial devotion. Bonaventure observes that encountering God's name engages both mind and heart, eliciting humility, trust, and love (Bonaventure 1268, 51). Augustine similarly emphasizes that Israel's covenantal relationship with God, prompted by His name, inspires reverence and devotion (Augustine 1998, 105). The divine name fosters both fear and confident reliance, forming the foundation of Israel's life before God.

Scripture illustrates this awe in pivotal moments: Moses hesitates before the burning bush, Joshua shows reverence to the commander of the Lord's army (Josh. 5:13–15), and the people tremble at Mount Sinai (Exod. 19:16–20). The revelation of God's holiness and name demanded respect, obedience, and acknowledgment of His authority. True worship involved ethical faithfulness as much as trust in God's provision.

Thus, the holy name of God was more than a theological concept; it shaped Israel's identity and mission. To know, honor, and live in awe of God's name was to participate fully in a life of wonder, devotion, and covenantal trust.

Jesus' "I Am" Sayings

Each of the "I Am" statements in the Gospel of John conveys, in both figurative and realistic terms, various aspects of Jesus' mission and character that address the deepest needs of humankind. Each statement presents a spiritual reality connecting Jesus' identity with God's fulfilling promises in Israel's scriptures.

Jesus states, "I Am the Bread of Life" (John 6:35). Understanding and living out this meaning is essential for all followers of Christ. While manna temporarily satisfied physical hunger, Christ offers eternal life and nourishment of the spirit to all who partake in or engage with Him (Augustine 1998, 215). The image invites reflection: the kingdom of God is not achieved by human effort alone but is cultivated by depending on the living Christ for spiritual satisfaction.

The same pattern is seen in Jesus' declaration, "I Am the Light of the World" (John 8:12). He illuminates not only the absence of goodness in the sinful darkness of ignorance but also personal spiritual blindness. Followers are liberated from ignorance and led into moral clarity and discernment (Gregory of Nyssa 1995, 142). Light functions as more than a metaphor for moral superiority; it enables believers to think and reflect with confidence, trust, and hope in God, replacing fear and uncertainty with assurance in His providential care.

The Good Shepherd imagery in John 10:11 further distinguishes Jesus from common depictions of shepherds. He willingly lays down His life, demonstrating that true power is paradoxically found not in force but in protective, relational service for His flock (Chrysostom 1986, 97). Unlike false shepherds, Christ exercises covenantal care that fulfills the relational promises of God's shepherding in the Old Testament. His leadership exemplifies sacrificial love and guidance that operates fully in His life, death, and resurrection.

Finally, Jesus declares, "I Am the way, the truth, and the life" (John 14:6). This statement assures those seeking eternal life that Christ alone fulfills the ultimate purpose of leading humanity to the Father. For Jesus, ethics is not abstract; it is the integration of person and purpose, rendering moral life trustworthy, meaningful, and complete (Calvin 1559/2006, 256). Christ demonstrates that He is not only Ruler but also Lord of the trust of His followers, exposing the inadequacy of any alternative path.

Collectively, the "I Am" statements reveal that Jesus, as the universal sustainer of creation, is also the personal sustainer of His people. Each metaphor articulates the particularities of nourishment, illumination, and relational care, offering trust, dependence, and worship as pathways to participate in His fullness.

Bread of Life for the Hungry

Jesus' statement, "I Am the bread of life. He who comes to Me shall never hunger, and he who believes in Me shall never thirst" (John 6:35), embodies a stark reversal of human expectation. Israel had expected physical sustenance in the form of manna to meet their need for life in the wilderness. Jesus, however, offers spiritual sustenance with an invitation to eternal life. While we might assume that turning away from earthly sustenance is the next step that requires discipleship, it becomes clear that the relationship of dependence on the Spirit is much more profound; the need that God meets, ultimately, is not a dependence on the provision, but a dependence on Christ. Wright (1996, 274) emphasizes that the feeding of the five thousand serves as an image that is more complete than this teaching reveals. While God provides for their needs, the people are invited to trust in the abundance of the Messiah.

Bread is representative of simplicity, universality, accessibility, humility, and provision. Augustine (1998, 149) states that Christ is the true food; only by consuming Him is the soul fulfilled. The image of bread suggests both belief and active participation: the disciple must receive Christ in faith and obedience, incarnationally; life is offered relationally, not abstractly. Lewis (1960, 101) reminds us that hunger exists both literally and spiritually, and Jesus' claim to being the bread of life speaks to the deeper desires of the human heart. The spiritual nourishment that Christ provides reinforces resilience, joy, and the determination to adopt ethical actions; trust in Him facilitates a life guided by God, rather than driven by desire.

Furthermore, the Bread of Life presents challenges to the communal facets of faith. The shared meal incites fellowship, reminding believers that sustenance is not just personal; it is relational, calling for acts of service, hospitality, and care (Chrysostom c. 347–407, 202). To feed the hungry, both physically and spiritually, foreshadows Christ's generous provision in our lives and enacts the Kingdom of God.

Therefore, to participate in the life of the Bread of Life ultimately means trusting in Christ's provision while living in dependent, relational obedience, not selfish self-interest. At the same time, His life nourishes, shapes, and directs us through our moral choices, deepens our love for Him, and sustains our life through every season. We recognize that God's care surpasses human expectations and fosters a continuous communion with God.

Light of the World for the Blind

Jesus' statement, "I Am the light of the world. He who follows Me shall not walk in darkness, but have the light of life" (John 8:12), radically converts our expectations of the spiritual realm. In a world accustomed to relying on human wisdom, authority, and tradition, Christ reveals the reality of seeing not only external knowledge but also a relational intimacy with Him. Nouwen (1994, 52) notes that spiritual blindness, as prideful self-reliance or moral ambiguity, is restored etymologically only through

Christ, who uncovers darkness while also providing access to guidance, understanding, and illumination.

The imagery of light is deeply rooted in the Old Testament. Isaiah mentions that the people who walked in darkness will see a great light (Isa. 9:2), affirming Christ's activity of fulfilling God's promises. As Origen (1994, 61) indicated, "light" represents God's presence, illuminating to inform, while also revealing, claiming, and transforming reality. The one who is aware of God's truth is also guided in righteousness. John intersperses physical and spiritual sight by recording that Christ healed the blind and then, further, claimed that He is the life-giving sight (John 9:5–7).

Augustine (1998, 172) articulates that following the light entails moral discernment, allowing the divine to shape knowledge, decisions, and relationships. The invitation is to participate; walking in light takes vigilance, patience, and obedience. Darkness is not just an external circumstance, but also an internal struggle, fear, sin, and self-deception. Through Christ, the disciple is enlightened to clarity, meaning, and direction that surpasses human ways of seeing.

Light carries a collective and ethical dimension as well. Following Christ as the Light of the World requires shining a light on pathways for others through acts of kindness, honesty, and faithfulness (Chrysostom c. 347–407, 198). Liberation and discipleship cannot exist solely as a personal compass; Christ cannot be partial; He must also be relational, illuminating pathways of solidarity and communion together. Christ, as the light for our lives, exposes our own blindness to a world shrouded in despair, silence, or moral obtuseness.

The invitation of Christ is illuminating, catalyzing reflection, demonstration, and response to obedience. Spiritual sight is not a static construct, but an ongoing cohort of consulting with Christ that allows us both sight and hope to act, with a prayerful and hopeful view towards transforming all dimensions of life (Wright 1996, 289), walking in His light from darkness to life, both personally and communally.

The Good Shepherd Who Lays Down His Life

Jesus' self-identification as the Good Shepherd in John 10:11—"I am the good shepherd. The good shepherd gives his life for the sheep"—demonstrates powerful changes concerning power, authority, and care. While many worldly leaders attempt to realize and gain power, prestige, or personal benefit, Christ demonstrates leadership sacrificially, protectively, and relationally. Packer (1973, 215) notes that the shepherd's point of view is grounded in relationships; the authority of leadership is legitimate due to the leader's devotion to the welfare of their people, rather than coercion or force.

It is important to recognize that this imagery is rooted in the Old Testament. Psalm 23 depicts God as a shepherd, guiding, protecting, and providing. Augustine (1998, 122) suggests that Christ embodies all the things these poetic assurances describe, particularly in bringing the personal presence of the divine shepherd to people. This metaphor embodies both vulnerability and power: it is one thing to lay down your life, an act of humility, and another to demonstrate complete authority over sin and death, a manifestation of power.

According to Origen (1994, 81), the shepherd's knowledge of the sheep extends to moral and spiritual intimacy. Christ knows the inner dispositions and struggles of believers. He needs to be in a way that enables Him to respond with care and protectiveness through His self-sacrificing love. Chrysostom (c. 347–407, 203) emphasizes that leadership measured by service and self-giving reflects divine authority, contrasting sharply with human ambition and self-interest.

With respect to restoration and safety, the Good Shepherd pursues the lost, wandering, or injured to seek their redemption (Luke 15:4–7) and commits to the value of those lost or unreached. Nouwen (1981, 67) makes an important pastoral point. As followers and disciples of Christ, the Good Shepherd's people both trust that Christ cares for them and enact mercy towards others, thus creating a community rooted in the love of relationships rather than competition or dominance.

In terms of practical application, the believer is enabled to imitate Christ's exemplary model of empathetic leadership, protective care for the vulnerable, and servanthood through self-sacrificing actions. Spiritual life with the Good Shepherd is not passive; it is a lived life of active discernment, obedience, and participation in redemptive work. Ultimately, to say that Christ is the Good Shepherd inherently comforts, challenges, and changes all believers as it asserts new forms of leadership and care based on love, sacrifice, and divine authority (Wright 1996, 305).

The Way, the Truth, and the Life

In John 14:6, Jesus says, "I Am the way and the truth and the life. No one comes to the Father except through me." This statement functions as an extraordinary claim of divine authority and as a troubling reversal of humanity's desires. Where humanity desires many avenues to their own satisfaction, fulfillment, or the innumerable ways to 'truth,' Christ declares that he himself is the only avenue to being one with the God of their creation. The uniqueness of this claim is neither binding nor suffocating but instead informative, restorative, clarifying, and granting words of eternal life (Carson 1991, 528).

The Old Testament background is integral to understanding this claim. In Deuteronomy 30:19–20, God indicates he is 'life' and life is a choice of the way to choose to follow. He calls Israel to choose his 'way' that leads to blessing. Augustine (1998, 367) interprets Christ's declaration as the fulfillment of God's covenantal direction, and that when individuals follow Jesus, they come to life, which is a fullness of life and wisdom. Truth, noted by Thomas Aquinas (1274, II-II, q.1), is more than propositional; it is personal. Truth is engaged in Christ, and 'truth' is a relational concept. Truth is meant to take humanity from a state of affairs to a focus of the heart toward God.

The metaphor of 'way' is dual in meaning; 'way' speaks of both direction and journey. Followers of Christ have a calling to walk in His footsteps by following His directions, which require the practice of being obedient, faith-filled, and humble. Henri Nouwen (1981, 88) challenges the ease of discipleship by articulating a total depravity of thought, word, and deed; he believes that discipleship promotes the interdependence of truth and life. Bonhoeffer (1959, 104) introduces the metaphor of the 'way' as costly grace, highlighting that living into the reality of life in Christ means surrendering oneself and inviting individuals to participate with God in the world's redemptive work.

Moreover, Jesus as life indicates the vigorous and spiritual relational living that is offered to believers through him. Jesus is not only another teacher conveying what is 'truth,' but he brings the conviction and active presence of God to shape how hearts and communities are transformed, forming a foundation upon which the kingdom of God is built. Origen (1994, 92) emphasizes that believers following Christ and in Christ who are being restored, also become empowered in their amending with God; the way to the Father was both unique and internal when they engage Jesus, finding that their unique 'way' is endowed with the convictions to join in contemplative prayer or go further and take action to participate in God's reparative purpose of 'the kingdom of God.'

Therefore, the statement I am the way, the truth, and the life evokes reflection and action. It reassures the faithful that God will guide their life actions, it confronts the earthly presumptions of who has authority and knowledge of truth, and it supplies a relational blueprint for individuals to live out their relationship with God. The way, as a means of participation, enables followers to be compelled by both the expected voice and intent, as well as the burdensome voice of God, and join in God's work of reconciliation, illuminated in the promise and responsibility of life in Christ (Wright 1996, 312).

The Paradox of the Eternal Word in Flesh

The incarnation is a paradox of the infinite God as a finite human existence. This is Jesus, the eternal Word, who entered time and space, who assented to vulnerability as a way of showing divine glory in our weakness and humility (John 1:14). The contradictions associated are overwhelming: the infinite Creator serves His creation. He was the Creator, the servant, the sovereign, and the suffering one all at the same time. Augustine of Hippo commented on this paradox and stated: "not lessened by the flesh the Word made flesh fully united divine nature and human, ordered and manifested the work of God's purpose in creation and redemption" (Augustine 1998, 214). In Christ, eternity touches temporality, and yet remains eternally the eternal Word, through whom humans can see the divine and have access to God.

From another perspective, Athanasius interprets it as "that God became man, that he might have a man" (Athanasius 1971, 47). It is a restoration to creation, the healing of humanity from its sin and death. The paradox presents itself with both theological and practical implications: as the eternal God, He guarantees the efficacy of salvation; as a human being, He assures believers that they will have a relatable and compassionate Savior. The infinite God enters into our suffering, grief, and temptation—not sin—demonstrating perfect obedience and love. The paradox of the human and divine is a tension that never fully reconciles, yet remains a mystery worth wrestling with and pondering in worship.

With respect to the practical element, this paradox means something for Christian living. The believer learns that divine strength is most often apparent weakness, power manifested by serving, and glory in humility (2

Cor. 12:9). The very incarnation that comes to reconcile heaven and tilt earth invites Christians to face the fundamental paradox of their own lives: meekness and gentleness, patience and not letting impulsivity control their actions, and love that elaborates "bearing suffering for the sake of others." The eternal Word who becomes flesh in servanthood is our pattern for a life marked by trust, obedience, and sacrificial love.

The incarnation is God's purpose and grace, united, open, and unbelievably accessible. The Word became flesh allows the eternal Word to reconnect, restore, and redeem both the infinite and the finite, creating intimacy and depth of relationship with the Creator. The paradox of wisdom in its fullest sense expresses that belief in Christ leads believers to build their lives upon the triangle of divine attributes—meekness, gentleness, and humility—to see for themselves that God's divine saving power leads to fullness of life through humility and gentleness.

The Infinite in the Finite

The mystery of the Incarnation opens up the door to the eternal God entering the temporal. In John 1:14, the Word was made flesh (the paradox of the infinite and the finite). The eternal Logos, which is unchangeable and completely transcendent, takes upon itself the limits of humanity; the mystery is unsettling to the human mind, and thus inspires awe and devotion (Wright 1996, 124). The infinite becomes not a distant thought or concept but is rather intimately present in the ordinary life of a carpenter from Nazareth.

Origen demonstrates that the entrance of the Logos into humanity is not a diminishment of divine majesty, but an expression of divine condescension and love; the infinite can become comprehensible by taking on flesh without having its own divinity diminished (Origen 1994, 87). So, the infinite becomes approachable, and humans get to experience God in findable, relational ways—people see Him eat, sleep, and weep. It is worthy of note that at each of these moments of need, emotion, or limitation, the infinite can occupy the finite. God's transcendence remains intact, where the incipient infinite occupies the shared coordinates of immanent, finite need, as the one who is the exalted King of the universe commits himself to washing the feet of his disciples (John 13:4–5).

For Aquinas, there are many implications to explore from this view, as noted earlier, that God is omnipotent, which means the divine essence can be present in anything finite. Thus, the Creator can venture and reach over the gap between Creator and creation (Aquinas 1981, II-II, Q.3, Art. 1). The Incarnation relates to the material world even as the incarnate God reconciles ordinary matter and makes it the space for a manifestation of the divine presence within the material world. Thus, every detail of Christ's humanity, from the birth in Bethlehem to his agony on the cross, uncovers the revelation of God's infinite love in the particularity of finite experience (Bonaventure 1268, 42).

For contemporary Christians, the paradox can inspire awe, as it also inspires imitation. To encounter Christ in His humanity reminds us that God cares about our closeness, recognizing human weakness (Nouwen 1981, 56), while also reassuring us that holiness can be infused into everyday life, thus demonstrating that the infinite reality of God can permeate our ordinary world. Because the Incarnation leaves us to reflect with humility—an acknowledgment that the infinite God, who rules the universe, denigrates for the sake of redeeming humanity, in so doing renders the incomprehensible God visible, open, and tangible; God invades temporalism to reveal eternity.

Augustine on the Word Made Flesh

Augustine of Hippo elaborates on this mystery of the incarnation, paying careful attention to the reality that the eternal Word took on human nature to restore fallen man (Augustine 1998, 204). In *Confessions*, Augustine explores the concept of God's humility. Despite being omnipotent and sovereign, he condescended to be located in time and place. The Word made flesh integrates the infinite into the finite, revealing God's mercy while providing a way for humanity to be saved (Augustine 1998, 210).

For Augustine, the incarnation cannot be divorced from grace. Because of sin, humanity cannot rise to God on its own. The eternal Word descends, dressed in flesh, to lift creation, providing an example of divine humility and self-emptying love (Edwards 1746, 88). Christ's humanity mediates wisdom and salvation; this is an incarnation, a living vessel, ego, bestowed by God, and a relational interface with God. Augustine affirms that believers "have received knowledge" of God as well as "the possibility of participation" in divine life (Aquinas 1981, II-II, Q.3, Art. 6).

Augustine also points to the instructive aspect of Christ's humanity. By assuming human form, Jesus experienced hunger, thirst, suffering, and sorrow. Following Christ, believers continue to model obedience, patience, and love for God and their neighbors (Chrysostom c. 347–407, 112, 202). The instructive aspect of Christ's life also provides an opportunity for believers to encounter God, not as an authority, but as a personal invitation to imitate Christ and be discipled. The Incarnation also gives rise to contemplation in Augustine. The faithful may discern the fullness of God's humility and love through contemplative meditation on Christ's dual nature (Bonaventure 1268, 53).

Practically, these reflections on the mystery of the Incarnation create encouragement for a devotional life of wonder and obedience. Believers are called to marvel at God's condescension while responding obediently through faithful service, a moral life, and loving others (Packer 1973, 215). The Word made flesh is therefore not only a theological expression, but it becomes a lived experience that forms the spiritual life, ethical life, and mutual witness. The incarnation is a historical, spiritual, and personal gift from God that reframes human understanding and encourages participation in the divine life.

Athanasius on God Becoming Man

In his seminal work, *On the Incarnation*, Athanasius began to construct the incarnation as God's plan for restoring humanity. He writes that it seems to follow that "he was made man that we might be made God" (Athanasius 1993, 35). This juxtaposition reveals that the eternal Word took on humanity to redeem it, to restore humanity to life in the divinity of God (Gregory of Nyssa 2001, 78). The incarnation, to Athanasius, is not simply historical, but God's most complete revelation of love and wisdom.

The linchpin to Athanasius' understanding of the incarnation is recapitulation; in Jesus Christ, humanity lives out their life of obedience, correcting Adam's disobedience and restoring God's creation to its former glory (Athanasius 1993, 42). By taking on the flesh, the Word links divine and human realities, sanctifies human nature, and reconciles all of creation back to God. In the incarnation, God exhibits both His infinite character and the proximity of His approachability, while distinguishing Himself from His creation (Bonaventure 1268, 57).

Athanasius adds a pedagogical dimension to the incarnation. He emphasizes that Jesus Christ exemplifies what God intended in terms of morality and spirituality when He suffers, is tempted, lives as a mortal, and embodies the divine will (Chrysostom c. 347–407, 118, 202). Ultimately, Christ's humanity serves as an accessible representation of the encounter with God, allowing believers to reflect on a transcendent Creator.

Athanasius's theological insight has great practical significance. Believers are invited into the transformative engagement with Christ's presence. The Word made flesh initiates human beings into divine life, but it necessitates yielding to the divine will (Packer 1973, 222). Worship, ethics, and community each experience the divine/human union of creation, beckoning believers into Jesus' humble obedience and sacrificial love.

In light of these observations, Athanasius believes the incarnation is indeed revelation, restoration, and formation. God's greatest act of love and redemptive purpose is historical engagement and an ongoing spiritual principle that takes shape in the way believers think, engage, and share in divine life. God becoming man has produced a renewed human experience of God, their lives, and salvation history.

Healing Through the Presence of "I Am"

The holy statement "I Am" in Scripture signifies both self-existence and intimate presence. It also offers significant healing for the human soul. The promise of God to Moses in Exodus 3:14 and the reassurance of God's promises in times of fear and uncertainty to the Israelites were marked by self-existence and presence, recognizing both powerful authority and seamless closeness. "Do not be afraid, I Am with you" (Isa. 41:10) is more than a declaration of power; it is a soothing consideration for a quivering heart, inviting a trustful response to a God-invited presence in a time of disorder. The knowledge of a God who is "I Am" cultivates awareness, ultimately freeing all who believe from fear and trepidation while restoring peace to seeking minds in a time of uncertainty and panic (Packer 1973, 215).

Furthermore, God's nearness, as the "I Am," is also restorative in all its relational gifting. Those ignored, abandoned, or disregarded are renewed in their personhood as they become aware of being introduced to a faithful presence embodied in the I Am, which, as Henri Nouwen notes, is a remedy to the loneliness we face in suffering, since "intimacy with God tells us that we are worth something in his love, not in the love of humanity" (Nouwen 1994, 47). When we understand that God is present, we are comforted and restored; we learn how to transform suffering into a grace experience. Making others aware of God's nearness in their plight and predicament is an unshakeable and inimitable comfort that eludes worldly consolations, for instance, "Even though I walk through the valley of the shadow of death, I will fear no evil; for You are with me" (Ps. 23:4). The presence of the I Am does not just surround; as a protector, the omnipresence and existence of God also restores.

Additionally, the incarnation of Christ and the healing power of God through his presence cannot be experienced only spiritually, but also found tangibly through Christ's enfleshing of the I Am, who comes particularly into our suffering. Where they need comfort in their bearing and compassion in their brokenness, Christ reveals himself as the I Am, sharing, feeling, and understanding their suffering (John 1:14). Trying to alleviate with compassionate sensitivity, Christ combines the union of divine power and receptive vulnerability in hope to be foundational for trust, hope, and ultimately renewal.

As Christians, it is essential to understand and learn practical ways to experience the gift of healing that occurs when we seek to become aware of the release of the I Am through prayer, meditation on Scripture, and receptive listening to the Spirit. The I Am is not simply seated on a throne far removed, but resides intimately in our hearts, healing our internal wounds of fear, loneliness, and despair. Knowing that God exists and is close by releases us to courageously face the fears of life ahead, to release our worries, and to sleep in peace while resting in love. Now, the presence of the I Am becomes a place where healing is a continued experience in the fullness of our whole being: body, mind, and spirit.

Freedom from Fear: "Do Not Be Afraid, I Am with You"

Jesus said, "Do not be afraid, I am with you" (Isa. 41:10; Matt 28:20) to emphasize that God, in human vulnerability, desires intimate companionship through the periods of life we experience as fearful events. Fear typically comes on the heels of events that rage beyond our understanding. However, Christ continually disarms fear with His presence. In scripture, God's presence safely shifts paralyzing anxiety into trust and courage. Consider Moses and the burning bush. God's proclamation - "I AM WHO I AM" (Exod. 3:14) - assured a hesitant servant that it was God's presence, not human ability, that would achieve God's purposes (Augustine 1998, 112). In the gospels, Jesus says almost the same thing to His disciples. Peter's fear of walking on water dissipates when he recognizes Jesus' presence (Matt. 14:27-31). The heart of these accounts illustrates that an understanding of God's continual presence, rather than fearing worldly events, is at the heart of spiritual courage (Calvin 1559, 45). Patristic writers, especially Gregory of Nyssa, have an organic concept of God's presence - it does not remove adversity or calamity. However, it transforms the individual's soul to endure the experience (Gregory of Nyssa 2001, 79). Fear has an isolating effect, but Christ's promise invites a relational response with the divine. Henri Nouwen claims that awareness of God's unending presence transforms loneliness into trust, anxiety into surrender, and ambition into spiritual formation (Nouwen 1981, 88). Application here is effortlessly practical: believers endure personal trials, such as sickness, grief, and uncertainty in the world, while focusing their attention on the eternal presence of the I AM, and recognizing that one does not have to fear. Therefore, "Do not be afraid" is more than a kind saying; it is a theological principle rooted in God's character and relayed in the person of Christ. Christians, who embrace this promise, touch the character of courage that is actual and deeply spiritual, because the eternal I AM walks with them in each moment to strengthen belief, endurance, and hope.

Healing the Lonely Through God's Nearness

Loneliness exists not only as a social phenomenon but as a spiritual state or a poor view of reality. Repeatedly in the Scriptures, God is described as near the lonely, the marginalized, or the suffering (Ps. 34:18; Matt. 28:20). Jesus' ministry as recorded in the Gospels demonstrates that he intentionally leaned into those who had been cast aside, the lonely, the lepers, and the widow, making it a point to provide not only words but the embodied presence of divine love to them (Mark 1:40–42; Chrysostom 202, 134).

For the early Christian father, Origen, "God's nearness, which is Christ's, is a dynamic identification that means through Jesus' nearness that God was willing to offer the person in isolation, marginalization, alienation, and/or suffering true restoration in a relationship that is spiritual in nature" (Origen 1994, 67). This was a particularly compelling idea, given that the standard twenty-first-century contemporary solutions to isolation were either distractions or accomplishments (i.e., achievement work). The alternative perspective offered by the I Am, what Jesus represents, is a relational approach to solitude that is attentive, patient, and sustaining. The story of Lazarus comes to mind, where a person's isolation was immediately transformed into optimal and wholesome communal living because of Christ's presence (John 11:1–44).

Jonathan Edwards observes that when the spiritual awareness of God's nearness is felt, the effect is profound, as it brings healing, aligns the heart with God's rhythm, and fosters trusting the relationship even when isolation is enduring (Edwards 1746, 55). Henri Nouwen also writes that from the moment one begins to see God in Christ as always present, one's marked vulnerability presents the possibility of being intimate with God. This recognizes God's intimacy with us, filling in the depravity caused by an overwhelming number of work activities and unrelated relationships characterized by a poor self-image (Nouwen 1994, 102).

As a final observation, this simple need to respond semantically and grammatically with a disability is a call for leaving behind unhelpful representations of God and one's loneliness. Substantively, this call is to develop a response prayerfully and attentively to God in prayer through the sacred word, the God of the word, and the Church. Through this act of submission to God, loneliness is not manifest as the absence of God, but rather as the beginning of a deep dependency on God through empathetic engagement with others. In a two-fold sense, healing is both inward, in the heart of the believer, and outward to the symbolically shaped relationships formed as representatives of God's sources of love (i.e., dualistic sets of relational forms).

Comfort in Suffering: God Who Shares Our Humanity

The incarnation reveals a profound truth: God is not distant from human suffering. Philippians 2:6–8 states that Christ "being in the form of God... humbled Himself," and entered completely into human weakness. By entering into the human experience, Christ offers unparalleled comfort, as God experiences grief, pain, and loss alongside His people (Wright 1996, 201). By becoming human, Christ bridges the infinite gulf between divine perfection and human finitude, offering believers a God who thoroughly understands their experiences and shares in their humanity.

Augustine reflects that the Word made flesh serves as a relational bridge for the suffering soul. The believer can fully disclose their brokenness to a God who has experienced it firsthand (Augustine 1998, 115). The gospels offer examples of this empathy: Jesus wept at Lazarus' tomb (John 11:35), healed the sick (Matt. 9:35), and took on the burdens of the oppressed. God's nearness is much more than passive; it invites active participation (Lewis 1960, 83). This incarnational engagement suggests that God's presence is not an abstraction, but rather a relational one, leading believers closer to comfort and hope.

Brennan Manning defines this divine solidarity as salve for those who suffer: suffering is no longer isolated but is absorbed into the tapestry of Christ's own life and victory (Manning 1990, 77). C.S. Lewis remarks that understanding that Christ is in solidarity with humanity in suffering transforms despair into hope and offers a model of patience, endurance, and empathetic ministry (Lewis 1943, 54). This theological point reiterates that the divine, empathetic presence not only removes suffering but also offers restoration, comfort, and an example.

Practically, believers experience consolation, yet it is not through the lack of suffering, but in bringing unavoidable suffering into the presence of the I Am. Through prayer, meditating on Scripture, and communal support, we experience God's care. The incarnation tells the weary that our suffering is not meaningless, nor is it suffered in isolation; God receives, redeems, and walks beside us with a loving presence.

Consequently, the comfort present through the incarnation of Christ completes a holistic and restorative triad of meaning—spiritual, emotional, and relational—revealing a God whose nearness heals, restores, and transforms hearts even while we struggle with temptation, loss, betrayal, and evil. Eschatologically, God fully enters into the human experience in Jesus to uniquely model empathy, solidarity, and divine love for His people across every relational dimension of suffering.

Joy in the God Who Is

True joy is the result of experiencing the unchangeableness of God. Joy is different from the temporary pleasures and changing certainty of the world. The God who said "I Am" (Exod. 3:14) offers a foundation for hope and joy we can rest upon, regardless of the circumstances of our lives. We rejoice in the God who is with us, who is faithful to His promises and unchangeable. He invites us as believers to rest in His providence. Psalm 16:11 states: "You make known to me the path of life; in Your presence there is fullness of joy; at Your right hand are pleasures forevermore." Joy is not based on your success, material possessions, or how much others like you; it is found in communion with the God whose nature is unchangeable, merciful, and loving (Packer 1973, 98).

Resting in God's faithfulness is central to joy. The Bible consistently speaks of God's commitment to His promises. Consider Lamentations 3:22–23: "The Lord's mercies are new every morning; great is Your faithfulness." The knowledge of His unchangeableness enables the believer to let go of anxiety, relinquish control, and trust that God is working all things for good. Luther reminds us that joy comes neither from what we have nor from what goes well; joy comes from the comfort and assurance of God's presence in all seasons of life (Luther 1957, 102). Even in complex trials, God's unchanging nature encourages perseverance, peace of mind, and resilience of spirit.

Joy is inherently relational. It changes how the believer relates to the world and injects hope into our relationships, work, and ministry. Henri Nouwen also notes that as individuals grow in their awareness of God's unchangeableness, it fosters a calm and generous spirit, enabling them to bless others by extending grace and encouragement (Nouwen 1994, 63). When we know God is by our side, whether in good times or challenging times, we are moved to worship, give thanks, and celebrate life in all its blessings and burdens.

On a practical level, cultivating joy in the God who is involves actively remembering, reflecting, praying, and pondering the implications of His immutable nature and faithfulness. The believer can then firmly resist despair and inhabit a posture of trust, thankfulness, and tranquility. Living in joy in the God who is becomes an experience lived out of our being, nourishing our character, shaping our choices, and enabling us to maintain hope-filled joy even in the challenges of all seasons. When I return to the place of rest in the unshakeable presence of the I Am, my heart rejoices and I dwell in the joy of His life.

Joy in God's Unchanging Nature

The unchanging nature of God provides believers with a stable foundation for enduring joy. Our human situations often rise and fall, generating anxiety as they do so. The assurance of God's immutability helps believers trust that His promises remain steadfast (Mal. 3:6; Heb. 13:8). Joy based on God's immutability is an abiding joy that does not rest on fleeting experiences but instead relies on the eternal character of the Creator. Packer (1973, 215) notes that assurance of knowing God's attributes to be unchanging leads to spiritual confidence and fortitude, enabling believers to rejoice despite adversity.

The Bible continually teaches this reality. The psalmist says, "The Lord is faithful in all His words, and gracious in all His deeds" (Ps. 145:13). Edwards (1746, 88) explains that when our hearts drift from God and become detached from Him, we have joy that extends beyond our conditional states because we are sure there is a constant, which is always God's goodness. Augustine similarly conveys that true joy can only be found in God, not in temporary pleasures outside of Him (Augustine 1998, 45).

Moreover, hope and trust in God's faithfulness help guide practice in discipleship. Knowledge of God's immutability fosters patience with one's own struggles, as well as with those of others. Lewis (1960, 76) highlights that joy based on eternal realities can provide inner peace, promoting gentleness and understanding as one lives in community. The settled nature of God's character avoids the friction of anxiety, so that the believer may act and speak from a place of steadfastness, guided by holistic integrity and hope.

In addition, joy in God's immutability provides continuity of thought in the relationship between theological contemplation and personal devotion. As we meditate on God's faithfulness, personal devotion manifests in a life that exhibits gratitude for God's gift, develops trust in His goodness, and enacts an ethical stance to live in alignment with His purposes and promises. Daily, one learns to appreciate God as omnipresent, characterized by unchanging love and goodness, while even seemingly ordinary situations become contexts for worshiping and enjoying Him.

Joy grounded in God's immutability is both theological and practical. It is more than a joy that withstands any situation; it is a joy that embodies

God's sustainable faithfulness, guides faith development, directs ethical outcomes, and fosters mature relationships. For believers who rest in the eternality of God's character, there is an inextinguishable joy that is constant when life rises and falls, drawing them closer to the heart of God.

Finding Rest in His Faithfulness

Rest in God, or rest in the faithfulness of God, comes from an assured trust in God's reliability. The world often grapples with uncertainty, anxiety, and unfulfilled desires. However, the unwavering message of Scripture is that God is steadfast (Ps. 91:1-2; Isa. 40:28-31). This assurance enables weary pilgrims to release their burdens and find spiritual, emotional, and even physical refreshment. Bonhoeffer (1959, 134) declared that the faithfulness of God is not just a concept; it is a relational offer of intimacy that calls believers to trust in Him communally and exchange their anxiety for His peace.

Scripture repeatedly portrays a witness to God's faithfulness in the biblical narrative. The Israelites trusted in God when they exited Egypt, and they claimed this historical testimony, passing it along to generations (Exod. 13:21-22). Furthermore, Jesus, the Word made flesh, was highly faithful to his promises, making provision for the marginalized, healing the sick, and ministering to the hurts of society's underbelly (John 14:1-3). This illustrates how God's fidelity is both characterological and relationally experienced. Nouwen (1994, 57) articulated that accepting God's constancy means being able to live with one's own limitations without despair, knowing that God's purposes will prevail.

Practically resting in God's faithfulness requires careful attention to His promises and reliability, as well as testing our impulses to be in control. Augustine (1998, 212) acknowledged that human rest means dependence on God—our complete satisfaction comes from him. Each day, practices of prayer, meditation on Scripture, and communal worship nourish a rhythm of dependence that fosters restorative rest.

Faithfulness provides a moral and emotional anchor. Trusting in God has stabilizing effects on decision-making, calms fears, and fosters patience when under challenging contexts. Wright (1996, 178) references the implications of rational stability brought about by God's trustworthiness, which fosters resilience and enhances the ability to increase hope and peace in one's community.

Rest given by God's faithfulness is a gift to the entire being: heart, mind, and spirit. When embracing God's constancy, believers can find respite from anxiety, assurance with uncertainty, and renewal of purpose from and by Him. Resting in God is an act of obedience, but also an encounter, bringing individuals into deeper intimacy with the One who is consistently worthy of trust and offers continued joy, peace, and flourishing.

Luther on the God Who Is Present in All Seasons

Martin Luther's theology places strong emphasis on the presence of God and the immutability of God in life circumstances. For Luther, God's presence, coupled with the immutability of God, provides believers with great assurance that God's care remains constant, regardless of human circumstances. Luther's remarks on Psalm 46:1-3 make sense. He saw God as a "very present help in trouble," a refuge, "always ready and unshaken" (Luther 1520, 57). God was not an abstract idea but actively storing up the experience of a believer's life in every season.

Luther's notion of the "God who is" is consistent with his Christological focus. This notion moves from the God of Stories to the Christ of living relationships that have a historical basis. In this way, the incarnate Christ expresses thoroughly what presence and while being in relation with something new is nourished by God. Luther made a point of saying, "in Christ, a believer is a self in Christ and partakes of this living relationship

God's Surprising Way

with God, where God participates actively, and meets fear or despair or uncertainty with reassurance" (Lowery 2010, 16). Luther's theology is practical, and he encourages believers to rely on God in the face of spiritual difficulties, poverty, illness, or social marginalization. Luther's insistence on God's presence during suffering aligns with Bonhoeffer's later understanding of God as "near to the suffering" (Bonhoeffer 1959, 134).

There is no doubt that historically, Luther displays a pastor's heart in his writings. In both sermons and letters, Luther assures believers that, regardless of the 'fallen world,' believers need to remember that God's presence is unchanged. N. T. Wright (2012, 188) accurately identifies Luther's call for God's constancy, urging modern believers to abandon self-reliance and learn to trust in God. Believers, particularly through daily prayer and reading Scripture, rely on God's promises. Reading Scripture and participating in the sacrament bring a sense of experiencing the reality of God's constant presence.

Additionally, Luther's understanding of God's omnipresence can have favorable psychological and spiritual consequences when the believer is deeply rooted in reliance upon God. Once a believer understands God as constant, their anxiety diminishes, and moral courage and spiritual perseverance increase in the presence of someone alive. Lewis (1960, 92) reveals that the notion of knowing God underlies human imagination, behavior, and ethical judgments, enabling us to be big, confident, and joyful with a satisfied life, knowing that God is sustaining us.

Luther's reflections offer insight into how one can live comfortably, confidently, joyfully, and satisfyingly in all seasons of life, because the omnipresence of God is comforting and reassuring. Trusting "the God who is" in ways of God, through the gospel, or in God's presence is how believers have an immutable reservoir of comfort, guidance, and courage at any point in their lives.

Love as the Overflow of "I Am"

The love of God is not an abstract notion but a real experience, made known in the person of Jesus Christ, the "I Am" (John 8:58) who lives in eternity. The nature of divine love emits waves of life from the ground of God's life for everyone who abides in Him. God's love becomes visible, tangible, and meaningful in Christ and is freely offered to the broken and the lost, in forgiveness and grace, and in communal intimacy without prerequisite. Love begins in God's life on God's action and existence alone, and flows from God's relational being as the "I Am" or Creator. God expressed His character in His self-existence (Exod. 3:14) and His fidelity as a covenant keeper. In the experience of love, the believer has met the I Am, and is invited to share in this love as a joyful response to being beloved, known, and accepted by God (Bauckham 1996, 147).

John Calvin cautions that believers become adopted children of God through union with Christ, and thus become participants in God's family and recipients of all appropriation (Calvin 1559, 502). Adoption is a remarkable expression of divine love: God deigns to call 'sinners' His own, thus altering their identity and capacity to live a life of witness to His love. For Calvin, adoption is more than just a legal standing; it is a relational reality, providing a foundation for the believer's increasing maturity, obedience, and service. In that sense, we love by virtue of God's love, as recipients and as sent bearers.

Henri Nouwen offers a contemporary witness, suggesting that the purpose of the Christian life with God is rooted in the awareness of being beloved (Nouwen 1994, 87). When believers finally understand what it means to be told by God, "you are Beloved," they discover that God provides love, exists in love, and love becomes the overflow that drives their existence. Love, the essence of being in God's presence, shapes relational experiences, fosters kindness to one another and to our neighbors, generates compassion, and is the catalyst for sacrificial love. It is the realization of being connected by that which is founded in love; it is selfless living by using God's grace to offer grace, patience, and mercy to a world of strife and selfishness. We can see each other as rivers flowing into the world as rivers that feed from an inexhaustible fountain.

In the end, love, as the overflow of the I Am, is both the ground and product. It begins in God (the I Am), and culminates in a relation that is both embodied and receptive. It is borne out of experience—being in the presence of a God of perfect love and goodness, and into the enfleshed realities of how we relate to family, community, and strangers alike. The believer, by abiding in Christ, dares not live for themselves, but rather, as emissaries of divine love, living like love, showing the world the I Am is tender and transforming in a world aching to be loved and wanted.

Divine Love Made Visible in Christ

Christ's humanity embodies divine love, expressible in relational and tangible ways. From Jesus' life and earthly ministry, it is evident that God's love is not theoretical—it is incarnate. God's love is made visible and tangible in acts of compassion, mercy, and sacrifice (John 13:34–35; Matt. 20:28). It is paradoxical—gentle yet powerful; humble yet transformative. In feeding the five thousand, raising Lazarus, and continuing to teach his closest followers, God's love encounters human vulnerability, meets basic needs, and restores dignity (France 2007, 442).

Richard Bauckham observes that Christ's actions embody a "personalizing love," wherein God speaks to them by name and relates to them in their particular situation (Bauckham 2008, 123). This incarnational love invites the believer to follow the pattern of self-giving and to seek to identify the 'other' not as an object of care, but as its subject. To be devoted to Christ means lavishing love on others through acts of mercy, kindness, hospitality, and patient presence (1 John 4:11–12).

In addition, divine love disrupts hierarchies and social norms among humans. It embraces the disenfranchised, the sick, and the socially fixed in a position of ignominy. It demonstrates that God's economy is designed to operate independently of human economies and structures (Luke 14:12–14). In reflecting on this love, Augustine notes that Christ's love, unlike something at rest, is constantly forming: love "forms or shapes" moral character, cultivates humility, and teaches self-forgetfulness (Augustine 1998, 54).

Visible love overturns challenges to embody some version of relational attentiveness and sacrificial love in our own lives. In addition, it reassures the faithful of the continued presence of divine love, active and present in suffering, loss, and uncertainty. Viewing the Gospels through a contemplative lens enables Christians to see not just Jesus' historical works, but the profound impact of God's love that transcends time, drawing human hearts into God's purposes.

Calvin on Adoption through Union with Christ

John Calvin regarded adoption as the highest gift of union with Christ, and that in relationship, believers are justified and incorporated into God's household (Calvin 1559, 294). Adoption is about relationship, but it is also transformational, bringing assurance that believers are no longer servants or strangers, but welcomed children in God's household. In Calvin's theology, union with Christ is the basis of all spiritual blessings, and the intimate way to experience God's covenant love is through adoption. Adoption is God's action, completely unmerited, and His gracious act toward humanity.

Calvin connects adoption to the believer's new identity, articulating that believers, in unity with Christ, share all the privileges and responsibilities of being a child of God (Rom. 8:15–17). They now benefit from God's protective, guiding, and loving love, providing a sense of spiritual security and the freedom to live holy and obedient lives. Importantly, union with Christ also challenges relational and moral lives, as the view of self as a child of God embraces a proper awareness of humility, gratitude, and dependence on God's wisdom. Calvin claims that this understanding renders spiritual pride impossible and fosters a sense of trust in God's providence, regardless of hardships or suffering (Calvin 1559, 296).

Fanatically, Calvin's apostle Paul's language in Ephesians 1:5–6 provides an interpretive foundation for Calvin's perspective, underscoring the relational aspect of believers' salvation. This is evident when Paul describes God as "predestining" believers for adoption through Jesus Christ. Calvin intentionally indicates that adoption cannot be attained without Christ's redemptive work; believers approach God, as Father, only through Christ's mediation and obedience. For this reason, Calvin's adoption model endeavors to blend theological depth with practical significance for everyday life, assuring believers of their inaugural status before God, while also calling them to believe and obey daily.

Practically, Calvin's considerations challenge believers to put into practice a pattern of prayer, worship, and involved ethics in relation to the very awareness that God is Father. Union with Christ and adoption lead to direct, relational, spiritual, and moral lives. In this context of awareness, one embraces the courageous act of confidence, gratitude, and love as an expression of God. Adoption is to be received as a gift, as well as lived as a calling: the vocation of embodying the familial love, service, and holiness of Christ indeed upon all persons united to him.

Nouwen on the God Who Calls Us Beloved

Henri Nouwen argues that the most basic way God speaks to humanity is through an ordinary, yet extraordinary, word: "beloved" (Nouwen 1994, 67). In Christ, God's call to be beloved is relational and personal. The belovedness means that everyone is known, accepted, and loved by God.

Our belovedness is not based on any human accomplishment, spirituality, or status. Our belovedness entirely rests in God's grace and initiative. Nouwen highlights that God's call to be beloved is transformative. It shapes identity, character, and vocation, especially for individuals feeling disillusioned, marginalized, or spiritually drained.

The parable of the prodigal son also depicts this divine hug (Luke 15:11–32). The father's welcome demonstrates how God's love restores dignity, inspires spiritual growth, and opens the door to reconciliation. Nouwen says that understanding yourself as beloved is fundamental to living a life of freedom, courage, and compassion. When believers grasp this calling, fear, insecurity, and the need for constant approval diminish—promoting the freedom to serve genuinely, love wholeheartedly, and live faithfully.

Nouwen acknowledges the communal aspect of being beloved. To hear "beloved" is not just something you receive as an individual; it is to be a part of a bigger family of faith. It shapes ethical behavior by encouraging believers to cultivate gentleness, patience, and compassion toward others. Recognizing God's loving, personal, and constant love fosters humility, gratitude, and an awareness of our obligation to the good of our community (Nouwen 1994, 71).

Practically, Nouwen urges believers to practice spiritual disciplines, including prayer, reflection, and contemplative reading of Scripture, to help them deepen their experience of being God's beloved. While doing these, believers open their hearts to God's presence, dwell in God's love, and participate in God's work in the world. This makes spirituality relational, not performative, based on the truth that human action flows from God's prior affection and acceptance.

Ultimately, our call to belovedness shapes the believer's entire stance toward life. The faithful believer is reminded that God is present, personal, and always loves us, regardless of our condition or desires. By receiving God's love, believers can live lavishly, extending grace, compassion, and hope into every aspect of their lives. Belovedness, then, is a gift and a vocation that is rooted in one's identity and spiritual formation, ethical behavior, and rest in God's eternal love, known through Christ.

Living with the "I Am" Today

There is something about daily existence that is immeasurably transformed when we live in the presence of Christ. Living in the presence of the I Am encompasses the realization that the I Am is not merely a disinterested God, but rather the Lord who dwells among us (John 14:23). To live in the presence of the I Am today means that there is a rhythm of intimacy established with God that provides regularity of prayer, reading of Scripture, and reflective attention to God's character for thought, speech, and action. Living in the presence of Christ brings a sense of security, as the eternal God who sustains the cosmos also sustains the individual believer; thus, there is rest to be had in uncertainty and courage to be cultivated in adversity (Psalm 46:1).

Viewing His sufficiency also shifts the focus tremendously away from human incapacity toward the divine capability. As believers face matters of work, relationships, and personal struggles, they acknowledge that the I Am is sufficient for every need they may face. John Calvin asserts that God's sufficiency enlivens and upholds God's people, enabling them to live faithfully and without relying on the power or respect of the world (Calvin 1559, 503). Likewise, Henri Nouwen observes that trusting in God's presence liberates the heart from anxiety as obedience and service naturally arise from a place of grounded confidence (Nouwen 1981, 52).

Awareness of the I Am today also emboldens believers to witness. Living in awareness of God's abiding presence alters how people speak, act, and interact with others. In the presence of the I Am, people make ethical decisions, exhibit acts of mercy, and uphold their integrity, becoming a reflection of God, who is unchanging and faithful (Wright 1996, 214). This confidence in God's abiding presence is not arrogance, but a humble boldness, grounded in the steady knowledge of serving a Creator and Redeemer.

The daily practice of prayer in the name of the I Am anchors life in divine reality. Life is always praying to the I Am, whether in a moment of tangible gratitude, intercession, quiet reflection, or some other way. Praying in the name of God reminds us we are part of a bigger story, in which the eternal God walks with us. Prayer creates a sense of being attuned to God, prompting us to align our desires with God's will, which in turn promotes expressions of joy, peace, and love in all aspects of life.

Abiding in the I Am today is discipline and delight; both abiding, being empowered, witnessing, and praying, all while being at rest in the sufficiency of the eternal God. As life daily unfolds, the presence of the I Am gradually breathes action into our ordinary routines, so what was opportunity to express grace, act with obedience, and develop a relationship with self, God, and others becomes actively possible, for we encounter an eternal God who is close, present, and worthy of trust in every aspect of life.

Abiding in the Presence of Christ

Abiding in Christ is necessary to living in the reality of the "I Am." Jesus invites believers to abide in Him and states that apart from Him, they can do nothing (John 15:4–5). Abiding with Him is relational, not ritualistic, and it entails a continual conscious awareness of His presence and guidance. By fostering this intimacy each day, believers experience God's sustaining presence, refreshed by the Spirit and participation within His redemptive work. Nouwen notes that abiding can foster a contemplative stance, where the mundane is simply a means of being present with God (Nouwen 1981, 56).

The Scriptures list just a few ways to abide—prayer, contemplation of Scripture, and listening to the Spirit. Paul specifically describes this as being "rooted and built up in Him, and established in the faith" (Col. 2:7). As it is relational, the abiding that Paul speaks of involves both God's initiative and human response: Christ resides within believers, and the believer focused on abiding continues to nurture a posture of receptivity, obedience, and reflection. Augustine asserts that God's presence is both immanent and transcendent; God desires that believers relinquish their attempts to control Him and trust His sustaining care (Augustine 1998, 214).

Abiding in the presence of Christ also has implications for community. Loving others in the presence of Christ enables believers to love well, bear spiritual fruit, and persevere through human suffering. The lasting awareness of abiding in God's presence fosters patience, humility, and hope, as one comes to realize that one's will and effort are subordinate to God's transformative work. Bonhoeffer emphasizes that this is where the disciple finds strength—not self-reliance, but the keeping of Christ's presence and steadiness in the face of suffering and uncertainty (Bonhoeffer 1959, 87).

Practically, abiding calls us into deliberate rhythms, substantive time in prayer and Scripture, and attentiveness to the Spirit. This even includes relinquishing distractions—not only surrendering to the time, but nurturing a disposition of openness. In abiding in Christ, believers experience the stability to act and the freedom to act in courageous love, as the very presence of God leads and guides them. In doing so, they embody the truth of "I Am," living each day simply as participants in His eternally transformative presence.

Drawing Strength from His Sufficiency

Christ's sufficiency is the heart of the believer's life. Jesus, the eternal "I Am," provides believers with all the necessary ingredients for spiritual living, moral strength, and devoted service. He says in John 6:35, "I am the bread of life: he who comes to Me shall never hunger." Here, Jesus is making it clear that sustenance and nourishment come not through human work and effort, but rather through His presence. Wright notes Christ's sufficiency does not merely replace an isolated, insufficient perspective; it radically disrupts a worldview of self-sufficiency, inviting individuals into a spirit of dependent freedom that nurtures spiritual maturity (Wright 1996, 452).

Christ's sufficiency is experienced through different aspects. First, spiritually, it gives believers an identity and purpose "in" Christ, not in sordid human praise or accomplishment. In an emotional sense, God's presence calms the hearts of those who are frightened, anxious, or sad, because His promises offer unceasing hope (Ps. 46:1–3). In a practical realm, sufficiency inspires the believer to depend on God for provision and make wise choices, knowing that the believer cannot navigate life based on their best insights; true wisdom and sound decisions come through Christ. Packer observes that the doctrine of God's sufficiency produces internal peace and contentment, thereby eliminating the anxiety of worry and striving for control (Packer 1973, 119).

The idea of sufficiency in relation to Christ also has an impact on discipleship. The believer is invited to depend on Christ for strength in evangelism, service, and obedience to God's will, surrendering their energy to Christ, who has invited them to relinquish their self-generated energy so that He might empower them. Bonhoeffer posits the idea that relating to Christ's sufficient presence in discipleship presents a paradox – freedom found through dependence. More clearly stated, the more the believer recognizes their insufficiency, the more they come to understand the power of God at work in their lives (Bonhoeffer 1959, 102).

In addition, sufficiency fosters gratitude and humility. When believers recognize God as their life and strength, they can cultivate an attitude of thankfulness rather than pride or self-serving independence. This recognition informs the believer's relationships, work, and community space, and the witness reflects trust and peace rather than anxiety and competition. As believers participate in the daily sufficiency of "I Am," through prayer, the Scriptures, and community worship, they entrust the developing reality of the "I Am" in their lives, drawing every ounce of sustaining strength from the unchanging Christ who satisfies every need and reflects the biography of "I Am."

Witnessing with Confidence in the God Who Is

Testifying for Christ springs from an adequate understanding of His identity as the eternal "I Am." John 8:58 shows that Jesus declared, "Before Abraham was, I am," confirming His eternal divinity. Understanding our worldviews is not just ideological, but it also strengthens people to be confident when Christ is the theological foundation behind their words, knowing that they communicate the sovereign God above the realities of time and place. Wright argues that the history of Jesus Christ provides believers with a bold witness, as they are not merely speaking about vague ideals or concepts, but about a tangible God who became visible in the world (Wright 1996, 481).

Confidence when witnessing stems from understanding that God holds authority, not the witness. The witness interprets and explains their faith in God through the Spirit, making the witness's words relevant to the heart in Christ. Paul affirms and reflects this principle in 2 Corinthians 3:5 when he said, "Not that we are sufficient of ourselves to think anything as of ourselves, but our sufficiency is of God." Therefore, witnesses practice dependence by speaking the truth while depending on the Spirit to move in their obedient words, so that God might use them in courting change for the recipient. As Packer notes, this means that both humility and bravery are present when the disciple understands his limitations as well as the limitless power of God at work to accompany the faith acts that witness to God (Packer 1973, 143).

Additionally, the eternal presence of Christ during witnessing provides courage to confront the opposition. Peter and John realized this when confronted by the influential people of their day in Acts 4:13. Even when they were viewed as ordinary people surrounded by influential individuals, they were so anchored in their understanding of God's person and identity that it led them to bold witness in their circumstances. Bonhoeffer argues that this confidence is gained through prayer, reading the Scriptures, and being in fellowship with others, where one realizes, through fellowship, that God is with His witnesses (Bonhoeffer 1959, 118).

Putting this into practice means expressing witness for faith deliberately and clearly, indicating both honesty and an awareness of humility to ensure the person is speaking of Christ, not themselves. Witness involves both declaration and the act of obedience to mercy and love. Lewis agrees when he argues that a life influenced by Jesus, who is incarnating Christ's person, testifies more than mere words (Lewis 1960, 82). Therefore, engaging with witnesses from the reality of "I Am" fosters tenacity, faithfulness, courage, and joy in the witness who believes their witness is referential and spiritually sustaining.

Daily Prayer in the Name of "I Am"

"The name 'I Am' grounds daily prayer and invites believers to relate with the eternal, self-existent God continually made known in Christ (Exod. 3:14; John 8:58). Daily prayer is more than ritual; it is relational, emphasizing dependence, intimacy, and trust. Daily prayer is dependence on 'I Am'; the believer remembers God's unchanging nature, God's faithfulness, and God's sovereign care over every sphere of life. Prayer becomes an animated conversation with One who is always present, altogether adequate, and incomparably sage. Nouwen notes that prayer nurtures humility and freedom, allowing the soul to yield to worries while resting in God's eternal presence (Nouwen 1994, 67).

The divine name is an indicator of the power of prayer embodied in identity. Jesus' use of God's name reveals His dependence on the Father (John 5:19), inviting Christians to align their requests, petitions, and praises with God's purposes, done in faith through submission to God's will and timing. Bonhoeffer attests that prayer under the authority of 'I Am' builds obedience and vigilance because it is 'infused' with daily life ordained by God's presence (Bonhoeffer 1959, 142).

Practical engagement encompasses both structured and unstructured forms of prayer, including reading Scripture aloud, meditating on God's promises, expressing gratitude verbally, and praying for others. Augustine claims that prayer, rooted in the fact of God's identity, becomes more than 'just words'; it becomes a phenomenological pathway of grace and a structuring of life if it becomes a formational prayer (Augustine 1998, 231). C.S. Lewis supports Augustine's point, explaining that prayer in awareness of God's eternity cultivates moral imagination, insight, and courage, and trains the believer to reflect God's love and kindness through everyday responses (Lewis 1960, 101).

Centering daily prayer in the name 'I Am' grounds the believer in ongoing transformation, fostering patience in suffering, clarity in decision-making, the courage to witness, and a rhythm of life responsive to God's presence. By establishing the name 'I Am' in the heart, mind, and will, continued engagement encourages transformation and change. Therefore, a believer can be in Christ, embody the sufficiency of Christ, and express love to others as existing in Christ. In other words, daily prayer in the name 'I Am' engages God's eternal reality while enabling human life to align with God in a practical, demonstrable way for joy pursued, peace obtained, and faithfulness expressed."

Chapter 4

Because He Is – I Am

The Reversal of Identity

In Christ, God does a radical reversal of the world's definition of identity. When people define themselves in terms of success, failure, social status, or moral performance/posturing, they are left with a conditional worth that is fragile and ephemeral. The gospel reveals the mind-boggling reversal: in Christ, our achievement no longer shackles us, nor ourselves ensnared by our shame—but are defined in terms of Christ through God's unwavering love (2 Cor. 5:17). In other words, by being given a rightful identity in Christ, our first love transforms our heart, and therefore how we see ourselves, and how we see others, and how we define and understand our purpose. Augustine explains that being at peace requires the soul to relinquish its self-created status and live in complete reliance on God (Augustine 1998, 102).

One of the most significant influences on identity is shame, and Christ's gentle covering meets its potential threat. The woman caught in adultery exquisitely illustrates this: neither condemning nor excusing, Jesus affirms her dignity and provides her with a vision to see herself from God's point of view (John 8:11). Where condemnation prevailed, healing and acceptance ruled. Similarly, freedom from striving (performance—and as it is contrasted against others) frees a believer from gravitating toward a consistent state of seeking approval for past and/or present social status and/or of performing in ways significant to others in order to feel significant or acceptable. Stott writes that spiritual maturity must not be evaluated based on external success, but rather on whether the believer is anchored in God's love; love is intrinsic to sustained purposeful integrity (Stott 1994, 112).

The restoration of wholeness in the image of God highlights the magnitude of this reversal. The believer who is broken by insecurity and the expectations of social norms is repaired and is now renewed (Gen. 1:27). Nouwen goes further to explain that to understand our God-given identity means peace in our being, peace in our relationships, and an outpouring of love and service in our communion (Nouwen 1994, 47). Such an identity influences our business, our relationships, and our existential ambitions, all of which are directed toward God-oriented ends.

The reversal of identity is both theological and practical in nature. By accepting and receiving Christ's covering, displacing worldly markers, and resting in terms of God's design, believers remain free, happy, and whole. Their identities are not static, nor are they dominated by shame, fear, or others, but rather deluded away by grace (Mary 2023, 126). This transition is astounding and is intended to allow the believer's soul to engage with God and one another unconditionally and in an unfettered manner, due to the valued other's unwavering truth—that they are God's beloved.

The World's Search for Self vs. God's Gift of Self

From the reflective narratives of Scripture and history, it is clear that humanity relentlessly pursues self-definition. The world seeks self-definition through success, position, or acclaim, which generates dissatisfaction and conflict within the self (Wright 1996, 215). The biblical narrative offers an alternative: the instruction of our true identity is found not in constructing our self, but in our communion with God. In Genesis, humanity is created "in the image of God" (Gen. 1:27), reflecting the worth bestowed by the Creator rather than something humans acquire. Augustine reflects that the restless heart of humanity seeks fulfillment in creation, although only God can truly satisfy (Augustine 1998, 12). This theological insight defines the nature of the radical reversal: instead of striving to define ourselves, we are offered our being as a gift, which is rooted in Christ.

The apostle Paul expresses this reversal in Galatians 2:20: "I have been crucified with Christ; it is no longer I who live, but Christ who lives in me." Our most actual identity emerges from our participation in the life of Christ, and it is this affirmation that transcends worldly identities. Bonhoeffer asserts that discipleship entails surrendering self-centeredness, thereby adopting a life of self-giving love, much like God (Bonhoeffer 1959, 48). This surrender does not involve loss, but transformation: a believer learns to find stability and worth through belonging in a relationship with God, rather than through social validation.

Practically speaking, this principle works against the modern fascination with personal branding, work ethic, or comparison. Packer describes this as part of the sacred experience of having a divine identity shaped by God, which creates space for the self that is shaped by performance (Packer 1973, 215). When we meet God relationally, we are allowed to meet and learn to abide in the knowledge that our value is given, predestined by God's love, and exists apart from the temporal merit of others (Lewis 1960, 73).

In terms of narrative, consider the story Jesus tells of the prodigal son (Luke 15:11–32). The younger son seeks autonomy and a self-defined identity that leaves him empty; however, upon return, the divine gift restores his identity. God accepts him not on merit, but on the relational call that God placed in both sons, who were made in His own image. Here, the gift becomes a model of a life lived in reversal: identity is received, not built. Therefore, the Christian journey is designed to go away from the self and to belong to God. The fruit of this journey will reveal joy, healing, and love, as the natural outpouring of an identity that is placed less in social interaction and more in belonging, whose worth is founded in God.

Losing Life to Find It (Matt. 16:25)

Jesus' puzzling teaching in Matt. 16:25—"For whoever desires to save his life will lose it, but whoever loses his life for My sake will find it"—speaks to the inverse worldly logic around identity. A person's actual life and identity do not come through self-preservation but rather by surrendering to Christ. The inclination to give over one's life stands in stark contrast to our contemporary cultural assumptions that emphasize autonomy and personal achievement. Calvin articulates that to attain one's own selfhood means to demonstrate humility and submission of one's will to God's sovereign reign; by recognizing that we appreciate our identity as a gift of grace, and therefore, it is less a matter of our human agency (Calvin 1559, 143).

This reversal is echoed in Paul's theological commitments. In Phil. 3:8–9, Paul invites the church to share with him the confidence that all that is associated with achievement and gain is nothing compared to the value of knowing Christ. Identity is not constructed, but received from being in Christ's death and resurrection. To "find" the life of the believer is to free a life not defined by lived experience that seeks worldly affirmation, as Augustine recognized: "To be empty of self, knowing only that God is my fullness" (Augustine 1998, 12)

Theologically, this principle reframes the concepts of success and failure. Owen opens the way to explore mortifying the self, which may seem absurd. However, it is the only way to experience spiritual vitality as we align ourselves to the desire of God (Owen 1677, 55). Mortifying the self requires letting go of the beliefs in personal importance, status, entitlement, and control, as well as acknowledging dependence before God. The narratives abound: the rich young ruler (Matt. 19:16–22) exemplifies the struggle between self-pursuit and surrender, while Christ demonstrates the epitome of losing a life to a life of self-emptying love (Phil. 2:6–8).

Paul's Confession: "It Is No Longer I Who Live"

Paul's statement in Galatians 2:20—"It is no longer I who live, but Christ who lives in me"—sums up a reorientation of identity. Personal identity, which has been based on self-identity, has been reconfigured through one's identity as a believer united with Christ. Origen noted that God's presence reassesses human existence, helping ordinary living become a sacred option for responding to God's redemptive purposes (Origen 1994, 92). In this sense, identity is relational: it is Christ's life in the believer, rather than the pursuit of personal identity.

Theologically, this involves the interplay of grace and response. Packer maintains that, in knowing God personally, a believer experiences support in both humility and confidence, because the believer rests in Christ's life, rather than an unstable self-definition (Packer 1973, 215). Chrysostom similarly observes that identity relates to the Christian's attention to live outwardly the life of Christ, even in how divine identity gives character, conduct, and community (Chrysostom c. 347–407, 202).

Narratively, one needs to reflect on the story of Lazarus (John 11:1–44) and note that his death and resurrection depict the believer's movement from a self-reliant existence to a life that Christ enlivens. In the same manner, Paul's foundational narrative, from persecutor of the church to apostle, illustrates how divine identity takes precedence over an individual's past failures, enabling them to move forward to a new life firmly secured in grace. This process encompasses healing and joy; the believer is now unyoked from shame, comparisons, and self-reliant pursuits (Lewis 1960, 73).

To engage this identity in practice means that even how I live out my identity in daily living is shaped by spiritual disciplines, the community that I serve, and obedient practice, which are no longer viewed as the source of identity, but as a marker of Christ's life in me (Nouwen 1981, 48). In this sense, Paul's confession assumes both a doctrinal and devotional nature for believers, as he invites them to step into the reality that the most authentic self cannot be separated from where Christ has been revealed, which opens the pathway to joy, healing, and relational love.

Identity in Christ

Christian identity is based on union with Christ. This is a radical theological truth that alters who we are and how we live. When Paul states, "Because He is, I am," he is affirming this union that is integral to our identity as Christians (John 15:5). Followers of Jesus are inserted into the life of God through Christ, such that they share in his righteousness, his love, and his eternal purposes (Billings 2011, 57). This union has ontological implications; who we are fundamentally, and how we engage in relationships with God and fellow humans, is fundamentally altered. Augustine reminds us that the only valid identification of the soul is in God, where the self is fulfilled and made small (Augustine 1998, 214).

Adoption into the family of God highlights the interpersonal dynamic. Romans 8:15–17 reminds us that we are children of God and heirs, no longer slaves to fear or sin. Adoption gives us security and belonging, and liberates us from the anxiety of proving our worth to God and others. John Stott suggests that understanding ourselves as God's children alters our moral motivation. When the imperative of obedience is driven from a relational base of gratitude, service without compulsion becomes possible—it arises naturally out of love (Stott 1994, 88). For Christians, this relationship of divine filiation empowers them to be brave, as their ultimate identity rests in God's love and care for them.

Additionally, identity in Christ has both corporate and missional dimensions. As a royal priesthood and holy nation (1 Peter 2:9), Christians are corporately empowered to reflect God's glory and carry out the values of kingdom living. Gregory of Nyssa views spiritual identity as both personal and communal, cautioning Christians to live in the world in a manner that reflects divine holiness and justice (Gregory 1995, 63). Given that the church is meant to be a gathering place for worship, service, and ethical living, it is a living document of what it means for Christians to demonstrate in this world a glimpse of the beauty of being a community of people in accord with their Creator.

As such, Christian identity has both intimate and expansive aspects. It is personal, grounded in union with Christ; it is relational, as we have been adopted into God's family; and it is corporate, as we are called to priestly and holy service. Knowing who we are in Christ means freedom, purpose, and a radically new manner of thinking that transforms our being, our relationships, and our mission in this world.

"Because He Is, I Am" — A Theology of Union

Union with Christ constitutes the theological center of Christian identity. It indicates that we do not exist independently, but with the triune God. The Apostle Paul captures that meaning with the statement, "It is no longer I who live, but Christ who lives in me" (Gal. 2:20). Therefore, the believer's life is encompassed and anchored to the life of the eternal "I Am," which indicates that the divine presence as well as the believer's existence cannot be separated. Augustine compares it to humans finding rest only when they willingly involve themselves in God's will, as he understands how Creator and creature are inseparable (Augustine 1998, 35). Aquinas likewise emphasizes that human nature does not need to merge with God through grace to participate in the divine life, but rather, human fulfillment is rooted in God's will (Aquinas 1981, I-II, q. 2).

Union with Christ may transform one's self-knowledge or simply the manner of engaging in obedience and love. Origen notes that through sharing in Christ's life, believers participate in God's activity and tend to manifest God's "activity" as a reflection of his character to one another in the daily rhythm of our lives (Origen 1994, 47). As a theological statement, this understanding of our union with Christ has implications for the idiosyncrasy of contemporary culture that emerges from an obsession with self-definition. Identity is not contrived; it is received, experienced relationally, and fulfilled through conformity to Christ. John Stott further notes that our human capacity to flourish is as dependent on Christ as humanity is when included in the "I Am, and because he is, I am" (Stott 1994, 82). This relational unity is also concretized liturgically and spiritually in prayers, sacramental participation, and worship practices, enabling the believer to be reminded of their identity as rooted in relation and continued to be distinguished in communion with "the Living Christ" (Nouwen 1981, 112).

Therefore, the statement "Because He Is, I Am" is both self-affirming and transformative; it asserts that one's existence is grounded in God while simultaneously enabling every believer to live epistemically in light of their union with Him. The "reality of Christ existing in me" functions as a centrifugal, first-helical, mental orientation outward upon one's desires, ambitions, and anxieties. Until a person experiences freedom from self-centered striving and attains true joy—whose satisfaction is found fully in God's sufficiency—they cannot fully implement the transformation reflected in Paul's journey from his conversion to his apostolic experience. This transformation witnesses a spatial and existential shift, moving the believer from engaging in self-imposed insecurity and striving to living from the root of God's love. The inner theological significance of this process, and its bearing on subsequent reflections on adoption, priesthood, or holy living, is intimately connected to the believer's grounding in their true identity.

Adoption into God's Family (Rom. 8:15–17)

Scripture makes it clear that adoption is the primary means by which believers come to discover their identity in Christ. Romans 8:15–17 reveals that through the Spirit, believers find themselves crying, "Abba, Father" (Rom. 8:15). This is not merely the recognition of God as Father, but the relational experience of being included as kin in God's family, which we signify in the Christian faith by calling God "Father." Calvin asserts that adoption restores a believer to the state of filiation that was forfeited in the Fall, reorienting human purpose and relationships toward both God and other human beings (Calvin 2008, 345). How Christians understand this divine sonship alters how they define themselves and their identity in relation to the world and the roles they inhabit as humans. By virtue of God's grace, Christians no longer measure their success, status, or independence by the world's standards; they belong to God. Accordingly, the believer's security, belonging, esteem, and love flow from God's gracious promise rather than from any modality of performance (Luther 2000, 92).

Henri Nouwen observes that adoption has significant consequences for spiritual formation: that living out one's identity as a child of God cultivates characteristics of being internally free, humbly dependent on God, and open to being led by God's Spirit (Nouwen 1994, 56). Theologically, it is worth noting how intimately adoption connects to our union with Christ, given that believers access God as Father through Christ. Chrysostom observes that God's invitation not only expresses a family relationship that is not merely an abstraction, but has tangible relational consequences; the Spirit not only dwells inside the believer but also comes alongside, guides, comforts, and affirms the believer's experiences daily (Chrysostom 202, 88). Adoption is, therefore, not only legalistic but decidedly experiential, shaping ethics, devotion, and interpersonal love.

Practically, adoption complicates the believer's understanding of their identity and vocation. The believer's relationship with God shapes their relationships with others, where the act of loving and being responsible for one another interlinks networks of relationships. Dallas Willard has commented on the significant difference between being a child of God, in that the focus for human beings is no longer self-preservation, but kingdom living (Willard 1998, 144). As sons of God, we can endure both joy and suffering, knowing both are participating in the Father's plan of redemption. The narrative of the prodigal son illustrates the almost limitless potential for change that adoption carries with it: a son returns home not by virtue of his moral adherence, but by the Father's relational commitment to receive him home.

As a consequence, adoption into the family of God serves as the foundation for Christian identity, not only cultivating assurance internally but also acting as an outward witness to the world. Believers receive belonging, affection, and power, which inform the vocation of believing, priesthood, and holiness.

A Royal Priesthood and Holy Nation (1 Pet. 2:9)

1 Peter 2:9 characterizes believers as part of a "chosen generation, a royal priesthood, a holy nation, His own special people" (1 Pet. 2:9). Believing is community, corporate, and missional; therefore, priesthood here does not only apply to clergy, but includes every believer responding to God's call to mediate God's presence into their daily lives through sanctification and service (Bonaventure 1268, 33). Additionally, the royal and holy identity of believers reminds us that identity is closely tied to dignity and holiness; believers are empowered to overcome sin through obedience and to serve others through their holiness.

Augustine recognized that the church's identity as a community embodies God's glory, as all members of the community are instruments God uses for divine purposes: to be holy in society while intentionally experiencing God in relationship (Augustine 1998, 215). Anselm of Canterbury emphasized that priestly vocation is not merely ritual, but ethical action where the believer is a living sacrifice that bears witness to the character of God (Anselm 2007, 48). In this way, we can understand how holiness is twofold: love and obedience; therefore, the identity of Christians is relational and embodied.

Brennan Manning explores the implications of contemporary royal priesthood as both gift and task; the assurance provided by Christ ignites boldness in mercy, courage in witness, and compassion in service (Manning 1992, 102). It is essential to remember that the history of Israel provides insight into the concept of covenant election, one of the contexts for Peter's teachings, and serves as a reminder to believers that their identity is derived from God's active initiative rather than their own passive achievement.

In practical terms, this identity provides an expression of vocation, community engagement, and spiritual formation. Believers are to stand in some ways distinct from the world, and in others, engage in God's redemptive mission through witness, prayer, and local ethical behavior. In whatever form—whether worship, service, or daily living—Christians must act as a royal priesthood, embodying the holy nation that has been called, and live out the reality that their most authentic self is found only in Christ (Stott 1994, 88).

Christ the Ground of Our Being

Christian identity is inextricably bound to union with Christ. Augustine often emphasizes that in God we can find true rest; apart from God, human striving is ultimately useless (Augustine 1998, 48). In *Confessions*,

Augustine reflects on the restless human heart and states that only in God do we find completeness in our work. This idea of rest in God is active trust and engagement in the life that God provides by grace. Believers are invited into the relatable intimacy with Christ in which ordinary life becomes a conduit for spiritual vibrancy.

Thomas Aquinas also develops our understanding of union with Christ by highlighting the metaphysical and participatory nature of the union. In *Summa Theologica*, he states that through grace, humans participate in the divine life, allowing the finite to participate in the infinite (Aquinas 1981, II-II, q. 2, a. 3). This participation is not merely an imitation; rather, it is ontological. The life of God is infusing believers and filling them with supernatural virtues. By being situated in Christ, the believer's holiness, joy, and love flow as an outpouring of unity with God. Spiritual habits, prayer, and sacraments usher in a life of participation, bringing believers into a tangible union with the eternal Word.

John Calvin employs a similar effort to frame union with Christ as the center of salvation, focusing on the relational and ethical dimension of Christ's union with God (Calvin 2008, 275). In *Institutes of the Christian Religion*, he argues that all spiritual benefits—justification, sanctification, and adoption—flow from the union. The union with Christ provides the firmest foundation for identity, posture of obedience, and confidence in God's promises. Calvin presents a view of the believer as being safe "in Christ," where one's interpretation of the biblical constitution, resistance to sin, and response to all of life occurs from a secure zone. The implications of being "in Christ" are staggering. When believers are "positionally" in Christ, legitimate worldly anxieties diminish, and they experience amplified joy and freedom.

In totality, Augustine, Aquinas, and Calvin provide a comprehensive theology of identity, grounded in Christ. Augustine provides rest and devotion; Aquinas gives ontological identity; and Calvin provides practical and relational integration. Together, the totality invites believers to understand their identity—not self-defined, but in union with the living God—and to embrace the reversal of worldly esteem and the enduring expectation of resting entirely in Christ (1 Cor. 1:30; Col. 2:6–7).

Augustine on Resting in God Alone

Through Augustine's theological understanding of identity, the human person is created with what can be best described as a "restlessness" until resting in God. In his *Confessions*, Augustine articulates, "You have made us for yourself, O Lord, and our heart is restless until it rests in you" (Augustine 1998, 3). For Augustine, this restlessness represents both humanity's longing for meaning and, ultimately, the futility of seeking identity in created things. In effect, it could be argued by Augustine that attempting to self-define through riches, honour, or power only ultimately leads to disappointing conclusions, since the human person is created to reflect God's glory and participate in His purposes. Consequently, identity is not self-made, but is an identity given as a gift of God.

For Augustine, rest in God does not imply inactivity, which is typical of a state of being, but, in actuality, represents a dynamic reordering of the will. In the view of Augustine, the human will is doubly divided; it is predicated towards temporal pleasure, while also having the unshakeable yearning for an eternal fulfillment (Augustine 1998, 62). It is worth mentioning at this juncture that, for Augustine, the term *conversion* stands for a reordering of orders of loves to the extent that the soul learns to worship God above all things. To have rest in God means the restoration from the breakdown of sin, and the discovery of oneself in divine love.

This notion of resting as the basis for identity has significant implications for the notion of Christian identity. First, stability: if identity arises from God, then even if all worldly markers are stripped from the believer, their identity remains in God and cannot be lost. Second, healing of shame and disconnected selves: in the love of God, the believer is fully known and fully embraced in their entire brokenness. Moreover, lastly, joy: by resting in God, the pressure of recognition is depleted, and allows the believer to centre themselves in the eternal act of belonging.

History reminds us that Augustine's vision and purpose accord with biblical text: "Come to Me, all you who labor and are heavy laden, and I will give you rest" (Matt. 11:28). In this sense, our requirement to rest in God becomes the beginning point for identity in Christ. That is what Augustine offers to Christians: to transcend identity as restless, self-defining agents and enter into the joy of belonging to God, where identity becomes an awareness of our true selfhood, discovered in that belonging.

Aquinas on Participation in Christ's Life

Aquinas places the believer's identity in the mystery of participation in Christ. Thus, for Aquinas, grace is not simply an added external factor but rather a transformative participation in the divine life, made possible in the Incarnation and mediated through the sacraments. In the *Summa Theologica*, Aquinas states that "the only-begotten Son of God . . . wished to make us sharers of His divinity" (Aquinas 1947, III.1.2). This means that believers do not simply imitate Christ externally. However, they are, in an ontological sense, incorporated into Christ's life.

Aquinas elaborates on this idea by speaking of *participatio divinae naturae*, or participation in divine nature. This concept is strongly emphasized in Scripture, which states that believers are "partakers of the divine nature" (2 Pet. 1:4). For Aquinas, union with Christ does not eliminate human nature; rather, it perfects it. Grace elevates human nature and heals it completely, enabling humankind to fully realize its purpose as an image-bearer of God. Human identity, therefore, finds its fulfillment not in autonomy, but in communion with the One who is Being.

Practically, participation is mediated by sacraments and lived ethically. In baptism, the believer is incorporated into Christ's death and resurrection

(Rom. 6:3–5), so their identity is grounded in this saving act of Christ. The Eucharist continually nourishes union, as Aquinas defines it, as "spiritual food," feeding the individual and, as such, strengthening the union with Christ (Aquinas 1947, III.73.1). Therefore, Christian identity goes beyond merely being a cognitive recognition; it is rather an embodied participation in Christ's life.

This theological framework also calls the believer to transformation. Since identity is grounded in participatory living with Christ, the Christian is invited to embody the virtues of Christ—charity, humility, holiness, all of which are signs of this new life. Aquinas stresses that grace does not supplant nature, but redirects it to its true telos—complete union with God (Torrell 2005, 152). To live in Christ is to live oneself authentically, reflecting the divine image.

Ultimately, Aquinas demonstrates that identity is a gift of grace: to belong to Christ is to participate in His very own life. It is solid assurance for the believer that their identity is not dependent on themselves, nor is it fragile—it is secured in the eternal Son.

Calvin on Union with Christ as the Center of Salvation

According to John Calvin, the essence of Christian identity and salvation is found in union with Christ. Calvin insists in his *Institutes of the Christian Religion* that unless Christ is received and remains firmly united in us, everything He has done is of no significance to us (Calvin 1960, 3.1.1). Therefore, union with Christ is not merely an unrelated doctrine, but is central to the gospel: it is the root of all the sources or blessings of salvation, that is, justification, sanctification, adoption, and glorification, which are born from this union.

Calvin draws deeply on the biblical witness. Paul explains, "It is no longer I who live, but Christ who lives in me" (Gal. 2:20), highlighting this idea of union. He also writes that believers are "seated with Christ in the heavenly places" (Eph. 2:6), already experiencing His exaltation. These types of statements convince Calvin that not only is Christian existence bound together with Christ's existence, but by the Spirit's work, what is Christ's becomes ours as well. This is a mystical and real participation; a spiritual identity that makes a profound and lasting impact on the believer's life.

Union with Christ also changes believers' views of salvation. Justification is no longer a mere legal pronouncement, but rather participation in Christ's righteousness. Sanctification is now not merely self-improvement but the outworking of the holiness of Christ. Adoption means sharing in Christ's sonship, and consequently crying out with Him, "Abba, Father" (Rom. 8:15–17). For Calvin, Christ is not only the giver of gifts, but He is the gift itself. Therefore, salvation is a comprehensive concept and cannot be fragmented, because it involves being in union with Christ (Billings 2011, 34).

In practice, union with Christ is assurance and identity. The believer rests not on fluctuating feelings or achievements but on the one who cannot fail. As Calvin states, "We are not our own; we are God's" (Calvin 1960, 3.7.1). This fact subverts pride and despair: pride because, in our lives, we are not self-made, and despair because, in our security, we depend on Christ.

Therefore, for Calvin, union with Christ is at the heart of Christian existence. To know who we are is to know who we belong to—inseparably bound to Christ, from whom every blessing flows.

Healing from Shame through Christ's Covering

Shame, one of humanity's biggest wounds, is rooted in the Fall. After Adam and Eve sinned, "they knew that they were naked; and they sewed fig leaves together and made themselves coverings" (Gen. 3:7). Their effort to hide themselves reflected the human impulse to hide brokenness and shame. God, in mercy, took their wrappings from their fragility and made clothing for them (Gen. 3:21). Since the beginning, the truth of Scripture has shown that it is not our efforts that will provide healing from shame, but God provides the remedy.

In Christ, this provision reaches completion. Scripture expresses that followers of Christ are "clothed with Christ" (Gal. 3:27), and we are covered not with fig leaves (our own accomplishment) but with the righteousness of God. Augustine said that the Gospel not only forgives sins but also grants dignity and restores the soul's order to its Creator (Augustine 1998, 10.29). The covering of Christ is more than external; it penetrates the heart with a new vision of who we are and, likewise, who the Father sees us to be.

The voice of shame cries out through the cross, the only place shame may be reconciled. Jesus "despising the shame endured the cross" (Heb. 12:2). Jesus experienced public disgrace so that the people who trust him would not be condemned and publicly humiliated. Bonhoeffer noted that Christ took up our frailty to humiliation so that his people could share in his honor before the Father (Bonhoeffer 1959, 45). The shame we fear now no longer defines us, for we share in Christ's honor and glory.

Practically, this gives believers the freedom not to hide, compare themselves to others, or hate themselves. In Christ, we can confess what is weak; we are still not identified by our successes, but by His finished work. The church witnesses to this when it emerges as a community of grace rather than shame, calling to remember that they share a covering in Christ.

All this leads back to the beautiful reversal that the Gospel tells: what began in the garden with shame and hiding transformed into being clothed with dignity and confidence in Christ. "Clothed in His righteousness," instead of living in self-contempt, we walk joyfully in a restored wholeness; once covered in shame, now reflecting the image of the One who fully covers us.

Freedom from Performance and Comparison

One of the more pervasive forms of bondage in modernity is performance and the ritual of comparison. Human beings have always struggled to validate their worth through performance, but the gospel breaks this endless treadmill. Paul reminds all believers that "by the grace of God I am what I am" (1 Cor. 15:10). Identity in Christ is not built upon; it is only received as a gift.

This message counters a culture of comparison that is based on appearance, production, or status. The temptation to compare oneself with others is not a new phenomenon. Cain's resentment of his brother Abel is a concrete example of the way comparison breeds envy, bitterness, and despair (Gen. 4:4–8). However, in Christ, we are liberated from the need to compete because our status before God is secure, and we can extend it to everyone else. Luther taught that justification by faith meant that a believer's worth is found, not in himself, but in the declaration of God (Luther 1960, 35).

Gregory of Nyssa offers a complementary approach. He did not view progress as a process of outpacing all of our neighbors, but rather as the continual ascent of the human soul toward God (Gregory of Nyssa 1995, *The Life of Moses*). As such, measuring life should not be in horizontal comparison but a vertical communion. This talk reframes ambition: instead of attempting to prove that we are better than one another, the believer desires to pursue confirmation in Christlikeness out of grace.

Practicing the freedom of performance and comparison in the reality of daily life reorients our daily lives. The parent who longs to meet impossible expectations, the student who can only feel satisfaction in outperforming their classmates, and the employee who is motivated by fear of incompetence, "enough," and has no rest in Christ. Jesus invites the weary, "Come to Me, all you who labor and are heavy laden, and I will give you rest" (Matt. 11:28). Rest, in this case, is not lazy, but a peace of living from acceptance instead of trying to attain it.

The church is called to the same embodiment. In a community where grace has shaped our collective identity, each believer freely rejoices in one another's gifts rather than feeling compelled to concern ourselves with competition. Freed from the grave burden of performance, Christians move securely and act in love without fear of being found wanting. Thus, the gospel is what uproots our desires to compare ourselves and invites us to rejoice in the greater joy of our identity in Christ, not as the sum of our human accomplishments.

Restored Wholeness in the Image of God

At the very beginning of the Bible, we learn that humanity is created in the image of God (Gen. 1:27). The reason this image is critical is that it underlies human dignity and purpose, even though sin has fractured this likeness. Sin distorts relationships—with God, for instance, but also with others, and as a consequence, within ourselves. The gospel presents not just forgiveness, but restoration: our likeness to God (the image of God) is being remade in Christ (Col. 3:10).

Early theologians of the church wrestled with this theme. Irenaeus described salvation as recapitulation—that is, Christ as the new Adam recovered what was lost in the first (Irenaeus 1997, *Against Heresies*). Augustine introduced us to the importance of grace. By affirming that while the image of God may be marred, grace can restore it through Christ's righteousness (Augustine 1991, *City of God*). Thus, Christian identity is about more than just avoiding guilt—it is about being conformed once again to God's design.

Thomas Aquinas extended this inner work of grace by teaching that grace perfects nature, which he saw as drawing the weight of human existence toward what it is intended to be, not by erasing what humanity is (Aquinas 1947, *Summa Theologica*). The self, which was once torn apart by sin and self-loathing, is transformed in Christ by moving toward its true end. Calvin understood this in the same human capacity, writing about the Spirit regenerating the believer to reflect God's holiness and righteousness (Calvin 1960, Institutes 3.3.9).

This doctrine of humanity being re-created in the likeness of God not only has profound theological significance, but it also has concrete pastoral applications. There are a great many people who live with a fractured self-image because of shame, trauma, and imposition of self from a disintegrated society. The good news that we are being made new speaks directly to those in a place of brokenness or worthlessness: God is not just covering blemished areas, but instead re-creating His likeness in them. Paul reminds us that, "If anyone is in Christ, he is a new creation; old things have passed away; behold, all things have become new" (2 Cor. 5:17).

Practically speaking, it matters for believers from an impact perspective in two different ways. First, renewing the *imago Dei* through grace in Christ produces hope, because believers can be sure no wound is beyond the power and grace of healing within Christ. Secondly (and somewhat related), renewing the *imago Dei* through grace involves humility, and believing that the renewed image is God's grace in us and not our own accomplishment (Eph. 2:8–10; Gal. 5:22). The gathering of the church is intended to be a community of restoration, seeing every individual as being created in the image of God and being made new. In a world filled with fracturing, the gift of the gospel, and its presence unmet, sees this hidden promise of wholeness working among us in the grace of Christ.

Joy in Belonging to Christ

The joy that accompanies the belonging of being in Christ comes from knowing and being known by God. It differs from the fleeting pleasures derived from human affirmation and achievements because it is based on the joy of divine intimacy that leads to unshakeable security. In Psalm 139:1–4, the psalmist speaks to the omnipresence of God and declares there is nowhere we can hide from His all-seeing eye. The idea of being fully known by God yet entirely accepted offers a state of liberation that surpasses any fear, anxiety, shame, or frenzied self-doubt (Lewis 1943, 112). Henri Nouwen captures the contours of joy that are birthed when we rest in the assurance of God's loving attention, which evokes a self-understanding and relational way of being (Nouwen 1994, 42).

The same sense of assurance that accompanies an awareness of God's abiding presence strengthens joy into deep-seated conviction. Romans 8:38–39 assures believers that nothing—neither heights, depths, adversity, nor rulership—separates them from the love of God found in Christ Jesus. This kind of assurance creates a sense of stability that is unattainable in the world, allowing a person to sit with uncertainty, suffering, or disappointment without feeling overwhelmed. Similarly, John Calvin noted that a believer's reliance on God's commitment brings comfort in their life and motivation to live faithfully. It further illustrates how joy is not disconnected from trust in God's providential care (Calvin 1559, 412).

The Reformation doctrine of justification also provides insight into the nature of this joy. Martin Luther boldly declared that being declared righteous on the grounds of faith was not based on merit or works. The definition of righteousness was not the striving and performance-sustaining burden of selfish ambition with every self-indictment, but rather freedom anchored in the joyful sanctification of all belonging in Christ (Luther 1520, 78). Not only does joy from belonging to Christ emerge from feelings, but also a lived reality that evidently shapes how believers love, serve, and witness to the world.

Therefore, the joy of belonging to Christ, as observed above, is complex: it involves knowing and being loved, being assured of God's abiding presence, believing in reconciliation through faith in Jesus and the Spirit, and also producing peace, fostering resilience, and inspiring devotion. As believers claim the joy that belongs to Christ, they inevitably become aware of the life-giving rhythm in which divine love perpetually renews their hearts, liberates their minds, and overflows with grace to others (1 John 4:16).

Joy in Being Known Fully and Loved Completely

People genuinely wish to be known and loved unconditionally. However, in our brokenness, we often fear that if people knew us perfectly and completely, they would reject us. The gospel announces a radical inversion: in Christ, God knows us better than we know ourselves and yet He loves us completely. As David says, "O Lord, You have searched me and known me" (Ps. 139:1). God's knowing is not just knowing from a distance; it is care, and God transforms knowing into comfort rather than fear in love.

Augustine wrote in *Confessions* that God is "closer to me than I am to myself" (Augustine 1991, 3.6.11). This gives him humility and joy, as the knowledge of God reveals his sin but also envelops him in mercy. Gregory of Nyssa follows this same thought, noting that God, in His infinite love, is not exhausted by knowing the weakness of humanity, but is instead revealed in His perfecting of that weakness (Gregory 1995, *On the Soul and Resurrection*).

In Christ, knowing and loving come together perfectly. Jesus knows the past of the Samaritan woman (John 4:17–18) and gives her living water; divine knowledge and divine grace come together in this act. Bonhoeffer pointed out that we can only be both found out and forgiven in Christ, releasing us from the burdensome masks of self-justification (Bonhoeffer 1959, *Life Together*).

Psychology today acknowledges our need for authenticity in relationships, but what the gospel offers that no human being can offer is perfect knowledge with perfect love. Paul assures believers that nothing "shall be able to separate us from the love of God which is in Christ Jesus our Lord" (Rom. 8:39). This assures us that our identity is not rooted in performance but merely in being infinitely loved.

The joy of being known and loved by God has some practical implications. It frees us from the fear of rejection, allowing us to confess honestly and be part of a genuine community. It inspires worship, because the One who knows every fiber of our hidden heart still calls us beloved. Furthermore, it brings us peace, because we never have to hide from the One who always holds us in truth and grace.

Assurance of God's Unfailing Presence

Abandonment is one of the greatest fears in the human heart. The Scriptures remind the believer, however, that God is always present, unchanging, and faithful. When the Lord gives Joshua the command "I will not leave you nor forsake you" (Josh. 1:5), the New Testament, too, repeated the same foundation for believers: "For He Himself has said, 'I will never leave you nor forsake you'" (Heb. 13:5). God's presence, when formed by His covenant love, does not depend on our faithfulness but rather His.

As Chrysostom stated in his homilies on Matthew, these very same words of Christ, "I am with you always, even to the end of the age" (Matt. 28:20), are not merely comfort, but something more profound and practical; they rest on the surety of Christ's resurrection and authorized power (Chrysostom 1986, *Homilies on Matthew*). Therefore, God's nearness can never be merely contextual or abstract, but actualized in Christ's Spirit abiding deeply with persons.

Thomas Aquinas taught in the *Summa Theologica* about God's omnipresence, which is both universal and deeply personal. He is present to creation in essence by sustaining all things, but is uniquely present by grace with the faithful to whom He assures intimate companionship (Aquinas 1947, I.8). This distinction shapes for the believer that God's presence is not simply metaphysical, but relational—even companionship with all of God's creations. God's nearness is a reminder that assures us He can even endure with us through suffering.

We get a glimpse of this remarkably illustrated in Paul's words: "At my first defense no one stood with me... But the Lord stood with me and strengthened me" (2 Tim. 4:16–17). In all that others may have been late to provide to Paul substantively, Christ clearly does. Bonhoeffer expressed this same assurance in writing *Letters and Papers from Prison*, noting that the very presence of God is the foundation of Christian assurance, for even where human companionship ceased, God's companionship and nearness endured (Bonhoeffer 2009, *Letters and Papers from Prison*).

The learned assurance in God's presence reveals tangible freedom: freedom to trust that we need not fear because trials cannot overwhelm us; freedom to find the courage to live faithfully; and freedom to breathe in comfort even in the midst of interminable sadness and despair. This recognition then forms us to rethink the nature of security or solidity from a frail definition, that security is not simply a guarantee that there are no dangers, but an abiding assurance of companionship. In all this, the believer walks in joy because no matter where life leads, the Lord is already there, leading, sustaining, and loving His people.

Luther on the Joy of Justification by Faith

For Martin Luther, justification by faith alone was not just a doctrine for discussion, but a truth that liberated his soul. Luther was tormented by guilt, trying to earn righteousness through works, but recognized in Romans 1:17—"The just shall live by faith"—that righteousness is not something earned but received. This truth brought him great joy, because in Christ he stood accepted and loved without worrying about self-justification (Luther 1957, 71).

Paul's statement, too, "Therefore, having been justified by faith, we have peace with God through our Lord Jesus Christ" (Rom. 5:1), reveals the fruit of justification: joy and peace. No longer distant, the believer is reconciled. Luther also emphasized that this peace is objective, as it is grounded in what Jesus has accomplished for believers, rather than in fluctuating emotions and deficient obedience. Stott concurs when he states, "people must never forget that justification means that God accepts them not because of what they have done, but because of what Christ has done" (Stott 1994, 123). Therefore, this hope transforms despair into joy.

Earlier, Augustine noted that true joy comes only as we find rest in the grace of God, rather than spending our lives defining ourselves through human striving (Augustine 1991, *Confessions*). Luther was rediscovering this truth, which kindled the church and awakened it to the center of the good news: a righteousness contrived from God, not achieved but imputed. For the believer, the despair to surety, bondage to freedom, and fear to joy take place.

Practically, this joy in justification will free the Christian from having to spend his life trying to live for the approval of others. Paul himself proclaimed, "It is no longer I who live, but Christ lives in me" (Gal. 2:20). Anchored by God's verdict, believers serve freely in love, not out of fear. Bonhoeffer would later remark that grace is free, but it is not cheap. Grace is costly because it does not come without a call to discipleship. Grace is joy (Bonhoeffer 1995, 45). Grace increasingly produces joy in the acceptance of God's love.

Thus, this joy of justification is not merely an internal feeling, though it most certainly is felt. Joy is a disposition based on peace with God that produces gratitude, worship, and confidence. Because Christ is our righteousness, we rejoice together every day in the joy of God's steadfast grace.

Love Flowing from Identity

Love exists and transforms not out of obligation or self-serving practices, but out of rest and in identity in Christ. When believers perceive their identities as fully known, fully loved, and adopted children of God, love flows as a gift that ebbs and flows. Paul encourages believers to "put on tender mercies, kindness, humility, meekness, and long-suffering," and above all of these to love as the reconciliation glue that binds all things together in perfect harmony (Col. 3:12–14). God's love is modeled as effortlessly flowing, non-reactive, and non-performance-based. This authentic love, modeled after God, reflects God's unchanging moral character towards all human beings (Packer 1973, 218). If love flows from being secure, there is room and space for others to develop and find their own identities, rather than feeding our lack of approval or neediness by using others, modeling God's self-giving heart.

Henri Nouwen asserts that the angry and demanding God is absent from those who live in the beloved, which offers them security in love, rather than in human love (Nouwen 1994, 53). Foundational relationship security dismantles fear, jealousy, or pride that impede love towards others, resulting in authentic love being patient, kind, and sustaining. A love that flows from identity is sacrificial, without manipulation, and does good for the sake of goodness. An identity in the Good Shepherd that laid his life down on behalf of the sheep (John 10:11) uniquely exhibits sacrificial love and care for the well-being of others.

When Paul speaks of "putting on" love as clothing, he reminds us of love, which is both a reality and a practice (Rom. 13:14), fueling a lifestyle supported by incarnational efforts in humility, service, and forgiveness throughout the full episodes of life, as determined by Christ's own character. Believers can live out security by enacting God's acceptance, thereby stopping the practice of making love contingent or self-expectation dependent on every social interaction, and making way for grace and kindness in each life circumstance, whether in family, church, workplace, or society.

Ultimately, love flows out of identity to say, God's relationship to me shapes my relationship to others. Love transforms the ordinary into ministry and witness when we put humanity back into the meanings of reconciliation, restoration, and the delight of a life lived in the love of God. As God's beloved, you are fully equipped to give love away, physically carrying the glory of Christ with your heart (1 John 4:19). In this practice of abundant giving and belonging in security, identity and love integrate. You live as you are committed to God's ongoing purposes.

Loving Others Out of Security, Not Neediness

Christian love originates not from emptiness but rather from fullness. When we are insecure in our identity, love often is self-seeking—an attempt to earn affirmation or fill a void. However, Scripture reminds us that we are secure in Christ and able to love others freely, without self-seeking motives. As John writes, "We love Him because He first loved us" (1 John 4:19). God's initial love provides our security. It gives us the freedom to love others without expectation.

Paul's admonition to the Philippian church in Philippians 2:3–4—"Let nothing be done through selfish ambition or conceit, but in lowliness of mind let each esteem others better than himself"—informs us of our security in Christ and empowers us to be free from any striving. When believers are not consumed by the desire to maintain their own reputation or recognition, they can genuinely serve others in love. Dallas Willard emphasizes that love is only possible when we are no longer preoccupied with self-preservation: "the abundance of God to us liberates us from being reliant on human approval" (Willard 1998, 123).

Augustine referred to this as rightly ordered love (ordo amoris). When the soul securely rests in God, it is freed from disordered desire. Love then is the overflow of a heart assured of divine acceptance (Augustine 1991, 3.6.11). This truth is powerfully evidenced in Christ's washing of the disciples' feet (John 13:3–5). John takes careful note: "Jesus, knowing… that He had come from God and was going to God, rose… and began to wash the disciples' feet." His knowledge of his identity and security, derived from his Father's love, freed him to serve others in humility. In a similar manner, believers who are grounded in their identity as God's beloved children can love without fear of rejection or exploitation.

Henri Nouwen offers a provoking pastoral insight: "When we claim and live from our belovedness, we can offer others a freedom that does not bind them to us, but points them to God" (Nouwen 2002, 58). Such love is non-manipulative, is liberation, and is a gift—a self-giving gift, resembling that of Christ.

To love from a place of security rather than neediness is to live out the gospel. Grounded in Christ's abiding love, we are free from relying on others for affirmation and empowered to be instruments of His grace joyfully.

Paul's Call to "Put On" Christlike Love

Paul often uses the metaphor of clothing, or "putting on," believers' new life in Christ. In Romans 13:14, Paul states: "But put on the Lord Jesus

Christ, and make no provision for the flesh, to fulfill its lusts." In Galatians 3:27, he speaks of the act of baptism: "For as many of you as were baptized into Christ have put on Christ." This clothing imagery, primarily when referring to love, emphasizes that human identity is inextricably linked to Christ's identity. While we intentionally select our clothing for the day, we also "put on" love as we engage in everyday actions with one another, seeking to embody the humility, patience, and self-giving nature of Christ.

C. S. Lewis takes this type of Paul imagery and provides a very suggestive interpretation in *Mere Christianity*: "moral change is more than obedience; it is surrender to the character of Christ" (Lewis 1943, 117). Love is not a suggestion; love defines who the believer is, the clothing of their identity, as a moral action. Paul encourages a type of ethical behavior in Ephesians 4:2–3 that can only be fulfilled once love has been put on: "with all lowliness and gentleness, with longsuffering, bearing with one another in love, endeavoring to keep the unity of the Spirit in the bond of peace." Paul goes so far as to consider how one embodies that kind of love and this unity, explicitly noting that it exemplifies God's love for his people, who together serve one another.

Origen captures the transformative quality of that type of clothing. In *On First Principles*, Origen notes that putting on Christ is an ongoing manner of thinking and doing, as it is led by God, thereby allowing us to produce love as an internal disposition that dynamically acts in external actions (Origen 1994, 82). Subsequently, love in many respects becomes identity and vocation that cannot be separated from our union in Christ.

In very practical terms, our putting on Christlike love is only as visible as it is reflective of our everyday lived choices, especially within the realm of relational behavior: forgiving those who have wronged us and not seeking revenge; serving others quietly, and not seeking to draw attention; speaking the truth to others in a manner that is tempered with compassion. Henri Nouwen offers this insight: "Our effectiveness in loving others is directly proportional to our willingness to let Christ dwell in us" (Nouwen

1981, 47). The act of putting on Christ is relational, ethical, and devotional as it emerges from our union with the God who first loved us. Christians are God-active collectively, serving one another. When believers intentionally put on Christlike love, they become visible witnesses of God's active presence in the world. They themselves become a space that embodies a tangible reflection of God's divine grace, which can transform both the individual and the community.

Nouwen on Living as the Beloved

Henri Nouwen discussed the believer's identity in Christ and how love can only move freely when one knows oneself and others as beloved. A significant source of this is understanding that our worth is received, not achieved; God's affirmation is for us to receive, not to gain through accomplishments. John 1:12–13 states, "But as many as received Him, to them He gave the right to become children of God, to those who believe in His name: who were born, not of blood, nor of the will of the flesh, nor of the will of man, but of God." This identity, the beloved child of God, can serve as the foundation for loving others with proper affection.

Nouwen (1994, 35) discusses the practice of living as someone beloved as an inward disposition of daily practice outlined as contemplation and prayer. By knowing this love of God that never changes and resting in it, we are liberated from faith based on performance, comparison, and fear. Paul in Galatians 2:20 states, "I have been crucified with Christ; it is no longer I who live, but Christ lives in me." In this way, we see that the believer's identity is never separate from union with Christ, which naturally expresses itself in love.

How does this awareness of identity challenge the cultural narrative of self-worth? In a world where self-worth is often measured by the scope of one's accomplishments or recognition, Nouwen directs the believer to the source of love —the Living God —and to the inherent nature of believers as children of God through Jesus, the source of identity. C. S. Lewis also argues that the emphasis of Christian love is not primarily emotional, but rather an extension of God's life through the believer's life (Lewis 1960, 93). To live and acknowledge oneself as the beloved means that grace is felt personally, and we allow that grace to inform our actions, which are then relational in nature.

Practical examples of this include demonstrating patience, forgiving without conditions, and extending oneself in service without seeking affirmation. Nouwen (1994, 52) suggests that recognizing oneself as the beloved fosters humility, generosity, and joy, which in turn enable one to reflect the true nature of Christ's love. Suppose a spiritual rhythm of initially receiving God's love builds our service. In that case, every act of service flows from a heart anchored in the loving embrace of divine affirmation.

Living as the beloved creates a positive cycle; as God loves the believer, the believer then replicates acts of love, creating spaces where communities are bound by grace, acceptance, and care for one another.

Biblical Anchors

The Scriptures often tie the identity and organic vitality of the believer to union with Christ. John 15:1–8 relates the Vine to branches: "I am the true vine, and My Father is the vinedresser. Every branch in Me that does not bear fruit He takes away; and every branch that bears fruit He prunes, that it may bear more fruit" (John 15:1–2). Here, Jesus asserts that his followers must abide in Him for life and fruitfulness. Bauckham (1996, 174) notes the significance of the metaphor of the Vine, which denotes both intimacy and dependence: that the believer is inseparably joined to Christ, receiving nourishment, direction, and power from Him alone. The spiritual implications are clear: faithfulness and obedience, as well as the vitality of a relationship with Christ, are not dependent on human activity but on an abiding relationship with Christ.

Galatians 2:20 provides yet another tremendous anchor: "I have been crucified with Christ; it is no longer I who live, but Christ lives in me; and the life which I now live in the flesh I live by faith in the Son of God, who loved me and gave Himself for me." Paul articulates that instead of an identity based on the self, identity is now defined by the life of Christ in the believer, which recalls Nouwen's (1994, 37) reflections on living as the beloved. Our old self has been crucified, and our life now flows from the indwelling of God. Such a union enables us to escape the performance-based aspects of spiritual practice. It provides us with safety and confidence to live holy lives.

Ephesians 2:6 places believers at a level that unites cosmic and spiritual reality: "And raised us together, and made us sit together in the heavenly places in Christ Jesus." Paul's imagery represents both present spiritual position and future hope. Augustine (1998, 112) reads sitting as a reminder to rest in God's sovereignty, indicating stress-fueled objectives can cultivate experiences of joy and peace that transcend earthly cycles. Practically, abiding, crucified with Christ, and seated all provide anchors for practical daily life or lives that are characterized by assurance in the storms of life, being courageous in obedience. Love flows from our security in Christ.

In bringing together John, Galatians, and Ephesians, the identity work of the believer is firmly rooted in Christ. Abiding in the Vine, participating in the crucifixion of Christ, and resting in a seated position produce a life characterized by joy, healing, and love, both received and expressed.

The Vine and the Branches (John 15)

In his declaration, "I am the vine, you are the branches" (John 15:5), Jesus emphasizes the complete dependence of his followers on Him. In this agricultural imagery, familiar to his audience, the vine represents the life-source, and the branches symbolize the community of faith that relies on Christ for its sustenance. Therefore, in addition to relational closeness, it also indicates spiritual fruitfulness. The branches are lifeless if they cannot remain one with the vine and produce life-giving fruit, which is a metaphor for the ultimate desolation that comes from separating from Jesus when we pursue life independently of God. As Augustine contemplated, the believer's life must remain "....entirely in God, for apart from Him we can do nothing" (Augustine 1998, 302). This imagery highlights that abiding does not mean simply visual attachment, but rather continual abiding, as in aligning oneself with Christ. Abiding encompasses prayer, obedience, and trust in God (Brueggemann 1994, 121).

Furthermore, consider John Chrysostom's view that the act of pruning the branches—while painful—will increase the fruit that one can produce and reflects suffering from God's loving discipline (Chrysostom 198, c. 347–407). The act of abiding in real life means that work, conversation, and worship can be spaces of divine presence. There is no way for fruitfulness to happen without the character and influence of Christ producing itself through the believer (Packer 1973, 215). The life of the early church, as depicted in Acts, demonstrates fruitfulness through a communal and sacrificial way of life that exemplifies the life attached to Christ.

The metaphor also conveys an eschatology of hope in that just as the branches attach to the vine, struggle, lead to life or fruitfulness, believers' experience of trials is designed to help them identify their faith and produce faithful character, pointing to the final union with Christ in eternal existence (Wright 1996, 412). Dependency on God is radical in a self-sufficient culture, so that there is a time to reflect and consider that identity, effectiveness, and joy must come from the Savior. One can practice, abide, and grow through disciplines in daily life (scripture meditation, corporate worship, sacraments), giving Christ the desire, motivation, and action. Abiding in Christ as life indicates that he is the only true life. So, John 15 is the framework for all Christian life and activity, as a dynamic, relational, and fruitful participation in the life of the eternal Vine, encompassing both present transformation and future glory.

Crucified with Christ, Yet Alive in Him (Gal. 2:20)

Paul's statement, "I have been crucified with Christ; it is no longer I who live, but Christ lives in me" (Gal. 2:20), establishes the unique transformational union believers have with the crucified Savior. The statement marks a theological watershed: death with Christ represents being freed from the power and dominion of sin, with life in him establishing a new identity that the Spirit empowers. In other words, Edwards points out that this union entails a profound renewal of one's support, allowing one to manipulate and structure one's affections and desires according to God's will (Edwards 1746, 98). The self of the believer is not lost but redefined; independence changes to fellowship. The believer participates in the ongoing life of Christ—a reality that is both mystical and practical.

Historically, Origen suggests that the believer's crucifixion will share a mystery and similarity with Christ's, involving the whole person—mind, will, and body—in the redemptive act of God (Origen 1994, 162). On a spiritual level, this participation changes or influences suffering: one sees their own hardship through the lens of Christ's death and resurrection, which provides a context for meaning and resilience (Nouwen 1981, 77). For example, we see this in the story of Stephen in Acts 7, where he mirrors dying with Christ with courage and grace—seeing the presence of God amidst persecution. Daily spiritual practices, such as prayer, fasting, and self-denial, provide concrete experiences of living in the crucified life, which cultivate a Christlike character in tangible ways.

The paradox of Galatians 2:20 can serve as a helpful reflection on identity, as the self is both surrendered and affirmed in Christ. Augustine points out that by embracing this paradox, one develops humility, obedience, and joy, because ultimately my life is the work of God's redeeming love (Augustine 1998, 312). There are ethical implications: living in Christ equips believers to love sacrificially, serve wholeheartedly, and do justice—practicing the life of the crucified Messiah in the world.

Practically speaking, the reality of being "crucified with Christ" instills courage in the face of failure, freedom from guilt, and the ability to defy cultural norms without fear of rejection. One experiences freedom not because they have managed to escape struggle, but because they have encountered Christ in the midst of it. As Paul articulates, the Christ that lives within me is the source of spiritual vitality, joy, and love. Suppose I take up this union every day. In that case, the invitation of this union is a reality that cannot be affected by anything in my life—I could be living in a life of death and experience a life of resurrection now.

Seated with Christ in the Heavenly Places (Eph. 2:6)

Paul's declaration, "and raised us together, and made us sit together in the heavenly places in Christ Jesus" (Eph. 2:6), reveals the believer's relationship to spiritual authority in union with the resurrected Christ. This theological position is not only positional; it is transformational. Paul emphasizes the reality that believers who are united with Christ, through faith, share in His victory over sin, death, and the principalities of this world (Calvin 1559, 278). The being "seated" signifies stability, rest, and authority. Believers are no longer under the power of sin, but they live in the reign of Christ, which has both theological and practical implications for daily living.

In citing the "heavenly places," Augustine sees both grace and obligation for moral vigilance, because reaching "heavenly places" involves having our minds and hearts aligned with God's will and living out a Christlike life in the daily realm (Augustine 1998, 415). The believer's earthly progression is inextricably linked to the raised position in the heavenly realm, providing a unique perspective on the believer's present struggles and disappointments. Origen points out that such a wonderfully intimate union brings an invitation to join the faithful in Christ's triumph, where prayer, worship, and obedience are part of divine empowerment (Origen 1994, 189).

Practical implications from Ephesians 2:6 are reflected in many biblical narratives. In every instance, exiles and prophets trusted in God while resisting the sufferings of life, embodying values derived from the heavenly perspective of Christ's authority and purposes. Like these faithful believers, Christians battling cultural pressures or personal life crises are invited to live from the vantage point of exaltation and draw confidence and peace from their identity in union with Christ. Henri Nouwen argues that the process of understanding this position grants profound inner freedom, allowing one to value Christ as the center of identity, even when earthly lives are precarious (Nouwen 1994, 84).

From an ethical perspective, the seated position helps alleviate preoccupations with status and self-sufficiency, and speaks to humility, service, and reliance on God's power in loving actions of justice, reflecting the reign of Christ through mundane earthly life. The "heavenly places" are not merely spatial abstractions; they provide normative interpretation and regulation for concrete living that shapes choices, relationships, and spiritual practices through Christian engagement. By embracing identification with Christ, Christians can cultivate joy, patience, and devotion to obedience, and live now in the fullness of Christ's victory and in expectation of its consummation in glory.

Living as Children of God

Embracing our identity as children of God is not merely an idea but affects everything we think, say, and do. This identity is not something we earn through achievement or morality, but is given to us through our adoption into God's family (Rom. 8:15–17). This identity transforms believers' lives as they live with confidence, humility, and a freedom from the fears of rejection and failure. In various ways, the Scriptures reveal and reiterate that being God's children carries with it both privilege and responsibility; we are to represent His character, honor His name, and further His work (1 Pet. 2:9).

Worship is where identity is embodied. Worship becomes an expression of belonging and therefore is our response to God's love and faithfulness. As we are lifted in adoration, gratitude, and surrender of heart, we develop a conscious awareness of God's presence among us that infuses our everyday existence (Augustine 1998, 112). Worship is not simply limited to liturgy and song; it can be expressed incarnationally, or in ethical living, servanthood, and relationships as we reveal God's imago in some of the most practical of ways.

Living by confidence instead of fear involves placing our trust in God's care and sovereignty. The fear of the known and unknown simply loses its grip on us when we remember that our Father is Sovereign over us, watches over us, provides for us, and orders our steps (Ps. 23:1–4). This confidence can lead us to live boldly in our spiritual formation, encourage us to be brave in witness, strengthen our capacity to endure trials, and find leisure in God's enoughness rather than seeking accomplishment through our own abilities (Calvin 1559, 421).

Living a servant life without striving is the paradox of living as a child of God; we exhibit power through gentleness and leadership through humility. We serve sacrificially because we are compelled by love, not because we expect recognition or reward (Matt. 20:26–28). The privileges of being God's image-bearers become our way of life; through our words, actions, and attitudes, we each reflect the reality of the Father's kingdom.

To walk in joy, healing, and love every day must be the prevailing evidence of what it means to be a child of God. We abide in Jesus who restores us, frees us from shame, and empowers us to love sacrificially. We live our lives as living prayers that might reflect the kingdom of God to the world (Nouwen 1994, 67). This rhythm of devotion, trust, service, and joy facilitates the best expression of life as a child of God that is both secure in divine belonging and transformational to those around us.

Identity Expressed in Worship

Worship is our primary means of recognizing and nurturing our identity in Christ. Whereas self-authenticity and self-identity are the focus in our secular society, Scripture calls believers to "offer your bodies a living sacrifice, holy and pleasing to God" (Rom. 12:1)—grounding identity not in self-fulfillment but in God's purposes. Worship is our human expression of our identity in relation to God, not a mere external ritual or ephemeral emotional response to aesthetics. Augustine emphasizes that worship arises from the heart's innate sense of God's majesty and our dependence upon Him, stating, "Our hearts are restless until they rest in You" (Augustine 1998, 29). Identity of the restless self is healed in encountering the God who defines us.

"Worship, therefore, operates in three distinct but complementary ways: it emphasizes what we have in Christ, affirming belonging and union; it shapes and/or institutionalizes identity; and it affirms the worth of the worship. Calvin remarks that when believers participate in liturgical life and the sacraments, they are reminded of their belonging and membership in the covenant family" (Calvin 2008, 415). Likewise, Aquinas notes that worship engages the reason and will to promote understanding and devotion (Aquinas 1981, II-II, q. 81). Worship is never passive; rather, it affirms and declares that the believer's worth is based on Christ (not raw accomplishment) over and above the will of man.

Practically, worship contemporizes the ordinary. Singing psalms, praying with purpose, and participating in the Eucharist cultivate an inner conscious possession of God's sovereignty. These acts can alter our self-understanding. The psalmist's declaration to God, "As the deer pants for the water brooks, so pants my soul for You, O God" (Ps. 42:1), illustrates the human desire to orient our person to a divine identity. Nouwen states that worship enables the believer to "live from the place of being loved by God," which in turn transforms relationships, priorities, and even vocational aspirations (Nouwen 1994, 78).

Therefore, identity expressed in worship is both faithful and revelatory. Worship reveals our identity to whom we are in Christ, while simultaneously forming us in the image of the God who calls us, redeems us, and sustains us. It is in worship that we find the freedom of self-obsession, as we rest in that assurance that our identity is secured in the everlasting, loving presence of the God who is I Am.

Living with Confidence, Not Fear

Confidence in the Christian way of life is based not on self-confidence but rather on God's unchanging presence. When the Word of God says, "For God has not given us a spirit of fear, but of power, and of love, and of a sound mind" (2 Tim. 1:7), it is a radical challenge to live audaciously in the security of God's identity and promises. Fear that tempts us toward inaction, or over- or under-reaction, stemming from failure, rejection, and/or uncertainty, is often present when believers define themselves through worldly lenses and not through their union with Christ. When we recognize that God is "I Am," a profound change occurs in the soul, giving us a firm footing and enabling us to stand unshaken in any situation (Exod. 3:14).

Augustine argues that trusting in God's sovereignty brings peace to the heart. True courage comes when the heart rests entirely in God, as opposed to resting in the transitory claims of (mere) humans (Augustine 1998, 28). Likewise, John Calvin proposes that our status as God's adopted children makes us bold, not in ourselves, but knowing that in Christ, we obtain a secure standing before God (Calvin 2008, 234). The psalmist expresses this state with great joy when he states, "The Lord is my light and my salvation; whom shall I fear?" (Ps. 27:1). Ultimately, faith and confidence are inseparable as each derives from an abiding knowledge of God's presence and care.

According to Dietrich Bonhoeffer, courage includes obedience and humility, discovering that believers may find fear diminishing when yielding control to God, trusting God when they move (Bonhoeffer 1959, 63). Practically, what does this mean? This means that in prayer, Christian vulnerability before the promises of God, intentional action in faith for obedience despite the fear creeping in, remembering the victory over fear in Christ in His life, death, and resurrection (John 16:33). When God's nearness is more real for the believer, they hurtched doubts and established unquestioning audacity in assurance and can love, witness, and endure the trials without fear.

Confidence develops because we recognize that our identity is rooted in the unchanging God. As we meditate on the security of God's promises, fear diminishes, and we can walk with courage. The world is offered evidence of a faith that is alive, grounded, and transformative (1 John 4:18).

Service Without Striving

Authentic Christian service does not arise from legalism or the need to perform or receive recognition, but rather from a secure sense of identity found in Christ. For example, when believers derive their identity from their union with Christ, their service is an outpouring of gratitude to God; it is a way beyond themselves, rather than a means to receive approval or recognition (John 13:12–17). In fact, Paul's instruction to serve one another in love (Gal. 5:13–14) presupposes a freedom from the finished work of Christ, providing believers with a sound foundation for accurate service, which is rooted in love. Without this grounding, seeking to serve out of ambition or self-interest can quickly lead to exhaustion, bitterness, and motives that distort one's service, as seen in the actions of the religious leaders of Jesus' day. Although their public acts could be viewed as honorable, their service often was merely a façade to conceal their anxiety and pride (Matt. 23:5–7).

Augustine profoundly states, "Our hearts are restless until they rest in You," to highlight that a person who rests in God alone can serve others with loving joy rather than much anxiety and self-concern (Augustine 1998, 28). Aquinas similarly teaches that our external actions do not simply perfect virtue, but by the movement of the soul to desire the good or will of God (Aquinas 1981, II–II, q. 23). Because of the love of God, one who serves from this love is responding from the interior space of a heart at rest by grace rather than reward.

According to Henri Nouwen, "authentic ministry is rooted in the awareness of our dependence on God and our vulnerability as human beings, for it frees us to serve without worrying about needing the approval of others" (Nouwen 1981, 45). Nouwen's observation resonates with the biblical model of Jesus, who humbly washed his disciples' feet, thereby teaching us about the importance of service and leadership that are integral to humility and relationship (John 13:14–15).

Otherwise, each day, believers are trained to take more time to be filled and reminded in the sufficiency of God through Scripture, prayer, and personal reflection. By realizing that every act of service has been received first as a gift from God, the Christian can rest in their service free of what they believe they are owed, experience the joy of freedom in their love, and develop meaningful purpose in their service (2 Cor. 3:5). Through letting go of ambition for our service and resting in acceptance by God, love becomes an act of self-giving modeled after Christ. These acts of love, therefore, foster a community based on mutual care rather than human approval.

Bearing Witness as God's Image-Bearers

As believers, we are called to reflect God's image. Each believer brings God's character more fully into the world and images God's presence as an image bearer. We read in Scripture, "You are the light of the world. A city that is set on a hill cannot be hidden" (Matt. 5:14). The very image of light serves as a powerful reminder of both the obligation and privilege we have to represent God's truth, love, and holiness before the world every day. When we bear witness to Christ, we are not merely publicly proclaiming Him in some formal way; we are living testimony to His work of transformation in us (2 Cor. 3:18).

Origen notes that every believer participates in God's glory in the liturgical sense of reflection, where we somehow reproduce the imago Dei through our actions, thoughts, and speech (Origen 1994, 112). Similarly, Gregory of Nyssa believed that as individuals grow in their spiritual faith, they mirror more of God's qualities, representing our incorporation of God into our lives through ethical behavior, mercy, and humility as actions originating from our union with Him (Gregory 2001, 87). When believers venture into the everyday and consistently imagine God, they are showing the world who the invisible God is through visible acts of mercy, justice, and love.

John Stott notes the interconnectedness between ethical witness, relational integrity, and doctrinal faith, that our actions ratify our message (Stott 1994, 59). Bearing witness, then, means both public acts of justice and mercy and private acts of devotion and discipleship. Acts such as serving marginalized individuals, exercising fiduciary responsibility in using our resources, listening with compassionate presence in vulnerable situations, and, before we utter a single word, demonstrating God's kingdom to the world. Paul models this reality in delineating that believers are "ambassadors for Christ" (2 Cor. 5:20), and heirs to the ministry of reconciliation.

In practice, bearing witness takes contemplation about one's own actions and motivation. It takes effort to consider your speech in light of the hydrostatic pressure of the Scriptures; consistent adherence to the character of Christ, the courage to confront injustice, empathy to appreciate individual experiences, and humility to understand that we rely on God. When we embrace our identity in Christ, we no longer act in fear or self-interest but from a firm footing in God (Rom. 8:29). Bearing witness becomes something we do not from a position of duty, but is the outflow from who we now are as God's children with God's character, which we have realized when we allow God's presence into all parts of our life even as we influence those around us for somebody else who bears God's image.

Walking in Joy, Healing, and Love Daily

Living the Christian life is not simply a succession of individual acts, but rather a walking in the reality of Christ's presence. In the Bible, we are commanded to "rejoice always in the Lord" (Phil. 4:4) and to "carry each other's burdens" (Gal. 6:2), equating joy, healing, and loving as aspects of daily discipleship. Joy does not depend upon circumstances but flows from the unchanging nature of God's presence, person, and acts in our lives. For Henri Nouwen, spiritual joy is rooted in the awareness of being God's beloved. It also serves as a reminder for believers that being close to God gives us an enduring inner vitality, because "when we give ourselves to God, we want to experience that the closeness in God—the Spirit's presence is vibrant" (Nouwen 1994, 56).

Healing is both personal and relational. Paul encourages the church to live lives of reconciliation and forgiveness with one another, recognizing that the Spirit uses the church and our relationships to mend emotional and relational wounds (Eph. 4:32). John Owen discusses the importance of mortifying sin because it is essential when walking in holiness, which opens our daily lives to both surrender and dependency upon God's grace (Owen 1968, 102). In practical terms, these words translate into habits and actions of confession, repentance, and seeking restoration with our neighbors. The Spirit is cooperating with us by working ongoing transformation in our lives, even reminding us of how we are to emulate Christ's overwhelming love through tangible actions.

Love, the ultimate fruit, is a natural outpouring of living a God-oriented life. Referring to the preeminent Christ-figure in the history of literature, C.S. Lewis, when describing love, says that love is not just a feeling but an act of the will that is disciplined and directed toward others as God commands (Lewis 1960, 78). When Christians live intentionally in joy and healing, love becomes tangible and visible to others, allowing us, in the words of Lewis, to "become a kingdom of merciful neighbours where hurts are healed" (Root 2014, 86); love comes as God's comforter for the diseased, the light for the weary, and hope for the hopeless. Our daily acts of rhythm, through prayer, meditation in Scripture, and serving others, sustain this walk by inviting ordinary, faithful practices into God's eternal purposes.

Walking in joy, healing, and love in a daily cadence is who we are in Christ. It requires some discipline, awareness, and dependence on the Holy Spirit, yet this life of "continual abiding" is available to everyone who "remains in him" (John 15:4-5). The more we embrace this walking rhythm, the more our lives will bear witness to the beauty of God's Kingdom and invite others into the forever-transformative aspects of the Christ-life.

Chapter 5
What We Are Called to Do

The Reversal of Vocation

God's calling is at odds with the goals society sets for us. Society promotes personal achievement, comfort, and recognition of authority as goals of success. In contrast, the Bible directs believers to a whole new vision of success, based on obedience to God's will (and not on likeness to authority), as participation in God's kingdom purposes. Jesus expresses this idea in Matthew 10:39: "He who finds his life will lose it, and he who loses his life for My sake will find it." It appears that when people seek worldly security or try to exalt themselves, they come up empty, but when we give ourselves up to God, we find true life. This reversal is essential to our view of vocation as a cross-centered journey, in which we use self-denial as the first step into spiritual vitality.

Augustine of Hippo states that human turmoil occurs whenever our desire is out of order; he further explains that we will only find proper rest when we shape our desires around God (Augustine 1998, 32). This quote helps to reinforce the idea that God's calling is more than a theological whim. It is a revolutionary principle that demands work and assures a daily life change. The paradoxes of the cross-centered life are evident in everyday things. A teacher chooses to serve, rather than earning their teaching credential and government title; a business leader chooses integrity as a stewardship over profit; and a parent chooses sacrificial love, often without fanfare. Bonhoeffer also explains that discipleship means finding the pathway of God, which appears different from that of society, and enjoying the freedom that comes with surrender (Bonhoeffer 1998, 45).

This call to inversion is God's call to see the ordinary as sacred. Our work, relationships, and everyday choices cannot be neutral; they are our places for obedience and participation with God. The first shall be last, and the last first (Matt. 23:11–12) reminds us not only that the kingdom operates by upside-down logic, but also that we must get on board with this reversal to a new way of understanding our life decisions. Stott emphasizes, "Every choice we make can therefore be of positive value, when it is guided by a purpose to reflect God through our choices; we will head for reflection to saturate our choices with humility, and we will head for active love in what we are about" (Stott 1994, 78).

The reversal of vocation indeed requires a great deal of freedom and holds great responsibility in service to God. It allows us to have a different understanding of what success looks like, creates a new identity, and helps us to be joyful in obedience. By abandoning our desires for exultation and preening ourselves, we can live a life of Christ and adopt a lifestyle of service, love, and humility, as a pattern set by Jesus. The call to re-orient our vocation around the cross allows us time for reflection and discernment as we allow our lives to continue aligning with God's redemptive work, everywhere shaping our character and our community.

God's Call vs. Worldly Ambition

God's call to His people often stands in stark opposition to what our world values. While human society may value wealth, fame, or influence, true life, according to Scripture, comes from obedience, humility, and participating in God's purposes. Matthew 6:19–21 reminds us of this difference between earthly treasures, which decay, and heavenly treasures, which last forever, as Jesus notes. While it is often human instinct to pursue our own self-advancement, God calls us to something that turns those instincts upside down and commissions us to live lives of surrender and servitude, not accumulation and recognition (Calvin 2008, 412). Augustine articulates that the human state of restlessness in desire is often misdirected—he states that the only place the soul can find peace is in God (Augustine 1998, 23). The biblical story is filled with portrayals of this unease: the rich young ruler, though living a moral life, could not respond to God's call because he was unable to let go of his possessions to participate in eternal life (Matt. 19:16–22).

Furthermore, Jesus, in the Sermon on the Mount, speaks directly against the values of the day, calling His followers to righteousness, ethical treatment of others, and humility over self-aggrandizement (Matt. 5:3–10). Rather than being a transaction, vocation is understood as a relational concept—it is viewed as God's redemptive work, not a map for advancing oneself (Origen 1994, 102). Ultimately, that means being discerning about God's priorities, particularly in the areas of career, leadership, finances, and relationships—obedience leads to the expression of devotion, humility reflects trust, and success is living fruitfully, not being acclaimed. The early church fathers wrote of vocation as finding joy by participating in God's purposes and being service-oriented, fitting into God's will (Chrysostom 1986, 142). This paradox shows that while those who yield their lives find freedom and abundant life, self-seeking is often marked by frustration and loss (Matt. 10:39). Engaging this divine call requires reflection, thinking about Scripture, having a practice of surrender daily, and creating a rhythm around obeying God's call on your life and being devoted to him in the ordinary. When Christians reorder ambition in service of God's kingdom, they are participating in this reversal that is so characteristic of the upside-down logic of the gospel: true 'greatness' is found in humility. Eternal gain emerges through faithfulness or service.

Losing Self to Find True Life (Matt. 10:39)

In Matthew 10:39, we find a succinct expression of the paradox that is Christian life: "He who finds his life will lose it, and he who loses his life for My sake will find it." This reversal of our natural human impulse toward self-preservation and comfort invites us to an altogether different posture. To "lose one's life for Christ" does not mean carelessly giving ourselves over repeatedly; no, it means to consciously reject our self-centered pursuits and align our desires, choices, and daily activities with God's reality and intentions (Calvin 2008, 487). In losing, we "go upside down" with the kingdom and its peculiar pathways, for we will never find freedom like losing control—and with it, a real and unshakeable sense of security (Packer 1973, 115).

The apostle Paul is a living example of this principle of union, as stated in Galatians 2:20, where he says he no longer lives for himself, but through Christ in him. Living in union with Christ transformed his understanding of vocation, relationships, and inward priorities. The early church writers emphasized the same idea: Augustine states that the heart, which was restless when surrendered to God, found peace, and the self became a servant, not a master, delighting in obedience (Augustine 1998, 52). Origen describes this loss of self as the involvement of the soul in the redeeming mission of Christ, which fosters both humility and "spiritual maturity" (Origen 1994, 77).

Losing oneself is also practical. We lose ourselves by resisting our culture's obsession with success defined by self-carving, riches, and recognition. Losing oneself is about consistent prayer, reflection, and intentional purpose to align God's will with our own, rejecting immediate comfort, and relinquishing personal gain for God. The biblical story illustrates this principle vividly, as the wealthy young ruler was unwilling to give anything up. In contrast, Peter and the disciples, who gave it all up for Jesus, found immeasurable joy and purpose in doing so (Matt. 19:27–30).

This paradox is an invitation always, not merely an assumption for theoretical consideration. Every day, in every decision, whether it may seem significant (e.g., work) or small (e.g., relationships), every moment is an opportunity to surrender. Moreover, slowly, surrender will shape identity, transforming the "I" into one that no longer derives significance from self, but from God's enduring purposes. When believers accept the paradox of losing themselves in the world, life will be characterized by joy, freedom from fear, intimacy with God, and a resistance to the desire for self. Engaging in this discipline cultivates spiritual resilience, aligning our hearts with eternal values rather than fleeting worldly gains. If losing oneself is salvation, it is the source of true life—a life rooted in union with Christ, motivated by the Spirit, and led by obedience rather than ambition (Matt. 10:39).

The Paradox of the Cross-Centered Life

The cross is central to Christian vocation, presenting the paradox that subverts the world's expectations: strength in weakness, life through surrender. Jesus' call to take up the cross daily (Luke 9:23) is a call to suffer, to humility, and to self-denial as pathways to abundant life. The cross is a symbol of atonement in the Gospel message; it also serves as a model for discipleship, influencing ethical conduct, spiritual formation, and vocation (Bonhoeffer 1959, 101). Early theologians consistently highlighted this paradox: the believer's desire to suffer in obedient response to God's call reflects participation in Christ's victory and purpose by releasing pain in divine fruition (Gregory of Nyssa 1995, 68). Chrysostom takes this further by stressing that the cross is not a burden, but the way of liberation, that even the soul must ultimately "ennoble the soul to value the eternal rather than the temporary things of a fleeting world" (Chrysostom 1986, 95).

In concrete terms, living a cross-centered life means that, from moment to moment, you choose to willingly put God and God's kingdom above your own needs, comfort, convenience, or prestige. This reorientation to the cross will require prayerful reflection, ethical discernment, and a willingness to serve others obediently and sacrificially, just as Christ's self-giving love (Bonhoeffer 2009, 84). The paradoxical and subversive nature of submission to Christ also extends to leadership and vocation, not as authority exercised over those subject to your power, but through your humble obedience and service to others, promoting their well-being, empowerment, and flourishing (Matt. 20:25–28).

This principle is repeatedly demonstrated in Scripture: Jesus' life and ministry invert all worldly hierarchies to show us that greatness is found in servanthood and that victory emerges from surrender. Paul, too, articulates the cross and movement of paradox in the letters to the Corinthians. His strength of faith is made perfect in weakness; he delights in weaknesses and insults and shortcomings and persecutions and difficulties, because they produce endurance, character, and hope (2 Cor. 12:9–10). Living a cross-centered life requires energetic and active trust, a willingness to suffer personal loss, and determined reliance on the indwelling Spirit within your heart to foster confidence and fortitude.

Suppose you engage the paradox of the cross. In that case, you participate in God's longing for His redemptive work in the world, experience freedom from a compulsive, ego-driven ambition for power and prestige, and discover depth and shalom joy in the Spirit (Bonhoeffer 2000, 86–87). For the Christian, the cross serves as a reference point for discerning the meaning of life and also a template for ethical discernment, dislodging the Christian from the notion that authentic human flourishing is separate from a response to Christ's sacrificial love. Obedience, humility, and surrender are not a disadvantage, but pathways to human flourishing (Luke 9:23).

Following Jesus in Practice

Discipleship consists not only in esteem or agreement, but also in the active obedience of daily surrender, self-denial, and service. Jesus calls those whom He knows as "the disciple" to "take up his cross and follow Me" (Matt. 16:24). Taking up one's cross may be value-laden, as there are carnal priorities in our lives, from which Jesus is inviting the believers to live, such that we may be free. The cross is emblematic of suffering and denial, but at another level, it signifies a decisive commitment to live one's life in service to God's purposes, away from self-interest. Practicing the way of Jesus and taking up one's cross may include, not exclusively, daily decisions that involve: humility in work, integrity in forming relationships, and engagement in sacrifice motivated by clear choices for loving devotion. Bonaventure (1975, 88) suggests that the Incarnation teaches us that God is revealed as the Servant, affirming that actual greatness comes from the surrender of status and power for love and obedience.

To deny oneself in a self-absorbed world presents unique challenges. Society today believes that ambition, comfort, and immediacy are normal. Scripture, on the other hand, calls upon believers to renounce comfort, ambition, and immediacy to flourish in the world as people with Kingdom values submitted to the will and purposes of God (Luke 9:23). As C.S. Lewis (1960, 101) articulates, fundamental self-denial is denying the good things the Father offers to open the door to God's best desires for our lives. Lewis also nudges us when thinking of holy surrender that self-denial, when properly understood, is about the deepest delight in God. When we relinquish control of our lives, including all their details, God orchestrates life in accordance with His provision and purposes for us. Practically, this could mean choosing integrity over expediency in business matters; choosing patience over irritation with our family; or choosing generosity over greed in our community. We perform acts of self-denial that mirror the love and humility of Christ.

The act of servant leadership is an affirmation of my orientation toward others in recognition of the upside-down values of God's kingdom. Jesus, in his own ministry, modeled that leadership is about feeding, shielding, and tending to those entrusted to my care, and not about lordship or popularity (John 13:12–15). Origen (1994, 77) observed that spiritual authority is not predicated on position but on one's willingness to exercise self-denying, sacrificial, servant leadership toward others. Contemporary applications of leadership include addressing the needs of younger believers, prioritizing the welfare of the team over personal gain, and calling a team to compassion that reveals the heart of Christ.

Thus, the process of following Jesus in practice transforms everything about how I live. The daily cross, self-denial, and servant leadership become a place where I am forming a character, deepening my faith, and embodying the values of God's kingdom. Discipleship, particularly in the world, exists as a distinctly different orientation from the burden of a requirement to live our lives for God and His purpose. Rather, it is a working out of one's participation in God's redemptive work, which involves overcoming barriers to holiness and flourishing as a community.

Taking Up the Cross Daily

Daily denial of self is one of the key marks of true discipleship. Indeed, Jesus said, "If anyone desires to come after Me, let him deny himself, and take up his cross daily, and follow Me" (Luke 9:23). This direction indicates that there is a continuing and conscious moment of surrender to God's will every day we live and breathe. The cross is more than a symbol of Christ's atoning sacrifice; it is a way of life, and Christianity intends for it to inform how we think, act, and make vocational choices (Bonhoeffer 1959, 101). Daily cross-bearing seems contradictory: it involves suffering and self-denial, yet leads to freedom, joy, and intimacy with God. The early church viewed this as the path to spiritual maturity. Augustine (1998, 52) notes that the loss of self, achieved by surrendering to God's purposes, frees the restless heart to embody divine love and peace. Origen (1994, 77) similarly understands taking up one's cross daily as participating in the sins of Christ's redeeming work, and thereby developing humility and endurance. This will require a degree of vigilance on the part of those aspiring to self-denial over personal will.

Therefore, we must resist, even educationally, the cultural assumptions that define success as self-promotion, wealth, and status. In practice, this means that we work prayerfully and wisely, ethically and responsibly, to prioritize God's kingdom; not at the expense of self, but motivated by concern for God's mission, not self-interest. The metaphorical language of Scripture presents life opportunities for daily cross-bearing, for example, as seen in the apostles who left their families and careers to follow Jesus, accompanied by both purpose and community (Matt. 4:19–20). Likewise, encountering cross-bearing in relation to service or relationships, where the choice between being selfless versus self-promoting is cross-bearing, requires efforts to speak with integrity, dignity, and sacrificial love (also keeping cultural acceptance in mind), placing oneself on the narrow road Jesus describes. The difference that results from cross-bearing creates character and identity, claiming Christ through our resilience in the midst of challenge, and through discernment and rootedness in relationship with God. In Galatians, Paul illustrated this point of personal attitude and identity development when he said he was crucified with Christ (Gal. 2:20); that is, he had crucified the self so that Christ may live through him. In practical terms, daily cross-bearing is characterized by working to become obedient, being secure enough in oneself to trust, and having an eternal focus instead of chasing ambitions that only hold weight in today's world.

Consequently, taking up the cross daily is not simply a theological thought process but is to become the reality of your life. It challenges self-indulgence in every decision and personal encounter. When we choose to deny ourselves, we have determined to suffer in the sense of participating in Christ's victory over sin and brokenness, and where all of life becomes an invitation to join in a witness for God's kingdom through the ordinary, to a life shaped by the cross. The call to self-denial by taking up the cross daily allows followers of Jesus to experience the freedom of being empty of ego-driven ambition, the joy of servanthood, and the embrace of intimacy with God, who invites, sustains, and empowers their lives (Luke 9:23).

Denying Self in a Self-Centered Culture

Self-denial is a persistent problem in a society that values individualism, self-advocacy, and comfort. Nevertheless, Scripture calls believers to live in a way contrary to the dominant culture: "for whoever wants to save his life will lose it, and whoever loses his life for my sake will find it" (Matt. 16:25). Denial of self is not a rejection of self, but a positive re-orientation of heart and mind towards God and others. Denial of self involves resisting the instincts of ego, entitlement, and immediacy in favor of humility, obedience, and service (Packer 1973, 115). Augustine (1998, 52) asserts that true freedom is found in subordinating self to God, and that the restless heart can only find rest in surrender.

Similarly, Chrysostom (1986, 95) affirms that self-denial liberates the soul, refocusing the will from ephemeral rewards to eternal rewards. In practical terms, self-denial will manifest in everyday life as choosing God's will over one's personal will, extending forgiveness, or opting to serve rather than prioritize convenience. Biblical narratives model this principle in their storylines—Jesus' ministry to those on the margins, Jesus' righteous anger at exploitation, Jesus' denial of the world to play out His ministry, and discipleship (Matt. 19:21–22)—all affirm that real life looks like laying down one's rights, occasionally at great peril. Self-denial fosters spiritual fortitude because it begins to reorient our motivations towards God's purposes rather than those of culture (Bonhoeffer 2009, 84). Self-denial in vocation might mean resisting the urge to prioritize profit and influence while maintaining integrity.

Self-denial in relationships with others may involve waiting until the other person is finished speaking or keeping one's thoughts to oneself, prioritizing humility and the well-being of others over one's own need for comfort. Self-denial is paradoxical; there is a sense in relinquishing control (and even desire for self-glory) that believers discover their true selves, freedom, and joy. Paul models this self-denial principle in Galatians 2:20, where he acknowledges that his life's purpose no longer revolves around self-interest, but rather his devotion to Christ, whose life in him transforms mundane tasks into sacred acts. Self-denial is a lifelong discipline that requires regular reflection and prayer, along with others in community who hold us accountable. In this way, self-denial is an active lifestyle choice to participate in the kingdom's upside-down values, which assert greatness arises in meekness and humility through service, not through social pressure or a desire to dominate. Self-denial is one of many spiritual disciplines that develop character, enhance intimacy with God, and cultivate a lifestyle characterized by obedience, love, and joy in God's actions and mission in the world.

Servant Leadership as Kingdom Practice

True servant leadership radically turns worldly power on its head in the realm of God's kingdom. Jesus teaches, "But whosoever will be great among you, let him be your minister" (Matt. 20:26). True leadership in the kingdom of God is not via domination and self-interest, but through humble, selfless, and caring service to others (Bonhoeffer 1959, 101). This model challenges our cultural paradigms, which often view leadership in terms of authority, wealth, or influence. However, the early church fathers assert that leadership grounded in service reflects the very essence of God and Christ. Augustine (1998, 52) notes that when leaders pursue their own self-glory, they violate the very vocation of their calling, while service leaders fulfill the divine order and grace. Chrysostom (1986, 95) amplifies this concept, suggesting that when leaders serve others, they become purified internally, develop ethical judgment, gain hope for spiritual maturity, and enhance the community.

Responsible servant leadership manifests in various spheres: the workplace, family, church, and society. In practice, leaders will prioritize the needs of those they serve, understand the ethical implications of their decisions for the common good, and cultivate environments that foster the flourishing of others. Biblical exemplars provide us with insights: Moses served as a leader of Israel humbly and in total dependence on God; Paul portrayed leadership through teaching, encouragement, and caring for congregations (Exod. 3:10–12; 1 Thess. 2:7–8). Servant leaders do not need recognition or a prize; they let go while trusting the outcomes to God's providence.

Trudging through the mundane, servant leaders embody and demonstrate kingdom values in their actions (Luther 1520, 63). Servant leadership also takes patience, courage, and reliance on the Spirit, especially during adversity and when leaders are misunderstood. By embodying humility, empathy, and accountability, leaders create communities where God's love and justice can flourish. Servant leadership is transformative: it shapes character, models upright living and ethical behavior, and empowers others to respond to God's purposes for their lives. Indeed, this perspective also indicates that greatness in God's kingdom is inextricably intertwined with service, as a reflection of the self-giving love of Christ and coupling leadership with divine wisdom and care (Matt. 20:28). Through daily practice and modeling self-giving love to participate in God's redemption, servant leaders flourish and cultivate obedience, love, and fruit for the advancement of the kingdom.

Biblical Models of Calling

The Scriptures also provide models of obedience that reflect the nature of God's call, which is often surprising or paradoxical to worldly expectations. Abraham exemplified the radical trust that defines the call of God. He was called to leave his place with his family, but he did not know the destination. Leaving his home demonstrates that God's promises are provided by faith and action (Gen. 12:1–4). According to Augustine (1998, 112), Abraham embodied obedience as a radical realignment of human will to divine purpose, noting that "True freedom is to will the command of God, and not to will anything contrary to the will of God." Abraham's call demonstrates that God's call reveals counter-cultural choices for the believer. Following the call of God requires a "depriving of habits and choices of what are socially acceptable," and allowing God's sovereign vocation to take precedence over and beyond human understanding and comfort (Conn 1999, 24).

Moses represented the tension between human limits and divine enablement, all the while struggling with reluctance and fear. In fact, Moses was afraid to be obedient and certainly believed he was not good enough, nor was he worthy of the call. In what may reflect a lack of self-confidence, Moses was obedient in response to God's call. He needed to be reminded of God's assurance, promise, and opportunity of God who accompanies his call: "I will be with your mouth, and teach you what you shall say" (Exod. 4:12). Gregory of Nyssa (2001, 145) underscores that when it comes to God's calling, we all are reluctant at first, and notes that God makes those feelings of hesitancy in people's lives a mode of God's power. Moses demonstrates that obedience to God's call is never self-reliance, but instead relying on the Spirit, who provides sufficient enablement to the obedient one, while offering a relieving model for today's believers who experience fear of the mode or terms of obedience to a call.

The narrative of David adds further insight into God's understanding of leadership. Politically speaking, David was not a likely candidate; yet, God crowned him as king through His call. God saw David's heart, and therefore, David is forever king because God called him. God's evaluation of leadership is based on the heart (1 Sam. 16:7). Chrysostom (1986, 233) observes that judgment regarding leadership tends to emerge according to competencies and other facets of external, outward behavior. However, David's value was about internal disposition, and God valued humility, devotion, and responsiveness to God's call as measures for service. David's ultimate triumphs and failures (returning to God through the Psalms) remind us that vocation pertains to responsibilities and privileges in proportion to one's internal character and disposition, as well as God's purposes.

These biblical examples remind us that there is a momentous calling and demand from God to transform us, in trust, surrender, and with an intent to God. We are not in control of God's call, and God's call does not conform to factors of human understanding or societal norms. With appreciation for Abraham's faith, Moses' reliance, or David's heroic heart, obedience to God's call means embracing a reality that breaks worldly expectations. Together with Abraham, Moses, and David, as explained herein, vocation is relational, abiding as a theology of communion with God; it is not only relational, but vocation is also practical and expressed through faithful and obedient service.

Healing in Obedience

To obey God is both a duty and a way to inner healing and to freedom. Our human drive for self-determination often creates anxiety, pride, and turmoil. The Scriptures remind us that when we give our will to Him we relieve ourselves of these burdens: "Come to Me, all you who labor and are heavy laden, and I will give you rest" (Matt. 11:28). John Owen explains that the mortification of sin that the believer is seeking occurs when they put away their self-rule and submits to God's authority, leading the believer toward emotional as well as spiritual healing and restoration (Owen 1968, 47). Thus, obedience becomes healing and puts the soul back in alignment with its intended creator.

One key impediment to a responsive obedience to God's call is pride. In commenting on the struggles of complying with God's direction, Jonathan Edwards observes that the inherent rebellion of the heart against God breeds discontent. At the same time, submission leads to humility and peace (Edwards 1746, 82). Obeying and letting God heal means we learn to say no to our limits as human beings and embrace God's sufficiency. When Moses realized he was not enough, he met God, who said, "I will be with you" (Exod. 3:12). Similarly, for a believer, when God directs that we turn from self-reliance to trust in Him, the anxiety vanishes, and the believer discovers a deep rest they could not find in their own striving.

Obedience also heals by bringing us back to who we really are, by reconciling us to our true identity. As Augustine states, when we free our will, which was once seeking fulfillment through self-promotion, and redirect it to God, who is the ultimate fulfillment (Augustine 1998, 121). In doing this, the believer experiences healing from the tragic impact of sin, as well as the internal rupture that occurs when we attempt to live submissively. Obedience reflects both moral alignment and psychological wholeness.

The practical application of these truths is not only abstract; any believer can apply them to their daily lives. When a believer obeys God at work, home, or in the community — i.e., they submit their planning and will to God — they soon discover freedom from fear and anxiety that comes, in part, from taking personal responsibility for the outcome. Its capstone is that in obedience to God, we have companionship with our creator. This obedience affects resilience, joy, and togetherness. God is restorative. Recall Ps. 138:8, "the Lord will perfect that which concern me." You can see that yielding to God's direction is inextricably connected to the healing and restoration of the human heart.

Healing in Obedience

Obeying God is not an oppressive adherence to rules; rather, it is a pathway for deep healing and spiritual freedom. True freedom cannot be experienced while believers cling to self-determination and the false notion that controlling circumstances or outcomes brings meaning to our lives. As Scripture reminds us, when we trust in the Lord and commit our ways to Him, He will guide our path, stabilize our souls, and provide refuge (Prov. 3:5–6). Obedience to God both invokes human desires and affirms divine purpose, allowing God to be at work restoring our hearts, healing our minds, and reconnecting with us.

Healing pride and submitting to God's authority are central to our obedience. The human propensity for self-exaltation, which encompasses facets such as self-sufficiency, independence, status, recognition, or privilege, can lead to spiritual anxiety and relational friction. Obeying God means we recognize that wisdom, power, and worth come from Him and not from our achievement or reputation. Augustine emphasizes that humility and submission are essential for opening the soul and allowing the infusion of God's grace, which forms personal character in patience, love, and abiding joy (Augustine 1998, 214). Jonathan Edwards, speaking in charitable forms of humility, argues that the agency of obedience that emanates from a respect and reverence for God awakens and nourishes our inner affections for the beauty and glory of Christ, beyond self-centered motivation (Edwards 1746, 87).

The anxious soul should find rest in this posture of obedience. Anxiety is often created from a desire to control what is, ultimately, God's business: relationships, resources, and outcomes. When believers surrender their efforts to control these things, they will begin to develop a rhythm of trusting and relying on God, which will result in peace that surpasses our understanding (Phil. 4:6–7). Jesus's invitation, "Come to Me, all you who labor and are heavy laden, and I will give you rest" (Matt. 11:28–29), implores believers to find refuge in His gentle and lowly heart. Obedience rests upon the act of belonging to God's restorative brand of authority and guidance through a faithful companionship.

Practically, the healing nature of obedience may be observed in daily choices. Obeying God throughout the day may look like sharing the truth in love, serving others sacrificially, and prioritizing God's will above our own. With each act of surrender, we increasingly trust, grow in humility, and see our pride dissipate, nurturing our resilient spirituality. Obedience to God is more than compliance with His commands; it is a vibrant and healing engagement with God's transformational presence, offering enduring peace, reestablished healthy relationships with others, and, more generally, a soul tuned to God's divine and preferred purposes.

Freedom from the Weight of Self-Determination

Human beings often live under the charade that self-determination is the path of fulfillment. From childhood, we are taught that personal choice, will, ambition, and control define who we are and what our future holds. That said, in contrast, Scripture bears witness that true freedom is not about self-determination but surrender to the will of God. Jesus teaches: "He who finds his life will lose it, and he who loses his life for My sake will find it" (Matt. 10:39). The profound paradox underscores the harsh lesson that seeking to carve out total control of one's existence apart from God is a weighty endeavor that does not ultimately allow for joy, peace, and spiritual development.

The burden of self-determination manifests through anxiety, perfectionism, and a sense of exhausting pressure to keep striving. Jonathan Edwards writes that when one relies solely on oneself, unchecked, it can darken the soul and close its eyes to the providential work of God, leaving individuals fatigued, restless, and spiritually impoverished (Edwards 1746, 72). Augustine writes that people desire to take absolute control of their lives, which leads to inner disorder, because only God has the knowledge and absolute power of wisdom and sovereignty to give things proper order (Augustine 1991, 311). Ultimately, understanding this is the first step to liberation and freedom.

Freedom comes when we emotionally and volitionally resign control and embrace God's direction, believing it will be better than our own intentions. Dietrich Bonhoeffer believes that discipleship rests not simply on obedience, but is aligned with God's will for our own wills and giving up the illusion of independence (Bonhoeffer 1959, 63). It may simply be emerging into life and making daily decisions by seeking God's voice in prayer, placing plans and ambitions before His wisdom, and allowing Him to establish priorities.

Even communal life can assist in attempting to release control. John Chrysostom emphasizes the importance of accountability, spiritual direction, and communal prayer (Chrysostom 1986, 54). As people gradually let go of their desire for dominance and their own perfect completion of desires, they begin to experience an emergence of peace in their inner being, which stems from confidence in God's providence rather than one's own force of will.

Ultimately, the experience of freedom from one's own self-determined life will be transformational. Life, professional skills, ambitions, plus domestic relationships, shall be entrusted to God, and your sense of purpose, and indeed joy and stability will emerge with greater depth. Although surrender may sound passive, it is a freedom to live life to the fullest, utilizing one's God-given skills in the wisdom, grace, and love of God. In this paradox, the cross-centered life, we observe that losing self-control and accepting the Lordship of God offers only the ability to be genuinely "controlled".

Healing Pride Through Surrender

Pride is one of the most subtle and universal hindrances to the spiritual life. It can hide behind a belief in competence, self-reliance, or superiority. Although worldly cultures can legitimize pride as a form of confidence or achievement, biblical scriptures reveal that spiritual flourishing requires humility and surrender. "God resists the proud, but gives grace to the humble" (James 4:6). This means that pride is not merely internal, but an obstacle to receiving grace from God and experiencing restored relationships.

The first step to healing pride is to notice it. The psalmist provides an invitation to self-examination: "search me, O God, and know my heart; try me, and know my anxieties; and see if there is any wicked way in me" (Ps. 139:23–24). Part of spiritual discernment involves reflecting on how the self, ambition, and ego distort relationships, service, and devotion. Augustine says that pride is often necessarily connected to our attachments to the world, honour, or personal achievement; restoration can only be found in turning the heart wholly towards God (Augustine 1998, 112). By giving direct attention to pride, the believer opens space for God to do his work of transformation.

Surrender is a matter of will and a condition of the heart. It does not mean discarding or abandoning one's gifts or responsibilities, but choosing to surrender them to God instead of self-orienting those gifts to exalt oneself. Thomas Aquinas emphasizes that actual virtuous behaviour looks like not just doing good acts, but doing them with the right, God-oriented motivation, free from self-seeking objectives (Aquinas 1947, I–II, q. 63). In practice, this can look like intentional humility as a leader, admitting vulnerability and mistakes, or living in a way that celebrates God's glory instead of personal glory.

We are compelled to heal because healing is a relational and communal process. John Chrysostom points out that living in humility with a "community of believers" sets up mutual accountability, grace, and encouragement (Chrysostom 1986, 54). Prayer, confession, and spiritual direction communalize the practice of surrender, helping believers rely on God's strength instead of their own.

Healing from pride returns spiritual freedom and relational wholeness. As believers relinquish control, submit their ambitions, and allow for God's direction, they discover that humility is not weakness; it is a threshold to exercising God's grace, to joy, and to faithful service. Surrender aligns the soul with God's kingdom, allowing for an orientation toward Christ, and as a result, for love, obedience, and wisdom to flow out.

Rest for the Anxious Soul

Worry is one of the unavoidable elements of living in a world that values independence, control, and constant accomplishment. The human tendency to micromanage events, to count calories (in some sense), to anticipate every variable, and to rely on human capacity often keeps the soul weary and unsettled. Still, God's word calls and challenges God's people to trust and surrender to Him: "Cast all your care upon Him, for He cares for you" (1 Pet. 5:7). This is not just for emotional relief but an invitation to cooperate with God's providential care and relinquish the false notion we can bear this life's burden independently. The psalmist reiterated this mantra of soul tranquility: "Be still, and know that I am God" (Ps. 46:10). From this vantage point, stillness is both an acknowledgment of God's rightful dominion and a lived experience that supports the healing of the soul.

Jonathan Edwards presents a balanced perspective on resting in God. Rest here does not mean irresponsibility, and yet we completely shift our attention and affections to the Lord's eternal purpose (Edwards 1746, 29).

When the believer rests in God, anxiety retreats and has no place because the believer's ultimate future is not decided by human effort but by the divine wisdom we call. This trust is further developed through spiritual disciplines practiced daily, including prayer, meditation on Scripture, and obediently responding to God's word, which serves as a rhythm of surrendering worry. Henri Nouwen states that once we enter into this rhythm, the soul is drawn to an intimate experience of God's presence, quieting the anxious soul and allowing it to experience quiet confidence (Nouwen 1994, 78).

Moreover, rest in God is a communal and relational experience. Anxiety becomes worse through isolation and the pressure to maintain some appearance. Participating in the church life, receiving encouragement, and providing intercession for another person acknowledges the reality that God's care comes through His people (Chrysostom 1986, 42). In a busy world, perhaps this would include practical actions such as scheduling time for silence, being intentional about establishing boundaries for emotional and mental health protection, and being graciously grateful for God's providential care each day.

In essence, rest for the anxious soul is a profound act of worship and obedience to God's kingdom and glory. When we surrender control, acknowledge God's dominion, and trust His providence, the believer enjoys a moment of immediate peace while developing holistic spiritual growth. This type of rest is not a moment of relief, but a gift of a transformative posture for living daily with faith, hope, and love. It is restorative rest that is available to the anxious soul, which counters the world of endless striving to perform, providing a grounded sense of belonging in God's kingdom and leading the disciple to live with peace and ever-increasing resilience to be faithful and serve.

Joy in God's Mission

Participating in Godly acts creates a joy that transcends circumstance. When believers engage in Kingdom work, they will discover that joy is not tied to personal accomplishment or recognition. Joy is intertwined with being in relationship with our Creator and integrating their work into God's mission and purposes. Jesus affirms this principle when he states, "These things I have spoken to you, that My joy may remain in you, and that your joy may be full" (John 15:11). Thus, joy is bound with obedience and taking part in God's plan.

This joy is heightened when believers serve in a capacity where they feel God's presence. Henri Nouwen comments that ministry is always personal and transformational; it is never just a task (Nouwen 1981, 56). When a believer sees a desperate need in the marginalized, a broken person who needs comforting, or someone who desperately needs teaching, they often find themselves in the presence of God, which also creates internal joy. Yet, this awareness of God's nearness does not diminish our fatigue and discouragement that may come from serving people sacrificially.

The joy of participating in God's work radically alters human priorities. Paul encourages believers to work heartily as for the Lord and not for men, because work that is done for an eternal purpose is more valuable than recognition from an earthly purpose (Col. 3:23). This joy reorients priorities because the focus shifts from achieving for the sake of self to achieving for the sake of God. Jonathan Edwards firmly believed that the heart only feels true satisfaction when reveling in God's glory as it participates in His redemptive purpose (Edwards 1746, 102).

Joy in God's mission is not esoteric; it is full of pragmatism. The parable of the Good Samaritan demonstrates that, although this service may have been costly, his act of service ultimately led to an internal joy that God provided, as well as wholesome spiritual growth (Luke 10:25–37).

Likewise, participating in modern expressions of community, family, or various types of church ministry relates to the manifestation of God's Kingdom on earth, resulting in joy, rest, and nourishment for the believer.

Most importantly, joy in God's mission is indistinguishable from being in God's presence. N.T. Wright observes that being an agent of God's work is a foretaste of the ultimate joy in heaven, which exists when service and obedience are completely in sync with God's will and God's ultimate mission (Wright 1996, 488). The delight of each believer increases proportionately to the believer's measure of surrender, humility, and dedication, and it can be concluded that the pathway of joy is paved by loving and faithful responding to God's work.

The Delight of Participating in God's Work

True delight in God's mission occurs not because we have completed the job or accomplished our will, but because we are involved in God's story and redemptive plan for all creation. The Scriptures emphasize that God has called His people into a partnership with Him, enabling them to become participants in His purpose. To quote Paul: "For we are His workmanship, created in Christ Jesus for good works, which God prepared beforehand that we should walk in them" (Eph. 2:10, emphasis added). Our calling in God invites us to reframe our understanding of success—we find delight when we are obedient to God's will, not when artificial standards dictate our worth.

When we see God demonstrate His presence in our midst through little, simple, and ordinary actions, we can appreciate the joy of participation. The account of Jesus feeding the five thousand demonstrates how everything is possible in God, and our little becomes quite large when it is done in reference to God's mission (John 6:1–14). The through line is the capacity and humility of participating in God's action, because the source of fruitfulness is in Him alone (Bonhoeffer 1959, 85).

Moreover, joy is a relational construct: we are called to a community of co-laborers. When Moses led the people, he discerned the presence of God among the people. He did not forge ahead or direct himself; he obeyed and depended on God's person and vision to guide him (Exod. 33:12–23). For the sense of joy to be realized, we must be attentive to God's voice, connect with God in prayer, and be open to God's direction (Packer 1973, 102).

Ultimately, delight in God's work stems from a spirit of gratitude. Where we see God's providential care and provision, the overflow of our hearts seeks to praise Him, reflecting the Psalms, "Serve the Lord with gladness; Come before His presence with singing" (Ps. 100:2). Delight in God's mission changes who we are and produces joy, endurance, hope, and love that spills into every area of life. This is a positioning of delight that finds its foundation not in our gain, but in God's eternal purpose, which allows us to offer ourselves as living sacrifices (Willard 1998, 210).

Experiencing God's Presence While Serving Others

Serving another is an expression of participation in the mission of God, in which joy arises when one experiences God's presence. When Jesus says, "Whoever desires to come after Me, let him deny himself, and take up his cross, and follow Me" (Matt. 16:24), the paradox is apparent: denying self and serving others opens oneself up to the presence of God who sustains, consoles, and empowers (Bonhoeffer 1959, 97).

The Gospels are rife with examples. The story of the Good Samaritan exemplifies attentiveness to God's desire for mercy, as the Samaritan cares for the victim without anticipating reward (Luke 10:30–37). Service, through the view of our spiritual engagement with God, is not a task or duty to be performed, but an encounter with the God who is present with both the one serving and the one served. Henri Nouwen notes that an act of ministry responsive to God's nearness transforms our mundane actions into vehicles of grace, generating gifts such as "joy, peace, and inner healing" (Nouwen 1994, 76).

Making ourselves available to God's presence takes humility and dependence. Moses' leadership conveys this well: he was aware of his limitations and sought God's guidance, enabling him to serve his people (Exod. 18:13–27). Likewise, when we remain aware that God is responsible for the fruit of our service, rather than a result of our own work, we free ourselves to rest and enjoy the comfort of our faithful obedience (Packer 1973, 215).

Prayer and reflection can allow space for God's nearness to ourselves or to one we may be serving. As illustrated by Jesus, who frequently withdrew to solitude with the Father, God's nearness was vital to Jesus as a model of dependence and communion in his work of ministry (Mark 1:35). God's work is inextricably linked to His experience of God in every encounter of service.

At last, joy in serving is inseparable from the presence of God. When we act out of love, God's and others' joy, and as humble servants of God, we embody and represent Christ's self-giving nature, showing the world in tangible forms what His Kingdom looks like. Before long, even amid fatigue, resistance, and suffering, God's continuing presence offers us courage, hope, and delight because serving others, all others, is an experience of God that matters in an eternal perspective (Wright 1996, 205).

Nouwen on Joy in Following Christ

Nouwen notes that joy in discipleship emerges when we relinquish control over our lives and surrender to the rhythms of being a disciple of Christ (Nouwen 1981, 112). Following Jesus is inherently a countercultural act: secular society encourages freedom and self-promotion, whereas the Kingdom of God encourages self-denial, obedience, and humility. What is paradoxical is that joy flows out of relinquishing self-seeking aspirations. Jesus promised, "He who finds his life will lose it, and he who loses his life for My sake will find it" (Matt. 10:39).

Nouwen notes that there is a relational aspect to joy. Joy flows out of abiding in Christ as disciples and being engaged in God's mission. The reality for the disciples was joy in relation to the experience of seeing integration occur. Seeing people and the Kingdom of God advance because of their obedience to Christ produced overwhelming joy for the disciples (John 15:11). The early church enjoyed a shared sense of communal joy through service, prayer, and dependence on one another (Acts 2:42–47).

Joy requires the experience of attentiveness to God's presence. Nouwen identifies that the spiritual disciplines of prayer, solitude, and contemplation foster a heart that is receptive to God working in our hearts and the world (Nouwen 1981, 118). Thus, when serving others, the awareness of God's leading becomes an encounter alongside and with God rather than merely fulfilling an ambition. Even the smallest acts of care—feeding the hungry, visiting the sick, comforting the afflicted, lending a sympathetic ear to someone—can encourage an engagement with the divine.

Moreover, joy is developed in trust. Once God has our plans and ambitions submitted to Him, He can change the service we render as well as the very characters doing the service (Bonhoeffer 1959, 85). The rich young ruler exemplifies this tension: seeing the joy in life surrendered following the dictates of Christ to neglect the enormous attachment to worldly possessions (Matt. 19:16–22).

Primarily, Nouwen speaks of joy not just as an ephemeral, happy experience, but as a stable joy—a delightful state grounded in the reality of obedience and communion with Christ, empowered by the Spirit. To persevere, sacrificial love, and embodiment of being His witness is ultimately to live in joy—the flip side of the world as God desires it to be possible because of the nature of the upside-down Kingdom of God (Willard 1998, 214). Thus, our joy in the experience of following Christ is inextricably bound up in surrendering our joy through serving others, as well as in the awareness of living life as part of God's eternal plan.

Love as the Fruit of Vocation

Love is conceived as the fruit of a vocation to which God has called you. Because vocation is the opposite of ambition, as believers turn away from the patterns of the world of ambition toward the vocation of Christ, love will emerge as the determiner in thought and action. This is affirmed by scripture in Philippians 2:3–4: "Let nothing be done through selfish ambition or conceit, but in lowliness of mind let each esteem others better than himself. Let each of you look out not only for his own interests, but also for the interests of others." No vocation is disconnected from a disposition of selfless love.

Paul reminds believers that letting others have consideration is part of God's heart and is a marker of living the Kingdom life (Rom. 12:10). In contrast, professional self-interest has impractically complicated the meaning of our calling; love, through self-determined sacrificial service, manifests that self-centeredness has little place in the believer's vocation when the vocation is centered in Christ. Dietrich Bonhoeffer observes that "It is costly because it costs a man his life, and it is grace because it gives a man the only true life" (Bonhoeffer 1959, 112). Love is costly because it requires something more than the ease, reputation, and attachable importance of being in the spiritual orbit of personal identity or non-identity. However radical it may seem, love is God's Kingdom realized; it tells the world of the transformative power of Christ.

The scriptures are filled with examples of active love. The parable of the Good Samaritan reminds us that love is not passive, but requires active action to meet the needs of another (Luke 10:33–35). When Paul urges the church to consider others above themselves (Phil. 2:4), he broadens the concept of leadership and relationship by demonstrating that Kingdom love is active, humble, and enduring.

As the fruit of vocation, love also cultivates the community of believers. Henri Nouwen notes that God invites each person into relationship, not merely to the task, but to be His love in relational contexts (Nouwen 1981, 79). Love in families, churches, and workplaces can bind broken and disjointed communities as everyone experiences joy in loving acts of encouragement and building others up, healing them, or projecting visible relationships with God's presence.

Love, as the fruit of vocation, aligns the believer to God's purposes and creates a lasting spiritual impact. As Bonhoeffer notes, the cost of true discipleship is abundantly repaid in action through the life-changing power of love (Bonhoeffer 1959, 118). The believer's vocation is defined not by what tasks they can accomplish, but by a selfless, Christlike love that directs each decision, engagement, and moment of service.

Loving Others Through Sacrificial Service

In Christian vocation, the abundant life is not measured by personal benefit or status but by how much our lives mirror the selfless love of Christ. The New Testament authors cannot say it often enough. Perhaps the best summary and exhortation are these instances in Scripture where Jesus states love is the ultimate essence of God's kingdom (John 13:34–35; 1 John 3:16). In this light, sacrificial service is at least the external expression of love that takes learning to live that love out of our lives by going outside the safety and limits of ourselves and cultural preconceptions. Jesus exemplified all this in His life and death. He would teach, demonstrate, and illustrate that authentic leadership, found in greatness, is only accomplished through an attitude of humility and servant-mindedness (Mark 10:43–45).

This sort of love requires intention; it is the willingness to give up or forgo self-interest, self-convenience, or personal desires to prioritize the needs of another. Augustine describes ambition and selfish consideration as abandoned in love, as this direction of love is seen; one's will becomes perfected outwardly—God is turned out (Augustine 1991, 212). We can reason, think, and even feel love, but love is an active, willful response to an expressed or unmet need or want within the other (whether seen or not). Ongoing care is often challenging to see. The Good Samaritan, as described by Jesus to illustrate love through serving and caring for others, provided care without any expectation of return, demonstrating God's mercy in the world, which is its essence (Luke 10:33–35).

Sacrificial service and care have the power to heal that inward self-focus, retraining the human heart's desires to align with God's objectives for Heaven on earth, as it is in heaven. As Packer observes in his interpretation, love rooted in God's grace produces qualities in life and action—such as humility, patience, and endurance—in the care of others and in their development and well-being (Packer 1973, 287). By entering into a life of service, a Christian partners in God's restorative enterprise in the world; love meets expressed spiritual needs, emotional needs, and sometimes physical needs.

In practice, sacrificial care and service can take many forms, including mentoring, responsiveness, providing necessary hospitality, advocacy, and performing acts of kindness and goodwill. Nevertheless, it does not matter if these actions are small or large. All share the orientation of oneness within the heart toward God and neighbor. Theologically, it is not voluntary, but part of the work of discipleship—a discipleship to Christ that responds out of love: "But if any wants to become my follower, let them deny themselves and take up their cross" (Matt. 16:24). Sacrificial love is our response to God's love for us, and it is a partnership that reflects Christ's ongoing mission in the world.

Paul's Call to Consider Others Above Self

Paul frequently encourages believers to consider the interests of others before their own, positioning love as a "moral responsibility" and as a form of spiritual formation. In the book of Philippians (2:3–4), Paul says, "Let nothing be done through selfish ambition or conceit, but in lowliness of mind, let each esteem others better than himself. Let each of you look out, not only for his own interests, but also for the interests of others." This paradox of the Christian vocation is that absolute joy and fulfillment are found in emptying oneself of self, not in promoting oneself.

Paul's intention for this ethic is to firmly ground it in the person of Christ, who, being in the form of God, emptied Himself of that status and became a servant, humbling Himself for the purpose of serving and redeeming humanity (Phil. 2:5–8). To obey this call requires a very intentional level of self-awareness, including awareness of our own natural tendencies toward pride, selfishness, and culturally defined parameters of success. In reflection on personal experience, Edwards notes that the lifestyle of the believer is a consistent learning in humility, and involves continuing the discipline of prioritizing God's purposes above personal desire (Edwards 1746, 117).

This ethic of love is not merely relational, but a theological foundation for the believer's actions. By esteeming others, believers imitate God's impartial grace (Rom. 12:10), creating a microcosm of God's kingdom in their families, communities, and broader society. In framing these practical expressions in the life of believers, we see where Paul encourages generosity, patience, empathy, and reconciliation as practical expressions of love connected to God's calling (Gal. 6:2).

Paul also challenges a cultural narrative of self-oriented ambition. Where the world raises the individual, the Christian vocation raises others. Moreover, the result of this shift is joy, peace, and spiritual development.

Stott observes that Paul's teaching provides for the flourishing and sanctification of the community. If one orders life toward others rather than toward pride of place, one cannot help but grow into a faithful likeness to Christ (Stott 1994, 159).

Bonhoeffer on Discipleship and Love in Action

Dietrich Bonhoeffer observes that Christian discipleship must include action and costly love. In *The Cost of Discipleship* (1959), he distinguishes "cheap grace" from the grace that calls believers to hopefully act with loving concern for others (Bonhoeffer 1959, 45). In this framework, love for others is not passive, sentimental, or easy; rather, it is a courageous risk that may require the sacrifice of oneself.

Bonhoeffer grounds this range of discipleship in the incarnation and crucifixion of Jesus. True discipleship entails following Jesus, which sometimes involves actions that may result in suffering, social alienation, or a threat to one's own life (Matt. 16:24). According to Bonhoeffer's idea, acting with love is not abstract but incarnational. Love is always both action and reflection, which adds value to the needy human condition. This action can take the form of feeding the hungry, visiting the sick, or clothing the poor (Matt. 25:35–36).

Bonhoeffer has also noted the communal dimensions of the church's discipleship. Believers are called to mutual commitment, to love one another by bearing each other's burdens and thus fulfilling the law of Christ (Gal. 6:2). Discipleship takes shape by loving one's neighbor like Christ in self-giving love through accountability and encouragement, in reliance upon, but not ownership of, God's resources for the benefit of the whole community. In addition, discipleship assumes that the church reflects a relational God. A culture of grace in the body of Christ assumes an understanding of generosity and un-ownership of community resources for the flourishing of all.

Finally, this love remains both spiritual and ethical; they are not hermetically sealed from each other. A substantial change in the heart can have a significant impact on an individual's behavior. Bonhoeffer contends that action without the lordship of Christ is not ethical action, and the opposite—deeming pious devotion to God without embodying *phronesis* through action—is also lacking (Bonhoeffer 1959, 98). Therefore, the disciple who desires to be ethical seeks to join faith and works, devotion and action in the service of life, reflecting God's kingdom on earth. In the discipleship of sacrificial love, sacrificial love leads to specific or tangible signs of God's dwelling presence in the world.

Theological Insights

Theological reflection deepens understanding of vocation, enabling practical obedience to emerge from the timeless wisdom of the Church. Augustine of Hippo reminds us that God's call is inherently life-giving: it takes the human heart away from self-centered striving. It gives it purpose in divine fulfilment (Augustine 1998, 102). Obedience is therefore not a burden but an invitation into fullness of life for each believer. This view of vocation reframes it; worldly successes do not measure vocation, but rather faithful alignment with God's purpose.

John Calvin reinforces this, where vocation is viewed as a divine appointment rather than an ambition. In whatever vocation, be it formal ministry, family, or society, every believer's life is found in God's providence (Calvin 1559, 234). Witnessing God's sovereign authority in one's calling diminishes anxieties about self-determination, resulting in the confidence to serve others faithfully in accordance with God's purpose.

Edwards offers an additional aspect: that joy must accompany obedience. Edwards avers that true delight is not finding recognition and fame in this world, but rather in sharing with God in His work of redemption (Edwards 1746, 88). Scripture affirms this, stating that believers are to find rest and satisfaction within God's purposes, rather than in the transience of our human endeavors (Matt. 11:28–30). This makes it evident that surrendering to God's call not only brings joy but also enhances one's effectiveness in Kingdom work.

The biblical narratives illustrate this further. In taking God's call to leave Ur, Abraham obeyed. Moses, although reluctant, took the call to lead God's people. David's pursuit of God's heart all highlight a string of divine calling that exceeds what humans call success (Gen. 12:1–4; Exod. 3:10–12; 1 Sam. 16:7). All of these illustrate that vocation is transformational because it shapes and encourages dependence upon God in character.

Theologically, to reflect is to embody humility, patience, and discernment. Reflecting on past historical knowledge through our reading of the Scriptures, it should become more apparent and believable to believers that vocation requires them to relate to, love, serve, and devote themselves to others in response to the communal call. The words of Augustine, Calvin, and Edwards are beginning to reveal that a calling represents a privilege and an opportunity for eternal joy. Therefore, it should now be concluded that every act of obedience, despite seeming ordinary, may have eternal significance.

Augustine on God's Call as Life-Giving

The call of God is the source of human life; it is the basis of human vitality. Augustine noted that life without God is life devoid of substance; only through God's call can we find a place of authentic being and purpose (Augustine 1991, 47). The divine call comes not just as a command to obey, but rather as an invitation to share life with God. Whenever God calls in the Bible, there is a call to transformation. When God called Abraham, Abraham left his country and his family without knowing where he would end up, because he believed God (Gen. 12:1–4). The call of God provides a vocation for the believer to experience life marked by joy, obedience, and eternal significance. Augustine asserts that the heart is restless until it finds rest in God: "You have made us for Yourself, and our heart is restless until it rests in You" (Augustine 1998, 49).

The response to God's call entails surrender and action. The calling of Samuel is an example from Scripture where God acted supremely; the believer must respond, but there is a need for attentiveness and willingness (1 Sam. 3:4–10). Augustine noted from the life of Samuel that our stories are illustrations of how a life-giving vocation is the coming together of grace and human response. The believer's challenge is to cultivate a response to God's will marked by humility, patience, and trust. The believer's life becomes animated by God's purpose as opposed to being motivated from a selfish place or the world of human ambition.

Practically, the call of God is present in day-to-day decision-making, which can bring both challenge and joy, such as personal moral choices in the workplace and engaging in acts of mercy in the community. Every minor cadence of the act of obedience is a participation in the larger stories of God's salvation (Ps. 37:5). When believers relate to vocation as a gift from God, the focus of their life shifts from what they create from self to being an agent of God. Sometimes relating to vocation means being happy in our stumbles and pain, and even sometimes finding joy in uncertainty. The reflections of Augustine on God's calling to vocation also remind today's readers that vocation is both personal and communal: by remaining faithful in our response, we deepen our own walk with God and provide a blessing to the larger body of Christ. Finally, God's calling is life-giving because it restores to human hearts their ultimate source and enables them to discern the holy in mundane routines, transforming them into holy acts of service in today's world, so that ordinary work carries the beauty of sacred work (Matt. 5:16).

Calvin on Vocation as Divine Appointment

John Calvin views vocation as a divine appointment, where everything we do—individually, socially, or vocationally—can be an avenue for glorifying God in the service of others (Calvin 1559, 431). The worldview focuses on vocation as a means of prestige, power, or self-promotion; Calvin frames calling as an act of God's sovereign purpose. God equips and positions a believer to carry out responsibilities as part of daily life, not just in public ministry or family; whatever a believer is doing is part of fulfilling a divine appointment. Colossians 3:23–24 declares, "whatever you do, do it heartily, as to the Lord and not to men, knowing that from the Lord you will receive the reward of the inheritance; for you serve the Lord Christ." This passage highlights the relational aspect of vocation, as it is oriented toward God, and how this occurs as part of a divine plan.

Calvin says vocation is not about tasks or roles, but the believer's theological goal is to be conformed to Jesus Christ through obedient living. God ordained a particular life, with unique circumstances, skills, and opportunities, so that every day's work—whether it is teaching, farming, serving, or administration—could be used for building God's kingdom. For example, in the Bible, the detailed account of Joseph's time in Potiphar's house and later in Pharaoh's administration captures how God's appointment in ordinary labor can also deliver extraordinary ends (Gen. 39:2–6). When a believer obeys God in faith, they exercise an opportunity for the work God will accomplish. This is evident in Jacob's prophecy about the land of Joseph, which will bring blessings to the tribe, echoing God's providential hand in making them fertile and productive.

Additionally, Calvin shows that vocation includes the core of responsibility and accountability. Human efforts are always subordinate to God's initiatives; nevertheless, while a believer is engaged faithfully, God is honored as one who does God's ministry (Calvin 1559, 438). This theological principle fosters a healthy humility that protects against pride or self-promotion and encourages believers to view their posts as divinely established instruments. Spiritually, accepting that God has appointed one for a vocation develops a sense of joy, peace, assurance, and purpose in engaging in mundane work as spiritually significant and in the context of eternity. Once the conjuration of 'work' becomes redefined from a casual noun into spiritual action, Christians can experience that they are not living for themselves, but for God (1 Cor. 10:31). Thus, they can find joy in obeying God and serve others as expressions of God's love; every calling, no matter how large or small, has eternal significance.

Edwards on Joyful Obedience

Jonathan Edwards foreshadows and asserts the simple, yet profound, insight that adherence to God is connected to joy; the Christian life is the delight of a gracious response to God's love. Being in love with God means being in alignment with His will (theologically, the term "purpose" is used). Living in harmony with God represents the highest level of spiritual maturity, and delight produced by God's purposes working in us harmonizes the will, heart, and mind of the believer. This joy is internal and relational; as believers participate in God's blessings, they reflect a sense of belonging and value as participants in God's redemptive purposes. Do not forget Psalm 119:2: "Blessed are those who keep his testimonies, who seek him with their whole heart." The blessedness of obedience is not merely external; rather, it is internally experienced delight that flows from communion with God.

Edwards's theology counters the maximalist rhetoric that religious disciplines are burdensome or austere. Instead, Edwards presents the act of submission to God's will as an obligation to pray, serve, or make an ethical decision, thereby being free to obey God. For example, biblical stories demonstrate that faithful obedience, such as Abraham offering Isaac (Gen. 22:1–14), can produce the joy, trust, and intimacy that come from allegiance to God's will. The believer's similarity to God's purposes allows for work, relationships, and the believer's discipline to be reformatted and reconstructed to express delight.

Joyful obedience practically means discerning God's will in everyday living, practicing prayer, reading, and reflecting on God's word. Edwards recognizes that joy and obedience practiced can ultimately have an impact on the believer to shape character, help nurture humility, and develop love for others, like a virtuous spiritual formation loop (Edwards 1746, 117). Edwards emphasizes that the internal pleasure of spiritual joy helps build resilience in the face of difficulty, as spiritual joy is anchored not in the distressing life experiences but in God's eternal faithfulness. Choosing to view "obedience as delight" allows the believer to freely move towards intimacy, instead of remaining in a performance-based engagement with God.

Concludingly, Edwards provides a coherent theological framework for understanding joy and obedience as cause and effect; when a person follows Christ, they ultimately receive a reward in the joyful development of their heart, in line with the divine will. The consequence of developing joy is that the believer can deepen their love for God and their neighbor, and further experience the peace that comes with entering into an anxiety-free state of joy (Matt. 22:37–39). Joy and obedience expedite expressing the abundant life Jesus speaks of (John 10:10) as a spiritual discipline and experience.

Living Out Our Calling Today

Christian vocation is a reality, not simply as an abstract idea, nor is it limited to religious or sacred spaces. Instead, the community of the faithful lives it out in the normal rhythm of life—in work, family, and community, and through every decision. Since faith and work are integrated, every activity embodied in the world, however insignificant, contributes to God's work of redemption. Colossians 3:23–24 encourages Christians to work heartily, "as for the Lord and not for men." These times remind the faithful that even in their faithful work, they offer it up as a spiritual sacrifice (Hauerwas 2001, 192). Calvin notes that God asserts particular callings on each person's life, and that even secular tasks can be used to serve the Lord (Calvin 1559, 431). Framing work as sacred can foster habits of integrity, diligence, and humility, and actively resist the temptation to define worth through accolades, achievements, or recognition.

Love through service to family and community relates vocation to relational reality. Galatians 5:13 encourages believers to love and serve one another, emphasizing that obedience to God cannot be separated from genuine care for others. For example, Stott recognizes that family and neighborhood provide immediate contexts for demonstrating love like Christ, and we form character through faith, including acts of patience, forgiveness, and attentiveness (Stott 1994, 88). Some practical examples of loving service include mentoring a colleague, helping a neighbor with a problem, or nurturing children in faith and virtue. In communion with each person, believers are called to share Christ's love and offer the kingdom of God as heavenly visions, lived reality.

Humility as a leader reinforces the trust that authority is to serve others, not an avenue for greatness. Jesus articulated this point, defining God's kingdom as based upon service, not authority (Matt. 20:26–28). Humility in leadership embodies active listening, empowerment of others, and working for the common good, leading to trust and cultivating a community attuned to God's desires.

Living a daily life of choices that align with God's mission, in all avenues of engagement, forms strands of faithful obedience. Proverbs 3:5–6 reminds us to trust God in all of our ways. Choices regarding ethics, finances, and relationships can be acts of worship in response to God's will, grounded in prayer and Scripture, as a means to develop devotion and discipline (Hauerwas 2001, 56).

Walking in joy, healing, and love through obedience exemplifies the holistic practice of this idea. Bonhoeffer notes that costly discipleship not only shapes the environment for others but also transforms a person by eliciting the heart to foster spiritual maturity in wholeness (Bonhoeffer 1959, 123). In doing so, it forms the intersection between vocation, devotion, and service, revealing an unencumbered life for themselves and others and suggesting that navigating the calling of God is equally available in all spheres of their lives.

Integrating Faith and Work

Christian vocation extends beyond the church and into the world, particularly in the workplace. Christians should recognize that integrating faith and work involves seeing our primary work not as a means to make a living, but as a means to show the kingdom of God. In Colossians 3:23–24, Paul encourages believers, "Whatever you do, work heartily, as for the Lord and not for men, knowing that from the Lord you will receive the inheritance as your reward." This invitation reframes even the most menial or tedious task as a form of worship; it places spirituality within the context of ordinary life. Thomas Aquinas said that human action participates in God's providence when it is rightly ordered to the good (Aquinas 1947, II-II, q. 64). So, efforts to make ethical decisions, work with diligence, and be as creative as possible are not peripheral, but central sides of Christian work: divine vocation.

Faithful work also cultivates virtues such as patience, humility, and integrity that counteract the cultural drive for self-gain, recognition, or competition in the workplace. According to Dallas Willard, when believers approach work from a contemplative perspective, the daily grind can become a space for spiritual growth and an opportunity to deepen character formation, developing reliance on God to navigate the entire system of character that develops through work (Willard 1998, 212). Similarly, Henri Nouwen states that when believers engage in prayer while doing menial work—work we do every day—we can transform what was mundane into a meaningful reflection, love, and relationship, even in the face of the obligation of repetition (Nouwen 1981, 47). Therefore, work is a vehicle not only for exhibiting the kingdom of God but also for becoming a witness to the kingdom of God to coworkers, clients, and the community through good moral behavior, a strong work ethic, and serving others.

Making work practical also means making decisions with discernment, meaning God's intentions. Good stewardship of time, money, and talent in the professional sphere means ensuring that what we undertake as professionals is not only carried out for self-serving purposes but also because it glorifies God. C.S. Lewis reminds us that mundane, ordinary actions, if we hold them in proper orientation toward God, can carry spiritual significance (Lewis 1960, 112). Christian integrity, justice, and compassion create spaces that ensure workplaces reflect the values of the kingdom and foster communities unified by respect, accountability, and service.

Ultimately, integrating faith and work means that something once seen by some as secular can be viewed as sacred—day-to-day work can be seen as a divine vocation. Implementing this vision creates a holistic spirituality and a sense of vocation, devotion, and ethical work that can become a lifestyle, nurturing spiritual transformation and community impact in the world. The work we do is always a witness to God's proximity to us in our situation, and it results in satisfaction and purpose for the believer (Matt. 5:16).

Loving Through Service in Family and Community

When a believer is mindful and aware of her family and community, Christian love, as portrayed and lived out in Scripture, is exemplified most tangibly in her service to them. Serving sacrificially is both a humble choice and a relational awareness. Paul indicates in Galatians 5:13, "For you, brethren, have been called to liberty; only do not use liberty as an opportunity for the flesh, but through love serve one another." The phrase, "serve one another," is not a suggestion that serving one another is an option to the vocation of a believer. Families and neighbors provide a practical context for expressing Christlike love, as the power of tangible care that sustains our ordinary life is grounding (Stott 1994, 88). It is in those shared and created spaces where discipleship is not a theory but a vocation to look with eyes wide open and perform active discipleship through words and deeds in the landscape of our daily lives, conversations, and decisions, all for the sake of God's grace.

The practice of love as an active response to love of Christ depicts Jesus taking the example in the parable of the Good Samaritan (Luke 10:33–34), where love cannot be abstractly ascribed to humanity. However, in practice, love is often intertwined with the needs of others, particularly those who are marginalized and the most vulnerable. Love in relation to family and community follows a similar pattern, involving giving and receiving attention, sharing burdens, forgiving wrongs, and utilizing time, energy, and resources to develop and nurture relationships with one another. As Brennan Manning posits, true love flows from an awareness of God's grace, which fosters a relationship rather than a desire for identity or reward (Manning 1993, 65). The practice of love, therefore, becomes an antidote to impatience, humility a counter to pride, and grace dissolves self-interest.

Living out this vocation in practice also requires mindfulness and intent. Every day, in various roles that define our identities as parents, siblings, spouses, and neighbors, we constantly set aside our self-interest for the sake of others. Along with spiritual practices such as prayer, reflection, reading Scripture, and supporting one another in our Christian faith, service has its locus in spiritual formation, attempting to cultivate love in response to the love of Christ, rather than merely checking off a list.

According to Henri Nouwen, we can share service, whether through God-memory through our ritual and shared experiences or creating God-memories of love through our day-to-day relationships, all of which turn the ordinary into encounters with the Holy Presence of God, where together we pursue personal holiness and holiness as a community (Nouwen 1994, 89).

Living out love in ordinariness in our everyday lives will incarnate in Christians the kingdom that is seen by the world as one of mercy, justice, and compassion. Some communities strive to express the sacrifice of loving one another, bearing witness to God's reign as a community united in love. God creates these communities, where members have the opportunity to be witnesses of hope and illumination, as they experience restoration, reconciliation, encouragement, and spiritual growth together. Service as practice resides in an embodied context of vocation, spirituality, and relational agency, suggesting that being called by God encompasses deeds of service, acts of care, and expressions of love for others. Love as a response in family and community practice is the way and the fruit of a Jesus follower's life, ongoing transformation, and continued movement of creating newness in families, communities, and the world (1 John 4:11).

Choosing Humility in Leadership

Humility is the foundation of Christ-centered leadership, standing in stark contrast to worldly models that emphasize prestige, power, and self-interest. Jesus outlines this principle clearly: "Whoever desires to become great among you, let him be your servant" (Matt. 20:26). Leadership is founded on selflessness, service, and accountability. John Calvin reminds us that for leaders, "every human authority is, according to the divine order, a trust given by God for the benefit of others" (Calvin 1559, 438). As leaders, we steward God-given trust and must seek to honor God's purposes in our leadership, steering clear of pride, ambition, and the misuse of influence for our own personal gain.

Humility in leadership encompasses listening, being receptive to feedback and correction, and prioritizing the well-being of others over personal interests. As Augustine points out, greatness in God's eyes is measured not by our worldly success, but by our love and faithfulness in service (Augustine 1998, 144). Humble leaders earn trust from those they lead, building a culture of collaboration, exemplifying Christ to others, and creating an environment where others can flourish both spiritually and in their organizations. The demonstration of servant leadership reveals a paradox: actual authority is best exercised by providing gentle guidance, encouragement, and sacrificial acts of service, rather than domination or coercive authority.

Scripture shares stories that reveal what humble leadership looks like. Moses is characterized by reluctance but is entirely reliant on God's leading (Exod. 3–4). The testing of David's heart demonstrates a prioritization of humility before ambition within God's will (1 Sam. 16:7). Together, these examples show that humility requires letting go and listening for God's directions while being sensitive to those we lead. Henri Nouwen notes that humble leaders relate to others' experiences, creating space for others to feel heard, seen, valued, and represented, thereby forming God's ethics of the kingdom in our everyday lives (Nouwen 1981, 67).

When we reflect on the application of humility in the present day, we can understand its broader implications in our families, workplaces, churches, and civic engagement. Choosing humility is to be countercultural against the inclination to self-promote in a world inundated with self-promotion. It is to model love, service, and accountability that takes into account the other. Through consistent, grace-filled choices, leadership can become a space for honoring God's purposes in the world and modeling God's kingdom in concrete ways. Humble leadership not only engages in God's mission, but it also shapes both the context and the leader's character, slowly developing patience, empathy, and reliance on God's guiding voice.

Daily Decisions Aligned with God's Mission

A believer's life is a life of decisions. In the same ways, we constantly make decisions, day to day, even in seemingly trivial matters, such as the use of our time and resources, to larger decisions where we might wrestle with a moral dilemma or a relational situation. Proverbs 3:5-6 tells us, "Trust in the Lord with all your heart, and do not lean on your own understanding; in all your ways acknowledge Him, and He shall direct your paths." One way to think about these verses from the scriptures is that they are telling us not to view daily obedience as incidental, but rather as a conscious commitment to our own and God's mission. We need to maintain that ethical discernment and faithful action is not something that only is produced in a moment, or because we have an epiphany, often while deeply and passionately in crisis, but rather ethical discernment and faithful action is at best a habit, nurtured by the consistent action of listening to Scripture, prayer, and the use of spiritual or church disciplines where we seek help from the Holy Spirit (Hauerwas 2001, 56).

So, in all of the moments where believers and disciples intentionally think decision-making relationally with spiritual discernment—even during the most trivial acts of faith, where we may not be consciously aware of how our faith is emerging—are practical ways in which believers thoughtfully engage to take full advantage of God's call and become part of God's mission for the continued growth, establishment, and expansion of the kingdom of God and the love, integrity, compassion, discernment, and frailty of humanness we have. Aligning the everyday choices of our lives with God's mission is an exercise in awareness and intentionality. Every decision we make—including our faithful stewardship of our finances, our engagement at work, and our anticipation and response to requests from family, friends, and our community—provides another opportunity to enact God's divine intention. A familiar example of this is the parable of the Good Samaritan (Luke 10:30–37). One individual had the opportunity to stop and care for another person who was hurt. The Good Samaritan was intentional in his decision to turn the time of travel into a world-changing, kingdom-focused activity. In the same way, the many small choices believers make together in faith are the actions that shape setting, character, culture, and communicate God's love through a person, action, or attitude. Dallas Willard describes the significance of personal, spiritual transformation when he says that transformation ultimately takes place in the mundaneness of daily life, where obedience becomes reflexive, habitual, and formative rather than episodic (Willard 1998, 212).

Additionally, it alters our understanding of vocation in relation to daily living within and around God's mission. Decisions that we often consider "just routine"—such as how we respond to episodes of relational conflict, how to prioritize obligations during preparation, or how to use our time—can be made with kingdom-focused intentionality and have eternal consequences when we practice awareness and attentiveness to the reality that these too are kingdom decisions. Henri Nouwen reminds us that an awareness of God's leading in our lives gives us both the opportunity and responsibility to make decisions, as well as to deal with the consequences and actions taken through a lens of love, justice, and mercy (Nouwen 1994, 59).

Cultivating a sense of awareness and intentionality in our daily living requires time, patience, discernment, and humility to acknowledge our vulnerability and, at the same time, God's sovereignty over our lives. A life lived under the guidance of God through holistic spirituality ensures that every action is ethically and prayerfully directed by our kingdom vocation toward human flourishing—both individual and communal—ultimately demonstrating what the transformative power of Christ looks like. Trusting God's leading in our decisions means we participate in the unfolding of God's kingdom, the fulfillment of God's mission, and obedience to God's redemptive purpose (Matt. 6:33).

Jeyran Main

Walking in Joy, Healing, and Love Through Obedience

Obedience to God is the mechanism whereby Christians are transformed, from the inside out, and develop joy, healing, and love. "Blessed are those who keep His testimonies, and who seek Him with the whole heart" (Ps. 119:2). This illustrates that blessings and fulfillment are two sides of the same coin of faithful obedience to God's Word. To submit to God is more than merely obeying rules; it is relational obedience—a responsiveness to God's love that fosters closeness of spirit. Bonhoeffer may be describing costly obedience when he insists that cost entails sacrifice, risk, and vulnerability, which is formative of spiritual maturity because it builds character and makes the believer a participant in God's redemptive work in the world (Bonhoeffer 1959, 123). Obedience is an act of commitment to participating in God's ongoing mission; it yields joy that is based on the presence of God's Spirit in the believer's life, rather than on circumstance.

Healing comes after obedience. When a believer's heart surrenders to God, the weight of pride, anxiety, and ego eases. By relinquishing their desire for control, a believer also relinquishes fear and doubt, allowing God to realign priorities, shift desires, and build trust. Nouwen notes: "When obedience leaves more room for God's transfiguring love to enter their inner life, it can create wholeness in the parts of their brokenness" (Nouwen 1981, 73), and wholeness in the realm of loving others as well. The walk embodies spirit and active involvement, addressing both spiritual and practical aspects of living, caring for one's family, one's neighborhood, and the collective world we inhabit. Jesus' call to abide (John 15:10-11) suggests that the ability to experience joy and love is contingent upon the intimacy of the abiding relationship with the Savior.

When actions of love occur as a result of obediently relating to God, love is effortless and a natural overflow of a heart attuned to God. Actions of kindness, service, and generous sacrifice emanate from a heart filled and renewed by the Holy Spirit, informed by Scripture. This love is not performative, but rather love that creates community, restores relationships, and, in the world of witness, bears eternal signs of God's freshness in the Kingdom. John Stott reminds us that "obedience and love must never be separated; to serve Jesus means to know love and to love concretely" (Stott 1994, 142), through action, deed, or skill.

Hence, joy, healing, and love as a walk unite vocation, devotion, and relational ministry in a single rhythm of life. It demonstrates that fidelity to God's call creates an abundance of life not just for the believer, but for those who surround and support them, evidencing the fullness of Christ's teachings and modeling, and demonstrating the Kingdom of God at work in the present time.

Chapter 6

Living in Surprise

The Reversal of Life's Expectations

Life rarely unfolds like we would like it to. We think through the steps, time frame, and intended results, but life tosses some unforeseen variables our way. The Scriptures repeatedly teach us that God's ways are not just different in meaning, but also in action. In fact, "My thoughts are not your thoughts; nor are your ways My ways," says the Lord (Isa. 55:8). What we must recognize is that the differences are not coincidental, but rather formative as God is actively taking us on a journey of spiritual formation and greater reliance upon Him (Packer 1973, 215).

The, at times, surprising (and counterintuitive) lesson of Jesus can be found in Matthew, chapter 5—the Beatitudes. "Blessed are those who mourn, for they shall be comforted" (Matt. 5:4). Often, as is our human experience (and proclivity), we assume a blessing means joy, success, or content; however, in Christ's teaching, He is declaring that despair can be a means to divine comfort. Mourning, while challenging and painful, can open our souls to God's sustaining presence, as we may experience blessings from the experiences we have lost or resisted. As Ortlund notes,

God subverts our assumptions about life through Christ's teaching, which highlights how often the way to spiritual fullness is contrary to our worldviews (Ortlund 2012, 88).

Like mourning, trials—regarded as painful experiences—are a regular part of life, albeit unwanted. James reminds us, "Count it all joy when you fall into various trials, knowing that the testing of your faith produces patience" (James 1:2–3). Our human tendency is to avoid that which is painful; however, God can, in part, use this discomfort to stretch and develop our reflective character and reliance upon Him. Here lies a compelling paradox: what we often consider bad by human rationale, when surrendered to God, can actually become a trajectory of grace, perseverance, and victory (Packer 1973, 221).

A better understanding of life's reversals encompasses a mindset shift. We are invited into a trust that God's timing, methods, and outcomes are bigger than our expectations or understanding. By learning to let go of our expectations of God's work—even when things do not go according to our plans—we open ourselves to hidden blessings in our suffering, comfort through mourning, and growth in our trials. As we learn to lean on God's sovereignty and leadership, we find that life's reversals can become portals for change and hope.

God's Ways vs. Human Plans

Human beings, by nature, are planners. They set goals and expect specific plans to produce expected outcomes. They behave as if hard work and good planning equal success. However, our scriptures tell us repeatedly that God has the capacity to think farther than humans do. The Lord says, "For My thoughts are not your thoughts nor are your ways My ways" (Isa. 55:8). This should remind Christians that life does not always unfold as we plan. God's plans are not arbitrary; they are systematic, designed to develop us into trusting, obedient, and spiritually mature individuals (Packer 1973, 215).

The struggle between human planning and God's providence is a common theme throughout scripture. Joseph had his life as he planned it taken away when his brothers sold him into slavery (Gen. 50:20). For all intents and purposes, Joseph's planning certainly probably felt sidetracked; however, it was the Lord's sovereign plan that positioned him to save the lives of many from famine. The example shows us God can redeem what humans call a disaster. In some of his writings, Ortlund notes that Christ's mission consistently inverts human assumptions and standards, or norms, and that God often does the same, contrary to human expectation (Ortlund 2012, 88).

This dynamic is evident in more subtle ways every day. People plan careers, relationships, and life events, and suddenly life is interrupted by loss, health reasons, or unexpected job offers, and they have to put their plans aside and respond. Rather than being defeated by the moment, we should recognize that we should trust God for his sovereign plan. Proverbs 19:21 tells us, "There are many plans in a man's heart, nevertheless the Lord's counsel—that will stand." Humans can only often plan on what we know—or think we know—about ourselves and our current circumstances. Nevertheless, God's plans—while comprehensive—have no limits, i.e., eternity, wisdom, and mercy.

Submitting our plans to God does not mean we stop being responsible; it just changes our viewpoint. We can relinquish certainty and accept being still and trusting. Turns in life, 'detours', are often God's plan; they are not setbacks, but invitations. Invitations to trust Him to allow us to see Him as wisdom, provision, and/or faithfulness. As we trust God in our situation and allow ourselves to rest, returning to what we know about God, it is mysterious, yet ultimately for our good and His glory.

The Paradox of Trials as Pathways to Growth

What we often regard as struggles in life could be obstacles we want to avoid. The Bible offers a helpful perspective on trials, viewing them as opportunities for growth. When James says to believers, "Count it all joy when you fall into various trials, knowing that the testing of your faith produces patience" (James 1:2–3), this is a somewhat counterintuitive teaching. Rather than simply viewing struggles as harm, we can see them as fertile ground for character, perseverance, and stronger faith.

The paradox is with respect to what we anticipated, not necessarily God's plan. We often think of blessings as ease and struggles as ill fortune—but God turns this perspective upside down. Trials are not evidence of a lack of provision by God; they are a provision. Peter says, "Beloved, do not think it strange concerning the fiery trial which is to try you, as though some strange thing happened to you; but rejoice to the extent that you partake of Christ's sufferings" (1 Pet. 4:12–13). In trials, the believer can identify with Christ, be tested in faith, and develop a genuine dependency on their God, that suffering alone can bring (Packer 1973, 228).

Joseph understands this principle. He suffered betrayal and imprisonment for many years, which must have felt like ill fortune. Yet, it had set him up for saving the nations from famine (Gen. 50:20). The believer today experiences trials too: loss, disappointment, or personal struggles, even though they may seem inconsequential along their journey. In the spiritual realm, we are actually preparing to have wisdom, compassion, and even faith in God's ready providence and plans, rather than their prosperity.

To see trials as a pathway to maturity means that you are not, "from now on," just looking at ease or opportunity to flee. You will appreciate and welcome the possibility of something transformative in struggle.

God's intentions are far more weighty than the temporary pain we experience from not driving through. He is developing us into containers of his grace and strength. We rest our trust in Him in "trial" (because we are unable to focus on our own behavior). We start to realize that the experiences we want to avoid may be the very ones that take our faith to new depths of maturity. Our character increases (Ortlund 2012, 95).

Joseph: From Prison to Palace

Joseph's life illustrates how God often acts in enigmatic ways, using even what appears unfortunate for a divine purpose. When administered betrayal by his brothers, sold into slavery, and wrongfully imprisoned, it would be easy to see disaster after disaster in Joseph's life from a human standpoint. Yet, the Scriptures do witness to God's providential provision in Joseph's life: "You meant evil against me, but God meant it for good, to bring it about that many people should be kept alive, as they are today" (Gen. 50:20). The saga demonstrates that God's providential purpose can continue to function despite the semblance of chaos or injustice in one's life.

Medieval theologians have much to say about the interaction between human actions and God's will. For example, Thomas Aquinas expounds that God can and does bring about good from those who do evil, because of God's providential will—literally in line with the example of Joseph (Aquinas 1947, II-II, q. 83, art. 3). There was no moral justification for Joseph's brothers to betray and imprison him; however, through those acts God dealt with those agents and brought interactions to fulfill His providential plan. In concluding this section, Aquinas states that God's wisdom is utterly beyond ours, and the point is that even in those situations, He is configuring the very circumstances to make the best of all that He created.

Joseph's experience demonstrates that virtue and patience do matter in the course of God's plan. In his exegesis, Origen states that suffering shapes the soul (McNamer 2021, 199) and cultivates spiritual maturity in believers, a process that takes time to teach them to endure and wait (Origen 1999, 215). Joseph's account—from Potiphar's house to imprisonment—shows that even at that stage, Joseph was obedient, waiting for God's purpose to unfold at the appropriate time without vengeance.

Furthermore, Joseph's life reminds us that there is a broader way to postulate what God is doing as we find ourselves in the apparently unknowing. Early Church theologians, such as John Chrysostom, posited that God works through suffering so that humble and faithful people who become blessings for others emerge (Chrysostom 1986, 122). Through stepping into the unknown and entrusting God's providence, Joseph transitioned from being an apparent nobody to an influential role, ultimately becoming the grand instrument of saving not just his family but entire nations from starvation.

To reiterate, Joseph's journey is a reminder to believers that God's providence is still at work, even when nothing appears to be going our way. Life's unexpected curves, which require us to depend on God's providence and act faithfully, create barriers and obstacles, turning suffering into an opportunity for blessing, leadership, teaching, and spiritual maturity.

Peter's Transformation After Failure

Peter's experience illustrates how failure can catalyze growth and transformation through God's grace. Peter made a bold pledge to be loyal to Jesus, and yet he denied Jesus three times on the night of Jesus' arrest (Matt. 26:69–75). Peter's failure revealed his fear and weakness, and it was an unfortunate blow. Yet Scripture articulates something essential for us to know: our failures do not constrain God's plans and purposes. Jesus restored Peter after the Resurrection, asking the question three times, "Do you love Me?" and ordering Peter to "Feed My sheep" (John 21:17). The totality of a three-part re-establishing, in contrast to Peter's previous three-part denial of Jesus, demonstrated Jesus' unwavering commitment to Peter. Peter's failure became a launch point for his restored ministry—not one of mere reactionary behavioral change driven by fear. However, one of the most significant sources of courage is generated through a deeper and more humble process of leadership, teaching us that God's grace can transform failure into a source of strength.

The theologians of the Reformation offer insightful commentary on the nature of the redemption process. Responding to God's grace, Martin Luther clearly stated that it is grace—not merit—that initiates spiritual renewal. Peter's restoration ultimately expressed Luther's persistent claim that God's forgiveness is, and can only be given freely to believers, allowing them to move past their failure into active participation with God in ministry (Luther 1957, 128). In a similar spirit, John Calvin noted that God often uses the difficulties and failures of a believer's life as formative trials to foster humility, dependence on God's power, and the perseverance required for effective ministry (Calvin 1960, 347). In Calvin's view, Peter's fall and restoration also illustrate humankind's weak nature, while being places where God's sanctifying power is at work—where failure does not disqualify a person from service but prepares them to serve from a heart grounded in empathy and dependence on the Spirit of God.

Many contemporary voices echo this truth. J. I. Packer asserts that God's grace can transform weakness into a place of growth, enabling the believer to respond with a stronger and even more faithful response (Packer 1973, 240). Peter's denial was a teaching moment, not only for Peter but also for the early church, of a relentless divine mercy that can, and will always, interact with and take account of human frailty. Peter's transformation calls all believers today to know that failure in community is not an end, but a starting point for God's redemptive work. Peter's experience continues to remind us of core themes in Scripture: knowing God who restores is knowing God who equips—taking our human weakness and transforming a person into an instrument for glorifying God.

Paul's Thorn: Weakness Perfected in God's Power

Paul's wisdom regarding his "thorn in the flesh" provides insight into God's power to redeem and reveal His strength through weakness. Paul rightly states, "…My grace is sufficient for you, for my strength is made perfect in weakness" (2 Cor. 12:9). God did not take away the infliction, but instead sustained Paul with it, so that Paul could recognize that he was never meant to rely on his own strength, but that all his strength comes from God. The paradox reveals a profound spiritual reality: God often turns barriers into opportunities for grace, growth, and influence.

The theologians of the Early Church had ideas about how suffering and weakness can be redemptive. Origen explains that affliction exists to purify the soul, allowing it to break free from worldly dependence and become solely dependent on God (Origen 1999, 228). In the midst of suffering and weakness, the person is being shaped in grace and formed in humility, patience, and spiritual discernment. Paul's thorn in the flesh is a powerful portrayal of this: prolonged limitation leads to persistent dependence upon God and the ability to showcase His strength in ways that success and ability cannot.

Likewise, medieval theologians were interested in the tension of human weakness and God's providence. In his teachings, Thomas Aquinas suggested that God allows suffering because it serves as a means to a greater good, for example, when virtue is developed or enhanced. The soul is being prepared for an eternal end (Aquinas 1947, II-II, q. 83, art. 3). If our view of Paul's thorn in the flesh is as punishment, we are missing out on the tremendous opportunity to appreciate the complementary modality of divine strength mediated through suffering and the extension of humanity that bears great potential for the developed embodiment of faith in God.

The perseverance Paul demonstrated formed his character and protected his faith, arguably preparing him for a ministry characterized only by God's sustaining providence and strength. For the believer, just like Paul, nothing is accomplished apart from the revelation of heavenly virtue. Paul willingly recognized his weakness as the means by which to glorify God and calls believers to lean into their limitations with trust and humility. Where the world encourages grievance for one's hardships, a believer's life is meant to receive hardship as an opportunity to engage with God, who acts through and in the believer's life.

As Chrysostom reminds us, the faithful, while being offered blessed immortality, still have to reckon with constant pain and experience the grace of God extended—and at the same time, the affliction of God's glory is transformed into their immediate reality, made available for them (Chrysostom 1986, 135). Finally, Paul's experience instructs both him and the believer that rather than weakness being a limitation, it is, in fact, God's strength, opening up possibilities for transformation. To yield to God's power, lean into dependence on Him, and trust God in His infinite wisdom is perhaps an acknowledgment for believers that what began as a burden or grievance is a means by which God brings to completion the work He is developing, etching His glory, and breathing endurance and greater faith into the faithful. Peter's transformation challenges the contemporary reader to reframe failings as opportunities for restoration and development in God. Dismissed failure by trusting God and humble surrender means obediently responding one more time to God's invitation to be entrusted to feed His sheep. Through humbling surrender, past failures may serve as opportunities for the believer to acquire and develop spiritually in their pursuit of maturity. Peter, like failure, does not indicate the absence of a future—as God meets us in our failure, prepares us with the strength for greater work, and leaves space for what will remain: strength. Easter remains, and Pentecost turned us into mobilizing agents for God.

Joy in the Surprising Ways of God

Joy comes as a surprise to the human heart, as our expectations and life seldom match up. That being said, God has a unique way of providing surprise to develop joy and depth of spirit. C.S. Lewis once suggested, "what we call 'goodness' in God is often beyond our expectations of goodness and that makes the experiences of joy exceed our ideas of what could be produced or manufactured" (Lewis 1960, 114). Joy can be experienced when believers relinquish their drive to be in control of themselves and their lives, and instead delight in God's will; they then embrace the otherwise unreasonable or unplanned elements of experiences, moments, and results.

I have often had to exercise faith for God's provision with respect to God's timing, when my circumstances felt beyond manageability. Henri Nouwen describes how God's grace is often experienced as elusive, and grace that works through small, hidden, or unexpected means often transforms ordinary experiences into extraordinary encounters with joy (Nouwen 1996, 88). The feeding of the 5,000 exemplifies this principle: creating the extraordinary from a minuscule offering in extreme need (John 6:1–14). The argument presented by Richard Bauckham highlights the relational aspects of God's providence, focusing not on moderating events but rather on orchestrating historical events for God's purpose while inviting humans to participate (Bauckham 2008, 143). Recognizing and embracing such experiences can deepen faith and foster spiritual expectation, leading to delight even when life is incomprehensible.

Life offers numerous additional opportunities to experience God's surprising grace. Nouwen argues that faithful persons who have long paid attention to God may lose touch with the idea of God's presence, which allows joy to emerge in ordinary routines of domestic life, ways of life, and service to others, bringing about an expectation of enjoyment and fair leisure (Nouwen 1996, 105). Brennan Manning further develops

Nouwen's thinking by arguing that God's grace often collides with us as we experience weakness or incompetence, resulting in a spirit of joy that is not dependent on life's conditions, circumstances, or accomplishments, but instead rooted in God's presence and awareness of God's favor (Manning 1990, 67). When God provides gifts, grace, or goodness, and believers recognize and receive them with thanksgiving, they can experience joy despite contextual reality, personal condition, or worldly measures of self-fulfillment and success.

Joy in the surprise of God begins with availability, trust, and awareness. Effort alone does not limit joy; God provides joy through the experience of His intentional, loving hand in the midst of uncertainty. By seeing God's provision, sharing in the joy of an unexpected gift, and receiving His grace in everyday life, believers experience a joy that endures change, is transformational, and is rooted in the truth of His presence and the freedom of choice.

Finding Delight in the Unexpected

Life is often accented with surprises that contain unknown blessings beyond the imagination of our minds. God delights in acting in ways that take us beyond what we have thought or imagined, allowing His believers to experience the unknowing. C.S. Lewis suggests that the deepest enjoyment comes not from our control over what our lives are like, but from allowing God to exercise His wisdom in sovereignty, which may sometimes remain unknown and mysterious (Lewis 1960, 114). Suppose we are no longer preoccupied with guessing or controlling what will happen. In that case, we can bear witness to God's delight in us as we become fully present.

Dallas Willard presents the idea of engaging in the present reality of the Kingdom of God in our everyday experience, rather than as a distant hope for the future. Engaging in awareness of God's presence—often through observation of His action in the ordinary rhythms of life—reduces barriers to experiencing delight, allowing us to appreciate that joy can exist even when we are not at our best (Willard 1998, 72). The operational view of attention helps transform unexpected or surprising moments into joy-filled moments as we notice God's presence in small, often undetected things.

The unexpected arrival of delight often upsets conventional pictures of success, safety, or comfort. Contemporary spiritual writers note that delight often arrives when we trust God's timing and intent, things we do not, in reality, control. Henri Nouwen reminds us that trust sometimes requires accepting the unexpected, inviting a posture of spirit that is flexible and open to God's unknown joy as an expression of love and care (Nouwen 1996, 88). When delight comes from the unknown, it is often accompanied by humility, openness, and gratitude that arise from experiencing the unforeseen, as we continue to build resilience in life's uncertain adventures.

Recognizing God's presence and work in unexpected moments is also a part of the spiritual formation process. Brennan Manning notes that much of our understanding of God comes through experiences of weakness, vulnerability, or a lack of expectation, all of which occur under God's grace and care. God's grace teaches us to find joy not in worldly expectations, but by abandoning ourselves to the presence of His delight (Manning 1990, 67). Believers are encouraged to embrace the unknown, becoming familiar with God while being nourished through the ordinariness of life.

Delighting in the unexpected invites believers to engage with curiosity, faith, and a sense of joy. It counters one of the most persistent distractions of the human condition: the need to control. Instead, it cultivates a posture in which we can see God's grace and goodness and receive joy through surprises, setbacks, or uninvited occurrences.

Experiencing God's Provision When It Defies Logic

God's provision often exceeds human understanding and challenges the ways humans consider reasonable. The Bible is filled with examples of God's provision, proving repeatedly that His provision does not align with human expectations. The feeding of the 5,000 (John 6:1–14) is an example of the illogical extension of God's provision through a small offering of loaves and fish multiplied to meet the needs of thousands. Examples of God's unexpected provisions in the lives of followers of Christ serve to remind them of God's limitless wisdom, which is beyond human comprehension, and that His provision can come in surprising, unconventional, or multiple forms, disrupting human conventions.

Respected biblical scholar F. F. Bruce identifies God's providential work as He supernaturally orchestrates human encounters through both ordinary and extraordinary situations, aligning them with His purposes (Bruce 1988, 162). What seems humanly limited or improbable may become abundant in the hands of God. Although people might attempt to witness God through organized faith, it often takes awareness and attentiveness to recognize that provision can emerge through ancillary means because God does not conform to human assumptions.

Similarly, Abraham Kuyper observes that God's provision extends beyond individual needs to encompass social and historical dimensions (Kuyper 1898, 43). What is miraculous is not merely a feature of biblical history; God provides care for creation and community—from temporal life to eternal destiny. Trusting God in provision requires both personal trust and acknowledgment of God's wisdom, as much of the outcome of God's providential orchestration surpasses human vision.

Experiencing God's providential provision in unusual ways also fosters spiritual maturity. Brennan Manning observes that God's provision often emerges through human weakness, reminding believers of their dependence on God rather than on human effort or reasoning (Manning 1990, 67). When one witnesses God's care in unlikely circumstances, they are strengthened, humbled, and genuinely grateful.

Expecting God's provision may seem illogical because it requires trust, patience, and openness. Yet God provides opportunities for care in all aspects of life. By embracing unexpected realities and maintaining awareness of God's provision, believers learn that God's ways and provision—material, emotional, or spiritual—are higher than human ways (Isa. 55:9). Recognizing provision in unexpected forms cultivates humility and fosters a deeper awareness of God's reality, often leading to experiences of surprise, delight, and gratitude.

Nouwen on Finding Joy in Daily Grace

Henri Nouwen points out that joy is not found in momentous or accomplished achievements. According to Nouwen, in *The Life of the Beloved*, the realization of God's presence in the ordinary dimensions of life cultivates a type of joy that accumulates and permeates beyond time and context: "Joy happens when we allow ourselves to be surprised by God" (Nouwen 1996, 105). Joy emerges when believers begin to pay attention to God's gracious actions and welcome those moments in which they encounter God as simple expressions of love.

C. S. Lewis asserts that the joy of God is frequently two-fold, with God revealing Himself through surprising moments: "What you realize is that joy is not a humble thing that reflects the good, convenience, and pleasure of the world but instead the goodness, and aesthetic that connects believers to the revelation of God's presence" (Lewis 1960, 114). Lewis continues to describe the beauty of humans learning to notice moments that go beyond the obvious bonds of life—to be aware of how the fullness of human life involves experiences of grace.

Dallas Willard further develops this idea, noting that spiritual disciplines, such as prayer, reflection, or intentional service, create environments where joy can arise. Paying attention to the grace of God and engaging intentionally in spiritual formation provides believers with opportunities to recognize God in surprising ways (Willard 1998, 72). The depth of these experiences can assist the spiritual person, as the discipline becomes an opportunity for the soul to experience God's provision, guidance, and presence while immersed in the routine aspects of human existence, allowing joy to become a natural component of their spiritual life.

Brennan Manning highlights that God's grace meets believers in their weakness, vulnerability, and imperfection. It is in welcoming God—where the grace of God's love replaces attempts to arrange one's perception of self-sufficiency and perfection—that believers have the opportunity to experience joy (Manning 1990, 67). Nouwen continues this exploration, expanding on the notion of joy as a receptive state of the soul to God's presence in ordinary demands, burdens, and routine human activities, which are part of human existence.

The search for joy in everyday living is cultivated through awareness, mindfulness, gratitude, and receptivity to God's presence. When perceived in the ordinary, believers begin to realize that joy is not something that can be purposely pursued. Joy sourced from God is a gift of the Spirit, rooted in the faithful, unchanging love of God. As believers grow accustomed to it, they become less moved by external circumstances and more able to receive the daily flame of unexpected grace. Their souls become attuned, aware, and sensitive to God's active providence in their lives, shaping joy as an enduring rather than fleeting experience.

Healing Through Divine Surprise

Healing, whether spiritual or emotional, takes on forms that astound the human heart. For example, anxiety thrives on our will to control situations and predict the future. The Scriptures put this to rest by inviting believers to cast their worry: "Casting all your care upon Him, for He cares for you" (1 Pet. 5:7). John Owen, Puritan theologian, explains that spiritual rest can happen when the soul trusts God's sovereign control, relinquishes worry, and knows that God's wisdom is perfect (Owen 1980, 214). A believer's anxiety is thus cast to God, liberating fear and laying the groundwork for joy, regardless of circumstances.

Dietrich Bonhoeffer supports this idea when he shares that faith is not living in the hope of controlling every junction of life, but rather faithfulness in God's presence during fog and doubt (Bonhoeffer 1959, 92). The healing journey from anxiety begins when believers shift their focus away from self-sufficiency toward God's providence. The believer's awareness can then perceive God's seemingly overlooked hand guiding and directing them, relieving them from the illusion of control over uncontrollable life outcomes.

Gregory of Nyssa argues that spiritual life can grow when a believer releases themselves from ideology, predictability, and control, allowing God to act in ways that exceed human disposition (Gregory of Nyssa 1991, 147). Similarly, Thomas Aquinas reminds us that God's providence enables God to create or draw together what may appear chaotic or illogical to bring about a greater spiritual good than human reflection could achieve (Aquinas 1947, II-II, q. 83, art. 3). Freedom from human control positions the heart to receive God's grace and experience healing in ways that may surpass human expectation.

Restoration of the human heart is often accomplished quietly, through means invisible to the human eye. Augustine of Hippo refers to God's healing work as gradually transforming the human heart from brokenness to wholeness, as God re-creates it through hidden processes (Augustine 2001, 311). John Stott adds clarity, affirming that God's work of transforming life in each believer is attainable, as all are made into vessels reflecting God's character and purpose (Stott 1994, 156).

Healing, through God's dramatic involvement, becomes a teacher—imparting trust, lessons in surrender, and focused attention. In openness to God's unexpected work, believers often find recovery, freedom from anxiety, and spiritual wholeness. This process may not be immediately apparent during times of confusion, but it is certain in the faithfulness of God's sustaining love.

Healing Anxiety Through Trust

Anxiety often results from the human desire to control or foresee the outcome of every situation. There really is a pattern in Scripture which reflects, again and again, God calling us to "cast our cares on him"—"Casting all your care upon him; for he careth for you" (1 Pet. 5:7). Healing anxiety requires the soul to transfer its securities from self-soothing security to looking for God's ultimate care and provision. John Stott notes, "Trusting God instead of the burden of our worries turns the fear into peace, and makes us strong for restoration and resilience in whatever we are facing" (Stott 1994, 156).

In his role as a pastor, Bonhoeffer discusses discipleship within the context of disabling circumstances. Letting go of control is a central tenet of being a disciple. Bonhoeffer states that people experience ease of anxiety and are at rest when they accept the reality of God's goodness in every circumstance, even when they are uncertain about whether, how, and when adversity and distressing circumstances will be resolved (Bonhoeffer 1959, 92). Trust is not passive; it is an active surrender of the illusion of control, while developing obedience, faith, and attentiveness to God's will and ways.

Henri Nouwen also reflected on the lurking inner pollutants that contaminate our souls when we allow our souls to care for themselves. Nouwen observes, "Anxiety decreases not because there is less danger, but because we become vigilant in the presence of God" (Nouwen 1996, 88).

When spiritual presence and understanding can inhabit the space in life and the soul that contributes towards emotional well-being and spiritual maturation, believers can face uncertainty with God's love as their basis of security, rather than self-security.

C.S. Lewis expresses a similar view, suggesting that joy and trust are about the transformation of happiness, innocence, sincere trust, and freedom (Lewis 1960, 114). When a believer surrenders to God's authority, anxiety gives way to peace, clarity, and purpose.

Ultimately, the therapeutic process of healing anxiety through the development of trust embodies both a spiritual and practical process for disciples. Trust appears as surrendering to the unknowables of life, gaining awareness of God at work in the essential unknowables, and faithfully preparing toward trust rather than control. By leaning into the true wisdom of God and allowing His providence to operate on His terms, believers can enter into a new experience of managing anxiety—strengthening themselves toward resilience, fostering relational connection with others, cultivating intimacy with the Creator, and experiencing the gift of a worry-free existence.

Freedom from Predictability and Control

As humans, we naturally seek to identify probabilities and exert control over our lives. While these instincts can be characterised as applicable, scripture teaches that spiritual freedom is found in surrender to the reality of our lack of control and trust in God's providential work (Prov. 16:9): "The heart of man plans his way, but the Lord establishes his steps." There is also a recognition in Gregory of Nyssa that spiritual formation occurs for believers when they release solidified plans and accept God's will (Nyssa 1991, 147). In this space of freedom, believers respond to the soul's invitation to openness in actively following the Holy Spirit as they posture themselves in humility and cultivate joy.

Thomas Aquinas offers theological insight into the capacity of humans to act with free agency in light of God's willful act. Aquinas believed that unpredictability and freedom to lose are gifts of God to exercise virtue and develop a believer's formation (Aquinas 1947, II-II, q. 83, art. 3). Thus, in willingly acting within their freedom to lose, an individual begins to see the presence of God, even in the unpredictable or potentially unsafe. Freedom from loss and unpredictability is freedom for spiritual maturity in discernment.

Dietrich Bonhoeffer similarly emphasizes the ethical and confessional aspect of relinquishing control. Within trust, discipleship, and the will of God, it is possible to engage believers in faithfulness without fear (Bonhoeffer 1959, 92). By continuing to surrender to the given expectations, we leave open the summons of God to create beloved surprises and transformation through His grace.

Henri Nouwen suggests that freedom from predictors opens up possibilities for both an interior experience of peace, while staying attuned to God's unending work, both inwardly and outwardly. A soul that is not clinging to predictables is a soul that is living and free (Nouwen 1996, 88). One of the rich potentials of the concept of freedom is that it opens up possibilities for delight and joy. Furthermore, it opens the integrity of resilience into deeper intimacy with God, even the mystery of an unknown future, taking on a foundational aspect of spiritual formation.

Freedom from predictability and control creates a tension for each of us to resist the temptation to grasp power in the midst of our circumstances. Nevertheless, this very space of surrender becomes a framework within which to receive the abundance of God's leading, the depth of his provision, and the accidental beauty of God's movement in our lives. To lose control is to gain trust, and, rejoicing in a new perspective on the Way of God, it is best regarded as a mystery.

Restoration in God's Unseen Work

Restoration often occurs in quietness, largely hidden from human observation. Scripture reminds believers that God acts in ways we cannot immediately register: "He restores my soul; He leads me in the paths of righteousness for His name's sake" (Ps. 23:3). Healing and renewal are rarely accompanied with fanfare, and may be invisible to believers, but we are assured, it is God's patient, faithful work in the soul. Augustine of Hippo notes that God's change or transformation is often slow and continual, as He reshapes hearts and conditions in ways we fail to recognize (Augustine 2001, 311).

John Stott also notes that God's hidden work produces a level pen, but at least we know, and often apprehend, tangible spiritual fruit in a believer's life. Blessed restoration encompasses movement of both the inner life by way of heart renewal and outward movement (expression) by way of Christlike character change (Stott 1994, 156). Believers who exercise trust in God's unseen work also learn the virtues of patience and faith. When inner and outer change is elusive, God's purposeful habits with the changed soul are maintained and are productive:

Dietrich Bonhoeffer importantly draws attention to the relational nature of God's often hidden transformative work in restoration. Discipleship also often occurs in even the most mundane conversations, in acted-out and often unfruitful trials of obedience, trivially disguised as inactivity and unconcerning actions (Bonhoeffer 1959, 92). When believers faithfully practice life's rhythms, they act as instruments or vessels of God's restorative power, which is not always evident in their own hearts, minds, lives, or in the lives of others.

Gregory of Nyssa observes that spiritual movements also often transpire in unnoticed and unapparent experiences or events. Gregory describes the spiritual journey to virtue, humility, and dependence on God as happening beneath everyday and visible obedience (Nyssa 1991, 147). The awareness of this essence of God's hidden work promoted spiritual discernment, waiting, and patience in a follower. When this occurs, a follower's growth embraces and waits on God, leaning on diversity when the preferred futility is immediately apparent, especially when their plans parallel ours.

Restoration in God's hidden work bids the believer to trust the divine process. Healing, renewal, and transformation often proceed, nevertheless quietly, and behind-the-scenes, but purposeful loads upon human measure, but they are. Thus, by trying faithfully when unseen before being processed, and being aware, exhibiting faith, patience, and being careful to pay attention to its most simple models, the soul bodies with God through the movements, experiencing wholeness and spiritual movements, secondary and more profound peace in exercising the yield and yieldedness of God's hidden, but purposeful providence.

Love Flourishing in Surprising Contexts

Love often expresses its most vibrant and powerful qualities in unplanned contexts that involve discomfort. Scripture calls upon believers to love not only easy people but those who reject, frustrate, or harm them: "But I say to you, love your enemies, bless those who curse you" (Matt. 5:44). Loving the difficult neighbor demonstrates a conscious act of choice, courage, and reliance on God's grace. C.S. Lewis notes that loving the unlovable is an act of will that transcends emotion and is guided by moral imagination and the pursuit of virtue (Lewis 1960, 102). When believers choose love over resentment, they create opportunities for transformation and reconciliation in relationships that seem irreparable and beyond repair.

Henri Nouwen writes that challenging relationships are places where we grow spiritually. When we love those who make it difficult for us to love them, we become filled with humility, patience, sympathy, and are shaped into vessels of God's grace (Nouwen 1996, 95). When we embrace uncomfortable expressions of care, we embody characteristics of Christ and allow ourselves to deliberately participate in God's redemptive activity in those relational spaces.

When we also respond to personal harm with unexpected grace and love, we amplify that same dynamic. Brennan Manning reminds us that God's transforming grace is all the more powerful when believers show forgiveness and kindness when it is least deserved (Manning 1990, 72). When believers choose love over resentment, they join God's restorative work, transforming painful experiences into potential healing, reconciliation, and spiritual witness. As Richard Bauckham explains, by entrusting all disruption to God's providence, believers are hopeful in the complexity of relational disruption, knowing that even when people are difficult, they can become part of God's loving and redemptive purpose (Bauckham 2008, 189).

As Dietrich Bonhoeffer explains, radical love is most evident in the most "disturbing or unstable" contexts. Christian love truly engages brokenness and offers mercy, courage, and reconciliation even when our love requires risk and sacrifice (Bonhoeffer 1959, 97). When Christians express radical and unexpected love, they become the heart of Christ by allowing God to demonstrate God's ability to transform lives through grace and intentionality.

Love is often expressed in the most vivid and surprising contexts when believers choose intentionality, grace, and trust. When Christians choose to love the difficult, respond to hurt with unexpected generosity, and experience that disruption as a space for radical care, they participate in God's ongoing work of transformation and God's redemptive love.

Loving the Difficult and Unexpected Neighbor

In a Christian life, loving the complex and unexpected neighbor is one of the most challenging calls to action. As stated in Scripture, "But I say to you, love your enemies, bless those who curse you, do good to those who hate you" (Matt. 5:44). That command is against human nature, which tends to pride, self-preservation, comfort, and reciprocity. It takes intentionality, courage, and reliance on God's strength, rather than human capacity, to love the hard-to-love.

C.S. Lewis said in his reflections on love in complex spaces that you can love through an act of the will, as opposed to merely an emotion one feels (Lewis 1960, 102). It requires will, moral imagination, and the ability to seek the good of another person, even as they are opposing, upsetting, or hurting you. Choosing to love the difficult neighbor is a humble and spiritual act of obedience that allows God to operate in our lives and express His graciousness in spaces that may feel anything but open.

Henri Nouwen also said that difficult people are often spiritual places of our own refining, or those around us (Nouwen 1996, 95). Loving those who oppose us expands our hearts to include and teaches us patience, humility, and empathy. Nouwen challenges us to accept relational discomfort by allowing God to be a partner in the relationship, while simultaneously shaping our character to relate as it is formed into the likeness of Christ, thereby allowing for the potential of reconciliation rather than hostility.

Moreover, engaging with the unexpected neighbor requires embodied perceptions of them in God's love, not judgment or fear. It becomes a starting point for what could be a restoration, and to enable gaps that we find between ourselves and others to be bridged when human agency is insufficient. The difficulty of loving the unknown neighbor becomes a divine invitation to reflect Christ's heart, revealing love that is not determined by preference, situational contexts, or social expectations.

At the heart of it, loving the complex and unexpected neighbor is a spiritual practice that transforms both those who give and those who receive shaped love. It is a practice that takes root in a disposition toward obedience to

God's Word and, by faith, influences moral imagination, being empowered by the grace God gives. By consciously choosing love over disdain, fear, or avoidance, Christians create relational spaces where love, God's presence, reconciliation, and transformative nature can unfold, even in the midst of challenging circumstances.

Responding to Hurt with Unexpected Grace

Responding to personal hurt or betrayal with grace is difficult because it runs counter to the instincts of humanity; however, it is a reflection of the heart of Christ. The Scriptures remind believers to forgive as they have been forgiven and turn from vengeance to mercy: "And be kind and compassionate to one another, tenderhearted, forgiving one another, even as God in Christ forgave you" (Eph. 4:32). While grace in painful moments can feel counterintuitive and contrary to human nature, extending grace is a magnificent witness to God's transformative love.

Brennan Manning reminds us that God's grace is most fully experienced through the weakness and imperfection of humanness (Manning 1990, 72). Responding to injury with unwavering grace requires dependence on God, whereby believers must confess that they, too, were given unmerited mercy and grace. In offering empathy, compassion, and forgiveness, as Christ forgives, Christians allow God's love to flow into this relational conflict and work on the Lord's behalf to restore what is broken and to reconcile the pain. Extending grace after relational hurt is not passive and emotionally disengaging; it engages the human heart in choosing mercy over bitterness, patience over resentment, and hope over despair.

Richard Bauckham states that the relational aspect of grace is at the heart of spiritual existence. Believers must remember God's providence; in the midst of responding to our injuries, we can often serve as a conduit of God's providential hand if we choose to respond in a way that allows us to be a mutually healing and restorative figure (Bauckham 2008, 189). Grace in unpredictable situations has the power to repair relationships by creating possibilities for empathy, understanding, and reconciliation. Unexpected kindness towards those who have injured us signals the kingdom possibility of God's loving embrace, which can change the wills and hearts of both the giver and the recipient.

Henri Nouwen reminds us that responding from a place of grace has the power to foster spiritual maturity in a believer, as it teaches a soul to depend on God and not on human judgment or retaliation (Nouwen 1996, 95). As believers adopt this grace approach to God's framework, they can align with God's purpose and begin to discover that extraordinary transformation often occurs after relational indignity or personal disappointment.

Responding to relational hurts with unexpected grace necessitates intentionality, patience, and an acute awareness of God's ongoing work at multiple levels. Responding to hurt with grace embodies the natural inclinations and impulses of our humanness. However, it demonstrates the reality of divine love and the potential to set things right, reconcile, heal, and restore. In short, extending grace enables a believer to participate in a way that leads in God's direction, bringing about God's presence in the midst of conflict and suffering.

Bonhoeffer on Radical Love in Disruption

Dietrich Bonhoeffer challenges believers to embody radical love, even when they are surrounded by societal confusion, placed in danger, or have disruptive relationships. In *The Cost of Discipleship*, Bonhoeffer argues that Christian love is not simply an idea of an abstract concept like "joy," but a lived concrete reality calling for courage, obedience, and risk (Bonhoeffer 1959, 97). Bonhoeffer's radical love is most authentic when found amidst uncertainty, injustice, or opposition, as it reflects the love of Christ who died for the unworthy.

Bonhoeffer makes it clear that genuine discipleship requires interaction with a broken world. Beyond real marks of love, disruption is not passive or ideational; instead, there is never a time when extravagant love is not active and costly. It can be doing whatever is needed to stand against injustice, advocate for the oppressed, or extend mercy to those who act against your comfort or expectations. When that happens, people bring God's healing and redemptive work, which brings hope and restoration in the midst of chaos and brokenness.

For modern readers, Bonhoeffer should provide a challenge to progress beyond normative and safe expressions of love. Love can be a transformative reality in society when people first break free from normativity, face their fears, and directly enter and engage with the unanticipated realities of unwanted human existence. Grace and mercy in contexts of disruption require humility, discernment, and absolute dependence on God, as human wisdom alone cannot produce the restoration that God has initiated in the world.

Additionally, Bonhoeffer's radical love, presented in the midst of disruption, is about shaping the Christian who engages with it. When disciples act to love in precarious and unsafe contexts, they are shaped even deeper into the *imago Dei*, learning dependence, compassion, and patience far before comfort can "teach" these qualities. The practice of love in contexts of disruption is faith-strengthening and fosters believers' spiritual formation, demonstrating God's transformative power to those around them.

Above all, Bonhoeffer encourages believers to recognize that radical love entails disruption. Disruption is an opportunity to be a witness and serve in spiritual ways. By taking up and embracing love that is courageous, sacrificial, and unexpected, Christians show the proximity of the heart of Christ to a world marked by brokenness and recognize the ways God is most evidently present and powerful in the disruptions that force reliance not on our strengths or norms, but on His guidance in every life experience.

Biblical Anchors of Surprise

The Bible reveals that God defies human notions of what is possible and feasible. Perhaps the most famous illustration of God's upside-down ability is the account of Jesus feeding 5,000 people (Matt. 14:13–21). In the story, Jesus takes five loaves of bread (half a loaf for each person) and two fish (a typical food for most families) and uses them to multiply the meal for thousands. Divine provisioning usually outstrips human considerations. F. F. Bruce notes that in this miracle, we see both the compassion of Christ and the underlying truth that God's norms for His restoration of creation are found in a greater context than human constructs could ever encompass (Bruce 1988, 162). Abraham Kuyper reminds us that God manifests His intervention in historical events as commonplace occurrences that invoke unbelievable realities, both physically and spiritually (Kuyper 1898, 43). Both stories teach the disciples about trust, obedience, and engagement in the divine work, and that God's surprising moments may expect human affirmation.

In the resurrection of Jesus, we have the manifestation of the ultimate upside-down event, as what looked like failure on the cross became the foundation of the most tremendous success in history (Luke 24:1–7). N. T. Wright unpacks the significance of the resurrection in transforming the believer's understanding of life and death, as well as the power of God, highlighting God's counterintuitive ways (Wright 2003, 412). The tomb was sealed to mark finality, but could not contain Christ's power. This episode also conveys a profound truth about the hopeful possibility in dire circumstances, and that God intervenes in ways and at times previously unknown to our earthly foresight.

Mary Magdalene's experience with the risen Christ signifies the personal and relational realities of upside-downs (John 20:11–18). Henri Nouwen observes, "'A sacred moment' occurs when ordinary experiences become extraordinary, redeeming restoration, recognition, and joy" (Nouwen 1996, 88). Mary, astonished, comes to recognize Jesus in time, emphasizing that divine surprises are personal, relational, and deeply disruptive. These biblical anchors serve as profound delights to believers, providing God's provision, victory in the human story, and relational intimacy in ways that surprise, amuse, and deepen faith, prompting trust in His disposition to refine.

Jesus Feeding the 5,000 (Matt. 14:13–21)

The feeding of the 5,000, arguably the most vivid instance of divine surprise in the Scriptures, involved Jesus taking five loaves and two fish, which looked like a pittance when compared to such a multitude, and multiplying them so that more than five thousand men, excluding women and children, could eat and have leftovers (Matt. 14:13–21). The event clearly illustrates that God's provision is often abundant and exceeds human imagination, transcending the limitations imposed by finite logic. F. F. Bruce notes that this miracle reveals something of Christ's compassion for human need and also the larger principle that divine resources are without limits and operate within a different paradigm than finite limits (Bruce 1988, 162).

Abraham Kuyper notes that the feeding of the multitudes demonstrates God's goodness in both physical and spiritual provision. The miracle is not simply a work of impressive power; it is, in a sense, God's work in ordinary ways to accomplish extraordinary things (Kuyper 1898, 43). The disciples helping to distribute the loaves and fish reinforce that divine surprises include human cooperation. Many times, the provision of abundance requires the qualities of obedience, trust, and courage to act on the little you have, allowing believers to become engaged and active in the work of God.

This event also taught the disciples something about faith. The disciples were focused on limitations and scarcity; Jesus focused on God's ability to meet every need. When the crowd, whom the disciples assumed would be unable to eat their share, learned from the multiplication of loaves and fish, they began to understand that God's ways often exceed human expectations, providing abundance in the face of perceived scarcity.

Moreover, the feeding of the 5,000 also anticipates and provides everything in the spiritual realm, already pointing to Jesus as the Bread of Life. Just as he multiplied the loaves physically, he gives the spiritual sustenance that it takes for believers to live forever in eternity. Henri Nouwen reflected that God's surprises often come in ordinary settings, where what looks small or insignificant turns into an extravagant blessing (Nouwen 1996, 88).

Fundamentally, this miracle encourages believers to trust in God's providence by acting faithfully with what they have. Also, it reminds them that God's provision will likely come in a way that surprises and discourages nagging doubts, serving as a means to promote faith while caring for their body and soul.

The Resurrection: The Ultimate Upside-Down Event

The resurrection of Jesus represents the ultimate divine surprise, upending human expectations and upending the fundamental realities we know about life, death, and the power of God. The supposed defeat on the cross became triumph; it reframed sin, humanity, mortality, and hope (Luke 24:1–7). N. T. Wright argues that the resurrection is not merely a fact of human history, but also a reality that reframes the world and the lives of believers by revealing something about the unexpected power of God (Wright 2003, 412). Notably, while empty tombs challenge human understandings of finality, they also reveal that God's work often transcends the logical views of humanity.

The resurrection indicates that God's kingdom operates according to a truth that is often opposite of what humans typically assume and have grown comfortable believing: defeat can become victory, suffering can add glory, and apparent endings can become beginnings. In this upside-down world, the believer is encouraged to trust God and the newness He is bringing, even when it might seem too hopeless to do otherwise. F. F. Bruce states that the resurrection marks God's decisive action in the history of the world, where He shows us that God is capable of sovereignty and power, bringing life from death and hope from despair (Bruce 1988, 235).

Furthermore, the resurrection beckons the believer into its hope and renewal. We see the disciples move from confusion and fear to bold proclamation and courageous witness because they encountered the unpredictable ways of the risen Christ. Transportation from humans often depends on their receptivity; our ability to appreciate the truly miraculous in God's active involvement in the events of our lives when we respond to God with faith and receptivity.

Henri Nouwen noted this personally: encountering the risen Christ changes the inner life; we are changed, possessing hope and restored to purpose (Nouwen 1996, 88). The resurrection confirms the nature of God's surprises: cosmic and personal, not limited to the whole world, but penetrating individual lives and hearts.

By God's design, the resurrection maintains its status as the ultimate upside-down event. It defies expectations, reverses human assumptions, and invites new participants to trust in God's capacity to act beyond what is humanly imaginable. By this thinking, the Christian bears witness to the radically surprising nature of God's love, which wins the day over life's dark experiences and assures us that whatever God does in the world will be surprising, because God is transforming and redeeming.

Mary Magdalene at the Tomb: Joy Amid Astonishment

Mary Magdalene's encounter with the risen Christ exemplifies the incredible joy and astonishment that often accompany God's surprises. On the first day of the week, Mary went to Jesus' tomb and discovered that the grave was empty. In her sadness and confusion, Mary suddenly recognized that it was Jesus standing before her. Day after day, God often surprises us by taking something that appears to cause mourning and transforming it into celebration, or despair into hope.

Henri Nouwen notes that in times of surprise, the divine moment is frequently relational and personal. Mary's recognition of Christ not only demonstrates that God is at work in the world in a cosmic sense but also that God is present in direct encounters between human beings at the microcosmic level. Mary Magdalene's astonishment demonstrates a heart open to God's unexpected work—a readiness to receive grace and notice God's surprising activity in and through humanity when our human eyes only see emptiness (Nouwen 1996, 88).

What is also revealed in this encounter is the relational nature of God's surprises. God chose Mary to be a witness to the resurrection and declared her to be the messenger of hope and life. God's surprises typically involve normal human beings in ways that have extraordinary significance. In the case of Mary, God intervened in a way that was personal, exciting, and disruptive—inviting her into action as part of God's redemptive work in the world. F. F. Bruce highlights this point when he states that God's work can actually change the way people view the world and one another, transforming them into messengers who proclaim the "good news" of Christ (Bruce 1988, 241).

In addition, Mary's final response indicates that the surprise was not lost on her and that she integrated her emotions with her sense of discipleship. The start of her surprise began with such a sorrowful loss that it, however, was not the final experience of the resurrection. Her openness to the unexpected presence of God was a transformative experience, shifting her from a state of fulfilled grief to one of joy and mission. This encounter teaches us that our actions in response to God's surprises can be filled with receptivity to God's goodness and that we can act faithfully, not disconnected and inactive.

Mary Magdalene's experience at the tomb reminds us that often the divine surprises come from the intimacy, relationality, and transformational experiences of God in God's world. Joy emerges with a context of astonishment, and sorrow opens the door to action by displacing our surprise and angst with faith. God, through Mary's encounter with the physical Christ, reminds Christians that God acts in our world from an intimate, unexpected, and life-giving place, inviting a personal response of worship through witness, rejoicing, and engagement in the power of God's mysterious work unfolding in the world.

Theological Reflections

Believers are invited to a theological reflection that prompts them to consider how God's surprising work is evident in everyday life. Often, God is surprising and hidden from human eyes, though the effects of His work are powerful. Augustine of Hippo points out that much of God's work is hidden in the shadows and behind the scenes; God is at work in things, events, circumstances, and hearts as part of His redemptive purposes. In *Confessions*, Augustine also reflects a sense that God's providence is often at work in life, as events unfold that, for us, exceed comprehension and at times are hard to believe even occur. He points out that God's providence, by nature, works in secrecy until a retrospective view reveals how God worked out His purposes (Augustine 2001, 311).

God's Surprising Way

The hidden and surprising nature of God's work invites believers to exhibit patience, humility, and faith, trusting that God is always at work behind the scenes, even when He seems silent, distant, and things are chaotic, uncertain, and delayed.

N.T. Wright also describes the concept of Kingdom reversal, meaning God often works in ways that are unexpected and surprising, and in the ordinary of life. Essentially, God can take something that appears weak, hopeless, or disastrous and bring a transformative outcome. With this principle in mind, part of Wright's point is that these Kingdom-reversing moments occur in relationships, at work, during personal hardship, and within the community. Thus, divine surprises are not merely cosmic events, but rather relational, practical, and formative events. Wright wants believers to embrace unpredictability. Specifically, God's power or agency bends toward humility, obedience, and faithfulness, which move to reshape a life or community (Wright 2003, 412).

J.I. Packer helps synthesize (and caution) the need to trust God's surprising agency in light of the sovereign nature of God. When Packer writes in *Knowing God*, he points out, "Providence—God's complete control of everything that happens, rather, for he knows it is only a short and uncertain distance he is going to have people go before they do not do anything he says, because the outcome is predestined" (Packer 1973, 215). This is to say that God's providence entirely governs the way we experience and expect the circumstances of life, and also considers that often God orchestrates parts of life we cannot know, because all the outcomes are outside our notion of comprehension. However, when we trust in God's sovereign plan, we can surrender our anxiety, anticipate the embrace of uncertainty, and even find peace, or at least a desirable steadiness. Then, we responsibly open ourselves to the unpredictability of life while waiting for God's divine surprise. Packer suggests that the surprises are also always purposeful, serving as goals for a Christ-like character, or deeper interactive dimensions of our faith, or even an exceeding realization of God's abundant glory.

As a set of reflections, these three voices provide a fuller scaffold for God's surprising work: Augustine shows us that it is hidden, Wright conveys the counterintuitive, transformative nature, and Packer emphasizes our need to trust God's sovereignty. In this sense, as believers, we participate in God's actions that are both personal and cosmic, relational, transformative, accurate, yet powerful in their hidden spirit. All of these theological observations encourage the user to trust, be faithful, and remain open, both administratively and spiritually, to the surprising capabilities of God, as collaborative participants in His redemptive and surprising work, within His redemptive and surprising plan.

Augustine on God's Hidden Work

Augustine of Hippo notes that much of God's work in the world remains hidden. Augustine describes this hidden work of God as quietly taking place behind the scenes, accomplishing God's purposes. In *Confessions*, he contemplates the mystery of how God involves Himself in human lives by shaping hearts and moving circumstances toward divinely ordained good, while much of the time the events in both the world and our lives seem confused and chaotic (Augustine 2001, 311). As Augustine shows us, believers can see this hidden work of God as an invitation to recognize that God's providence is often not visible at the surface level. This phase of divine action within our lives requires both trust and humility in the Christian pilgrimage.

The hiddenness of God's action also brings a sense of patience and dependency on divine wisdom to understand what and how God is doing things. As limited human beings, we often fail to see how a series of seemingly inconsequential or delayed events is working toward reforming us into the image of God. Augustine observes that God is prone to (or will) have us undergo slow, stabilizing events that cultivate virtue, alter our individual character, and produce spiritual fruit over time, rather than measuring our progress by immediate consequences. Augustine reminds us that through trust in God's invisible activity, the Christian pilgrimage fosters obedience and perseverance, essential elements of hope, and a faith that transcends circumstantial evidence, demonstrating that God approaches, acts through, or produces humans.

Augustine again notes how the nature of God's hidden work is relational. God's action, as divine providence, is all about relationship, not only cosmic design. God's shaping work helps people to accept God's will graciously. This hidden shaping brings humbled obedience and invites the saint to love, encouraging the faithful to partner with God not only in response to visible blessings but also in things that are not visible, embracing the ongoing grace and work of faith.

The theology of hidden work speaks to another reality that believers are called to reflect on when trials, suffering, and uncertainty abound. Augustine observes that all of these events and circumstances will, often over time, be part of the work of divine providence when shaping character and strengthening reliance on God. The reality of all of God's working, though often hidden, calls the traveler to unshakable faith, trusting that God's providence is wise and loving.

Augustine's reflections help remind Christians that God is at work in all things, even if they are not visible to human eyes. When believers embrace and welcome the hiddenness of God's activity, they do so in patience and trust in God's purpose, not in a loss of hope or an enthusiastic pursuit of abstract faith, even if they suffer from unresolved disappointment. They see how God's unseen work is purposeful, illustrative, transformational, and faithful in wisdom and love.

Wright on Kingdom Reversals in Daily Life

N.T. Wright points out that God's kingdom operates in surprising ways, often upending human experience. Wright writes about "Kingdom reversals," in which God honors the humble, empowers the weak, and changes loss to victory (Wright 2010, 98). Wright employs Kingdom reversals to prompt believers to recognize that God's priorities supersede human reason, and His purposes are fulfilled, at least at times, through the apparent absurdity of human logic.

Kingdom reversals are not only cosmic, but they are also down-to-earth, practical, and relational. Wright addresses the role of context in these surprising instances, noting that they typically occur in the ordinary settings of human experience, such as relationships, workplaces, families, and communities (Wright 2010, 102). Ultimately, one act of obedience, humility, or kindness may have ripple effects that human estimation cannot comprehend. By participating as followers of Jesus in these instances, they are invited to witness the surprise of God and how, in the case of these Kingdom reversals, God can inversely bless almost counterintuitively by upending human action in circumstances otherwise defined by success.

Wright states that faith and a posture of openness contribute to the experience of these reversals. Just as the early disciples could not fully grasp Jesus' mission, modern-day disciples face difficult situations of unfairness, despair, or discouragement. Kingdom reversals remind Christians that God's intention is not always clearly revealed; usually, our success, power, or influence, as measured, is not enough to assume any action by God. Trust and attention are necessary if one is to notice God's surprising actions in life itself.

Additionally, recognition of Kingdom reversals fosters hope and encourages perseverance. Believers understand that disappointments, setbacks, or social injustice do not define the absence of God, but rather are moments that offer an opportunity to recognize God's presence in unexpected ways. Wright encourages Christians to demonstrate humility, patience, and courage, and that living with the "upside-down" Kingdom is a reflection of God's wisdom, justice, and power (Wright 2010, 101).

Essentially, Wright's reflections encourage believers to live with their eyes open for God's surprising interventions. By living out Kingdom reversals, Christians embrace God's redemptive work in their lives and situations, build resilience, and bear witness to the Kingdom of God, which they recognize is amazingly transformative and often nonsensical to human understanding.

Packer on Trusting God's Sovereign Surprises

J.I. Packer emphasizes the importance of trusting God's sovereignty in the face of life's unexpected events. In *Knowing God*, Packer writes that God rules all events with wisdom, purpose, and power, even when human beings cannot see what God is doing in particular circumstances to achieve His divine purpose (Packer 1973, 215). God's surprises can take the form of joyful changes or challenging life transitions. Regardless of the situation, surprises are not meaningless events; they are opportunities to experience God's providential and continual care. Trusting God's sovereignty enables believers to surrender their anxiety, allowing them to rest in God's faithfulness.

Packer points out that God's sovereign surprises will often feel paradoxical from a human perspective. Discouraging and chaotic situations can sometimes be ways God is using them for growth, refinement, or blessing. When believers acknowledge God's sovereignty, it changes the way they view their trials and setbacks. Rather than reacting to trials with fearfulness or resentment, Christians are invited to respond with faithfulness, patience, and obedience to God, because God is at work behind the scenes in every circumstance (Packer 1973, 215).

Additionally, trusting in God's sovereign surprises means the believer is maturing spiritually. Packer writes that trusting in God's providence leads to humility, as believers acknowledge that they do not have a complete understanding of God's timing or ultimate plan. This also cultivates peace and confidence as believers do not carry the burden of predictability or control in situations. Embracing God's sovereign surprises teaches Christians how to live a gracious and resilient life, one that is reliant on God's supernatural wisdom (Packer 1973, 215).

Packer goes on to say that God's sovereign surprises are relational, as God desires to draw believers into deeper fellowship with Him. Unexpected events become occasions for prayer, intimacy, and discernment. When Christians remain trusting of God's guidance, they become fellow workers in God's redemptive work, even in the face of events that may feel challenging or forced upon them. God uses all events to nurture spiritual growth and to bring Him glory (Packer 1973, 215).

Most centrally, Packer reminds Christians that God's sovereignty remains a comfort to faithfulness. None of life's surprises—joyful, puzzling, or painful—are meaningless. When Christians embrace trusting God's sovereign control, they are actively seeking all of the life stages and finding themselves interacting with God's plan and experiencing God, not just through intellect but in tangible ways, to nurture a faithful life that holds a reliance on God that carries hope, peace, and joy among the unexpected (Packer 1973, 215).

Living in Surprise Daily

Living in God's surprises daily entails leaning fully into an approach of openness, attentiveness, and a disposition of trusting in God's providential work. Scripture tells believers "to trust in the Lord with all your heart, and lean not on your own understanding" (Prov. 3:5). Living with an openness to God's surprises requires releasing our own agendas, surrendering to the

Holy Spirit's leading in our lives, and being willing to make changes to our habitual routines based on His guidance. As Dallas Willard states, "Spiritual formation is an expression of God's presence in movement, a waking up all at once to what has been taking place, and now we will let God take the lead" (Willard 1998, 44). Learning to live with openness can transform the ordinary into a creative, divine surprise and provision.

Another primary component of living in God's surprises is finding joy in the little things and unseen parts of life. Henri Nouwen's assertion, like Willard's, hinges upon intentional openness to God in the art of living: spiritual delight often emerges in tiny, unnoticed moments—a kind word, a small act of service, reflection to listen—that point to God's active presence, even when hidden from view (Nouwen 1996, 88). Recognizing and celebrating these small invitations to grace nurtures gratitude, attentiveness to the Spirit at work, and a gradual awareness of God's ongoing providential work.

Living in God's surprises molds relationship expectations. Brennan Manning feels strongly that we will benefit from the capacity to give each other grace and flexibility, particularly in times when misunderstandings arise or when we are angered or disappointed with someone (Manning 1990, 72). Of course, patience, humility, and mercy aimed at one another can heal a wound, open the possibility to trust again, or enable God's intent to be woven into what might appear as our impotence, disillusionment, or dishonesty. The unseen moments are also ideal times to love when life becomes disoriented or disrupted. Love seen becomes radical love throughout interruptions to ordinary life; it is in those moments of sacrifice and love challenged that Kingdom priorities or values flow into a life: Kingdom priorities to discuss one another, Kingdom responses to interact kindly with one another, Kingdom commitments to care for one another—Bonhoeffer called this Practical Christianity or the way of Jesus (Bonhoeffer 1959, 97).

Walking in God's surprise daily also means we are walking in the upside-down rhythm of the Kingdom. N.T. Wright suggests Kingdom life has the incessant feel of unduly inverting human community; the rhythms of humility, mercy, and generosity supersede control and self-centeredness (Wright 2010, 98). Engaging the Kingdom invites a tremendous privilege to participate in the witness of giving it up and mutual forms of provision in service to one another, to follow one's faith when living life according to multiplicity, finding joy in what is often ordinary, quotidian routine, or that peak of grace when ordinary everyday life is transformed into the majesty of God's creativity.

As a result, being surprised in everyday life involves and nurtures attentiveness and flexibility, allowing us to be open to God through trusting resilience and the detours of seeking delight, which are created wholly with God's ongoing, sometimes surprising presence.

Practicing Openness to God's Unexpected Plans

It is vital and powerful to practice openness to God's unexpected plans when living a life full of faith and spiritual attentiveness. Scripture teaches us to "trust in the Lord with all your heart, and lean not on your own understanding" (Prov. 3:5). Openness is more than mere acceptance; it is active attentiveness, humility, and readiness to abandon our own plans to pursue God's plans. Life does not usually go as planned, and being open helps us to notice what God is up to in the moments of disruption, uncertainty, or difficulty.

Dallas Willard notes that spiritual formation entails cultivating an awareness and sensitivity to God's presence in everyday life. In this sense, being open to God's unexpected plans requires a heart and mind that are tuned to the Spirit, to catch even the subtlest nudge or opportunity (Willard 1998, 44). When we practice active attentiveness and openness so that everyday decisions do not seem mundane, they can become spaces for God's activity.

Openness also means letting go of control. As human beings, we tend to prefer predictability, security, and certainty. However, God's plans often move outside of predictability, security, and certainty. When we relinquish our insistence on controlling God's plans and instead pursue His plans, we discover that we are lifted and transformed into beings of patience, trust, and reliance on His wisdom. Henri Nouwen emphasizes that this "letting go" transforms God's work, including aspects that we might tend to regard as insignificant or hidden, into a journey where incredible spiritual fruit becomes observable (Nouwen 1996, 88).

Additionally, openness fosters flexibility with how we respond within relationships, ministry, and self-development. The practice of openness allows us to bend plans to see how they evolve, to allow forgiveness in the face of unexpected events, and to participate in God's redemptive work as it is revealed. This practice of openness encourages the spiritual shaping of us as we become more disposed to spiritual engagement due to our developing trust in God. Openness encourages us to deepen our trust in God's providence, and it can help us develop joy in perceiving God's surprising presence in our everyday lives.

Practicing openness to God's unexpected plans is both a discipline and a spiritual posture. It compels us to let go of our control and rigidity that we impose on the work that God wants us to accomplish, to become open to God at our center—paying attention to the Spirit, approaching sometimes unwanted surprises with humility and trust. In the practice of openness, allowing God to work in the ordinary moments and interruptions of life, we live into the very real possibility of God's work of encounter, reformation, and redemptive ends.

Finding Joy in Small, Unseen Ways

Discovering delight in small, unnoticed ways is a vital practice for cultivating spiritual attentiveness and fostering a relationship with God. While humans tend to focus on significant accomplishments or visible gifts, Nouwen states that true joy often comes from the subtle, ordinary, and unnoticed aspects of life (Nouwen 1996, 88). The ordinary, the word of encouragement, quiet reflection, or the unexpected act of kindness typically invites all believers to catch a glimpse of God's continuing presence and grace, often amidst a busy or mundane day.

Encountering delight in the unseen comes from awareness. Nouwen states that the spiritual life is nurtured by attentiveness, which enables us to pay attention and see the hands of God at work in the ordinary aspects of life. When believers pause and pay attention to the small blessings surrounding them, they not only become aware of God's sustaining presence but also cultivate an awareness of their own gratitude, wonder, and closeness to God. This practice leverages humans' tendency to measure significance solely in terms of visibility or magnitude, while cultivating a more spiritual sensitivity to the subtle ways in which God nurtures, heals, and delights.

In addition, embracing delight in the unseen also breeds resilience and hope. Life is a regular, and often unpredictable, stream of difficulties, distortions, and disappointments, both personally and collectively. At the same time, by discovering and paying attention, however subtle, to experiences of blessing, believers can perceive and experience God's sustaining presence and grace in every circumstance. Dallas Willard asserts that practicing major spiritual disciplines, such as meditation, prayer, and attentiveness, enables Christians following the way of Jesus to notice aspects of God's leading and provision that might otherwise go unnoticed (Willard 1998, 44). These small joys can be constant anchors of hope, life reminders that God is at work even when operating in the background of life.

This practice transforms perspective and relationships. By seeing and celebrating small, unnoticed delights, believers cultivate a habit of attention and encouragement. They are witnesses to joy and affirmation in the lives of others. Similarly, paying attention to the unseen enhances gratitude. It fosters humility, awareness, and generosity within oneself, thereby improving a believer's inner life and their interactions with others.

Recognizing delight in small, unnoticed ways fosters and deepens spiritual formation, nurtures attentiveness, and trains the heart to see and learn to recognize God's continuous, quiet work in their lives. When believers grow to embrace the ordinary as a source and uncover the divine delight in their everyday routines, they begin to experience and appreciate every moment of life with renewed purpose, wonder, gratitude, and a lasting awareness of God's abiding presence, even amid the unusual rhythms and expectations of daily life.

Healing Relationships Through Flexibility and Grace

To live in God's surprises requires a flexible relational posture, recognizing that life's surprises impact our relational other-centeredness based on both expectation and experience. Brennan Manning reminds the reader that moving beyond misunderstanding, conflict, or disappointment in any relational circumstance requires being grace-filled partners (Manning 1990, 72). Grace fosters a posture of non-anxious presence, manifesting in patience and loving-kindness rather than reactionary judgment amplification, which may only serve to deepen any entrenched disappointment and hinder future relational repair.

Flexibility is a vital component of the outpouring of grace. Humanity does not live life in the precise ways it expects. It is a fact that everyone will act in unhelpful ways toward others at times, and that such actions may elicit disappointment, anger, or necessitate self-advocacy. Flexibility generates a context to acknowledge and name disappointment or difficulty in relationships while cultivating space for reconciliation and transformation. In Manning's view, grace, by definition, requires us to acknowledge ourselves as flawed, imperfect beings who also have the benefit of human example, i.e., other people whom we may call friends or members of our community. When forgiveness and understanding become the baseline for relationships, it enables us to bring our honest selves into relationships with self and others, holding Christ's redemptive work as the model for enacting mercy and loving-kindness relationally

Encouraging the act of healing relationships through grace asks believers to be alert to God's ongoing leading. Instead of acting out of impulse, prayer, reflection, and response to the Holy Spirit will help discern our response to conflict and relational repair. Pursuing God's guidance with the acknowledgment of one's condition invites believers to model confrontation that conveys respect for honoring God's wisdom or dignity toward others. Flexibility and grace, combined with spiritual discernment, transform potentially damaging relational incidents—characterized by consistent failure and disappointment—into active opportunities for personal and corporate growth, intimacy, and the mutual humanizing traits of simply being human.

More than specific relationships, as described above, God surprises us with communication systems and relational methods on neighborhood, regional, and institutional levels, meaning the opportunities for practicing grace and flexibly responding leave examples of engaging conditions for trust, relational communication, and joint actions. Being in the moment in grace results in creating collective environments where the reality of God's Kingdom is palpable in our lives and experiences with one another. A reminder that God frequently invites us to exercise His outpouring in little and sometimes mundane ways to show God to others. Do not doubt where His transformative work began: in visible acts of forgiveness, patience, and kindness.

When healing relationships with flexibility and grace, believers enter places of participating in God's redemptive work. Christians model a posture of humility, not seeking to be in control while responding with God's flexibility and merciful nature, fully committing to restoration, reconciliation, and flourishing for all in the relationship(s). This is a purposeful redemptive practice with personal implications for one's own development as well as the community's transformation, representing God's unexpected regenerative and life-giving capabilities to move between peace, healing, and love.

Loving Generously When Plans Are Disrupted

Life's unpredictability can often interrupt well-planned intentions. However, such moments can offer specific opportunities to exercise generous love. Bonhoeffer points out that true discipleship is revealed not when things happen smoothly but when disruptions, crises, and sacrifices require radical responses aligned with Christ (Bonhoeffer 1959, 97). In the context of bigger picture disruption, generous love reflects the upside-down values of God's Kingdom, where service, mercy, and compassion take priority over comfort and control.

Disruptions, whether sudden disturbances in personal rhythm, challenging relationships, or unexpected life circumstances, provide believers with an opportunity to reevaluate and reprioritize. Instead of responding with frustration, resistance, or self-centered instinct, the Christian response is to respond with creativity, patience, and love for others. Bonhoeffer notes that such responses take intentionality and courage because they take seriously what it means to respond faithfully, not just in a self-protective manner, to God's calling, and then to act. This radical generosity explicitly reflects the Kingdom of God in real time and space; these disruptions allow us to transform the frustration of disruption into acts of witness and blessing.

Loving generously in the face of disruption also contributes to spiritual growth. Each disruption provides an opportunity to practice humility, selflessness, and trust in God's invisible affirmations. Brennan Manning notes that grace and generosity are most vividly present in disrupting experiences that fall outside one's comfort zone (Manning 1990, 72). By accepting these disruptions positively, the Christian learns to look toward God's capacity to sustain their trust, allowing for action that expresses love directed by God's values and priorities.

In addition, generous love in the midst of disruptions helps build stronger relationships and a more cohesive community. Responding to the expectations of mercy, patience, and providing practical care supports the process of reconciliation, trust, and shaping among others, exemplifying the behavior of Christ. Thus, demonstrating active expressions of God's Kingdom shows continuity, indicating that it is neither timeless and unattainable nor a process that is expected.

Learning to love generously in disrupted circumstances trains the believer to hope in the way God chooses, to see surprises not as negatives needing a corrective pathway, but as opportunities that arise invisibly. Therefore, when one's actions align with the will of God, Christians are immensely gifted by God's goodness when they can discover how to make something out of these challenges—using their radical images of discipleship as a means of unending surprise that reflects the nature of God's love: surprising, healing, and life-giving love. Through occasions of disruption, the ability and willingness to create opportunities for this life-giving nature reveal that one's desire embraces dramatic generosity, and is not limited to those convenient and uncharacteristic moments, but can flourish the most in disruption when life is asking each of us for faith, courage, and sacrificial love.

God's Surprising Way

Walking Daily in the Upside-Down Rhythm of God's Kingdom

Routine daily life in the upside-down rhythm of the Kingdom of God involves embracing principles that often contradict what we expect as humans. N.T. Wright poignantly expresses that the Kingdom operates on values that turn the world order upside down: humility, service, mercy, and selflessness take precedence over status, power, and control (Wright 2010, 98). Living in a Kingdom rhythm means that ordinary life is the context in which God's surprising work of transformation is made known. This requires our attention, obedience, and trust.

The upside-down character of the Kingdom challenges us as believers to reorient our perspectives. Success in God's Kingdom does not align with achievement or recognition. It focuses on faithfulness, love, and small—and sometimes unnoticed—actions. Everyday life—work, family life, and community life—is an opportunity to express our practice. When Christians are open to the unexpected, they recognize that God uses ordinary life and the unexpected twists that occur to produce amazing things.

This rhythm also fosters flexibility and resilience, aligning with God's upside-down rhythm of life. Because life is unpredictable, living in the rhythm God intends trains us to respond with patience, flexibility, and grace. According to Dietrich Bonhoeffer, radical discipleship is characterized by Christians aligning their lives with the priorities of the Kingdom, as it demands faithfulness to God, even unto sacrifice, disruption, and self-denial (Bonhoeffer 1959, 97). Practices like these demonstrate the active, relational, and responsive faith that we are looking for, as opposed to a rigid, unilateral expectation of ourselves.

Additionally, this active daily rhythm can foster spiritual growth and community transformation. The impact of even small acts of service, humility, and mercy radiates through relationships and communities, modeling the values of the Kingdom of God. Henri Nouwen skillfully outlines how being attentive to God in the ordinary allows us to experience God's grace and joy in all the ways He works—even in very ordinary ways (Nouwen 1996, 88).

The invitation and challenge to walk in the daily upside-down rhythm of God's Kingdom call believers to trust in God's wisdom, take hold of the surprises, and allow God's values to inform our actions, thoughts, and relationships. For Christians to live consistently with this rhythm allows them to engage in God's transformation of the world, experiencing and demonstrating the perhaps counterintuitive, life-giving movement of God's Kingdom in ordinary lives.

Chapter 7

The Power of the Cross

The Reversal of the Cross

The cross of Christ is an example of the radical reversal of God's Kingdom, where shame becomes glory, apparent defeat becomes victory, and human wisdom is confounded by divine purpose. The paradox of the cross is striking: the very thing that the world despises, scorns, and condemns will be the means of salvation for the world. It is a paradox that Paul notes, for he says: "For the message of the cross is foolishness to those who are perishing, but to us who are being saved it is the power of God" (1 Cor. 1:18). At the cross, humanity's understanding of success—that which is good is power, prestige, and honor—is overturned in the wholeness of humility, sacrifice, and obedience (Wright 1996, 152).

Isaiah prophesied the reversal in the suffering servant: "He was despised and rejected by men, a Man of sorrows and acquainted with grief" (Isa. 53:3). The suffering, shame, and death of the servant are not evidence of God's absence, but instruments of redemption, foreshadowing Christ's crucifixion. Likewise, Psalm 22 begins with lament but ends in praise, revealing the intertwining of apparent despair and humiliation with God's redemptive story (Ps. 22:1–31). When Christ takes on shame in the crucifixion, He fulfills Scripture in the process. He directly evokes suffering as a necessary disposition of humility and obedience to God.

As Augustine of Hippo notes, we should see the cross as the ultimate testimony of God's wisdom, in that in human weakness, God's strength is perfected, and in disgrace, glory is attained (Augustine 2001, 311). John Stott further elaborates by arguing that the cross, in itself, communicates a profound notion of love while inverting the expectations historically associated with reward, inviting Christians to lives characterized by Christ-like humility and servanthood (Stott 1986, 42). Ultimately, the consequence of accepting death is a new human understanding of victory, in which eternal significance is achieved through obedience to God, even in the face of painful suffering.

Practically, this radical reversal enables Christians to reimagine suffering, disappointment, and apparent failure as rich opportunities for spiritual development. By accepting the paradox of the cross, believers discover that grace calls them to see shame transformed into glory, that death can produce life, and that God's wisdom surpasses human reasoning. Therefore, the cross calls believers to see from a Kingdom perspective, where what the world sees as weakness may actually be strength, loss may be seen as gain. God will fulfill His purposes in dramatically transformed ways, often in ways that have not been seen before.

From Shame to Glory: The Paradox of the Cross

The cross serves as the supreme paradox of God's redemptive plan: absurdity and humiliation in the world become a means to glory and life. The crucifixion of Jesus—a device of public execution and humiliation—reveals that the Kingdom of God is predicated on principles that often run counter to human expectations. As Paul explains, "For the message of the cross is foolishness to those who are perishing, but to us who are being saved it is the power of God" (1 Cor. 1:18). In human thought, success is often equated with mastery over, influence upon, and honour with respect to others, but the cross declares that God's power is made perfect in weakness and humility (Wright 1996, 152).

This paradox is seen in Isaiah's prophecy of the suffering servant centuries earlier: "Surely he has borne our griefs and carried our sorrows; yet we esteemed him stricken, smitten by God, and afflicted" (Isa. 53:3). The servant's suffering, shame, and death were not a demonstration of God's abandonment, but rather the means by which God brings restoration and redemption. In the synoptic gospels, Christ willingly enters into this shame, embodying proper response and love to the point of death. The rich young ruler (Matt. 19:21) is another example; worldly status and security must be sacrificed so that one can be incorporated into God's Kingdom. Both encounters invite believers to confront the shockingly paradoxical way of God.

Augustine of Hippo has aptly summarized the cross as that which is disgraceful in our temporal context, yet becomes the locus of glory in God's eternal plan. He articulates that God's power is rendered great upon earth in human weakness and suffering, such that folly in the eyes of the world accomplishes God's highest purposes (Augustine 2001, 311). John Stott makes a similar observation, noting that the cross relays God's love and the radical inversion of worldly values, from which believers are compelled to light the path for humility, obedience, and self-denying service, as identities of the Kingdom (Stott 1986, 42).

As Christians today, the cross speaks to our conventional measures of success, achievement, and honour. Daily experiences of failure, disappointment, or shame need not lead to a feeling of defeat, but rather to an opportunity for spiritual growth, humility, and a deep reliance on God, as participants in His redemptive work on earth. In the paradox of God, shame becomes glorious, weakness is emboldened, and the cross serves as a sign and symbol of God's wisdom and redemptive agency.

Christ's Death as Victory, Not Defeat

The crucifixion of Christ represents the supreme triumph of God over sin, death, and the powers of darkness. Although the crucifixion is a moment when it seems that Christ is at his most humiliated and suffering point, God sees it as the most exalted point of God at work. As Paul notes in 1 Corinthians 15:17–18, "And if Christ is not risen, your faith is futile; you are still in your sins. Then also those who have fallen asleep in Christ have perished." And while the cross here seems weak, it hides the profound victory obtained through Christ's obedience and sacrificial love (Wright 2006, 214).

Isaiah's prophetic words foreshadow a victory, as in the suffering servant who dies for the sins of many: "Surely He has borne our griefs and carried our sorrows" (Isa. 53:4). The servant is pierced and oppressed, yet his death brings life to others; this is a reversal of defeat, as surrender to death becomes salvation. The Gospels reinforce this divine logic by demonstrating that the willing, sacrificial suffering of Christ is not defeat, but rather a necessary step in restoring humanity. This lies at the heart of the events in the Garden of Gethsemane, whereby Jesus obediently submitted to the Father's will to show that true victory is obedience rather than self-preservation (Matt. 26:39).

Origen builds on this paradox, noting the revelation of God's power at the cross in a moment of weakness. The humiliation of the Savior demonstrates that divine strength cannot be contained, transcending worldly conditions of triumph to surrender suffering in favor of salvation ultimately (Origen 2001, 78). Similarly, John Chrysostom demonstrates that Christ did not simply endure, but intentionally embraced death as a means to victory, as God's purposes transcend human reason (Chrysostom 1987, 214).

This third point of view on victory as a means to draw meaning from loss and suffering for believers today situates life experiences when the presence of God's fullness can seem absent. Suppose God was able to turn shame at the cross into victory. In that case, personal trials can transform daily life experiences into trusting God for a redemptive end. As believers in what God has accomplished, Christians can embody Christ by understanding obedience, humility, and faithfulness, even through suffering, which brings them as participants into God's own victory over evil. Thus, the cross convinces Christians that what was their defeat is to be the very site of God's victory, demonstrating that God's glory is revealed most mightily through the actions of the lowliest of means, which is how the world would see humanity as weakness.

God's Wisdom Confounding Human Wisdom

The cross is the ultimate example of the perverse nature of human knowledge: God's wisdom looks foolish to the world. Paul expresses this tension in 1 Corinthians 1:25 when he writes, "For the foolishness of God is wiser than men, and the weakness of God is stronger than men." Humanity often values intelligence, power, and success based on the current worldly knowledge, but God is up to something different. God's plans operate on a different level that often seems contradictory to the wisdom of the world. The cross represents a moment of failure and shame, yet it is the very divine wisdom of God that overwhelms any human understanding (Packer 1973, 215)

Isaiah's prophecy also demonstrates this same pattern, in which God's wisdom appears foolish from the human perspective. The servant of the Lord, "despised and rejected by men" (Isa. 53:3), accomplishes salvation through what seems to be the weakness of being the suffering servant. Similar to Psalm 22, it begins with lament and ends in praise (Ps. 22:1–31). These two examples demonstrate that self-pity and shame do not indicate that God is detached from reality; instead, they are opportunities for God's work of redemption. The world views failure, shame, and suffering as evidence of loss; God's wisdom, however, acts upon these experiences as opportunities for mercy, restoration, and glory.

Origen says that the cross is the supreme example of God's unintelligible wisdom. It was through what looked like foolishness and weakness that God accomplished salvation, because His salvation plan cannot be neatly fitted into the human intellect (Marciano 1994, 82). He goes on to state that what seems to demonstrate foolishness or weakness is merely the tool God uses to accomplish His salvific purposes, because God operates at a level that the world did not expect (Origen 2001, 82). John Calvin claims, in a similar way, that God's order "transcends human understanding," in which the cross reconnects the adversaries — God and humanity — through Christ's obedience to God and death (Calvin 1960, 178).

In a practical sense, understanding God's wisdom through apparent weakness challenges the believer to live with humility, patience, and trust. Life is full of moments that pose challenges that seem contradictory, unfair, or disastrous. We learn to value God's wisdom and intentions through the cross of Christ, which creates space for Jesus to build faith in the rough moments of life that occur along the journey through trials, surrender, and uncertainty.

The ultimate complexity of God's wisdom, demonstrated through the cross, is the height of paradox: strength born in weakness, life born in death, God's glory revealed amidst what human wisdom interprets as failure or defeat. The believer is invited into an established upside-down Kingdom, which invests in trusting God's wisdom in counterintuitive times in life, where trust is difficult simply because it contradicts human wisdom.

God's Surprising Way

Biblical Witness to the Cross

The cross is the ultimate example of the perverse nature of human knowledge: God's wisdom looks foolish to the world. Paul expresses this tension in 1 Corinthians 1:25 when he writes, "For the foolishness of God is wiser than men, and the weakness of God is stronger than men." Humanity often values intelligence, power, and success based on the current worldly knowledge, but God is up to something different. God's plans operate on a different level that often seems contradictory to the wisdom of the world. The cross represents a moment of failure and shame. Yet, it is the very divine wisdom of God that overwhelms any human understanding (Packer 1973, 215).

Isaiah's prophecy also demonstrates this same pattern, in which God's wisdom appears foolish from the human perspective. The servant of the Lord, "despised and rejected by men" (Isa. 53:3), accomplishes salvation through what seems to be the weakness of being the suffering servant. Similar to Psalm 22, it begins with lament and ends in praise (Ps. 22:1–31). These two examples demonstrate that self-pity and shame do not indicate that God is detached from reality; instead, they are opportunities for God's work of redemption. The world views failure, shame, and suffering as evidence of loss; God's wisdom, however, acts upon these experiences as opportunities for mercy, restoration, and glory.

Origen says that the cross is the supreme example of God's unintelligible wisdom. It was through what appeared to be foolishness and weakness that God accomplished salvation, because His salvation plan cannot be neatly fitted into the human intellect (Marciano 1994, 82). He goes on to state that what seems to demonstrate foolishness or weakness is merely the tool God uses to accomplish His salvific purposes, because God operates at a level that the world did not expect (Origen 2001, 82). John Calvin claims, in a similar way, that God's order "transcends human understanding," in which the cross reconnects the adversaries — God and humanity — through Christ's obedience to God and death (Calvin 1960, 178).

In a practical sense, understanding God's wisdom through apparent weakness challenges the believer to live with humility, patience, and trust. Life is full of moments that pose challenges that seem contradictory, unfair, or disastrous. We learn to value God's wisdom and intentions through the cross of Christ, which creates space for Jesus to build faith in the rough moments of life that occur along the journey through trials, surrender, and uncertainty.

The ultimate complexity of God's wisdom, demonstrated through the cross, is the height of paradox: strength born in weakness, life born in death, God's glory revealed amidst what human wisdom interprets as failure or defeat. The believer is invited into an established upside-down Kingdom, which invests in trusting God's wisdom in counterintuitive times in life, where trust is difficult simply because it contradicts human wisdom.

Isaiah's Suffering Servant (Isaiah 53)

Isaiah 53 represents one of the deepest prophetic understandings of the mystery of Christ's redemptive work. In this chapter, the author describes a figure who bears the suffering, rejection, and punishment that humanity deserves: "Surely He has borne our griefs and carried our sorrows; yet we esteemed Him stricken, smitten by God, and afflicted" (Isa. 53:4). This suffering servant experiences humiliation and affliction not for personal sin, but for others, which serves to highlight the substitutionary dimension of Christ's death. In the rejection and suffering of the servant, God demonstrates wisdom and a plan that sometimes seems foolish to human thinking—and even at times brings about human shame—and creatively reinterprets weakness or shame for the ultimate act of salvation (Wright 1996, 170).

The servant's rejection—"He was despised and rejected by men" (Isa. 53:3)—mirrors Jesus' experience in the Gospels. From the mockery of religious leaders to the derision of the crowds, Christ's suffering on earth fulfills Isaiah's prophetic message. It provides a concrete model of obedient humility. The chapter emphasizes that suffering brings healing: "With His stripes we are healed" (Isa. 53:5). This principle provides a theological basis for conceptualizing the cross not as defeat, but as God's gift of restoration and reconciliation.

Origen reads the text both allegorically and literally when he notes that God's wisdom works through what seems foolishness to the world. The suffering servant also embodies God's strategies and reveals that God's purposes unfold not through human glory or power but in humility, obedience, and self-sacrifice (Origen 2001, 79). Augustine of Hippo also highlights that it is when humanity perceives only weakness that God most clearly reveals his plans, highlighting how redemption often comes in forms contrary to human expectations (Augustine 2001, 313).

For example, for believers today, Isaiah 53 calls for reflection on the agony of suffering, obedience, and divine love. The servant's willingness to bear the burdens of others is a challenge to Christians to practice sacrificial love, humility, and trust in God's plan even when circumstances lead to pain or are challenging to bear. The suffering servant demonstrates that what appears to be shameful temporally becomes a vehicle for eternal glory—and this serves as a model for how to think about Christ's death on the cross as the quintessential act of God's redemptive wisdom.

Psalm 22: Lament Turned Praise

Psalm 22 provides a powerful biblical lens through which to view the cross, highlighting the relationship between suffering and God's vindication. The psalm opens with the anguished cry, "My God, My God, why have You forsaken Me?" (Ps. 22:1), indicating extreme human distress and reminding us of Christ's cry from the cross. The anguish in the psalm is a lament, but it is a lament of someone entirely dependent on God, driven by discord and suffering, demonstrating that faith is both a belief in God and a faith that God is required (Packer 1973, 225).

The speaker recounts the physical and social sufferings, mocked by enemies, bones out of joint, and isolation (Ps. 22:6–8, 14–15). Each of these images points toward the brutal experience of the crucifixion, which combines the inner experience of suffering of the individual with the public experience of suffering that is deeply meaningful because of its intensity. Then the psalm shifts from lament to praise—moving from anguish to trust: "All the ends of the world shall remember and turn to the Lord, and all the families of the nations shall worship before You" (Ps. 22:27). Suffering that is passed on to God has meaning as part of the narrative expanding across time to new creation and glory.

Origen utilizes this psalm as a prophecy about Christ's suffering. Divine purposes are often expressed through weakness and vulnerability. What inhuman eyes perceive as tragedy emerges, for God's providence, as the instrument of salvation, and ultimately victory (Origen 2001, 85). Likewise, John Chrysostom emphasized that the psalm foresaw the cross, demonstrating how lament and suffering reveal God's power and glory in a different way, one that is not limited to showing strength (Chrysostom 1999, 221).

For contemporary believers, Psalm 22 serves as both a mirror and a guide. It calls believers to voice their pain honestly and then to voice confidence that God has a redemptive purpose. Suffering with isolation and notions of defeat does not equate to abandonment; it can produce greater dependence on God, deeper spiritual growth, and prepare the believer to serve in God's kingdom work. The psalm ultimately reflects God's power to convert lament into praise. While the cross may be a moment of human suffering, it will also become a moment of revelation of God's glory and power.

Paul's Theology of the Cross (1 Cor. 1:18–25)

Paul's understanding of the cross in 1 Corinthians 1:18–25 provides a profound theological framework for God's power and wisdom as demonstrated in and through weakness, shedding light on what it means to be a Christian. Paul writes, "For the message of the cross is foolishness to those who are perishing, but to us who are being saved it is the power of God" (1 Cor. 1:18). Paul's contrasting language above highlights the paradox of being a Christian: God's power is revealed through weakness (Calvin 1960, 182).

The Corinthian situation must be examined; in a cultural context where rhetoric, wisdom, and status were highly valued, the weakness of the cross was also perceived as scandalous and foolish. Paul reframes the foolishness by indicating that God can use the foolishness of the cross for a greater wisdom than any wisdom this world can provide: "Because the foolishness of God is wiser than men, and the weakness of God is stronger than men" (1 Cor. 1:25). The cross exposes worldly standards for power while also showing a form of God's Kingdom where humility, obedience, and sacrificial love are paramount (Packer 1973, 220).

On a more theological level, Paul's understanding connects the usage of the cross to the Old Testament expectation of suffering. Isaiah 53 (that suffering is redemptive) and Psalm 22 (that suffering is transformative) play a role in Paul's understanding of Christ's death as intentional and in line with God's established plan for salvation. Seen through the direction of the cross, believers can see that what appears to be defeat in worldly terms is, in fact, victory through the apparent loss of lives being reconciled to God and the new creation being recognized (Wright 1996, 175).

Origen emphasizes Paul's wording, the ever-present paradox of God's intentionality with the cross. Moreover, God's design is that what we perceive as weakness in humanity is actually the means by which God brings redemption (Origen 2001, 88). For Christians today, Paul's theology serves as a model of faith for navigating a world that will be opposed, marked by trials, and rejection. The suffering, rejection, or apparent defeat that each person faces can be a part of God's power and transformative plans. The cross is both scandalous and glorious—a revelation of God's power and wisdom and an invitation for believers to live in God's upside-down Kingdom, a place where humility and sacrifice mean more than pride and worldly power.

Healing Through the Cross

The cross is more than a demonstration of divine supremacy; it is also a source of genuine healing, offering restoration, freedom, and wholeness to those who embrace it. At its core, the cross is a mechanism of forgiveness, thereby restoring the brokenness between God and humanity. Where humans fall short in reconciling, the death of Jesus is enough. As Paul writes, "In Him we have redemption through His blood, the forgiveness of sins, according to the riches of His grace" (Eph. 1:7). Forgiveness moves outward from God to humanity, producing healing among humans, restoring the relationships that creation longs for (Calvin 1960, 190).

In addition to restoring relationships, the cross liberates one from guilt and shame. Isaiah points to this pattern as he writes, "He was wounded for our transgressions, He was bruised for our iniquities; the chastisement for our peace was upon Him" (Isa. 53:5). When believers identify with the death of Christ, they are liberated from the weighted guilt and shame of their sin and free to experience spiritual freedom and live in empowered obedience and intimacy with God. John Stott writes, "Realizing the cost of forgiveness in Christ gives rise to greater appreciation, and modifies the whole moral and relational existence of the believer" (Stott 1986, 53).

Finally, the cross also brings healing from the brokenness caused by suffering. Each of Christ's own experiences of suffering, rejection, pain, and disparagement demonstrates that God's redemptive work attends to the actuality of vulnerability that comes with human frailty. Henri Nouwen states that the cross shows God the Father engaged within human suffering; thus making its meaning at least somewhat redemptive (rather than absurd). God can now move productively through suffering as a redirecting vehicle for divine healing and spiritual growth (Nouwen 1992, 112). This productivity not only encompasses the cognitive connections to healing in an emotional, relational, or spiritual sense, but it also models for believers how our own vulnerabilities can become galvanizing agents as we surrender to, and trust God to transform personal suffering, pain, grief, and loss into service and transformative growth.

For the believer today, the cross is both a theological and a practical reality. The cross heals relationships, helps alleviate guilt, and transforms brokenness into health and grace. As believers lean into the cross and make it part of who we are through faith, reflection, and obedience, and apply our whole selves to the expressed purpose of healing relationally, emotionally, and spiritually, we are, in effect, employing the whole of healing through the life of the cross. The cross becomes the embodiment of a divine paradox: profound healing, yielded through suffering and apparent defeat, provides an unprecedented demonstration of God's power from the most vulnerable human moment; that power is most fully realized at the most significant level of human frailty.

Forgiveness as Restoration of Relationships

The cross serves as a graphic representation of healing, beginning with forgiveness. This forgiveness causes us to reorient our relationships vertically, in our relationship with God, and horizontally, in our relationships with others. It is significant that the sacrificial death Christ died on the cross is the definitive model of reconciling love, and shows us that forgiveness is not simply a virtue we ought to practice in the abstract; rather, it is a transformative reality that heals damaged relationships. Paul writes, "In Him we have redemption through His blood, the forgiveness of our trespasses, according to the riches of His grace" (Eph. 1:7). The vertical and horizontal position of forgiveness comes from God, flowing downward to us. Forgiveness is the foundational basis of communion with God, and it serves as a model for believers on how to offer grace in their relationships with others (Calvin 1960, 190).

The cross, additionally, reveals to us that forgiveness seldom occurs without both surrender and humility. Take, for example, Jesus' prayer to the Father as he hung on the cross, "Father, forgive them, for they do not know what they do" (Luke 23:34). He exemplifies the depths of relational power in forgiving those who perpetrate evil against him. This act of divine mercy creates transformation, creates an adjusted understanding of justice and reconciliation by communicating how God's way of doing things is different from our natural inclination toward tit for tat. John Chrysostom offers helpful insight when he writes that forgiving injustice as Christ does reveals not only a Kingdom ethic but states, "Forgiving injustice is at the heart of authentic community life and an authentic spiritual formation" (Chrysostom 1999, 221).

Forgiveness is more than a unifying dynamic in our interpersonal relations; it restores the interior life of the believer. Unforgiveness breeds bitterness, resentment, ultimately leading to spiritual dryness and disconnection. Holding onto forgiveness is an act that sets believers free to participate, both emotionally and spiritually, in the life of the Kingdom of God, released through the freedom brought about by the death of Christ. Augustine has rightly contended that divine forgiveness changes the human heart, enlarging its capacity to love God and others (Augustine 2001, 317).

In a practical sense, Christians are called to embody the ongoing reconciliatory work of the cross in their everyday lives. We are called to give grace to others, readily forgiving those who have harmed us, seeking reconciliation where relationships have been fractured, countering vengeance with an attitude of mercy and humility. The cross continues to shape a living pattern: the ability to forgive others is a gift from God, and when we receive that gift from God, it is our responsibility to share that forgiveness with others. Forgiveness restores relationships, liberates the heart, and continues to renew lives in the redeeming work of Christ across space and time.

Freedom from Guilt and Shame

The cross offers believers incredible freedom from guilt and shame, reaching the deepest places of hurt in the human heart. In Christ's voluntarily suffered death, the penalty of sin is taken, leaving believers forgiven before the God of the universe. Isaiah has prophesied about the servant Jesus: "But he was wounded for our transgressions, he was bruised for our iniquities; the chastisement for our peace was upon him, and by his stripes we are healed" (Isa. 53:5). This text boldly proclaims that the suffering of Jesus is redemptive. It offers human beings spiritual and deep emotional healing and restoration. By accepting the freedom found in the gospel, Christians can release themselves from the guilt deeply rooted in their hearts, which often serves as a barrier preventing them from drawing closer to God and growing spiritually (Wright 1996, 178).

Paul relates this life-changing freedom from the cross in Romans 8:1 when he states, "There is therefore now no condemnation to those who are in Christ Jesus." Christians are not simply forgiven; they are counted as righteous, far removed from the cycle of self-hatred and fear of punishment from God. According to J. I. Packer, when grace is understood as revealed through Christ's death, it changes the conscience of the believer—living not in a sense of lack and not having value is not the rhythm of one's life. Instead, it is characterized by confidence, obedience, peace, and the absence of guilt (Packer 1973, 228).

The cross addresses relational shame. When sin disrupts our relationship with God, ourselves, and fellow humans, and guilt involves the responsibility to act, it can become very cumbersome. Through Christ's atonement, believers are invited to experience a reconciliation that unites the self with God, themselves, and their communities. Henri Nouwen suggests that the guilt people have experienced and internalized has become a maxim, which becomes spiritually formative. The cross ultimately reveals itself to be one of the greatest imaginable stories of transformation, rather than highlighting our levels of human imperfection and inadequacy (Nouwen 1992, 118).

Practically, living into the freedom of the cross means actively claiming the freedom of forgiveness, rather than succumbing to the lies of shame we feel due to our failings. This must mean acknowledging the mistakes of the past and still framing our lives and identity without being tied to past transgressions, presenting lives of humble, obedient love, so clearly modeled from Jesus as ontological revelation by way of death—where losing in appearance became the ultimate way to triumph over a life that constricts or restricts the intimate giving and receiving of forgiveness (the basis of love) from God as transformative power toward daily transfigurative life into purpose from God's moment of grace.

Healing Brokenness Through Christ's Sacrifice

The crucifixion of Jesus Christ provides a unique and powerful means of healing and restoration, acknowledging the inherent brokenness of human life. Human brokenness can take many forms: fractured relationships, personal failure, emotional injury, or spiritual disorientation. The cross proclaims that through His death, Jesus paid the penalty of sin and healed the brokenness of all who believe in Him. In fact, the prediction of the messianic suffering servant in Isaiah 53 states He took all the weakness of humanity: "Surely He has borne our griefs and carried our sorrows" (Isa. 53:4). The cross changes pain into redemption; it says firmly that divine power is to be seen when human weakness is at its apex (Wright 1996, 182).

Paul's theology also affirms the healing dimension. Paul viewed life in Christ in 2 Corinthians 5:18–19: "All this is from God, who reconciled us to himself through Christ and gave us the ministry of reconciliation: that God was reconciling the world to himself in Christ, not counting people's sins against them." Paul collaborated with the teachings of Christ, as he relied on Christ's suffering to be part of a way of redemption that healed problematic relationships and restored one's integrity. John Stott reminds us we are justified and sanctified in Jesus through the cross; it offers "spiritual clarity" and, therefore, the moral will and strength to live with restoration (Stott 1986, 65).

Origen counters the purity of the suffering servant because in and through Christ's sacrifice, God enters into the very brokenness of human life (with all its dimensions). Therefore, the cross of Jesus Christ enters the depth of humanity's pain to bring reconciliation and healing, as wholeness living in brokenness has a context for God's grace and power to be seen (Origen 2001, 91). Similarly, Augustine reminds us that human brokenness is a reality; however, in Jesus, God can redeem not only humanity's external sin but also the disordered affections of the heart, bringing peace and growth (Augustine 2001, 320).

Thus, for contemporary believers, the acceptance of life's brokenness—as emotional scars, guilt, estrangement, or whatever it may be—can find its way into the hands of Jesus Christ. Physical healing is the healing of pain, but true healing restores purpose, harmony, and spirit. The cross of Jesus Christ invites the recovery of wholeness; it teaches us that God's love transforms weakness into strength, sorrow into expectation, and brokenness becomes a pathway for God to work through in redemptive glory. In leaving this comment, let me say this: the cross of Jesus Christ is the basis of forgiveness as an act of grace, redemption, healing, reconciliation, and a channel of spiritual flourishing.

Joy in the Cross

While the cross is predominantly seen as an instrument of suffering and apparent defeat, it also serves as a source of great joy for believers. This joy is fundamentally rooted in the redemption made possible through Christ's suffering. Paul states, "For since the death of his Son restored our friendship with God while we were still his enemies, we will certainly be saved through the life of his Son" (Rom. 5:10–11). Through the act of redemption, despair is transformed into hope, guilt into grace, and loss into gain. Thus, joy that is solely rooted in the cross has nothing to do with circumstances, but is dependent upon the firm reality of God's saving work (Wright 1996, 190).

Often, suffering is used as a means to channel divine joy. As stated in James 1:2–3, "Consider it pure joy, my brothers and sisters, whenever you face trials of many kinds, because you know that the testing of your faith produces perseverance." The cross exemplifies this reality because what the world sees as humiliation or weakness, in God's plan, actually fulfills His faithfulness and power. In Packer's words, joyful confidence in God's loving sovereignty and grace amid suffering is the key, because suffering can bring us to greater spiritual closeness and strength (Packer 1973, 233).

According to Henri Nouwen, daily acceptance of the cross is how we can achieve this joy. Joy does not mean the absence of suffering; instead, true joy goes alongside it with God present in the experience, or in the gracious way suffering finds meaning in God's purposes. Believers are challenged to embrace even the small sacrifices, disappointments, and frustrations that come with walking in the way of Christ. Living a cross-focused life day by day helps train the heart to experience joy in God's redeeming work and recognize God's presence transforming all situations (Nouwen 1992, 125).

Practically, joy at the cross challenges believers to re-imagine their understanding of trials, suffering, and weakness. The unpleasant experiences we encounter are not simply trials we have to endure; they are also opportunities for growth and equality in God's redemptive work. Who we are becoming in the cross means that joy does not come from our comfort or control, but from God's wisdom, to whom we surrender everything in pursuit of the values of His Kingdom. The cross inevitably changes, producing joy through human suffering because God's love, power, and glory are expressed when our human expectations are deconstructed.

Joy in Redemption Achieved

Through the cross comes the ultimate redemption! With redemption comes an ultimate joy—a joy that is not circumstantial but is found forever in Christ's accomplished reconciliation through His sacrificial death. Romans 5:10–11 declares, "For if when we were enemies we were reconciled to God through the death of His Son, much more, having been reconciled, we shall be saved by His life." Such redemption is both a locus of divine grace and a reality that we live, restoring believers once again into right relationship with God and enabling them to enjoy a joy that exceeds human comprehension (Wright 1996, 190).

The redemption achieved at the cross brings relief from guilt, fear, and spiritual disunity. Christ bears the weight of sin that rightly belonged to humankind: "He Himself bore our sins in His own body on the tree" (1 Pet. 2:24). Now, through this substitutional sacrifice, believers are offered divine forgiveness and liberation to enjoy intimacy with God without shame and condemnation. Theologian J. I. Packer states that to understand the nature of God's redemptive work is to find joy that is secure and abiding, rooted in the assurance of God's love and promise of salvation (Packer 1973, 235).

Notably, the joy of redemption is a communal experience. Through the cross of Christ, reconciliation extends beyond the person to the community of believers. Relationships broken by sin can be healed, and the Church becomes a living testimony of God's mercy and grace. Augustine of Hippo writes about how God's divine redemption renews the human heart, enabling individuals to learn to love correctly and join in God's Kingdom mission (Augustine 2001, 322).

Lastly, the joy of redemption has a quality of action. It inspires believers to live obediently, in gratitude, and in servitude. It must not be normative or informal, but an action-oriented response to God's work of transformation. Henri Nouwen writes that the depth of God's redemptive work produces a spiritual vitality that is an expression of the totality of one's inner devotion and outer action (Nouwen 1992, 128).

As such, the cross, with its connotation of suffering and defeat, becomes the fountain of joy in redemption. The invitation for believers each day is to participate in and accept this joy, to recognize that God's power, displayed through Christ's death, restores life and freedom, and invites the faithful into a rhythm of gratitude, worship, and action for transformation.

Celebrating God's Faithfulness Through Suffering

The cross represents an intriguing juxtaposition of suffering and joy. It reveals that suffering is an experience whose purpose is not a sign of God's absence, but an invitation to experience God's steadfastness in the world. In the context of our suffering, we are challenged, as believers, to recognize that there is an even larger and ongoing redemptive story in which suffering is part of the process. James 1:2–3 tells us, "Count it all joy when you fall into various trials, knowing that the testing of your faith produces patience." In teaching us to "count it all joy," James turns suffering on its head, asking believers to find grounds to rejoice in God's unending love even when circumstances seem dire (Packer 1973, 238).

Jesus' experience on the cross serves as the most compelling example of why we should celebrate God's faithfulness in the midst of suffering. He chose to submit himself to betrayal, ridicule, and overwhelming pain. His desire to see the Father's will triumph above personal desire reiterates that suffering can teach, be infused with meaning, and purpose (Matt. 26:39). As Augustine of Hippo stated, "God often works through trials to transform us spiritually, for as we learn to hope and trust in his providence, we become open to growing into greater awareness of God's grace" (Augustine 2001, 328). The cross shows that when the world sees defeat, providence can leverage all circumstances to fulfill God's purposes, demonstrating infinite wisdom, power, and steadfast love.

Suffering also invites us into a communal and relational dimension of faith. As believers trust God during our suffering and continue to act obediently, we remain witnesses to God's faithfulness in the world and an inspiration to others, even if it is simply to comfort them in their own suffering. John Stott noted that rejoicing while suffering does not diminish the suffering, but rather glorifies God by demonstrating confidence in God's ultimate purpose (Stott 1986, 72). The cross powerfully demonstrates this: we see that the suffering of Jesus produced a deep golden thread of God's faithfulness towards humanity and opened the way for salvation.

For a modern believer, celebrating God through suffering involves trusting and reflecting on our experience, while also making a discernment between trusting the suffering and trusting God in the process. It means we are to embrace suffering as an opportunity to grow spiritually and mature, to lean into and rely on His sustaining presence, while also considering how we are helping to build God's redemptive work in the world. If we can and do this consistently as we believe with faith, Henri Nouwen would argue we begin to transform our suffering from a source of despair, pain, and anguish into grace that matures us, builds resilience, and deepens our understanding and experience of God's unending love (Nouwen 1992, 132).

Nouwen on Embracing the Cross Daily

Henri Nouwen offers a profoundly pastoral and reflective perspective on the ongoing engagement with the cross, stating that we can realize its power through salvation. However, we can also realize its power through the life of the believer. This daily engagement involves embracing the essential rhythm of vulnerability, surrender, and awareness of God's presence, even in the mundane struggles of personal limitations (Nouwen 1992, 135). Nouwen suggests that the cross is not merely a theological concept, but a part of life that shapes one's character, relationships, and spiritual formation.

This daily participation begins by recognizing human weakness. God's call to "my grace is sufficient for you, for My strength is made perfect in weakness" (2 Cor. 12:9) invites believers to move from reliance upon self to a place of surrender and engagement with God's sustaining provision. Nouwen also shares that daily participation in the cross allows individuals to be shaped in humility, reminding Christians that God's work is never built upon the power of humanity, but rather to accept the invitation to participate in God's redemptive purposes (Nouwen 1992, 138).

Nouwen notes further that the cross transforms suffering into opportunities for grace. He advocates that by leaning into the cross with the trials, disappointments, and relational difficulties, Christians begin to see God's redemptive presence in what may seem an ordinary or painful experience. Writing about this hidden work God does in human weakness, Augustine reflects that it produces some of the deepest spiritual growth (Augustine 2001, 331). Daily participation in the cross enables believers to perceive their ordinary lives in a sacred context, where God's power and love are evident and transformative.

In practical terms, this means there must be intentionality in praying through situations with cross reflection, responding to God's call in obedience, and nurturing compassion for oneself and others. Nouwen expresses that when believers live faithfully in respect to the cross, they become places of God's love, healing, and reconciliation. The great paradox of the cross, where weakness reveals God's strength, can establish a spiritual posture of hopeful resilience and joy (Nouwen 1992, 140).

In the end, Nouwen invites the Christian community to occupy the cross daily, recognizing that it is not some distant power, but a nearness. This exercise for believers fosters spiritual renewal, deepens Christian communion with God, and cultivates a credible ability to extend grace, forgiveness, and love in the rhythms of everyday life. The cross, which was once the source of suffering, is now the very structure where they might find ongoing hope, strength, and spiritual vitality.

The cross teaches us about joy and suffering: they are not mutually exclusive. Christians find in Christ that the challenges of life, when brought to God, become opportunities to celebrate His faithfulness, which reveals the truth about God's power being made perfect in human weakness.

Love Demonstrated in Sacrifice

The cross exemplifies the greatest manifestation of love, revealing the sacrificial love that God has for His creation, which is both relational and transformative. On the cross, Jesus exemplifies the self-giving that Christians are called to exhibit in the broader context of love for others. Romans 5:8 states, "But God demonstrates His own love toward us, in that while we were still sinners, Christ died for us." This divine action exemplifies the nature of love being given without merit or repayment; this love is freely given to even those who would curse and harm us (Packer 1973, 241).

Jesus demonstrates that love and sacrifice must be intertwined; love toward our enemies and neighbors must include suffering for the sake of others. Jesus states, "But I say to you, love your enemies, bless those who curse you, do good to those who hate you" (Matt. 5:44). Love, to be authentic at some level, must hinder our comfort and convenience through vulnerability, self-denial, and sacrifice of our time for others, with the understanding that love and sacrifice are often inseparable. In this regard, Augustine notes that Christ, through his sacrificial love, inspires humans to love others beyond their natural inclination to do so; therefore, Christians, by engaging in love, participate in the ethic of the Kingdom of self-giving (Augustine 2001, 338).

Dietrich Bonhoeffer's thoughts on costly grace further elucidate the practical outworking of sacrificial love. In his text *The Cost of Discipleship*, Bonhoeffer notes that genuine Christian love frequently entails tangible risks and heartache, and that love, as exemplified by Christ, is not merely an idea pursued in comfort (Bonhoeffer 1995, 112). In summary, the cross serves as both inspiration to love and a guide in doing so; that love is not an ideal we can subscribe to, but a practice that sometimes requires suffering and commitment.

For Christians today, this means living out the love of Christ every day and in everyday forms: forgiving those who wrong us, giving generously without expecting anything in return, and consciously working to help others experience life and health. Each time Christians choose to love others through self-giving love, they are agents of reconciliation, healing, and life. The cross demonstrates that love does not flourish in self-interest or ease, but in self-giving, obedience, and trust in God's purposes for redemption and renewal. Seen in this way, Jesus' sacrifice on the cross has become the ultimate witness to this transformative hunger for life, dedicated to challenging believers to regard their lives in recognition of the cost of following Jesus by encircling ourselves in love rooted in suffering, just as He did.

Christ's Love Poured Out on the Cross

The cross stands as the supreme demonstration of divine love, where the Son of God willingly endured suffering and death for the redemption of humanity. Romans 5:8 proclaims, "But God demonstrates His own love toward us, in that while we were still sinners, Christ died for us." This passage reveals that Christ's love is proactive, unconditional, and sacrificial. It is not contingent upon human merit, righteousness, or repentance; rather, it originates entirely from God's gracious initiative (Packer 1973, 241).

Christ's self-giving exemplifies love in its most profound form. On the cross, Jesus bore the full weight of human sin, experienced abandonment, and embraced suffering in obedience to the Father. Isaiah 53:5 affirms this, stating, "But He was wounded for our transgressions, He was bruised for our iniquities; the chastisement for our peace was upon Him, and by His stripes we are healed." Here, love is inseparable from sacrifice; it requires taking upon oneself the consequences that rightfully belong to others. Augustine of Hippo emphasizes that Christ's sacrificial love transforms the human heart, making it capable of receiving and extending grace, even in the face of injustice and hostility (Augustine 2001, 338).

The cross also demonstrates the relational dimension of love. Christ's death reconciles humanity to God, bridging the chasm caused by sin. This reconciliation is not merely juridical but relational, restoring fellowship, intimacy, and communion. The depth of Christ's love invites believers to participate in a similar pattern of self-giving, extending mercy and forgiveness to others (Stott 1986, 77).

Practically, understanding Christ's love on the cross reshapes the believer's ethical and spiritual life. It challenges Christians to prioritize others' needs above self-interest, to endure personal cost for the good of the community, and to embody compassion even toward those who oppose them. By reflecting on the magnitude of Christ's love, believers are called to imitate His example, making the cross a daily model for living sacrificially and relationally. The love poured out on Calvary thus becomes a transformative lens through which all human relationships, acts of service, and moments of suffering are interpreted and redeemed.

Loving Enemies and Neighbors in Christlike Imitation

In conclusion, the cross emphasizes to believers a radical ethical position on love. This love transcends our comfort and familiarity, even with those who are adversaries or harmful to us. Jesus is teaching in Matthew 5:44, "But I say to you, love your enemies, bless those who curse you, do good to those who hate you, and pray for those who spitefully use you and persecute you." This instruction goes against our natural inclination to repay evil with evil or to ignore those who oppose us. Jesus beckons us to be in Christ, to be drawn into a higher relational integrity which we imitate in Him, rooted in loving as He sacrificed loving (Packer 1973, 245)

Loving our enemies begins with recognizing their inherent value and humanity, and loving as Christ loved, even toward them. In this case, Jesus on the cross serves as an accurate model: Jesus forgave those that crucified Him, "Father, forgive them for they do not know what they do" (Luke 23:34). As Augustine notes, Christ forgives us not because we deserve it, but to transform our hearts by demonstrating divine love beyond our human imagination and capacity, and we are to love like Him (Augustine 2001, 342). Here, we see that love is more than a concept; it is a concrete action that can transform into relational reconciliation, overcoming bitterness.

Following Christ's likeness toward love of neighbor is inseparable. In the parable of the Good Samaritan (Luke 10:30–37), Jesus illustrates how our love for even strangers crosses ethnic, social, and relational lines. Real, neighborly love knows a type of compassion that is active, costly, and regards attentively the needs of others, regardless of their background, status, or other relationship we might have with them. John Stott helps us remember that love is not a suggestion; it is the essence of discipleship, which Jesus embodied on the cross by calling on us to understand that love includes a willingness to take a risk, capacity for humility, and extend beyond our comfort for the sake of another (Stott 1986, 80).

Practically, our practice with these teachings would be patience, forgiveness, and proactive kindness. Contrasted with the impulse of favor exchange or retribution, we teach a way that is countercultural to social norms held by the created but offers a posture of the created adopting that which models the self-giving love of Christ. In this way of life, we are given able bodies and intentions to participate in God's reconciling work for the good of others, as we accept participants in a Kingdom where mercy triumphs over vengeance and compassion subverts conflict. The cross is the ultimate framework, embodying the epitome of love, which is sacrificial, forgiving, and restorative, while bringing hope and the presence of God into every context of our relationships.

Bonhoeffer on Costly Love as Kingdom Witness

In Dietrich Bonhoeffer's reflections on costly love, he describes the interests and realities of Christlike self-giving in the life of the individual Christian. In *The Cost of Discipleship*, Bonhoeffer emphasizes that genuine Christian love is never comfortable or safe and is not merely sentimental; it calls for concrete action, personal cost, and sacrifice, as well as faithful obedience to God's calling (Bonhoeffer 1995, 112). The cross of Christ exemplifies such costly love, where Christ suffers and dies not for Himself but for the redemption of humanity, thus establishing the ultimate pattern for Kingdom living.

According to Bonhoeffer, costly love acts as a witness to the reality of God's Kingdom. In Matt. 5:16, it exhorts, "Let your light so shine before men, that they may see your good works and glorify your Father in heaven." Through costly love, Christians demonstrate God's power and presence in concrete forms of action and witness, thereby revealing God's justice, mercy, and grace. This type of love is not passive; such love confronts injustice, serves the vulnerable, and actively seeks and cultivates the flourishing of others, expressing the self-giving nature of Christ on the cross (Stott 1986, 85).

Bonhoeffer's theology also includes a foundational understanding that costly love often involves personal risk. The cross demonstrates that obedience and compassion can risk suffering, being a target, and being misunderstood. However, through costly love, the believer is active in God's work of redemption in creation, embodying the values of human flourishing that God offered in the Kingdom, and ultimately providing visible proof of God in the great center of redeeming value (Bonhoeffer 1995, 118). Additionally, Augustine views God's love for the world as shaped through love, enabling humans to act courageously and humbly in ways that serve others (Augustine 2001, 345).

Practically speaking, costly love requires discernment, effort, and commitment. Costly love involves making intentional choices for the best interests of others, forgiving those who have wronged you, and enduring suffering for the sake of righteousness. Bonhoeffer's vision of discipleship compels the believer to respond faithfully in a world that often does not appreciate grace, acting in ways that prove the cross is not simply historical but alive, as a model for ethical, redemptive engagement. Costly love is transformative for the believer and a witness to God's Kingdom, demonstrating the depth of God's mercy and an invitation into the believer's costly, sacrificial obedience.

Theological Reflections

The cross not only illustrates God's redeeming love, but also provides an opportunity for theological reflection on God's paradox of weakness and power. Augustine of Hippo describes God's strength as most evident through humanity's weakness. In *Confessions*, he notes that while it is futile to rely upon self, submitting to God's providence enables God's glory to shine through (Augustine 2001, 350). The cross brings this to light; as an illustration of humiliation or weakness, it is the instrument of God's ultimate victory. Therefore, believers are invited to acknowledge their own weakness through vulnerability, believing that God's power works through their weaknesses to fulfill His purpose.

Martin Luther notices the primary issue of justification through the cross. In his Reformation theology, righteousness is not earned by a believer's work, but given as a reward of faith that exhibits Christ's sacrifice (Luther 1520, 118). The cross becomes the ultimate instrument of God's divine grace, justifying sinners before God and producing a peace that surpasses all human understanding. The wording in Rom. 3:24–25, where Paul expects believers to be "justified freely by His grace through the redemption that is in Christ Jesus," illustrates the power of the cross. He explains that the cross removes human boasting, as salvation comes entirely from God's merciful initiative (Wright 1996, 205).

John Calvin highlights the glory revealed in Christ's obedience—according to his theological perspective, Christ's voluntary obedience to the Father's plan for all humanity glorifies God. In *Institutes of the Christian Religion*, Calvin describes the disposition of God's glory as being understood and seen through perfect obedience (Calvin 1559, 402). The cross reveals both God's holiness and God's redemptive plan, as an innocent act of obedience is intertwined with suffering and enduring distress for the salvation of humanity. This theological examination invites believers to imitate Christ's obedience, humility, sacrifice, and trust in God's providence.

As a combination of Augustine, Luther, and Calvin, the cross illuminates how it is a place for knowing God's paradox of divine weakness and strength, granting justification through grace and showing glory through obedience—the cultivation of humility, trust, and faithful obedience. Collectively, these theologians inspire believers to cultivate humility, faithfulness, and trust. The cross as a historical event illustrates God's glory and the all-powerful nature of God, viewed through both an additive and a theological lens, shaping the believer's understanding of living out the Christian faith through worship and ethics.

Augustine on the Triumph of God's Power in Weakness

Augustine of Hippo's theology embodies the paradoxical nature of human weakness and the power of God, as amply demonstrated in the cross of Christ. Augustine's phrase in *Confessions* reminds us that God reveals their great power where humans recognize their feebleness: "You have made us for Yourself, O Lord, and our hearts are restless until they rest in You" (Augustine 2001, 351). The believer's reliance on God, especially in times of suffering, becomes a vessel of divine glory and power. The cross is a demonstration of this reality because it was an occasion of shame and defeat. God's victory is realized in Jesus Christ's apparent disgrace.

Scripture reminds believers that divine power is made perfect in weakness. Paul refers to this in the second letter to the Corinthians: "My grace is sufficient for you, for My strength is made perfect in weakness" (2 Cor. 12:9). Augustine interprets passages such as this as a call for the believer to let go of independence and take on a posture of vulnerability, which is a spiritual discipline. Only in authentic vulnerability can the believer experience the paradox of the cross; human deficiency becomes the means by which divine sovereignty and grace are effective for the believer (Augustine 2001, 352).

Augustine also reflects on the transformation of God, showing power through weakness. When believers rely on themselves and their professed limitations, they begin to develop humility, self-control, patience, and a stronger will. This was the essence of the cross, and it taught that suffering, hardships, and defeats should not be perceived as abandonment by God, but rather as opportunities for God's glory to come forth. In Jesus' obedience to God, wisdom and strength have placed God's weakness in a position to surprise the world with God's victory, redeeming it and granting eternal life (Wright 1996, 210).

On a practical level, Augustine's reflection reminds believers to face life's challenges with faith rather than despair. It will not be weakness or failure, but the spiritual space for God to express God's love and power in the believer's life. Careful vulnerability and denying the need to control will position the believer to really experience the triumph of the cross, as believers are assured that God's strength is at play where human strength fails. In this light, Augustine's reflection conveys a profound spiritual truth: God's power is most evident when human weakness is most apparent, and the cross stands as the most conspicuous symbol of this paradox.

Luther on Justification and the Cross

Martin Luther's understanding of justification by faith is centrally focused on the cross as the location of divine grace and human redemption. In a seminal work of the Reformation period, notably *The Freedom of a Christian*, he stated that righteousness is freely imputed through faith in the sacrificial death of Christ, and not by anything that is morally achieved or self-imposed (Luther 1520, 118). The cross is thus both the means of, and the evidence of, God's mercy in reconciling sinners to himself, and of bestowing peace for those who trust themselves to Christ.

In Romans 3:24-25, we are told, "Being justified freely by His grace through the redemption that is in Christ Jesus, whom God set forth as a propitiation by His blood, through faith." Luther understood the great significance of these verses: the believer's relationship with God is not changed simply by anything we do, or by striving or performing, but through the efficacy caused by Christ's obedience and His atoning death. Additionally, the cross represents both the cost and the gift of salvation, demonstrating the extent of divine love while also assuring us that justification is purely based on the merit of Christ (Packer 1973, 248).

Luther's reflections provoked the paradox of the cross—what seemed like humiliation and weakness in human terms was, in fact, victory in divine terms. Focusing on Christ's crucifixion, the believer presented God who was both just and merciful. The cross ensured forgiveness, obliterated condemnation, and conquered shame. Calvin aptly notes that Christ's obedience through the cross reveals the glory of God and the perception of divine love (Calvin 1559, 402).

Practically, Luther's theology was designed to promote believers in freely living out the nature of assurance. Trust in the cross freed the believer from self-justification and invoked humility, gratitude, and obedience. The believer's life became a free response of devotion, rather than a performance to earn merits. This free devotion was an expression of trust, conscience, ethical development, and social relations. The cross is not simply our history, but rather a current phenomenon that affects one's faith, character, and witness today. In complete trust in Christ, Christians ultimately experience profound joy, peace, and security, which can only be provided by the redemptive worth of God, demonstrating that justification and salvation remain a gift to receive and a celebration of transformed lives.

Calvin on the Glory Revealed in Christ's Obedience

John Calvin's theological reflections on the cross emphasize the glory of God revealed in Christ's perfect obedience. In the *Institutes of the Christian Religion*, Calvin explains that Christ's obedience, even to the point of death, glorifies God's holiness, justice, and mercy. He explains the consistency of God's redemptive plan (Calvin 1559, 402). The cross, in itself, is not merely a historical episode of suffering, but a theological revelation; it demonstrates God's glory in uniting human salvation with God's purpose.

At his crucifixion, Christ's obedience to the Father in complete self-giving love and humility is the most radical embodiment of God's will possible. In Philippians 2:8, we read: "And being found in appearance as a man, He humbled Himself and became obedient to the point of death, even the death of the cross." For Calvin, it is at the point of impotent submission to God here in time and space that Christ reveals the grandeur of God's plan of reconciliation and redemption. Calvin highlights the same idea in his comment that the glory of God is revealed not through outstanding human accomplishments or worldly victories, but through humble obedience in the face of suffering. In humility, demonstrating human understanding is not to be preferred to divine wisdom (Wright 1996, 215)

In reference to Christ's obedience, Calvin continues to assert that the emphasis in our texts is not merely to describe and evaluate Jesus as submitting entirely to God, but also as an example for the believer, who is called to a life of humble submission aligning with God's will. When Christians contemplate the cross, they receive revelation and are reminded that glory is not separate from service, sacrifice, and obedience in the midst of trial. Likewise, Augustine emphasized that divine power is often most paraded in weakness and humility, reinforcing the reality that God's glory is easily mistaken for defeat through conventional worldly understandings of winning and losing (Augustine 2001, 353).

In terms of practice, Calvin encourages Christians to view obedience to God as participation in God's ongoing work of redemption, rather than a grievous obligation. Each day of being faithful in every act of honesty and service to God is an act of obedience, like those of Christ, that contributes to the ongoing revelation of God's glory in the world. The cross is revealed in the place of not only theological education but also practical, ethical, and Christian leadership education. God's glory is revealed most completely when Christlike obedience transforms suffering in Christians into a vehicle of salvation, hope, and renewed spiritual well-being.

Living the Cross Today

Living the cross today means that the truth of the cross is applied in every facet of life. When people face personal challenges, bearing them with a view toward the kingdom of God is what transforms suffering into spiritual growth; James reminds them to "consider it all joy when you fall into various trials, knowing that the testing of your faith produces patience" (James 1:2–3). Paul exemplified this, rejoicing in the midst of persecution because he was able to see suffering differently as an opportunity for the power of Christ to be revealed (2 Corinthians 4:8–10; Packer 1973, 215).

The outflow of Christ's heart is living a life of serving others in love. Jesus taught that the kingdom of God measures greatness in humility, meaning that to be great in God's kingdom means to be a servant: "whoever desires to be great among you, let him be your servant" (Mark 10:43–45). From comforting those in need to mentoring the marginalized, selfless acts are the love of the cross (Carson 1991, 58). Walking in humility and strength follows the same pattern of self-emptying sacrificial love. The strength God requires is accepting His will, obedience, and submission to it (Philippians 2:5–8; Moo 1996, 143). Humility is what God uses to provide believers with an opportunity, from an eternal perspective, for spiritual growth, reconnecting and deepening relationships in Christ, and focusing on God's purpose rather than our difficulties.

Forgiving others involves living the cross. Believers are called to forgive just as Christ forgave (Ephesians 4:32; Colossians 3:13). Forgiving each day allows a person to experience the peace of Christ, even if they have been wronged or are experiencing a painful loss; it also reflects God's love in transforming and redeeming (Wright 2006, 91). Even in the pain, the believer can still experience the joy of being in Christ. Paul and Silas sang praises to God while in prison, demonstrating rejoicing in adversity (Acts 16:25; Packer 1973, 220).

The cross illustrates the nature of the relationships one should have with people and, likewise, guides them in their relationships and decisions. It reflects the nature of sacrificial love for family, friends, relationships, and communities (Ephesians 5:25; Moo 1996, 158). Incorporating the cross into decisions throughout the day, not just for career choices, prioritizes God's desire in every daily action, with each moment reflecting eternal values and glory (Romans 12:1–2; Wright 2006, 112). Sharing the hope of redemption with someone extends the power of the cross to the potential of redeeming others, and when others accept Christ, they are transformed in both deeds and words (1 Peter 1:3–5; Carson 1991, 72).

Living the cross today is not an abstract concept; it is practical, direct, and transformative. Each trial, each act of service, and each daily choice allows believers an opportunity to embody the realm of Christ's love, humility, and redemptive power.

Bearing Personal Trials with Kingdom Perspective

To endure personal suffering with a biblical mindset requires the ability to look beyond the experience of pain to see the all-encompassing, eternal purposes of God through pain and suffering. Personal trials are not purposeless experiences; they are meaningful experiences that foster faith formation and renew the mind. The apostle James encourages his readers: "My brethren, count it all joy when you fall into various trials, knowing that the testing of your faith produces patience" (James 1:2–3). Rather than merely seeing discomfort or trouble, a biblical perspective enables us to recognize that God is using adversity to cultivate perseverance, faithfulness, and dependence on Him (Packer 1973, 215).

We can observe how a biblical mindset was evident in the life and letters of the Apostle Paul. In the midst of imprisonments, beatings, and countless other trials, Paul saw suffering as the medium through which God's power would be revealed: "We are hard-pressed on every side, yet not crushed; we are perplexed, but not in despair; persecuted, but not forsaken; struck down, but not destroyed" (2 Corinthians 4:8–9). Paul, in his letters, viewed trials again as the work of God's Spirit and as something believers can grow into, testifying about how we can overcome the suffering and difficulties of life through the power of God.

A biblical mindset holds significant importance in shaping our internal perspective on a particular trial, influencing how we respond emotionally and cognitively. Rather than potentially seeing ourselves as bitter or in despair, a trial can actually help us cultivate patience as a virtue, or regain our empathy and gain wisdom from what we are suffering. Romans 5:3–5 depicts, "Not only that, but we also glory in tribulations, knowing that tribulation produces perseverance; perseverance, character; and character, hope." What we have in Paul is a tracing of the movement from suffering to spiritual maturity, or virtue character growth toward hope. In a biblical mindset, you can endure while going through, hoping to maintain and remain steadfast through the process, and trust in the sovereignty of God and His care for you as you cope with hardship (Moo 1996, 142)

In terms of practice, for some individuals, holding a biblical mindset may involve more prayer, scripture meditation, and conversations with other Christians to gain support and encouragement. Seeking God's guidance and comfort in the experience of trials helps bridge the individual's suffering to some larger purpose that God has in mind for it. When one comes to the understanding that suffering is only "for a moment" as 2

Corinthians 4:17 states, and that God has pre-planned for us an "eternal weight of glory beyond all comparison," we begin to grasp how we can build resilience during times of hardship, and be able to relate to Paul's mindset around judgment when living with hope, rejecting the critical, sinful dimensions of our experience while being able to rejoice in the bigger picture of transformation that is happening in us (Colossians 3:23).

To develop a biblical mindset in the midst of personal trials does not imply passive resignation; it fosters a faith-driven response. It counters making sense of hardships on our own or reshaping our thinking in order to bring to prominence how God wants a transformative purpose to be achieved through the present troubling trials, as we think, prayerfully dependent, to convert this earthly inconvenience into an opportunity of witness-statement, spiritual maturity, and to strengthen our love and intimacy with Christ. Engaging ourselves with our suffering is not merely a sense of despair, but also an excellent vehicle of spiritual formation, with hope (Wright 2006, 91).

Serving Others Through Sacrificial Love

At the core of practicing the idea of the cross is serving others through self-denial and sacrificial love. Jesus perfectly models this love when He says that greatness in the Kingdom of God has nothing to do with power and status, but everything to do with humility and service. He commanded His disciples, "Whoever desires to become great among you, let him be your servant" (Matthew 20:26). Sacrificial love encourages believers to prioritize others' needs over their own comfort and security, as an expression of the heart of Christ.

Paul shares a similar idea with the Philippians in Philippians 2:3–4: "Let nothing be done through selfish ambition or conceit, but in lowliness of mind let each esteem others better than himself. Let each of you look out not only for his own interests, but also for the interests of others." When we serve with sacrificial love, it typically requires effort on our part. It will likely be inconvenient, potentially resulting in personal sacrifice and suffering. There is nothing that we go through in these scenarios that is wasted; they are all opportunities to demonstrate God's love and advance His kingdom (Packer 1973, 287).

Sacrificial love can be both practical and relational. Sacrificial love can be as simple as encouraging a friend who is struggling, providing material support to someone in need, or forgiving those who hurt you. Sacrificial love can involve greater engagement on your part, such as being in mentoring relationships, volunteering in a ministry capacity, or advocating for justice. Regardless of commitment, the motivation must come from genuine care for the person being served and obedience to God—not as a means to garner attention (Moo 1996, 178).

While living a life of sacrificial service, it also builds community. Acts of sacrificial love foster trust, promote unity, and enable those served to experience the reality of the gospel. Jesus' own example of washing his disciples' feet (John 13:14–15) teaches that if it is done out of love, no act is too humble. When believers serve others from the posture of sacrificial love, they typify the redemptive work of Jesus, and thereby serve as an example of the gospel through their practical expressions of love, showing others the grace of God already given to them.

In ultimate terms, sacrificial love changes everyone involved. It creates humble hearts, it inspires thankfulness in those served, helps others appreciate the mercy of God, and moves people towards the ultimate act of love: the cross of Christ (Wright 2006, 114). Serving others from a posture of sacrificial love is never just a duty; it is an honor and a way to express the heart of God every day.

God's Surprising Way

Walking in Humility and Strength

Being humble and being strong is the means of living the essence of the cross. Authentic Christian strength is not asserting itself through power, pride, or self-sufficiency, but by total surrender to God and dependence upon His power. Jesus exemplified this humility and strength in relation to His calling. Philippians 2:5–8 describes Christ's humility, which challenges our perceptions of authority and dedication to a greater purpose: "Let this mind be in you that was also in Christ Jesus, who, being in the form of God, did not consider it robbery to be equal with God, but made Himself of no reputation, taking the form of a servant, and coming in the likeness of men." Christ's humility did not diminish His authority or negate His purpose; it amplified His impact and revealed the true strength of submission and obedience to the Father.

To walk humbly requires one to accept their limitations, acknowledge their need for God's guiding presence, recognize the contribution and strength of others, and accept their way as just one part of the truth. James 4:6 encourages all believers: "God resists the proud, but gives grace to the humble." Humility does not mean we should make ourselves weak; it means we are willing to lay down our ambitions, willingly surrender control, and put God's will above our own. Strength is drawn through humility because God enables us to endure trials, stand against opposition, and courageously do His work.

Humility and strength practically connect us. A humble person listens intently, forgives often, serves sacrificially, and lives with courage to uphold truth and righteousness. The apostle Paul embodied this dynamism in his life and acknowledged his weaknesses and reliance upon God's strength when he shares, "for when I am weak, then I am strong" (2 Cor. 12:10). He revealed the unique paradox in that humility empowers God's strength to work through our weaknesses, and even our vulnerability becomes spiritual authority.

This humility and strength must be evident in all aspects of our lives, particularly in our interactions with others, our responsibilities, and the way we lead and make decisions. For example, humility softens and identifies the pride in our hearts, gives us appreciation for others, and even compassion. There are distinct ways that strength provides endurance, discernment, and a means to do something brave and faithful to God, such as not quailing in the face of opposition.

When we live out the example of Christ, we reflect God's glory and invite others into the transformative power of Christ that is offered to us. Living out humility and strength is not simply something we do, but rather the posture we must adopt for the duration of our lives. God has clearly stated that our hearts should be shaped by the cross and becoming Christlike (Packer 1973, 215; Wright 2006, 132).

Practicing Forgiveness in Daily Life

Forgiveness is at the center of living the cross today, revealing the heart of Christ and His redemptive work. However, it also reminds believers that while they received unearned forgiveness from God through Jesus' death on the cross, they are also to extend similar grace to those who have wronged them. As we are instructed in Ephesians 4:32, "And be kind to one another, tenderhearted, to forgive one another, even as God in Christ forgave you." This exhortation challenges Christians to put aside their resentment, anger, or bitterness and to replace them with love and reconciliation.

When it comes to practicing forgiveness, it is rarely easy. Forgiveness can be especially challenging when a serious or repeated wrong has been committed against a person. Forgiveness requires intentionality and prayer, as well as recognizing that strength does not come from within oneself. Jesus' teaching, found in Matthew 18:21–22, encourages this, as He instructed Peter to forgive not seven times, but seventy times seven.

Jesus was symbolically indicating forgiveness without limit. True forgiveness does not mean that justice is ignored or accountability is overlooked; it means releasing the burden of holding resentment and vengeance to God, so that He can work on the hearts of those who wrong us.

Forgiveness can take many forms in daily life. For instance, forgiveness may involve letting a coworker move on after holding a grudge against them, reconciling a family relationship that needs restoration, or offering grace to someone who has emotionally or spiritually hurt us. Often forgiveness can start with smaller acts of mercy and grace—not holding onto feelings of being wronged, listening to someone without interrupting, choosing gentleness instead of retaliation, or speaking words that build instead of wound. Furthermore, forgiveness is also self-protective, as it frees a person from the corrosive effects of bitterness, anxiety, and emotional captivity.

Another aspect of forgiveness is that it models Christ to the world. When believers forgive, they are acting to exercise the values and qualities of God's kingdom in tangible ways, which can offer testimony and hope for restoration in broken relationships. Furthermore, Colossians 3:13 reminds us of the importance of transparency with others: "Bear with one another, and forgive one another, if one has a complaint against another; even as Christ forgave you, so you also must do." Living life daily in a state of forgiveness not only preserves relationships but also enables a believer to transform ordinary conversations into moments of spiritual growth and kingdom impact, while reflecting God's mercy (Packer 1973, 218; Carson 1991, 145).

At the root, forgiveness is a practice that should be pursued as long as we remain in our prison cells of bitterness, resentment, and unforgiving actions. It demands humility, processing, dependence upon the Holy Spirit, and commitment to following Christ's example. Ultimately, the cross, in some form or another, demonstrates that forgiveness is not optional; it should be a hallmark of a life lived in the full reality, love, and grace of Christ.

Finding Joy Amid Pain

Living the cross today is the challenging yet transforming reality of discovering joy in pain. The Christian life does not sidestep suffering (the call of the cross summons believers into and through suffering), but voluntarily chooses suffering to grow, struggle, and depend on God. James 1:2–3 states it clearly, "My brethren, count it all joy when you fall into various trials, knowing that the testing of your faith produces patience." When believers see pain differently (not as meaningless and purposeless), but as some means by which God is forming character, perseverance, and faith, they can rejoice as James has instructed.

Joy in suffering does not come from denying the reality of suffering or pretending it does not exist. Joy comes from acknowledged suffering and crisis, and trusting God's greater purpose. The apostle Paul exemplifies this when he writes in 2 Corinthians 4:17–18, "For our light affliction, which is but for a moment, is working for us a far more exceeding and eternal weight of glory, while we do not look at the things which are seen, but at the things which are not seen." For a believer to cultivate joy in trial, they must first trust God and place their focus on eternal things instead of the temporal things. Joy then becomes a choice of faith, and is not dependent on circumstance.

Practically, joy in pain can be cultivated through prayer, Scripture meditation, and fellowship. In prayer, believers invite God's presence into their suffering, which brings them God's peace and comfort. In Scripture meditation, God's promises (His faithfulness, love, and sovereignty) engender hope, even in terrible circumstances. By fellowshipping with other believers, they can receive encouragement, perspective, and tangible support through shared burdens, fulfilling Paul's instruction in Galatians 6:2 to "Bear one another's burdens, and so fulfill the law of Christ."

As a tangible example of our joy in the midst of pain, the cross itself stood as Jesus' model, experiencing unimaginable suffering. Hope stems from a greater purpose for the sake of humanity, and believers model this hope when they endure hardships that God is using for His redemptive plan. Romans 5:3–5 connects us to this narrative of hope, "…we glory in tribulations also, knowing that tribulation produces perseverance; and perseverance, character; and character, hope. Now hope does not disappoint, because the love of God has been poured out in our hearts by the Holy Spirit who was given to us."

Taken as a whole, joy in the midst of pain rehabilitates pain and suffering; it transforms it into a crucible for spiritual formation (a process not easily recognized). It replaces despair with hope, self-pity with faith, and temporal concerns with eternal ones. The cross undeniably reveals to believers that joy is not the absence of pain, but the presence of God through every trial (Packer 1973, 229; Stott 1986, 112).

Sharing the Hope of Redemption

Living the cross today is about sharing the message of hope of redemption. The gospel is both an exciting personal message and a message of proclamation. The gospel offers hope to a world in sin and despair. As Christians, we are ambassadors of this message. 2 Corinthians 5:18–20 states that all things are of God, who has reconciled us to Himself through Jesus Christ and has given us the ministry of reconciliation. Now, we are ambassadors for Christ, as though God were pleading through us. Before we can share the hope of redemption, we must first recognize our own reconciliation and extend that same grace and care to others.

Redemption is more than forgiveness; it is life restored and purpose in Christ. Romans 1:16 declares the power of the message of hope: "For I am not ashamed of the gospel of Christ, for it is the power of God to salvation for everyone who believes." Christians living into this truth empower themselves to approach others with care and kindness, in light of the redemptive work of Christ, which has both present and eternal implications.

At the practical level, sharing the hope of redemption will require compassion, active listening, and courageous testimony. In hearing from those who are struggling and in pain, believers can discover where the message of Christ meets them in their needs. Our testimonies, which speak of God's redemptive power in our own story of moving from rejection and brokenness to forgiveness and purpose, are living testimonies of that redemptive power. In Acts 4:20, the apostles tell the authorities, "For we cannot but speak the things which we have seen and heard," outlining their responsibility to testify to the message of the gospel.

Finally, loving and serving people builds upon the message of the gospel. Addressing the marginalization of people, comforting those who grieve, and advocating for justice are just some of the redemptive works of Christ lived out through practical means of serving in our neighborhoods. Believers in Christ, as described in Colossians 1:27, "Christ in you, the hope of glory," are evident when seeking to love and serve people in these communities.

At the root, sharing the hope of redemption has a profound impact on both the giver and the recipient. It takes the personal faith of the giver into the public space, where it has a shared impact; despair is transformed into hope, and separation is turned into reconciliation. Living into the cross—connected by our words and our actions—ultimately allows believers to contribute to God's plan of redemption and shed His light of salvation in a dark world (Packer 1973, 241; Stott 1986, 175).

The Cross as Model for Relationships

The cross is not only at the heart of salvation but also serves as a model for how believers should act in their relationships. At its core, the cross represents selfless love, humility, and reconciliation—all behaviors essential for healthy, people-changing relationships. Jesus' sacrifice indicates love is active, costly, and it works for the good of others first. Ephesians 5:2 says, "And walk in love, as Christ also has loved us and given Himself for us, and offering and a sacrifice to God for a sweet-smelling aroma." If believers show sacrificial love, the relationship becomes a foretaste of the kingdom of God.

Forgiveness is another crucial aspect of the cross's involvement in relationships. The cross reminds believers that no matter how hurtful we may be, reconciliation is possible. Colossians 3:13 states, "Bear with one another, and forgive one another, if anyone has a complaint against another; even as Christ forgave you, so you also must do." Suppose we consciously remember the forgiveness on the cross. In that case, it allows us to extend grace to others, and conflict can become a means for reconciliation.

Humility is another aspect of what the cross teaches. Like Christ's willingness to suffer, we sometimes learn to endure suffering in relationships. Philippians 2:5–8 states, "Let this mind be in you which was also in Christ Jesus, who, being in the form of God, did not consider it robbery to be equal with God, but made Himself of no reputation... humbled Himself." Listening, understanding, and valuing others' interests above our opinions and pride is the essence of humility in relationships.

The cross also teaches patience. Relationships bring with them inevitable misunderstandings and trials, but the cross inspires perseverance founded on love and hope. Romans 12:10 encourages us to "be kindly affectionate to one another with brotherly love, in honor giving preference to one another." The sacrificial spirit of Christ in relation to God will inevitably inspire sacrificial behavior in our daily relationships.

Applying the cross is a great model for relationships, meaning they can become less about transactional interactions and more about the expression of God's love. When a believer demonstrates humility, forgiveness, and selfless love, they are not only loving God but also creating an environment of grace, empathy, and reconciliation for others (Packer 1973, 267; Stott 1986, 189).

Integrating the Power of the Cross into Everyday Decisions

The cross itself signifies reconciliation, but it is also a practical framework for everyday life. Influenced by God's guidance, each day presents us with the opportunity to reflect Christ in every decision we make, no matter how big or small. The heart of considering the cross as a practical framework for daily decision-making is understanding that Christ's investment of Himself is a call to submission, obedience, and humility. Paul articulates this perspective in Galatians 2:20: "I have been crucified with Christ; it is no longer I who live, but Christ lives in me; and the life that I now live in the flesh I live by faith in the Son of God, who loved me and gave Himself for me." God's mercies prompt the decision-making process to shift from a self-centered model toward a Christ-centered choice.

When we consider the cross as a framework for our everyday choices, the first step of moral consideration is a step of discernment. As believers, when discerning moral choices, we might ask questions like, "Do my choices imitate the love and integrity of Christ?" Conscientiously choosing actions based on integrity, justice, sacrifice, and kindness is a way to remember and pay respectful tribute to the incarnational and sacrificial life of Christ. Proverbs 3:5-6 says, "Trust in the Lord with all your heart, and lean not on your own understanding; in all your ways acknowledge Him and He shall direct your paths." When we trust in God's presence, guidance, and sovereignty as we consider our everyday choices, we begin to think about our lives in terms of God's kingdom purposes rather than fleeting personal desires.

Another aspect of a cross-shaped life is sacrifice at the level of thought. Sacrifice is a reminder that true life exists in giving rather than receiving personally, particularly in the choices we make for everyday activities (e.g., how we spend our time, money, and resources) that involve relationships. To bear witness to Jesus and act in often sacrificial and other-centered ways prompts us to think about how devotion to others mirrors and encapsulates Jesus' acts of self-sacrifice. Romans 12:1 says, "I beseech you therefore, brethren, by the mercies of God, that you present your bodies a living sacrifice, holy, acceptable to God, which is your reasonable service." In this scripture, even the most mundane acts of service can be transformed into spiritual service.

In addition, considering the cross in our decision-making often fosters resilience with hope. Life will bring trials and challenging times, but perceiving these situations through the lens of the cross creates a more measured perspective. Moreover, life is not void of suffering; it is primarily an opportunity to accompany Jesus and trust God, whether in good times or bad. James 1:2-4 reminds us to "count it all joy when you fall into various trials, knowing that the testing of your faith produces patience."

Most centrally, making decisions daily influenced by the cross transforms the mundane aspects of life into God's living proclamations of love. Every decision becomes an opportunity to honor Christ, love your neighbor as yourself, and demonstrate the effects of His redemptive work on earth (Packer 1973, 301; Stott 1986, 212).

Chapter 8

The Spirit of Work in Us

The Reversal of Human Strength

The Christian life can be regarded as a paradox: God's power is on most display through human weakness. Throughout Scripture, we see a reversal of the normal understanding of strength, as believers are invited to rely on the Spirit rather than on human effort. Paul's acknowledgment of the grace of God in his life (1 Cor. 15:10) suggests that productivity in God's kingdom does not arise from personal gift or ambition but from God's gracious enablement. He also describes this connection between human fragility and divine presence as "treasure in earthen vessels" (2 Cor. 4:7), emphasizing that what is weak or common serves as channels for great power when God dwells in them (Calvin 1559, 118).

It is in this sense that we can understand God's power is perfected precisely in weakness (2 Cor. 12:9), a concept established throughout Scripture. Moses, despite his deep-seated self-doubt, was empowered to lead Israel to freedom; Gideon, initially feeling inadequate, achieved victory by relying on God (Judges 6–7). The apostles (untrained, marginalized) boldly proclaimed the gospel on the Day of Pentecost (Acts 2). In fact, the human experience of insufficiency is the platform where God's glory shines through. The paradox is apparent: dependence on God, not self-reliance, produces enduring fruit and spiritual authority.

The writings of the Church Fathers and theological reflection offer further perspective. Augustine recognizes God "chooses the weak to shame the strong" (1 Cor. 1:27) and emphasizes that we must have an awareness of our grounding and humble surrender to see God act (Augustine 1991, 74). John Chrysostom observes that God often operates through the least capable and weakest, which suggests that our vulnerabilities amplify divine action (Chrysostom 2000, 105). Considering our everyday lives, the challenge is to learn how to corral our awareness of our weak personas and to allow ourselves to be dependent on the Spirit through prayer, study of Scripture, and service as acts of utter dependence.

The upside-down approach to experiencing human strength appears free yet transformative. It liberates believers from faith driven by performance, shifting attention from self-display onto God. Our neediness is not a deficit but the obvious connection to God's power; spiritual effectiveness has little to do with our natural abilities and falls entirely within the realm of faithful surrender. To live into this, Christians must continue to appreciate a kingdom where weaknesses are transformed into strengths, human limitations usher in God's glory, and ordinary lives are transformed by an extraordinary being who lives through us (2 Cor. 4:7; 12:9).

Spirit Empowerment Over Human Effort

The Christian life sets up a rigorous challenge to natural views of strength and success. It insists that true power is never self-generated and that it flows from the Spirit of God. Jesus repeatedly contrasted human effort with divine enablement. He taught that those who abide in His presence accomplish fruit-bearing beyond their natural boundaries: apart from Him, "you can do nothing" (John 15:5). The point here is that living in dependence on the Spirit is critical for ministry, obedience, and transformation. No amount of human effort, no matter how diligent or disciplined, is capable of producing lasting fruit apart from a Spirit-empowered life (Wright 1996, 182).

Scripture is filled with examples of spiritual empowerment. The biblical accounts of the apostles before and after Pentecost are telling. They were timid and uncertain, but empowered by the Spirit, they boldly proclaimed the gospel at Pentecost (Acts 2). They were not persuasive men or clever strategists, but the Holy Spirit filled them. In the same way, Samson accomplished feats of strength supplied by the Spirit that exceeded human capacity (Judges 14:6). These examples illustrate that divine enablement can take an ordinary human and bring them into extraordinary service for God, such that God works through what the world sees as weakness.

Voices from patristic history affirm this biblical pattern. Augustine observes that human striving, independent of God, is ultimately pointless; true accomplishment flows out of God's grace, which flows to and through the believer (Augustine 1991, 74). Origen notes that the Spirit can enable even the unlearned person to accomplish God's purposes, arguing that divine empowerment can truly transform (Origen 1993, 215). These reflections have carried over into modernity. J. I. Packer observes that while moral effort may help people become better, obedience and devotion empowered by God's Spirit go far beyond this limited definition (Packer 1973, 215).

For today's believer and Christian community, Spirit empowerment changes our everyday lives. The everyday-looking tasks of changing a diaper, listening to a friend, or working faithfully at your workplace all become potential venues for divine power when done under the direction and guidance of the Spirit. Our limitations remind us to entrust ourselves in humility, dependence, and trust; these laborious and mundane acts become vehicles of extraordinary blessing. Spiritual empowerment raises questions in our lives that prompt self-examination and surrender: a believer will never discard human effort; it will always be transformed into something greater when presented in the presence of God, as in "everyday worship." In this way, weakness becomes strength, and ordinary lives begin to take on the extraordinary work of God's Spirit (Philippians 2:13; John 15:5).

Weak Vessels Carrying Divine Power

When Paul states, "But we have this treasure in earthen vessels, that the excellence of the power may be of God and not of us" (2 Corinthians 4:7), he creates a stunning paradox: the most incredible displays of God's power are often found in the weakness of humans. The metaphor of an "earthen vessel," as depicted by the apostle, reminds us of our fragility and limitations, signifying that divine glory is not dependent on human strength, wisdom, or resources. Ultimately, it is the lack of what we need that accentuates God's power, making the work of the Spirit indisputable (Wright 1996, 212).

Scripture provides all kinds of illustrations. Moses, being self-conscious of his oratory ability, led Israel under the authority of God, not his own capability (Exodus 4:10–12). Gideon fought the Midianites, not from human strength, but from God's instruction through the Spirit (Judges 7:19–22). When you link all these stories together, you find something akin to a pattern: God revels in working through vessels that appear weak, showcasing His power as a means of redirecting all credit and glory to Him.

Patristic writers concur. John Chrysostom observes that if we are to receive the power of God, then we must be humble and dependent on Him; the more the earthen vessel's weakness is displayed, the more remarkable God's excellence becomes (Chrysostom 1988, 104). Gregory of Nyssa states that spiritual formation requires us to acknowledge our insufficiency, because God's Spirit can transform our fragility into channels of grace and effectiveness (Gregory of Nyssa 1993, 89). Modern theologians make similar statements: J. I. Packer insists that God's power in believers is never self-generated; instead, it operates through human agents who are surrendered and imperfect (Packer 1973, 215).

For believers today, the idea of using weak vessels requires us to embrace encouragement with humility. Understanding our limitations should compel us to trust in God, rather than ourselves. Everyday situations—relational issues, ministry demands, or personal battles—offer moments for God's power to be revealed. When we are vulnerable, God's glory is often clearer; when we depend on His strength, the treasure we possess in the gospel is also more valuable (2 Corinthians 4:7). This reminds us that weakness is not a hindrance to God's work. Instead, weakness can be used as a channel of divine strength, demonstrating that transformation and impact are only from God, not from us.

God's Strength Perfected in Our Weakness

The Apostle Paul writes, "Therefore I take pleasure in infirmities, in reproaches, in needs, in persecutions, in distresses, for Christ's sake. For when I am weak, then I am strong" (2 Corinthians 12:10). This statement reveals a profound theological truth: God's strength is not merely compatible with human weakness—it is perfected in it. Rather than lamenting our limitations, believers are called to embrace them as avenues for divine empowerment. Paul's thorn in the flesh exemplifies this paradox: his personal struggle became a conduit for God's sustaining grace, demonstrating that spiritual strength is ultimately God-given, not self-generated (Calvin 1559, 287).

Scripture repeatedly affirms this principle. The shepherds, lowly and marginalized, were the first to receive the announcement of Christ's birth (Luke 2:8–20), illustrating that God's redemptive purposes are often accomplished through those considered weak or insignificant by the world. Similarly, Jesus' servanthood, culminating in the cross, demonstrates that divine power operates not through force or domination but through humility and surrender (Philippians 2:5–8). The paradoxical kingdom of God lifts the weak, confounds the strong, and glorifies God through human insufficiency (Wright 1996, 456).

The Patristic tradition underscores this truth. Augustine observes that our weaknesses cultivate humility, making the soul receptive to God's transforming power; when we admit our inadequacy, God's grace achieves its fullest effect (Augustine 1993, 112). Origen likewise emphasizes that divine strength is most evident when human effort reaches its limits, for the glory of God alone is manifested in the triumph over impossibility (Origen 1987, 76).

For contemporary believers, this principle offers both encouragement and perspective. Trials, personal limitations, and moments of insufficiency are not hindrances but opportunities for God's power to be perfected. Whether in ministry, relationships, or spiritual formation, acknowledging our dependence allows God's strength to sustain, equip, and bear fruit beyond human capability. Recognizing that "When I am weak, then I am strong" cultivates humility, reliance, and a deeper experience of God's transformative presence in daily life (2 Corinthians 12:10). In embracing weakness, we encounter the power of God in its most profound and practical form, revealing that true strength is inseparable from surrender.

Biblical Work of the Spirit

The presence of God's Spirit in both the Old Testament and the New Testament is vital to understanding how God committed Himself through the revelation of Scripture to empower, renew, and sustain His people. An example is Isaiah 61:1–3, where the Spirit of God anoints the Messiah to proclaim good news to the poor, bind up the brokenhearted, proclaim liberty to the captives, and release those who are bound. In the prophetic view found in Isaiah, God's redemptive activity operates in a Spirit-driven sense, where the Spirit establishes a function whereby divine power can harness itself through human vessels to deliver justice and restoration (Wright 1996, 322)

The experience of Pentecost shows that these Old Testament promises are fulfilled. The early church's experience is recorded in Acts 2, where the Holy Spirit accompanies and empowers the disciples, enabling them to speak in languages and proclaim the gospel of Christ boldly. In this instance, we see how the Spirit redeems the limitations of humankind so that fear becomes courage, ignorance gives way to perspective, and wisdom begins to shine through weakness as a channel for the power of God (Bruce 1990, 145). The Spirit empowers ordinary believers for the extraordinary work of God's kingdom, establishing God's transformative presence as active and available.

In John 14:16–17, Jesus promises that "the Comforter" is coming, and the Spirit's indwelling will remain with and in believers. In this sense, the Spirit's presence is relational and practical. When characterized as relational, the Spirit teaches, convinces, sustains, leads His children into all truth, and enables obedience that is beyond their human capacity. Bonhoeffer (1959) explains that the key to Spirit-led discipleship is surrendering to a way of life that produces the spiritual fruit of the Spirit's discipline (Galatians 5:22–24); love, joy, peace, and patience are not the result of human striving but of God's initiative beyond human capacity (Bonhoeffer 1959, 102).

The writers of Scripture demonstrate, through prophecy and fulfillment, that the Spirit emboldens believers through the transformative work of God. The Spirit restores, empowers, and sustains believers in their relationship with God, providing a reminder that humans do not generate the only spiritual life that truly matters. Engaging the Spirit's work opens the heart to what it means to be dependent, humble, and participants in God's redemptive work. By living in the Spirit, Christians are enabled to reflect the values of God's kingdom, to live obediently, and to bear witness to God's presence in both ordinary and extraordinary situations.

The Spirit's work is a reminder that human dependence on the divine is sufficient to build lives and futures characterized by empowerment, renewal, and joy, demonstrating what God can accomplish through His Spirit beyond human effort.

Old Testament Prophecies of the Spirit (Isaiah 61:1–3)

In the foretelling of the Spirit's work in Isaiah 61:1–3, we see a splendid vision of God at work long before Jesus emerges. The biblical text reveals that God is always at work to restore, heal, and set people free: "The Spirit of the Lord God is upon Me, because the Lord has anointed Me to preach good tidings to the poor; He has sent Me to heal the brokenhearted, to proclaim liberty to the captives, and the opening of the prison to those who are bound" (Isaiah 61:1–2). The Spirit demonstrates that it is God's power that accomplishes God's redemptive purposes—and that pure human agency cannot achieve the restoration and justice that God intends.

The Spirit's purpose in Isaiah involves proclaiming good news and a commitment to action. The anointing enables Jesus, and by extension, the people of God in general, to lift and restore those on the margins, bring hope to the hopeless, and provide tangible help to individuals who suffer. As Gregory of Nyssa notes, the Spirit works upon the heart to renew it, aligning it toward becoming divine and equipping it for holy action (Gregory of Nyssa 1991, 87). The Spirit is both a changemaker and an enabler, for internal transformation and outward ministry.

Isaiah 61 demonstrates the work of the Spirit as restorative and a source of joy by replacing mourning with praise and despair with beauty. The phrase "the garment of praise for the spirit of heaviness" (Isaiah 61:3) embodies the idea that the Spirit goes beyond temporarily relieving suffering to establish spiritual restoration. This timeless vision is fulfilled in the New

Testament; for instance, Jesus claims this prophecy in Luke 4:18–19, declaring that the Spirit has anointed Him to bring salvation to the oppressed.

Isaiah 61 provides a framework for reflection, especially when considering the broad movement of God's Spirit through Scripture. The Spirit endows capability, empowers hope, and propels transformation. For Christians today, Isaiah 61 serves as both a source of consolation and a challenge: it offers comfort and reminds believers to depend on God's power rather than their own fortitude, fundamentally calling them to engage in the work of justice, mercy, and restoration enabled by the Spirit. By recognizing the Spirit's activity both historically and presently, Christians are invited into God's account of divine empowerment, which transforms ordinary lives into vessels of extraordinary ministry.

Pentecost: The Spirit Empowering the Church (Acts 2)

The Day of Pentecost is viewed by many as a pivotal moment in redemptive history, when God the Holy Spirit descends upon the early believers, fulfilling the promise of the Holy Spirit, marking the launch of the church's mission, and manifesting the Spirit's work in tangible ways (Acts 2:1–4). The event reveals Luke's intended universality and the dynamic nature of the Spirit's arrival: "And they were all filled with the Holy Spirit and began to speak with other tongues, as the Spirit gave them utterance" (Acts 2:4). The occurrence highlights that God's power is not merely abstract; it is relational, enabling ordinary followers of Christ to participate in extraordinary action in the work of His kingdom.

Pentecost is the fulfillment of Jesus' promise of the Comforter, connecting the prophetic word of the Spirit in the Old Testament with the reality of the new covenant (John 14:16–17). The Spirit prepares the church to proclaim, heal, and witness boldly, and divine power surpasses human weakness. John Chrysostom comments on this moment, noting how the apostles' ordinary status is inverted, as weak vessels are transformed into channels of divine power. Ordinary fishermen speak with authority; the power of the Spirit flows through the coordinated work of the apostles (Chrysostom 1993). Additionally, the manifestation of spiritual gifts underscores that while the work of the Spirit may be individual, it is corporate in purpose, for the "building up" of the church, rather than for private edification.

The narrative of Pentecost reveals the Spirit's work in removing human barriers—linguistic, cultural, and social—and foreshadows God's inclusivity as King. Through the gift of tongues, the apostles can share the gospel with people from multiple nations, symbolically representing the convergence of diverse peoples in the Spirit. Wright views Pentecost as both the end of the beginning and the beginning of the end: the Spirit enables the church to operate according to the upside-down values of the kingdom, transforming fear into courage and limited possibilities into expansive opportunity (Wright 1996, 275).

Pentecost is paradigmatic and challenges today's believers. Human initiative and creativity alone cannot produce the outcomes of the kingdom; only through the Spirit can ordinary lives achieve extraordinary results. This moment invites believers into the ongoing reality of the Spirit, calling them to openness, obedience, and boldness, so that God's power can work through their everyday words and actions. Pentecost reminds the church that transformation is God's work, with believers participating faithfully as conduits of His purpose (Acts 2:1–4; John 14:16–17).

Jesus Promised the Comforter (John 14:16–17)

In John 14:16–17, Jesus assured His disciples with a firm promise: "And I will pray the Father, and He will give you another Helper, that He may abide with you forever—the Spirit of truth." The Comforter, or Paraclete, is not merely a nebulous reality but a personal, sustaining, and guiding presence in the lives of believers. Jesus noted that the Spirit was not only meant to dwell within, direct, and empower, but also because the God of the universe will not abandon His followers in the reality of discipleship.

The Comforter's work involves theology in teaching, reminding, and convicting, representing an ongoing presence of Christ in the believer's experience (Chester 2010, 141). In Book 1, Section 8 of his commentary on John, Origen notes that the Spirit is the means by which divine wisdom is mediated to the faithful, which imbues them to know God's truth that exceeds human understanding (Origen 1996, 88). This divine indwelling also indicates a reversal of the standard human way of thinking about dependence: accurate spiritual understanding and enabling were not derived from human knowledge and ability, but instead came from God's empowering Spirit. In this sense, Paul's assertion in 2 Corinthians 12:9 that God's strength is made perfect in weakness is particularly relevant. However, perhaps one can say that God goes even further than this (in that He works to provide the ability to think, desire, or act in ways that cannot be reduced to weakness).

Also, speaking of the Comforter as the Spirit of truth refers to being able to see things morally and spiritually. The Spirit supplies the clarity that is needed to discern God's voice and call in the present age, surrounded by lies and unanswered questions, directing believers toward obedience, love, and justice. N. T. Wright concludes that the Spirit's work is "not only an individual or subjective experience, but a communal one." The Spirit sustains the Church (with Christ as its head and its body) and the Spirit cultivates the values of an upside-down kingdom (Wright 1996, 282)

Practically speaking, the promise should foster ongoing dependence on God and reflect the attitudes of humility, receptivity, and attentiveness. The Spirit can take decisions that in and of themselves seem to be "just a normal thing" and reorient them toward faithful "done in obedience." As noted in Galatians 5:22–23, practically, the believer should be growing in holiness to bear fruit in love, joy, and peace, among many other characteristics. The Spirit's role in this process is both intimate and far-reaching; He guides the believer in private devotion to God while, at the same time, equipping the Church for public witness.

As the final point, Jesus' promise of the Comforter invites believers to begin living with an awareness of the presence of the Spirit of God and to hear the guiding of the triune God through their thoughts, actions, and relationships. In this sense, faith is more relational than purely moralistic; the Spirit shapes and illumines our hearts and minds, compelling the ordinariness of human experience to participate in the extraordinary work of God.

Healing Through the Spirit

Healing is defined by the Spirit, which has physical, emotional, and spiritual implications, clearly demonstrating that God cares holistically for His people. The Scriptures assure us that the Spirit will bring wholeness and move devotees from brokenness toward the health derived from God: "He heals the brokenhearted and binds up their wounds" (Ps. 147:3). Healing is never static but relatively progressive, and the Spirit wants to heal the cause of our pain, guilt, fear, and sin while nurturing a consequent and renewed Spirit-filled life (Bauckham 1999, 188).

The healing action of the Spirit begins by renewing and sanctifying us inwardly, and we confront the reality of sin and its consequences while experiencing release from bondage to the old way. According to Chrysostom, the Spirit restores the soul first. Then it may proceed to change behavior, demonstrating what Phillips Gregory would describe as God reaching into the heart and lighting the soul to fill each aspect of our lives (Chrysostom 1998, 74). Paul said it another way in 2 Corinthians 4:16, where the outside is falling apart and passing away. However, the Spirit leads to an inward unveiling: "Though our outward man is perishing, yet the inward man is being renewed day by day."

Emotional healing is achieved as the Spirit softens hardened hearts that are burdened by resentment, fear, and guilt. Nouwen describes this in *Denial with God* as a gentle work of God that brings many of us to the point of being broken enough for God to use our brokenness as a means to evoke empathy and compassion in others, thereby profiting from our brokenness (Nouwen 1992, 45). Spirit-filled healing enables a person to trust the Spirit and offer forgiveness to oneself, thereby releasing the burdens of the past and achieving freedom from despair and shame.

Healing from the Spirit can also act to restore relationships. The Spirit equips individuals with the capacity to forgive, to be patient with others, and to be understanding, thereby facilitating reconciliation within families, communities, and the church. The model for this can surely be found in the ministry of Jesus, as He healed both physical ailments and relational breakages, emphasizing holistic healing intended by the Father through the ministries of the Spirit on earth (Matt. 9:35–36).

In essence, healing through the Spirit requires a partnership between human openness and divine grace. Healing through the Spirit calls for prayer, thoughtful reflection, and the intentional application of Scripture to the day-to-day aspects of life. When believers place their minds in the open hands of the Spirit and realize they have been changed to be vessels of God's restoration, they get to finally be God's love in action through the presence of a renewed heart, a resilient spirit, and reconciled relationships. Accordingly, healing represents a reality that comes from the inside out and serves as an outward testimony of the Spirit's effect on God's people.

Inner Renewal and Sanctification

The Spirit's transformative work in the believer's life is rooted in inner renewal and sanctification. Essentially, sanctification is not the improvement of ethics for ethics' sake; it is the Spirit's continual displacement of the heart and mind in alignment with the image of Christ (Rom. 8:29), which begins inwardly as the Spirit transforms desires, thoughts, and motivations, to ultimately outward obedience and holiness (Calvin 1559, 342). Paul explains this process by calling believers to "be transformed by the renewing of your mind" (Rom. 12:2), and this understanding fits the believer's perspective that spiritual transformation is a result of the Spirit's work internally, not just what humans can do.

Scripture illustrates sanctification as a cooperative work between God and humans. God initiates and empowers, while believers believe, obey, and respond to God's grace. Augustine assessed our own attempt at providing a sense of rest for ourselves apart from God, while equally asserting the human heart could only find rest through the work of the Holy Spirit renewing it (Augustine 1998, 101). In renewing the heart and mind, the grace of God in the Spirit shapes and prods, issues a response not only to fundamental moral failings but rekindles and re-prioritizes even our moral dispositions—the feelings or inclinations behind actions—who we are "becoming" as we move toward a reconciled and mature life in Christ. The Spirit of God renews and reformulates fully, intellectually, emotionally, and volitionally.

The Spirit desires to cultivate spiritual sensitivity and give discernment to believers, prompting them to act in response to God's presence and the decisions they make, aware of God's purposes. Henri Nouwen writes that when the inner life has been renewed, "true life takes on the shape of humility, trust, and love, and still allows God to let the believer's own life take place," as if the life of the believer becomes grounded in God's loving presence (Nouwen 1992, 37). John Owen, in discussing sanctification, defines it as killing sin and bringing life to virtue. We can delight in life because we do so as evidence of Christ's life living within us (Owen 1674, 58).

The narrative examples found in Scripture exemplify the renewal process once again, helping to formulate an understanding of the process itself. The narrative of Saul's transformation to Paul illustrates the inner renewal and establishes a renewal of both mission and character (Acts 9:1–22). The parable of the prodigal son features elements of repentance, including a personal process of restoration and a renewed character of life, made possible by God's overwhelming merciful grace (Luke 15:11–32).

Sanctification is a gift from God, and each believer's predicaments call for movement in the everyday process. Through prayer, reading, and engaging with Scripture responsibly, and being willing to respond to the work of the Spirit, we participate in the process of renewal. The benefit offers opportunities to grow closer to holiness, participate in fruit-bearing through the Spirit, and reflect character in daily life, which expresses freedom, more profound effects of love for God, deeper compassion for others, and the joy that emerges from experiencing life amidst good and evil, with joy that sustains our ability to be conformed, unlike any other.

Freedom from Guilt, Fear, and Bondage

The Spirit's work in the life of the believer has a wonderful liberation from guilt, fear, and spiritual bondage. Paul asserts that "therefore, there is now no condemnation for those who are in Christ Jesus" (Rom. 8:1). This is a reminder of the significance of the Spirit's work in bringing assurance of God's forgiveness and love. Freedom does not begin with self; it is a gift from God, given to us by the Spirit. The Spirit convicts of sin, leads into all truth, and renews the heart (John 16:8–11). The Spirit brings conviction, and the weariness and anguish associated with guilt enable true repentance that leads to reconciliation with God. Peace replaces shame (Packer 1973, 215).

One of the greatest hindrances to the human heart is fear, which disrupts obedience and trust in God. Scripture repeatedly maintains that the Spirit is the source of life. That perfect love casts out fear: "For God has not given us the spirit of fear, but of power and of love and of a sound mind" (2 Tim.

1:7). Augustine comments that when the heart rests on God's sovereignty, the believer lives in view of God's providential care, and anxiety fades away (Augustine 1998, 122). The assurance of God found in the Spirit produces empowerment in the face of life's trials, uncertainties, and spiritual opposition. We are not yielding to firm beliefs in personal strength, but trusting in the constant presence of the Spirit.

The Spirit also liberates from bondage, whether to sin, harmful habits, or oppressive conditions. According to John Chrysostom, "I concluded that Christ's death was a ransom to subdue sin's enslaving power, enable full obedience and righteousness" (Chrysostom 1896, 47). The work of the Spirit releases one through a practical, ongoing process of deliverance, where the mind is renewed, and responsible choices are displayed in the way we live our lives. Over time, the formerly yawning gap narrows as the Spirit replaces crippling influences.

Many moments in Scripture suggest this kind of deliverance. Although Peter was paralyzed by fear, he was empowered by the Spirit to speak to the people (Acts 2:14–41). The demon-possessed man of the Gerasenes received complete release through Christ. His life is a remarkable witness to the Spirit's capacity to restore dignity and freedom (Mark 5:1–20).

Freedom provides the believer with liberation that is both internal and relational. Freedom reconciles the believer to God, restores trust, and enables a life of holiness. Through the believer's prayers, Scripture meditation, and reliance on the Spirit, they will find liberating experiences that not only restore the inner self but also become embodied in an outward reality of loving God and neighbor through the empowered Spirit.

Emotional and Spiritual Healing Through God's Presence

The very act of Spirit work in believers creates space for deep emotional and spiritual healing. In this way, it restores the soul to experience wholeness. Scripture reminds us that God being present with us is itself restorative: "The Lord is near to those who have a broken heart, and saves such as have a contrite spirit" (Ps. 34:18). We are not to ignore emotional wounds, such as grief, anxiety, and bitterness, but rather spend time in God's presence where the Spirit can minister comfort and renewal (Nouwen 1992, 78).

Healing begins with acknowledging brokenness. Often, the psalmists express an authenticity of human emotion that models transparency before God. In doing so, they demonstrate that emotional honesty is part of spiritual growth (Ps. 42:5–11). When we learn to yield all our emotions to God, the Spirit meets us there, bringing a peace that surpasses all understanding, and is particularly effective in changing our hearts towards trust, gratitude, and hope (Phil. 4:6–7). As Packer observes, the Spirit helps believers to experience God as a present companion who loves and hopes to lead them toward reconciliation and emotional stability, rather than as a distant judge (Packer 1973, 211).

Spiritual healing is a much broader experience than just finding relief from negative emotions; it is about restoring the inner life of the person so that it is aligned with God's purposes. Bonhoeffer articulates this well when he observes that Christ-centered presence does not avoid suffering to heal; instead, suffering is transformed into a means of grace that invokes deeper communion with God (Bonhoeffer 1959, 89). Ultimately, the Spirit brings insight and discernment to the actions of forgiveness—of self and others—for believers who become stuck in the suffering of trauma and sin.

There are many biblical examples of restorative work. Jesus and the leper, Jesus and the woman at the well, and Jesus and Lazarus all demonstrate a holistic approach to healing, encompassing body, mind, and Spirit (Mark 1:40–42; John 4:1–30; John 11:1–44). Each of these encounters demonstrates that God's presence, mediated through the Spirit, is central to complete healing.

In practice, awareness of the Spirit involves prayer, meditation on Scripture, and a willingness to be guided by God. As believers practice dwelling constantly with God, their emotional wounds are healed, their spiritual vitality is renewed, and they, along with their lives, become works of testimony to God's transformative love, manifesting His kingdom on earth.

Joy in Spirit-Filled Living

Joy is a significant sign of a Spirit-transformed life. Joy is not to be confused with happiness, which is dependent on circumstances. Joy is not dependent upon circumstances, but instead is based upon communion with God and the development of a Christ-like character. We see this when Paul identifies the Fruit of the Spirit as love, joy, peace, longsuffering, kindness, goodness, faithfulness, gentleness, and self-control (Gal. 5:22–23). Each of these will contribute to a holistic joy that is durable enough to sustain one's life even through trials. In fact, joy is not simply to be thought of as an emotional state. Still, rather, it is a spiritual reality rooted in God's presence and promises (Wright 1996, 132).

Living in a Spirit-Filled joy, we need to begin by understanding that we are not living life on our own, but rather on the Spirit's guidance. Our lives are centered on God's nearness and purposes, which illuminate God's will and good plans. C.S. Lewis makes an intense observation that joy typically manifests as a surprise when a believer moves from one moment of self-willed striving to a moment of surrender to God's will, in which the Spirit harmonizes the circumstances of their lives with the purpose of spiritual growth (Lewis 1960, 89).

I should say that every day of feeling delight in God's direction requires an effort of tense awareness. Understanding Henri Nouwen's teachings, the Spirit leads in a gentle, patient, and often imperceptible manner, which opens the individual to a contemplative rhythm of listening, reflecting, and discerning God's Spirit actively at work (Nouwen 1992, 65). Therefore, regular moments of prayer and meditation on Scripture, and experiencing the reality of God's presence, cultivate an awareness of this sort of direction, while sustaining a dream of joy that goes beyond any predicament.

The Gospels present narrative examples of joy filled by the Spirit. Examples include Mary's song of praise at the annunciation (Luke 1:46–55) and the shepherds' exultation at Jesus' birth (Luke 2:17–20), whose joy was rooted in what God was doing, not in the circumstances. The early church's joys of fellowship included confusion, persecution (e.g., Acts 16:25), and spread of evil; but they knew the Spirit in their worship as joy, which is a witness to others of who God is and the joy of sustaining presence.

Joy in Spirit-filled living is the disposition of the heart and a witness to others. It takes form in how one engages with people, in love, service, and faithfulness, all of which witness to God's kingdom and the transformative power of God. When living by the Fruit of the Spirit and residing in God, the delighted joy of the Spirit will flow into their lives as they cultivate this transformation. All joy is deep, expansive, and reflective of the Spirit's indwelling work in their lives.

Fruit of the Spirit as Pathway to Joy

The Apostle Paul's description of the Fruit of the Spirit in Galatians 5:22–23 exemplifies a kind of joy that transcends circumstance. Joy is characteristic of the fullness of spiritual virtues. Joy is a transcendent quality, a gift, and a response to the Spirit transforming a believer. Paul juxtaposes the works of the flesh with the fruit of the Spirit, suggesting that true joy is produced not merely from human effort but from abiding in God's presence and discovering our place in the Spirit's enterprise (Gal. 5:22–23). John Stott notes, "The Spirit gradually adds these graces to the lives of believers, as he shapes their character, so that joy develops naturally in the life of a believer who is aligned with God's will" (Stott 1994, 212).

Spirit-empowered joy is more than mere pleasure or a fleeting emotional high. The joy of the heart develops in people who practice love, develop patience, and engage in kindness—types of virtues that connect others and resolve conflict, while also fostering broader peace within the heart's desire. Faithfulness and self-control strengthen joy as additional virtues of the Spirit develop, ensuring that personal joy is not disturbed by fear, whether from temptation or suffering (Packer 1973, 215). This transformative approach extends to all aspects of daily life, as the primary purpose becomes connected to divine delight, even in the face of trials.

The connection is vividly demonstrated biblically. The early church, despite persecution, rejoiced in their faith (Acts 16:25). This reaction demonstrates that genuine joy is not about ease; rather, joy, even in difficult circumstances, is rooted in the sustaining presence of the Spirit. Paul, in his letters, details that believers, by virtue of the fruit of the Spirit, are those who testify to the power of God transforming through relational and communal expressions, highlighting the agency for joy experienced personally (Phil. 4:4).

The joy from a Spirit-filled life stands as both interior and exterior. The joy motivates service, strengthens through perseverance, and externally allows for beauty and testimony to God redeeming His creation through the church. N.T. Wright notes that joy is "when we enter into God's upside down kingdom and find our fulfillment not in things that satisfy but a radical life of obedience, humility, as well as a willingness to share in God's Mission to the world" (Wright 2008, 147).

The Fruit of the Spirit leads to joy in that the fruit aligns human hearts with God's desires. When believers develop love, gentleness, patience, and all the other fruits of the Spirit, joy becomes their lasting delight and evidence of being in union with God through His Spirit. This joy comes from God as they suffer, delight in relationships, and show Christ's character to the world.

Experiencing Daily Delight in God's Guidance

The Christian life is not defined by obedience but by the way one joyfully responds to God's leadership daily. The Scriptures state that God, through His Spirit, leads believers into all truth and empowers them to live a life of faithfulness (John 16:13). Delight arises in the life of the believer who responds to God's leading with a heart attuned to the process. The believer lives within a rhythm of relationship as they listen, discern, and respond to God's leading. Henri Nouwen observes that abiding in, and the way in which the Spirit leads, are best realized when the believer possesses attentiveness and internal receptivity, allowing God's wisdom to guide their decisions, feelings, and relationships (Nouwen 1992, 57).

Believers can experience daily delight in God's guidance when they begin with a prayerful awareness, seeking God's presence at the start of each day. In this way, a believer also recognizes the presence of the Holy Spirit in their everyday life as they ask God to help and lead them through the various decisions, actions, and encounters that constitute their day. Psalm 37:23–24 states, "The Lord orders the steps of a good man, and He delights in his way." The Holy Spirit leads them in trustworthy and joyful delight even when their circumstances appear unpredictable. Delight is not the absence of challenges but the assurance of God's sovereignty and love.

Scripture shows us that God's guidance is both instructive and providential. The Israelites, led through the wilderness by a pillar of cloud by day and fire by night, represent their attentive dependence on God's guidance (Exod. 13:21–22). Similarly, in the New Testament, the early church was guided by the Spirit to direct their acts of mission and fellowship (Acts 13:2–4). These narratives reveal that daily delight comes from recognizing God's movements in both major life choices and mundane daily activities.

More than the joy of God's everyday guidance, delight turns ordinary obedience into a joyful experience. Daily steps, such as honesty, encouragement, or patience, become moments of communion with God, revealing that God's presence saturates our entire life. Dallas Willard emphasizes that the practice of awareness and responsiveness trains Christians to see God as the one who acts continually, leading to an awareness that cultivates a life of joy and peace (Willard 1998, 103).

As such, daily delight in God's guidance is a spiritual discipline of attentiveness and trust. As believers lean into the leading of the Spirit, respond to Scripture, and walk in faithfulness, they discover that God is pleased with their hearts as they lean into divine purposes. Delight comes from a relationship of joy, not just in outcomes, but in relational intimacy with the One who lovingly orders their lives.

Nouwen on the Spirit's Gentle Leading

Henri Nouwen offers a profound teaching on how the Holy Spirit guides believers in a spirit of gentleness, attentiveness, and relational connection to God. Nouwen points out that the work of the Spirit does not lead through coercion or demands. Instead, God's leading and guidance often occur through inner promptings, spiritual intuition, and a deep sense of inner peace, which shapes decisions and priorities (Nouwen 1992, 61). Nouwen urges an understanding that the Spirit's leading and guidance will take place not in extraordinary events, but through the rhythm of ordinary life; that is, the invitation to posture oneself as open and receptive.

The New Testament describes the Spirit as a Comforter and a Counselor, who "will guide you into all truth" (John 16:13). This promise reminds believers of God's ongoing, relational guidance. Nouwen emphasizes that recognizing the work of the Spirit as a gentle movement can only take place through stillness, prayer, and reflection. It can be challenging for believers to discern God's prompting and direction amidst the noise and haste. Nouwen's hope is for greater spiritual attentiveness among Christians; he urges the creation of space where listening, reflecting, and obeying God, in the form of the Spirit's gentle prompting, is possible (Nouwen 1992, 63).

Scripture demonstrates the Spirit's patient and guiding work within the life of individuals and in the life of the community. The Spirit guided the church in sending Paul and Barnabas as missionaries (Acts 13:2–4). The Spirit's leading does not necessitate widely known or spectacular manifestations of divine providence, as it can also evolve through communal discernment and responsive individual action. Jesus demonstrates the Spirit's guiding and attentive presence when he withdrew to pray, fasted, and responded to God's timing (Luke 4:1–2). Jesus' example makes it clear that gentle leadership may require waiting, trusting, and humility.

Nouwen frames the concept of spiritual attentiveness as having direct application in a believer's life, where daily choices and encounters with other people are times when we exercise and practice discerning God through the gentle leading and guidance of the Spirit. Nouwen understands this as finding meaning behind often ordinary acts when believers surrender their lives to the Spirit's gentle action; therefore, all things can now have significance in God's kingdom and the life to come. Dallas Willard expresses a similar sentiment: spiritual sensitivity allows God's power and purpose to be demonstrated in ordinary, routine life, and routine acts of obedience are often decisive actions with deep intentional meaning (Willard 1998, 110).

In closing, Nouwen encourages Christian believers to think and behave as dependent, patient, and delighted in the guidance of God in their lives. A Christian believer who lives with a receptive disposition toward the Spirit's gentle leading will experience life rich with God's discernment, peace, and joy in obedience, reflecting the transformative movement of God amidst the ordinary activities of life.

Love Expressed Through the Spirit

The New Testament consistently emphasizes that love is not merely a human emotion, but a genuine act performed by the Spirit. A Spirit-enabled love must surpass the intimate and inadequate impulses that followers of Jesus have to love their neighbors sacrificially, granting generous forgiveness, and displaying compassion as an unbreakable bond, all while exhibiting love enabled by the Spirit (Rom. 5:5). This love ultimately originates from God, sent through the believer submitting to the Spirit's influence, emphasizing John's declaration, "God is love, and he who abides in love abides in God" (1 John 4:16).

Spirit-enabled love for neighbor is vividly and actively displayed in Jesus' parables. Jesus' parable of the Good Samaritan, for example, displays love over prejudices, social customs, and personal convenience (Luke 10:25–37). In this illustration, love is not passive; it is sacrificial and costly, clearly demonstrating Jesus' example of costly love in relation to human beings. Dietrich Bonhoeffer offers a moment of clarity when he notes that discipleship involves living a costly love that is willing to follow Jesus into relationships each day, through acts of self-denial and inconvenience (Bonhoeffer 1959, 115). The Spirit enables believers to love with a love that demonstrates patience, kindness, and forgiveness —essentially, a love that is Spirit-enabled. Jesus even calls this love the "fruit of the Spirit" (Gal. 5:22–23).

Patience and kindness are not virtues developed by human determination, but a work of divine cultivation by the Spirit within us. John Stott notes that every aspect of love reveals the character of God, who is slow to anger and abounding in mercy (Stott 1994, 87). Surrendering to the Spirit, the believer is now free to respond to injustice, answer offense, or meet needs with calm endurance and practical love. This habit-forming spiritual formation produces a community of particular care and mutual compassion.

Paul reveals that love and a life in the Spirit are of equal importance when he commands followers of Jesus to "walk in the Spirit" (Gal. 5:16–25). The fruit of the Spirit will emerge as believers obey the Spirit. When love, a fruit of the Spirit, emerges from each believer who obeys the Spirit, it will shape their behavior, relationships, and ethical responses in all situations. This means that allowing the usual way we engage with others can suddenly become conduits of God's grace for others, making the believer a willing servant of a God who calls them friends in this kingdom work every moment. Ultimately, love through the Spirit is relational, transformational, and reflective of God, drawing the believer into manifesting God's act of reconciliation and redemption every day.

Spirit-Enabled Love for the Neighbor

Love for one's neighbor, instilled and fueled by the Spirit, lies at the heart and center of believers and their work, demonstrating the influence of the Holy Spirit in and through ordinary circumstances. While human love is often conditional or self-serving, love in the Spirit is God-like and, therefore, patient, kind, and sacrificial (Rom. 5:5). Love is not an abstract concept but a relational and practical reality that is constantly extended in every direction towards family, friends, strangers, and even enemies. Jesus summarized this practice as the second of the Great Commandments: "You shall love your neighbor as yourself" (Matt. 22:39).

The biblical witness offers numerous examples of how love, expressed through the Spirit, is practically demonstrated. The parable of the Good Samaritan (Luke 10:25–37) is a poignant example of care that transcends regional, national, ethnic, social, and personal differences. This suggests that loving one's neighbor in the Spirit often exceeds an individual's comfort and is expressed to others regardless of differences. The early period in Acts (Acts 2:44–45) provides a narrative of communal sharing, exemplifying practical, neighborly love in tangible and relational practices of sharing. Notably, love, like faith, becomes visible and expressible through the unfolding of one's life toward serving and attending to the needs of others. This reflects Origen's observation that "Divine love—and love, more generally—constitutes the optic through which one experiences others' relationships, seeks to provide for unconditionally, and will no longer ignore their suffering" (Origen 1996, 72).

The love described here is transformed by the Spirit both in terms of our relationships and our community with others. Love provides space where conflict once existed, brings patience where provocation happens, and sees empathy where suffering has taken place. Augustine reminds us that the love of the Spirit is God's mercy within the believer, which frees them from self and motivates them to encounter others (Augustine 1998, 214). Abiding in the Spirit allows believers to embrace love that is not passive but responsive to every person and circumstance, persistently and abundantly producing fruit.

As believers engage in love that takes a practical shape and form, it entails listening actively, speaking hope, forgiving genuinely, and serving sacrificially. Love is relational, responsive, and continuous, just as God is relational. This picture of walking and engaging one another in love by the Spirit fulfills both the ethical and spiritual capacities for Christ, effectively calling believers to be vehicles of grace or conduits of God's care and service to the world. Ultimately, Spirit-enabled love expressed toward one's neighbor is a routine, lived-out expression of the kingdom, a modus vivendi that connects hearts, facilitates transformation in lives, and points the way to all love that comes from God (1 John 4:7–12).

Patience and Kindness as Divine Work

Patience and kindness are not something that humans can develop through their own moral worth; they are the fruits of the Spirit, made possible through Godly grace and presence in believers' lives. As Galatians 5:22–23 declares, the Spirit bears love, joy, peace, patience, kindness, and more, illustrating that the ethical transformation of individuals is never just due to human self-control; it is God's work in our lives. Patience enables believers to endure suffering, delay, and even provocation, while kindness allows them to demonstrate their consideration and regard for others through generous deeds of compassion.

The biblical witness provides many examples of how these virtues originate from God. The example of Joseph, who was sold into slavery by his brothers, was patient through suffering and finally kind in the way he cared for them (Gen. 45:5–15). In the same way, Paul's exhortation to the Colossians encourages believers to "put on tender mercies, kindness, humility, meekness, and patience" (Col. 3:12), indicating that patience and kindness come from God, not from human ethics that are decided upon independently. John Chrysostom argues that patience occurs when humans align their will with God, and suffering for the wrong done to them becomes a focus on the relationship, rather than the suffering. Thus, the believer perseveres, not as a resigned "waiter" but as a participant upheld and empowered by the Spirit of the living God (Chrysostom 1999, 132).

When the Spirit enables patience and kindness, they allow relationships and communities to be reshaped. They enable individuals to work through conflicts gracefully, engage misunderstandings with compassion, and offer service to others without expecting reward. Acts of patience and kindness are evident in all that Jesus did when he interacted with the sick, the marginalized, and even the socially excluded, demonstrating that patience and kindness often run contrary to societal standards and human nature (Matt. 9:36; Mark 10:21).

Practically, believers can cultivate the virtues of patience and kindness by relying on the Spirit through prayer and God-focused contemplation of the Word, as well as by being earnest about loving others through acts of kindness. Reflecting that feelings of kindness and patience originate with God helps cultivate humble self-dependence on God and develops our hearts to be aware of those in need of kindness and patience. In the human frame of mind, Thomas Aquinas states the virtues grow through God's grace, as grace is the readiness for human disposition to live out the character of God in everyday life (Aquinas 1947, II-II, q. 23). Spirit-enabled patience and kindness become ways of participating in the life-giving work of reconciliation, healing, and witness.

Paul's Call to Walk in the Spirit

In his exhortation to the Galatian believers in chapters 5, verses 16–25, Paul outlines a process for walking in the Spirit. "Walk in the Spirit, and you shall not fulfill the lust of the flesh" (Gal. 5:16) encourages believers that moral and spiritual change is not just a matter of sheer will, but rather a matter of submission to the Spirit's leading. Paul contrasts the works of the flesh (selfishness, envy, immorality) and the fruit of the Spirit, nuancing that authentic Christian living is birthed out of Spirit-empowered compliance, as opposed to legalistic efforts.

Walking in the Spirit entails an ongoing relational interaction with God. It is a process, not an event. Our hearts and minds must be continually directed towards God's influence. John Calvin noted that believers are never separated from Christ, but rather included in him as the Spirit of God facilitates the believer's evidenced practical holiness and victory over sin (Calvin 1559, 345). Walking in the Spirit requires awareness, reliance through prayerful dependence, and the development of spiritual disciplines that foster relational building in an attitude of communication with the divine.

The story of the early church provides tangible expressions of what it means to live in the Spirit's guidance. After being empowered at Pentecost, the apostles exhibited courage, patience, and love in their ministry; this walking in the Spirit is characterized by both inner transformation and outward effectiveness (Acts 2:1–4). Paul himself displays, through his letters, both the tension and triumph of being Spirit-dependent, as his weaknesses were God's strength fittingly displayed, with newfound freedoms to witness the tension of practicing the paradox of being a Spirit-filled person (2 Cor. 12:9).

Walking in the Spirit also restructures community life. Someone who has been Spirit-led in their actions produces fruit, which reflects unity, and gives room for humility and mutual accountability on their own or in association. Brennan Manning noted that the Spirit allows believers to demonstrate love and patience in relational interactions with one another by expressing God's embodied character (Manning 1990, 112). Therefore, Galatians 5:16–25 presents an ethical perspective not only on behavior, but also on theology: that Christian virtue and character are only separated through the functioning maturity of divine power.

In summary, Paul aimed to lead the Galatian believers on an intentional, Spirit-led lifestyle, where obedience to life in Christ is a devotional rather than burdensome experience. Joy is derived from submission to God's purposes, with transformation occurring both personally and communally. The invitation to walk in the Spirit is the lived experience of believers. It is within the kingdom agenda to live in weakness, allowing grace to flow, so that the consequences of everyday life demonstrate the Father's power, love, and holiness.

Theological Reflections

The indwelling and transformative work of the Holy Spirit has long been a topic of rigorous Christian theological reflection, spanning the centuries from the early Church to the present day. For example, Augustine of Hippo emphasizes the Spirit's deep presence among believers and argues that, through the Spirit's work, the Spirit guides, sanctifies, and strengthens the ordinary believer's soul from within (Augustine 397, 1.1–2). The Spirit is not a measure of assistance in Christian practices that occur outside the believer; the Spirit animates the believer's entire inner life, transforming our hearts and minds to the will of God and making otherwise ordinary lives pathways for divine grace (1 Cor. 6:19). This view represents spiritual growth as relational and transformational, bound to God's initiative that exceeds any human efforts.

In the contemporary period, J. I. Packer gives voice to the work of the Spirit through each believer's identity in holiness and obedience. Most compellingly, he observes that a believer's moral and spiritual transformation is not self-generated but is a work of God's Spirit, who energizes faith, guides discernment, and produces the fruit of God's Kingdom in each believer's ordinary life (Packer 1973, 215). He writes about practical theology in which Spirit-led living is not only instantaneous but also ongoing, requiring daily surrender and attentiveness to God's nudges. This emphasis aligns with the biblical pattern of more than just inner transformation as a framework for discussion and thinking (Gal. 5:22–23).

Pushing reflection in a different direction, Dietrich Bonhoeffer articulates the ethical or relational character of the Spirit's work in the context of discipleship. The Spirit enables believers to act boldly and lovingly, to turn against injustice, and to embody the upside-down kingdom of God through service, patience, and humility (Bonhoeffer 1959, 82). He reminds the Church that spiritual and other life tendencies can articulate a way to construct a meaningful faith that will occupy all aspects of their lives, including personal relationships and social interactions with people.

Together, the points made in each of these theological reflections converge on a significant truth: We can recognize that the Spirit will create in and through an individual believer true weakness as strength, ordinary obedience into extraordinary fruit, and therefore human limitation as the pathways through which believers experience God's redemptive power. Such ongoing Spirit-activated work requires that we reflect on and be involved in a life of devotion and obedience, and to visualize our Christian lives as relational, transformative, and filled with the Spirit of God. It means, through Augustine, Packer, and Bonhoeffer, that theology is not only thought, but also action, and not only action, but action that reaches the heart through individual engagement.

Augustine on the Spirit's Indwelling

The mystery and power of the Holy Spirit's indwelling is a rich topic of unique description by Augustine of Hippo. He writes in *Confessions* that God's Spirit does not exist somewhere as an agent "out there," but is intimately present and transformative of the human heart and life from within (Augustine 397, 1.1–2). The Spirit shared within the believer enables them to know God experientially, allowing for both relational and dynamic communion. This indwelling is more than symbolically true; it is the center of spiritual renewal, where divine grace encounters human fragility, vulnerability, and weakness, ultimately transforming us into instruments of God's power (2 Cor. 12:9).

Augustine's understanding of the Spirit is also relational. He insists that the Spirit cultivates love, humility, and discernment, and leads believers to align all their thoughts, desires, and actions with God's will (Augustine 397, 3.5). Thus, he understood the Spirit to be, in many ways, an internal teacher, reflecting Christ's promise of a Comforter who would abide with the people of faith (John 14:16–17). By placing significant emphasis on internal transformation, Augustine shifted the nature of the Christian life from external observance to ongoing cultivation of interior devotion and obedience.

At the same time, Augustine emphasizes the paradox of divine-human interplay or engagement. While the Spirit cultivates and works apart from human effort or deserved entitlement, its fruits are intentionally realized in the response of faith and love made by the believer in place of all other efforts (Rom. 8:11). This engagement reveals an important relationship for Augustine: the Christian life is both a gift and a responsibility for the believer, where participation in God's work of transformation requires prayerful reflection and moral engagement.

The practical implications of Augustine's relationship are profound. A Spirit-filled life is characterized by ongoing attentiveness to God, who is never absent, and involves the formation of character, renewal of hope, and energizing of resolve through prayer, meditation, and the reading of Scripture. The Spirit ensures that those who live in relation with God are never alone in their troubles or burdens, encouraging and empowering their faithful response. Thus, Augustine clarifies the indwelling of the Spirit as the source and sustainer of the Christian life, defining intimacy with God. This approach suggests that followers become the very reflection of God's glory in all their ordinary lives.

Packer on the Transforming Power of the Holy Spirit

J.I. Packer insists that the Holy Spirit is fundamental to the transformation of every believer, making it possible for a life to reflect the holiness and power of God. Although Packer is clear that human efforts cannot produce authentic spiritual change, he maintains that transformation is possible because of the work of the Spirit; the Spirit works to conform the believer to the likeness of Christ in a way that produces fruit that glorifies God and affects the world (Packer 1973, 215). Packer is adamant that this transformation is not merely surface-level; it reaches the mind, heart, and will, impacting the character, affections, and conduct of the believer in accordance with divine purposes.

God's Surprising Way

Packer illustrates this using a combination of promises made in Romans 8:13 and the fruit of the Spirit as described in Galatians 5:22–23, expressing that the Spirit works in two ways, internally and externally, as believers are brought to renewal of thought, repentance, and moral discernment, and externally as the Spirit gifts them for godly actions as believers demonstrate love, patience, kindness, and integrity towards others, especially where it feels challenging to do so. In the context of his argument, this dual work—where the Spirit does internal work on the believer while producing physical acts of righteousness in the community of faith—reinforces the integrated nature of transformation when the Spirit leads believers.

Packer also emphasizes the necessity to cooperate with the work of the Spirit. There is an intrinsic nature to transformation, where surrender, prayer, and attention to God and His Word must direct the believer. It is through God's display of mercy and grace that transformation can occur (2 Tim. 3:16–17). Even in the midst of human frailty or inconsistent behavior, the power of the Spirit will still be adequate, just as Paul notes in assessing that the strength of God is made perfect in human weakness (2 Cor. 12:9). Consequently, spiritual maturity is a work of grace that calls the believer out of self-sufficiency and into reliance on God's enablement.

In practical terms, Packer counsels believers to take note of what the Spirit is doing and cooperate with Him on a personal level in their everyday lives. Each decision, interaction, and trial in daily activities provides the Spirit with the opportunity to develop character and demonstrate God's power for transformation. As believers grow to integrate attentiveness, obedience, and trust in their relationship with Christ, they will find themselves in a pattern with the Spirit that God uses to transform them for the rest of their lives, providing opportunities to witness the authentic and productive reality of God's kingdom in heaven and on earth.

Thus, Packer presents the Holy Spirit not as a blind theological concept, but as a permanent, personal, and active agent of spiritual transformation, making lives of holiness, joy, and effective witness possible (Packer 1973, 215).

Bonhoeffer on Spirit-Led Discipleship

Dietrich Bonhoeffer's theology of discipleship is grounded in the understanding that being a follower of Christ is only possible through the work of the Holy Spirit, who guides and empowers believers to live faithfully in a fallen world. Discipleship is far more than ethical or moral striving. It is taking part in the very life of Christ, in the relationships with both Christ and others, that the Spirit provides. He argues that Christ calls His followers to a costly, dynamic obedience, while the Spirit is equipping them to live lives that reflect the kingdom of God in everyday contexts (Bonhoeffer 1959, 86).

The paradox of divine empowerment through human vulnerability is a crucial aspect of Bonhoeffer's overall argument. Just as Christ came down in humility, revealing God through suffering and trial, those disciples who depend on the Spirit are now called to be servants in the same way, trusting in the Spirit to guide them and empower them. The Spirit enables the disciple to act rightly, not merely through human willpower, but through the Spirit producing the godly sense of discernment and courage even amid persecution, pressure from institutional religious bodies, or other social pressures (Acts 1:8). Bonhoeffer's primary emphasis of "costly grace" emphasizes that obeying the Spirit of God often calls us to align ourselves absolutely in God's purposes, rejecting the prevailing social mandates, and our warped ideas of comfort.

Bonhoeffer emphasizes that Spirit-led/exhorted discipleship is always communal. The power of the Spirit unites the church. It forms the type of relationships that are characterized by love, forgiveness, and a commitment to encourage one another, as was true of the first disciples (John 13:34–35). Every believer, in duly submitting to the Spirit's leading, contributes to the overall spiritual vitality of the greater body of Christ. Practicing obedience, which Bonhoeffer encourages, cannot be separated from listening attentively, praying with discernment, cooperating with Christ, and following his example with appropriate humility (Gal. 5:25).

Finally, Bonhoeffer characterizes the Spirit as a personal and present force, not simply a mystical companion that maintains the good work of discipleship across the ordinary and extraordinary. The Spirit gives disciples life to witness to the word and deed of God's kingdom; the Spirit's presence can transform fear into courage, lethargy into engagement, and indifference into exceptional sacrificial love. This means that Spirit-filled discipleship is a comprehensive process that includes character, relationships, and faithful action. Ordinary life can be the site of extraordinary grace and the presence of God.

Essentially, Bonhoeffer encourages Christians to remember that true discipleship is never unmoored from the Spirit, who enables believers to become Christ-like instruments of God's love, justice, and truth.

Living Spirit-Filled Lives Today

Living a Spirit-filled life requires daily intentionality and being aware of the necessity of depending upon God's power over human strength. Paul reminds us, "For we have this treasure in earthen vessels, that the excellence of the power may be of God and not of us" (2 Cor. 4:7). Living a Spirit-filled life begins with being aware of limits and that God's empowering presence can tense and hold in every moment of life. This awareness and dependence on God's power foster humility, enabling believers to submit their plans, thoughts, and actions to the Spirit's call (Packer 1973, 215).

A natural part of such humility is service to others. When the Spirit shapes our hearts, our actions of love, patience, and kindness become expressions of God's grace rather than self-interest. For instance, the way Jesus washed the disciples' feet (John 13:14–15) reveals that acts of service also portray the upside-down world of God's kingdom, where significant measurement is a product of selfless care for others (Bonhoeffer 1959, 86). Even the smallest acts of obedience can have a greater impact than we might imagine, as the Spirit multiplies faithful actions without the benefit of human eyes to see the results. Joy is not a product of completion but of being in alignment with God's Spirit. In addition, joy emerges from seeing real conversion in the lives of people being transformed by Christian obedience empowered by the Spirit (Gal. 5:22–23).

The Spirit also empowers the work of reconciliation. Spirit-empowered words begin to bring healing to the brokenness in relationships where forgiveness and understanding have been replaced by resentment (Eph. 4:32). Likewise, divine enabling empowers love without conditions. In every sense, believers reflect God's grace toward humanity by acting in patience, empathy, and mercy. Encouraging family or community to understand the various facets of the fruit of the Spirit—love, joy, peace, patience, kindness, goodness, faithfulness, gentleness, and self-control—illustrates how God's Spirit changes us in tangible, relational ways.

A Spirit-filled life also includes an evangelistic element. Living out the upside-down values of God's kingdom, believers witness to a world that is defined by self-interest and battles for power, offering examples of God's transformative love (Matt. 5:16). Walking consistently in joy, healing, and love demands vigilance, prayer, and surrendering normal, daily time to the Spirit, transforming simple, ordinary time into extraordinary channels of grace. However, we see all of this taking shape as the Spirit continues to make us little mirrors of Christ, guiding men and women to holiness, and thus helping each other take part in God's redemptive work in the world through the Spirit's unseen and powerful work.

Daily Dependence on God's Power

The believer's life is characterized not by self-sufficiency but by reliance on the Spirit's power. Scripture is clear that without the Spirit, our effort, no matter how sincere, will not bring about the transformation of heart or the impact for the kingdom of God that is necessary to live up to God's call. Paul explains, "I can do all things through Christ who strengthens me" (Phil. 4:13). There is nothing we can do without reliance on God's strength, not because we lack the ability, but because we lack the proper understanding of the true source of our strength. This kind of dependence requires humility each day, acknowledging our weakness while allowing God's grace and power to work through it (2 Cor. 12:9).

Practically, this dependence means turning to God in daily surrender, which begins with prayer and verbally acknowledging God's presence in our everyday lives. The human heart is restless until resting in God, Augustine notes, suggesting that every action, decision, and thought is meant to include conscious dependence on God (Augustine 1998, 42). Instead of living out of pride or self-reliance, believers take a posture of openness to incorporate the Spirit in decision-making, allowing the Spirit to add extraordinary significance to ordinary tasks.

Reliance on God's power enhances spiritual discernment. The more believers depend on God's power, the more they can discern the difference between God's will, human ambition, or cultural pressures. Daily dependent living can cultivate habits of turning to Scripture and listening for God's voice and guidance in engaging with neighbors, coworkers, and other relationships. As Dallas Willard observes, a life that depends on the Spirit is a life in which our awareness of God's goodness is habitual and part of the flow of time; a Spirit-dependent life lives at a deliberate pace whereby God is part of all actions in every moment, spontaneous but habitual (Willard 1998, 76).

Trust in God grants the believer the endurance to endure suffering. Our human strength will fail us in suffering, but God's power sustains, gives wisdom, and brings peace. When a believer lives in daily dependence on the Spirit, they can experience a rhythm of grace that enables them to take on each challenge with faith and without fear as they navigate their trials (Isa. 40:29–31). In the end, daily dependence on God transforms common life into a place for God's activity, as God's power is made perfect in human weakness, and God's glory is revealed through humble, Spirit-led living, forming unique and meaningful opportunities for altruistic action.

Serving Others in Spirit-Led Humility

Christian service is never rooted in human ambition or the thirst for accolades, but rather the product of the Spirit's work to create humility in us. Jesus demonstrated this fact in His ministry with His disciples when He washed their feet, showing that "Whoever desires to be great among you, let him be your servant" (Matt. 20:26–28). From an understanding of Spirit-led humility, Christ-followers can prioritize what others need over their own wants, thereby allowing their acts of service to be gifts of Christ's love, rather than something they do to elevate themselves in the world.

Service in humility begins as an attitude that depends on God. When we recognize that everything we have—gifts, opportunities, and resources—comes from Him, it encourages an attitude of gratitude. John Stott remarks that this is not accidental, concerning genuine service as an integral part of spiritual formation, and that "humility helps form our hearts" so that when we serve, we act out of love rather than obligation or social expectations (Stott 1992, 104). Paul also prepares our mindset, stating that we are to "do nothing from selfish ambition or conceit, but in humility count others more significant than yourselves" (Phil. 2:3).

We see several practical examples of Spirit-led service found in Scripture. The Good Samaritan provides us with an excellent model of sacrificial care for the marginalized (Luke 10:30–37). We also see Dorcas's ministry in Acts, which provides evidence of what unguided, selfless acts can mean to a local community (Acts 9:36–39). In each of these examples, the emphasis of service is Spirit-empowered and informed by compassion rather than the vanity of human accolades.

Spirit-led humility also reminds us of the expectations that come with relationships. Any service performed humbly has a profoundly positive influence on people. When we serve with humility, we practice being patient and understanding; we gently guide ourselves and others, creating space for love and reconciliation. As Henri Nouwen observes, a humble servant listens, walks with, and allows God's love to flow through small actions (Nouwen 1989, 58).

Taken together, to serve in humility is to be transformed, so that with those we serve, we demonstrate the kingdom of God's values—where love measures greatness, and power is expressed through gentle service. When Christians take the position of humility, they can experience their lives as a lifestyle of ministry that is pleasing to Jesus. Our lives can become like His: a presence in a world that brings healing and encouragement, a tangible representation of God.

Joy in Unexpected Fruit from Simple Obedience

Obeying God may seem commonplace or burdensome, but over and over again, Scripture demonstrates that faithfulness in small things can produce incredible results. Jesus teaches this very principle: "He who is faithful in what is least is faithful also in much" (Luke 16:10). Simple, Spirit-led obedience opens up the possibilities where the living God delivers unexpected and immeasurable blessings. It illustrates that a life of joy is often the byproduct of faithfully moving through life in accordance with God's leading, rather than joy being sought out on its own.

The account of feeding the five thousand (John 6:1–14) displays this reality remarkably. A young boy presents his lunch of five loaves and two fish, a humble act of obedience. Jesus takes the seemingly insignificant act and multiplies it to provide for thousands. This illustrates how God transforms the seemingly ordinary act of faithful obedience into a profoundly life-altering impact on those who follow it. The Spirit empowers the believer to realize that their act of simple obedience, albeit unnoticed and unrecognized, is part of something bigger in God's kingdom work.

Spiritual joy arises as the believer sees God's provision and transformational work as a response to obedience. Jonathan Edwards insists that true delight in God comes when our will is in line with God's, even in seemingly insignificant acts (Edwards 1957, 87). The joy is not self-generated but flows from the Spirit, who recognizes and affirms our responsibility within God's community and ultimately His glory, even on a small scale. Likewise, C.S. Lewis notes that if one acts from love, even in small ways, their acts connect to outcomes that far exceed any immediate result (Lewis 1960, 102).

Spirit-led obedience allows us to witness the Holy Spirit's transformational work of humility. The believer realizes that the outcome is God's work, not theirs, allowing them to set aside pride and any sense of performance-based faith, and practice obedience as a relational act of trust toward God's wisdom, timing, and sovereignty. As we are obedient in the seemingly insignificant moments of life, the Spirit grows joy by reminding us that the life of God's kingdom is often counterintuitive, yet still bears great value.

At its core, simple obedience is a pathway to spiritual fruitfulness and profound, lasting joy. The unexpected fruit that sometimes appears is equally a testament to God's powerful work as it is a reminder that even small, faith-filled acts, if led by the Spirit, participate in God's redemptive mission in the world.

Healing Relationships Through Spirit-Guided Words

Words matter in relationships. Scripture makes clear that speech is a pathway to life or death: "Death and life are in the power of the tongue, and those who love it will eat its fruits" (Prov. 18:21). In relation to others, words inspired by the Holy Spirit are conduits for reconciliation, healing, and restoration, not conflict and separation. Spirit-led words are not only about politeness; they reflect the character of Christ and allow Christ's peace to flow through.

Jesus illustrates this throughout the Gospel accounts. Consider the gentle yet firm words He spoke to the woman caught in adultery, which defused possible violence and invited repentance and restoration (John 8). In that instance, He shared truth, mercy, and empowerment simultaneously, and His response illustrated that Spirit-filled communication allows wholeness in relationships to flourish. Paul challenges believers to "let your speech always be gracious, seasoned with salt" (Col. 4:6). Through the Holy Spirit's inspiration, he alerts us that every word has the potential to build up and bring healing and clarity when spoken in the Spirit (Packer 1973, 142).

Words can often bring healing and restoration, but such words arise out of discernment and humility, not instinct or reaction. Henri Nouwen emphasizes that listening closely to the Spirit within us develops sensitivity to the correct timing, tone, and content of our intended speech, while seeking reconciliation over defensiveness (Nouwen 1989, 56). Spirit-imbued communication enables us to share confession, forgiveness, or affirmation, allowing believers to restore fractured relationships with authenticity and love. Words of empathy or encouragement, even when simple in form, and spoken in accordance with God's Spirit, can profoundly alter the dynamics of a relationship by allowing God to become present and tangible in others' lives.

Additionally, Spirit-empowered words foster spiritual growth. As believers become accustomed to pausing, praying, and letting God shape their response, they embody the patience, gentleness, and wisdom of Christ. Conflict becomes a vehicle for grace, not resentment. We experience the power of His Spirit overcoming our dependence on our own strength to restore someone, and relationships are healed. Relationships healed through Spirit-led words reflect the Kingdom of God, contribute to the community of faith, and generate peace, trust, and growth together.

Daily dependency on the Spirit's leading of speech empowers believers to speak life, reconcile, and fulfill God's redemptive action in their community. Spirit-inspired words enable us to be a living testimony of Christ's transformative presence, serving as conduits of hope and reconciliation in a broken world.

Loving Without Conditions Through Divine Assistance

As Scripture teaches, true love transcends personal preference, convenience, or righteousness. The command to love is not an issue of worth but rather depends on God and His character: "Beloved, let us love one another, for love is of God; and everyone who loves is born of God and knows God" (1 John 4:7). Human love is usually conditional, reactive, or partial, but believers can love unconditionally through the presence of the Holy Spirit. True love is a reflection of God's nature in our daily relationships.

Throughout His ministry, Jesus demonstrated unconditional love. His interactions with the marginalized, sinful, and social outcasts, like the Samaritan woman at the well (John 4) or Zacchaeus (Luke 19:1–10), demonstrated that human love is conditional and limited. In contrast, divine love flows not based on human sensitivity but on the work of God's grace in and through the believer. Dietrich Bonhoeffer theorizes that Christlike love is costly and disciplined, calling the believer to become grounded in God's Spirit instead of their proclivity (Bonhoeffer 1959, 122).

Unconditional love is both a divine gift and a spiritual discipline that involves purposeful dependence upon God. To soften the heart, to be patient, or to have empathy for another under challenging circumstances is truly remarkable. Spirit-fed love allows a believer to forgive offenses, to sacrificially meet needs, or to care for another with hope in return. Paul articulates the transformative nature of this selfless commitment in Romans 5:5: "Now hope does not disappoint, because the love of God has been poured out in our hearts by the Holy Spirit who was given to us." The Spirit is the origin and sustainer of unconditional love, empowering believers to operate beyond their limitations.

In practice, this love shows itself through acts of kindness, encouraging words, and enduring patiently in family, workplace, and community environments. This is God's upside-down kingdom, where He perfects strengths through weaknesses, and it is more blessed to give than to receive. When a believer yields to the Spirit, they exhibit a kind of love that blesses, heals, and restores, as a witness to God's transformative presence in a relationally fractured world.

Unconditional love, as a fruit of the Spirit, is a showcase of God's redemptive work—a lofty invitation for others to discover the same grace that ignites, motivates, and sustains the believer's heart.

Cultivating the Fruit of the Spirit in Family and Community

The fruit of the Spirit, which Paul describes as "love, joy, peace, longsuffering, kindness, goodness, faithfulness, gentleness, self-control" (Gal. 5:22–23), is not simply an abstract ideal but a reality that helps people live relationally and faithfully. In family and community settings, such virtues are both reflections of God's presence and avenues for fostering habitation, development, and encouragement. The fruit of such Spirit-led living is a deliberate cooperation with God, resulting in grace and blessing in everyday life.

Family life provides a primary context for Spirit-activated living. Daily events—including parenting, marriage, and sibling relationships—offer opportunities to exercise patience, gentleness, and self-control. For example, when parenting a misbehaving child, choosing kindness instead of irritation models God's grace, as He instructs in Ephesians 4:32: "Be kind to one another, tenderhearted, forgiving one another, even as God in Christ forgave you." In such family interactions, relational safety and spiritual formation are fostered, creating an environment that nurtures love, faithfulness, and Spirit-responsive behavior.

Community life extends these principles beyond the family. Volunteering, helping neighbors, or simply being a supportive friend allows believers to bear the Spirit's fruit outwardly and to demonstrate God's kingdom tangibly. John Stott notes, "Christian ethics are not restricted to private devotion, but to social engagement," illustrating how the Spirit transforms everyday relationships (Stott 2006, 178). Acts of patience, kindness, and goodness can generate trust, encouragement, and care that ripple beyond immediate interactions.

Spirit-led formation is intentional and relational. It involves prayer, waiting upon God, personal reflection, and a willingness to accept critique. Henri Nouwen observes, "The Spirit works with us, including our resolves and actions that are visible, as well as attitudes and urges of invisibly rooted embodiments" (Nouwen 1992, 101). The significance of a believer's life unfolds gradually through this progressive work of transformation; it requires surrender, obedience, and grace.

The fruit of the Spirit demonstrates believers' capacity to be conduits of God's love, joy, and peace to others. When their lives bear witness to the Spirit active within them, discipleship extends beyond personal piety to reveal the tangible reality of the Spirit in their families and communities.

Witnessing to God's Upside-Down Kingdom in Daily Life

The kingdom of God revealed by Jesus is an upside-down kingdom, one that differs significantly from the world's expectations. In the upside-down kingdom of God, the first are last, the strong are weak, and humility is honorable (Matt. 20:16; Luke 22:26–27). Witnessing to this reality requires more than telling others; it is manifested through observable, Spirit-led behaviors. When believers act in ways that reflect the values of the kingdom, they become living testimonies to the transformative power of God.

In daily life, there are numerous opportunities to live this reversal of values. Choosing restoration through forgiveness, generosity over selfishness, or service over advantage represents an expression of Christian witness. It embodies the Spirit at work in the believer. The rich young ruler (Mark 10:17–22) and the shepherds who visited Christ at his birth (Luke 2:8–20) provide evidence of an upside-down kingdom full of surprises—it blesses the humble, elevates the lowly, and invites the faithful to costly devotion. Living out these realities embodies the gospel and speaks powerfully in ways words cannot.

The witness of an upside-down kingdom is also relational. It compels believers to live out patience, kindness, and mercy in workplaces, schools, and neighborhoods. N. T. Wright emphasizes that kingdom ethics are not meant to be lived only in ecclesial or spiritual domains, but rather in ordinary spaces (Wright 1996, 412). When Christians embody Christ-like priorities in their daily encounters, they help others see God's kingdom and invite them to break free from conventional societal thinking, experiencing God's love.

Spirit-led discernment and action are essential. Through the power of the Holy Spirit, believers can discern the tension between cultural values and kingdom values, acting justly, loving mercy, and walking humbly (Micah 6:8). Bonhoeffer notes that such divine discipleship often comes at a cost; however, it can lead believers to a change in consciousness, recognizing that God's power is revealed to the world through weakness and sacrifice (Bonhoeffer 1959, 86).

Witnessing to God's upside-down kingdom is living theology. Every decision made in humility, service, and sacrificial love is a prophetic sign that God's reign is alive and real. With Spirit-enabled obedience, believers make the extraordinary visible in the ordinary, embodying the gospel before the eyes and hearts of those who observe, interact with, and are inspired by their lives.

Walking Consistently in Joy, Healing, and Love

To walk in the Spirit is not to walk occasionally, but rather to live a life of continual transformation characterized by joy, healing, and love. The apostle Paul challenges believers to "walk in the Spirit" so they do not carry out their desires of the flesh (Gal. 5:16). When we live continually in the Spirit, our lives develop a pattern of living in which we are aware that God's presence permeates both our cognition and our relational interactions as we make decisions. A consistent walk in the Spirit does not mean that we will be perfect in our endurance, but that we are committed to continually orient our lives towards embodying obedience, repentance, and relational wholeness.

Joy, as a fruit of the Spirit, is integral to this walk (Gal. 5:22). Joy is not merely happiness determined by a currently favorable event or situation. Rather, it is found within a believer's heart when they commune with God.

Even through difficult days, believers can experience a sustaining inner joy when they hold onto God's promises and recognize the continual, transformational work of the Spirit in their lives. Healing—emotional, spiritual, and social—follows as the Spirit changes and renews minds, forgives burdens, and heals broken relationships. Henri Nouwen emphasizes how embracing naked vulnerability and operating under the direction and leading of God's Spirit during the restoration process produces relational wholeness far beyond human ability (Nouwen 1989, 73).

Love, as the highest expression of Spirit-filled living, motivates believers to be consistently ethical and relational. It causes believers to seek to forgive, serve, or bless others, nothing less (1 John 4:7–8). Consistent love can only be developed through a disciplined approach to spiritual disciplines, through active prayer for attentiveness to the needs of others, and by the believer providing the same relational recognition to directions from the Spirit, even in the smallest context of everyday life. Stott observes that practical obedience in love demonstrates how genuine faith transforms lives and communities (Stott 1991, 205).

Walking consistently in joy, healing, and loving others requires humility, perseverance, and work empowered by the Divine. When believers, through the daily regularity of practices that align their lives with God's will, consistently embody these virtues and values, they create a fellowship of the kingdom of heaven on earth by bringing joy, healing, and love into their ordinary work. In fact, every decision, every conversation, and every service that a believer engages with in the community gives evidence of a life that is consistently Spirit-empowered, proclaiming the gospel, in which God's kingdom is all around for the person reflecting God's glory and inviting others to belong to the reality of God. Finally, the Holy Spirit enables believers to live in this way specifically because their lives reflect God's glory and invite others to a new reality of hope.

Chapter 9

The Coming Kingdom

The Reversal of the Future

The expected kingdom of God will come in a manner that defies all human expectations, revealing instead a divine reversal that will dismantle worldly hierarchies. Our scriptures remind us that God's kingdom is firmly against the pride of the mighty, and comforts the sad and downtrodden by inverting and reshaping lives that find hope in the sovereignty of God (Matt. 19:30). The identity of Jesus encapsulates this kingdom ethic when Jesus declares, "the last shall be first and the first last" (Matt. 19:30). Within this economy of grace, God does not simply align situations; God will impact our hearts, our priorities, and our communities with the just, merciful, and faithful vision of God. Believers are invited to exist in this upside-down reality as obedient and humble acts of devotion (Augustine 1998, 112).

God's attempt to engage in making wrongs right extends beyond ethical correction. The hope of God promises restoration and renewal. In Isaiah, prophetic vistas proclaim a kingdom where oppression will cease, justice will flow like a river, and consolation will be experienced even amidst suffering (Isa. 9:6–7). John Chrysostom explains, "it is not just that one community will be…its promise fulfilled; but that each…will experience the living of this promise and be challenged to live ever more rightly, rightly, in how they carry on in their being, as opposed to the world, in hopeful anticipation of God's ultimate, vindicating, unqualified fullness" (Chrysostom 1986, 72). This means believing that God will fulfill His justice by demonstrating it through our faith as we lovingly visit those who suffer and forgive those whose actions represent societal injustices.

Similarly, Origen demonstrates that to comprehend God's coming kingdom, one needs to interpret Scripture both literally and allegorically, for the 'upturning' of oppression is the spiritual truth and expression of God's active, divine love and power (Origen 1994, 45), embodying regenerative hope. In reflecting the promises of God, believers should be encouraged to seek the fullness of their object, which was previously delineated for our benefit. The 'upturning' of oppression reflects the active desire of hope of God, while the theological perspective affirms God as the active agent and the centre of faith; a grace that is the indistinguishable hope inviting us, as Christians, to mirror Kingdom values as a first taste of the visible eschaton (Bauckham 1996, 118).

The enacting of the coming kingdom is both a promise and a predicted outcome that occupies one's conscious thoughts and actions upon reflecting on the following: the coming kingdom invites us into a reality where we model the future embodiment of God's restorative efforts in the present, anticipatory reality. Through acting as we would when God and we meet in a future eschatological state, we become those who wait patiently in suffering, visibly engage with the dispossessed, and act, believe, endure, and trust that God divinely impacts our legacy, rather than through humanly possible attempts to alleviate oppressive outcomes. This full enactment of the coming kingdom occurs through the lens of reflective trust, as we consider and choose both ethical behaviors and embody those ongoing choices shared in cooperation with God (Wright 1996, 214).

God's Kingdom vs. Human Expectations

God's kingdom transforms human expectations of power, status, and success. With worldly kingdoms, the means of coercion, wealth, or hierarchical status, as the rationale to claim authority should you achieve those ideals, is now placed alongside the humblest of circumstances in the kingdom of God that raise the humble, comfort the oppressed, and for which status has no value in human expectations of human freedom (Matt. 5:3–12). In the same way, the Old Testament addresses human expectations in contrast to divine intention, portraying God as the just and merciful ruler who raises the lowly and causes humans to be inverted in their prioritization (Isa. 55:8–9). For those who hear the call of God in the life of Christ, the perspective of this inversion must be recognized, which affects the spiritual and moral actions of believers.

Augustine of Hippo draws on the notion that it is human to desire dominion and status, while the kingdom of God calls for submission and humility (Augustine 1998, 112). The spiritual joy of knowing that God's economy is based on grace, not merit, allows believers to be relieved from comparisons to worldly standards. John Calvin suggests that human anticipation is often misguided; one can only truly value a legitimate good deed by understanding God's perspective and intent (Calvin 1559, 45). The point here is that one cannot live in God's kingdom without an inner change that allows one to value righteousness, mercy, and faithfulness above worldly status or material gain.

Scripture stories have also portrayed this point in striking ways. The tension that accompanies the story of the rich young ruler offers insight (Matt. 19:16–22). The rich young man had everything we could desire, and when he saw the light of Jesus' kingdom, he asked about eternal life; when asked what he considered worthy of his "one thing necessary," he could not give up his possessions and walked away sorrowful. This story undermines a purely human or religious perspective because God, through the kingdom of Jesus, can use a person, or the person may miss out on God's grace due to human ambition. The narratives of Jesus with tax collectors and sinners reveal that God does not prioritize the religious component of repentance. However, God's invitation of love, the means by which God has organized a tempo for justification, involves a person joining God's mission to affect change in the community by creating a new sociality that acts for repentance for their sin in community (Luke 19:1–10). The relationships are based on the ethics of being human. Origen observes that these inversions are ethical instructions not simply referential to human behavior, but they express spiritual realities; hidden in our world is God's wisdom, which intends to reveal itself to those who trust and obey (Origen 1994, 58).

The availability of this truth in practical performance is adequate. Believers operating in dependence on God's kingdom begin to recreate empathy, justice, and humility while experiencing the kingdom in each moment. Stanley Hauerwas argues that living the values of the kingdom under God-as-king will challenge the ethical norms of society, inviting Christians to participate in life where their ethics are counter to the world and anticipate the coming restoration (Hauerwas 2001, 77). Therefore, it is possible that through daily cooperation and reflective obedience, trust creates new spaces for believers to replace lost human expectations, freeing them for the greater joys and peace of living under God's reign, which can in turn affect individual lives and communities of faith.

The Last Shall Be First (Matt. 19:30)

Jesus' proclamation that "the last will be first, and the first will be last" (Matt. 19:30) expresses the radical character of the kingdom of God. This principle reverses all value systems that lead human beings to measure worth based on their position, achievement, and status. Entering into the life of the kingdom is an invitation to humility and servanthood, met by the grace of God rather than human merits. It is a theological statement that suggests God's evaluation of life extends beyond winning, human approval, and success (Wright 1996, 213).

Martin Luther provides an extensive treatment of this theme when he contends that salvation and righteousness are pure gifts of God. Salvation is not dependent on human status and accomplishment (Luther 1520, 67). Because of this reality, the last—those socially marginalized, economically impoverished, or spiritually bereft—are the ones who are included, not excluded, in God's grace in the kingdom of God. Jonathan Edwards identifies this reversal as provocation for gratitude and reliance. At the same time, this is a demonstration of the creative power of God's grace, as well as the redemption and restoration of the seemingly powerless (Edwards 1746, 94).

The scriptures repeatedly highlight this principle. The parable of the laborers in the vineyard (Matt. 20:1–16) illustrates workers receiving the same wages, even though they worked different hours. The master illustrates that human standards of fairness should not be used to judge God's justice and generosity. Similarly, the centurion, a Roman officer, is commended because of his faith, not because of his rank (Matt. 8:5–13). In both cases, faith and trust are acknowledged and give credence to the present character of God's kingdom, rather than established social status. Gregory of Nyssa recognized that this reordering of spiritual realities suggested that believers should embrace opportunities for humility as the pathway toward union with God (Gregory 1995, 123).

In a practical sense, this teaching reorients Christian communities to express an ethic of inclusion and service. Those Christians who seek lowly offices in church or society do so because they encounter the reality of the kingdom and the blessings of the kingdom. This is the logic of the reign of God, which devalues the one and blesses the one who has taken a lowly place. Brennan Manning considered this idea significant in that to live last means to live in radical dependence on God, leading to meaningful intimacy with God and compassion for neighbor (Manning 1990, 57).

The last is first as it expresses or demonstrates the upside-down character of the kingdom. It is both a theological principle to consider in daily living, trusting God to work out His justice, and operating with a low measure of value placed on others, while serving without seeking to be recognized. As we embody this kind of ethic in the world, God is transforming our practices to be consistent with His redemptive work, which is already underway, a foretaste of the ultimate reversal of God's kingdom in the age to come (Wright 1996, 214).

God's Plan to Right All Wrongs

Three aspects of God's character stand in meaningful connection with the righting of all wrongs found in the redemption of creation: God is a righteous judge whose primary disposition is restorative rather than punitive; God's work of restoring justice is not simply directed towards the righting of all wrongs, but also the healing, reconciliation, and flourishing of creation; and thirdly, God's work in bringing justice is what enables Christians to act likewise in their own lives and communities together.

Chrysostom also recognizes that God's anticipation has both temporal and eternal elements, balancing God's justice with accountability for oppressors and comfort for the oppressed (Chrysostom 1986, 72). In all, expectation anticipates the realization of justice. It ensures that hope can flourish amongst those who are suffering by reassuring them that their suffering is not extravagant nor ignored. Origen, on the other hand, interprets this type of promise in an allegorical way, expressing that God, by no other means than some form of radical transformation, rights the spiritual and moral disorders of His people beyond the conscious moral imagination (Origen 1994, 45).

Scripture shows God's restorative work in marvelous ways. We see this in Exodus where God appropriates Israel "out" from their unjust oppression as slaves, and thus puts right centuries of oppressions (Exod. 3:7–8). In prophetic literature, God promises to put right injustice by judging oppressors while restoring shalom to the poor, disadvantaged, and marginalized communities (Isa. 9:6–7). Even in the New Testament, the fulfillment of this grand plan for restoration is present in Christ, who reconciles humanity to God, inaugurating the kingdom of God where shalom, forgiveness, and healing are present (Col. 1:19–20).

Theologically, this perspective offers a picture of God's sovereignty and faithfulness. Augustine reminds the church that humanity's efforts toward justice never measure up, yet God acts upon humanity, guaranteeing justice and enacting or restoring right (Augustine 1991, 215). Additionally, N.T. Wright explains that this eschatological vision instructs behavior in the present: Christians anticipate a future time when God's restorative reign will be brought about through mercy and reconciliation, while refusing to promote injustice in their day, and hoping for a future time when justice will be realized (Wright 1996, 218).

In practical ways, trusting God to fulfill all wrongs encourages believers with hope, expectation, and space for a response of service to injustice. Trusting God also inspires faithful witness, even when confronted for their faith amidst oppression and injustice, because they know one day God's reign will bring complete restoration for everyone. By living out the values of his kingdom (as an alternative culture) of justice, mercy, and love, Christians become agents of God and participate in the restorative purposes God envisioned for creation, experiencing a foretaste of the kingdom (Bauckham 1996, 118).

Biblical Promises of the Kingdom

The biblical witness provides a future hope for God's kingdom by showing its present reality. The kingdom of God promises restoration, justice, and blessing for those who follow him. For example, Isaiah 9:6–7 anticipates the Messiah as a ruler with a reign characterized by wisdom, peace, and justice: "For unto us a Child is born... and His name will be called Wonderful, Counselor, Mighty God, Everlasting Father, Prince of Peace" (Isa. 9:6–7). God promises through this prophecy that He will initiate a plan to reverse human suffering and bring an end to oppression, while assuring His people that the outcome is determined by divine authority, not worldly authority (Bauckham 1996, 214).

Revelation 21:1–5 continues this hope for restoration by describing the final renewal of creation: "Then I saw a new heaven and a new earth... Behold, I make all things new" (Rev. 21:1–5). This vision highlights the promise of the end of pain, death, and injustice, while clarifying that God's restorative work is cosmic in scope, encompassing the entirety of the gospel. Many scholars have noted that these types of promises offer spiritual resilience and ethical motivation, compelling believers to understand their place in God's plan of mercy and justice (Wright 2006, 212). This conviction has been passed down through the church since Patristic authors, such as Gregory of Nyssa, explained how such visions are transformative in directing believers toward holiness and citizenship in anticipation of the final restoration (Gregory of Nyssa 1995, 72).

The Beatitudes (Matt. 5:3–12) illustrate the values of the kingdom through practical discipleship. Jesus announces blessedness for the poor in spirit, the meek, and the merciful, thereby reinterpreting flourishing under God's reign: "Blessed are those who mourn, for they shall be comforted" (Matt. 5:4). The ethical and spiritual implications of these principles embody the reversal described in prophecy, where communities are directed by God's work in the hearts of believers (France 2007, 49; Chrysostom 1986, 78).

All of these passages affirm that God's promises are nuanced in different aspects: eschatological, offering ultimate restoration; ethical, providing patterns for living; and relational, building trust and obedience to God. Therefore, biblical hope is present-shaped and future-oriented. The biblical vision invites believers to embody justice, mercy, and humility in their lives as meaningful representations of the coming kingdom (Hauerwas 2001, 157). For these reasons, the promises of the Bible compel Christians to live faithfully in the present as they await the future fulfillment of God's reign with joy, compassion, and hope.

Prophecies of Hope (Isaiah 9:6–7)

In the book of Isaiah, we find a prophecy of hope anchored in something greater than themselves and even their vision for the future: the sovereignty of God over His plan to restore His people. Isaiah 9:6–7 reads, "For unto us a Child is born, unto us a Son is given; and the government will be upon His shoulder. Moreover, His name will be called Wonderful, Counselor, Mighty God, Everlasting Father, Prince of Peace." This declaration anticipates the Messiah, a King whose reign will activate justice, embody wisdom, and secure peace. In light of the suffering of the Jewish people during this time, Isaiah's prophecy offered both short-term comfort and a long-term, transformational vision of restoration. Specifically, through the language of governance—government on His shoulder—there is a reversal of human oppression signaled, with God coming behind and under these promises. In fact, for John Bauckham, Isaiah's portrayal of his sovereign peace fulfills a promise of establishing a kingdom (Bauckham 1996, 214).

Isaiah's imagery also aligns with the eschatological hope that runs throughout Scripture: the brokenness and marginalization in the earthly situation will be vindicated, and God's reign will establish order in a world of injustice. Patristic interpreter Origen read these prophecies allegorically, seeing in them a Word that simultaneously described Christ's first coming to earth while also unfolding the nature of Christ's reign, continually unfolding in the hearts of believers (Origen 1994, 57). Similarly, modern biblical scholar N. T. Wright affirms that promises such as Isaiah's function in both a historical and theological understanding, offering an invitation to the believer to live faithfully into those promises while awaiting God's fulfillment (Wright 1996, 83). Both represent an understanding of the expected hope for the future that encourages a reader's self-reflection on the present experience, based on the present expectation of the promised future. While the anticipation of hope is a passive experience, it clearly requires an activity of some kind by the believer, one that embodies God's active kingdom and what it looks like to have hope in the midst of a broken and suffering world (Hauerwas 2001, 119). Through the invitation to connect prophetic vision and lived experience, Isaiah serves as a model for how the anticipation of God's kingdom helps enrich a believer's spiritual resilience and joy, despite the suffering that accompanies it.

Isaiah 9:6–7 serves as a theological and practical blueprint. The promise of the coming Messiah signifies a God who is about the business of undoing worldly expectations, rooted in establishing the decree of justice, wisdom, and peace. Offered to believers is the satisfaction of the expectation of participating long before its ultimate fulfillment or realization. Living out, embodying those things of the kingdom now while awaiting the realization of their ultimate kingdom reign is a uniquely Christian pursuit. This pursuit of hope fosters an embrace between present obedience and future expectation (Edwards 1746, 45).

Revelation's Vision of Renewal (Rev. 21:1–5)

Revelation concludes with a breathtaking vision of cosmic renewal, affirming God's ultimate rejuvenation of His entire creation. "Then I saw a new heaven and a new earth, for the first heaven and the first earth had passed away...Behold, I make all things new" (Rev. 21:1–5). The imagery is relative to God's redemptive actions from start to end; human sin, suffering, and death are decisively eradicated. God's being is entirely present among His people. Scholars contend that there is an eschatological continuity running through the Old Testament prophecies and the book of

Revelation, with God's covenant promises culminating in Christ (Bauckham 1999, 178).

The passage has spiritual and ethical implications. Spiritually, it assures believers that the struggles of the present are temporary, evoking hope that extends beyond the distractions of the world. Ethically, it calls believers to relational work in God's mission in ways that reflect God's justice and mercy in their communities (Wright 2006, 212). The notion of new creation is about restoring social relations: mourning, pain, and death fade away, and humanity flourishes under the reign of God's righteousness.

Patristic writers, including Gregory of Nyssa, emphasize the vertiginous imaginings of such visions that inform the present and grant believers agency beyond a future. Renewal is not just a prospect; it also shapes and informs the believer's present spiritual formation, directing them towards the hope of love and endurance (Gregory of Nyssa 1995, 72). Current theorists, including Henri Nouwen, speculate that Revelation's vision motivates contemplation of God's presence and, more significantly, invites participation in God's work that continues the mission of healing a broken world (Nouwen 1992, 84).

The statement "Behold, I make all things new" expresses a divine verb that implies God's authority and agency in renewal: the renewal is God's action, not one we create. Indeed, believers have responsibilities to live in terms of this vision, drawing their lives into personalized reflections of renewing creation as a gesture toward the prospect of ultimate reality while waiting for the finality of God's reign (Stott 1994, 53).

Revelation 21:1–5 conveys a universal hope: God renews creation, reconciles humanity, and possesses them eternally. The vision of total renewal makes space for endurance and ethical responsibility toward His people. It enables believers to connect eschatological expectations with active spirituality, thereby expressing praise for God. It prepares believers for the opportunity to witness the active and now-reigning God for the age to come.

The Beatitudes as Kingdom Manifesto (Matt. 5:3–12)

The Beatitudes in Matthew 5:3–12 provide a concrete manifesto for living under God's kingdom: "Blessed are the poor in spirit, for theirs is the kingdom of heaven... Blessed are those who mourn, for they shall be comforted" (Matt. 5:3–4). Jesus's pronouncement turns worldly values upside down, defining blessedness in terms of humility, mercy, and righteousness rather than wealth, power, or prestige. These teachings function as both ethical guidance and spiritual formation, highlighting how kingdom principles shape character and community life.

Scholarly analysis emphasizes the eschatological dimension of the Beatitudes. France notes that Jesus' words echo prophetic promises, situating present discipleship within God's future fulfillment (France 2007, 49). N. T. Wright further interprets the Beatitudes as an invitation to participate in the "already/not yet" kingdom, where God's reign manifests in relational, ethical, and spiritual transformation (Wright 1996, 112).

Patristic voices, such as John Chrysostom, emphasize the moral and pastoral implications of the Beatitudes. Believers are called to cultivate inner virtues, practice compassion, and seek justice, modeling the kingdom in everyday life (Chrysostom 1986, 78). These virtues are not mere rules, but relational dispositions that shape how Christians interact with their neighbors and those who are marginalized. Similarly, contemporary theologians, such as Stanley Hauerwas, highlight the Beatitudes as formative for community ethics, fostering faithful witness in both the church and society (Hauerwas 2001, 157).

Spiritually, the Beatitudes cultivate joy rooted in dependence on God. Mourning, meekness, and mercy become pathways to blessedness, reflecting God's reversal of worldly expectations. Believers experience both comfort and empowerment, finding hope in divine faithfulness (Edwards 1746, 60).

Matthew 5:3–12 serves as a kingdom manifesto, articulating ethical, spiritual, and communal dimensions of discipleship. It bridges the prophetic promises of God's reign with present-day obedience, inviting believers to embody humility, mercy, and righteousness as a tangible foretaste of the coming kingdom. Through this lens, the Beatitudes shape a life of hope, joy, and transformative witness (Bauckham 1996, 226).

Joy in Anticipation

The hope of God's kingdom shapes the believer's life now by filling the day with strength, joy, and hope. Hope works as the primary source for spiritual joy. The Scriptures repeatedly remind believers that God can be trusted to keep His promises. The psalmist states, "You will show me the path of life; in Your presence is fullness of joy; at Your right hand are pleasures forevermore" (Ps. 16:11). This hope is not a passive hope relying on blind faith; it is an active trust in God's promises—one that can flourish even under the burdens of life as expressions of courage and gratitude arise (Edwards 1746, 92). As believers, our hope will be active based on God's character, and we will experience joy regardless of our circumstances—a foreshadowing of the eventual fulfillment of God's kingdom.

Trusting God for His faithfulness is a critical part of sustaining our anticipatory joy. Paul writes, "And we know that all things work together for good to those who love God, to those who are called according to His purpose" (Rom. 8:28). This hopeful baseline is where Christians trust God in His providence. God takes control of history as He plays it out to His glory and ultimately for the good of His people (Wright 1996, 84). Early Christian theologians, such as Augustine, who drew parallels with Paul, reasoned that hope holds the soul firm and links believers to eternal existence rather than the fleeting expectations of this life (Augustine 1991, 45). Trust nurtures patience and perseverance, which can transform the regular complications of our daily lives into opportunities for spiritual growth and a deeper relationship with God.

Paul's thoughts about "the glory to be revealed" in Romans 8:18–25 add a dimension to our understanding of anticipatory joy. He reflected on his current suffering, stating, "For I consider that the sufferings of this present time are not worthy to be compared with the glory which shall be revealed in us" (Rom. 8:18). He re-envisioned his sufferings, disappointments, and yearnings as temporary circumstances, and was propelled towards perseverance through the hope of redemption and ultimate glorification. The appearance of creation as groaning in eager expectation reminds believers that anticipatory joy is both personal and cosmic in nature. The anticipation of the glory to be revealed links believers to God's redemptive hope for his creation (Nouwen 1992, 66).

Overall, anticipatory joy is a kind of hope—or rather hope and trust in the glory promised to us—but it is also a trust that helps to shape our hearts and actions as we await the kingdom of God through daily life. It can be a practice of spirituality and expectation that elicits feelings of joy and fulfillment. More importantly, it allows Christians to engage with the present with faithfulness, courage, and gratitude while awaiting the complete promise of God's kingdom.

Hope as a Source of Daily Joy

Hope is a vital source of joy for believers, providing a spiritual foundation amidst life's uncertainties. The biblical picture of God's kingdom illustrates a future filled with justice, peace, and restoration, encouraging followers of Christ to remain expectantly joyful. Scripture supports this realization by stating, "You will show me the path of life; in Your presence is fullness of joy; at Your right hand are pleasures forevermore" (Ps.

16:11). Joy is not based on situational factors for the believer; instead, it comes from confident expectation of God's faithful promises, creating resilience and a more profound sense of purpose (Edwards 1746, 92).

Hope shapes how a believer sees their daily life, allowing them to experience spiritual growth through ordinary experiences. Focusing on God's future deliverance enables Christians to experience enduring joy, regardless of the outcomes. Early church theologians, such as Augustine, emphasized that hope enables the soul to endure suffering with patience and trust during adversity. From the believers' perspective, the present is viewed as temporary, while they place their hope in the future that awaits them (Augustine 1991, 45). This view offers a reframing of adversity, encouraging Christians to respond with gratitude, endurance, and active love for others.

In addition, hope is the impetus for active spiritual engagement, informed by the anticipation of God's purpose unfolding. Hope is what moves from prayer to worship and ultimately obedience as believers await God's next part of His plan, a plan they want to align their lives with. As Brennan Manning points out, hope is tied to intimacy with God, as a heart aware of who God says He is will actually experience joy and peace (Manning 1992, 58). Henri Nouwen also notes that hope allows Christians to be themselves while being vulnerable to hope, because in hope, we are not timid; instead, we root our joy in God, not in situational human experiences (Nouwen 1992, 66).

Practically speaking, hope transforms every day into an extraordinary life as we grasp the moment and deliberate on our experience with God, finding delight in the spiritual quality of life, embracing gratitude, and cultivating endurance. Regularly turning to God's promises and meditating on His faithfulness enables believers to find joy that pervades every aspect of life, allowing all-of-life relationships, work, and service to take on spiritual dimensions. Therefore, hope is not a passive feeling but an active life source that can fuel joy regardless of suffering, encourage faithful living, and provide the spiritual energy for the believer's soul, as God has promised (Edwards 1746, 93).

Trusting God's Faithfulness for the Future

Belief in God's faithfulness is the foundation of Christian hope; it is what enables Christians to live confidently and peacefully in the face of life's uncertainties. As the stories of the Scriptures show, God is faithful to His promises, and His people can rest assured that He will do what He has determined to do. For example, Isaiah says, "For I am the Lord, I do not change; therefore you are not consumed, you sons of Jacob" (Isa. 46:4). Believing in this faithfulness means Christians can set their expectations on God, and not on the constantly changing conditions around them (France 2007, 212).

The New Testament also expresses this idea of trust, highlighting it specifically in relation to the work of Christ in redeeming believers and the promise of God's kingdom. By recalling God's faithfulness in previous deliverances, Christians gain boldness to face present difficulties with hope and assurance of the coming glory. N. T. Wright emphasized the importance of trusting God's faithfulness in relation to the "already/not yet" understanding of the kingdom; God's ultimate plan has been inaugurated through Christ and is yet to come (Wright 1996, 88). Trust also transforms uncertainty into intentional ways to grow spiritually by bringing about change in attitudes, actions, and relationships.

Historical theologians also acknowledge the significance of trust in God's faithfulness. Augustine noted that faith was increased as the believer believed in the consistency of God's character. This faithfulness was a source of peace and humility while waiting for God to fulfill His promises (Augustine 1991, 215). John Calvin said something similar about believing in God's promises, with a person leaning into obedience, prayer, and service under the belief that God's "providential care" is better than the understanding of our own reason (Calvin 1559, 317). This imagines faith as more than the simplicity of belief; faith is an engagement with our hearts in obedience, prayer, and service, while being assured that God will fulfill His promises when He desires and decides.

In practice, trusting in God's faithfulness through hope enables believers to confront fear, anxiety, and doubt without succumbing to them or letting them take control. Trust lets our hearts become free from the control in which we often live, enabling joy, generosity, and compassionate action in our daily lives. Trust fosters faith in the community, encouraging one another to love with care within the body of Christ. Our hope is placed correctly on the faithfulness of God's promises, rather than on temporal factors, leaving more room for the kingdom of God to be lived out as a normal existence in a reality of joyful endurance, patient trust, and faithful living as a testimony to God's promises that are fulfilled.

Paul on the Glory to Be Revealed (Rom. 8:18–25)

Paul's reflections in Romans 8:18-25 offer an unforgettable depiction of hope, providing an audacious definition of suffering and present realities that both pale in comparison to the glory God will reveal in the end. Beginning here – "I consider that the sufferings of this present time are not worth comparing with the glory that is to be revealed to us" (Rom. 8:18) – Paul is illuminating the disparity between the immediate realities of living (in this case, wrestling) with the greater, eternal, abiding, and even transformative glory that awaits God's children in the future. The present reality of God's incomparable glory reframes the way we consider this life; it calls believers to pay attention to "what they are going through" (France 2007, 334). Paul carefully illustrates the brokenness of creation awaiting redemption: "for the creation waits with eager longing for the revealing of the children of God" (Rom. 8:19). Paul is purposefully indicating to his audience that his vision of hope extends past human suffering and onto cosmic realities, in which all of creation is enveloped in God's restorative purposes (Wright 1996, 102). By not offering this eschatological hope as an abstract thought and evoking a present experience of living into God's ongoing purposes, Paul invites believers to hold on with the expectation of God's fulfillment as they are obedient and actively participate in God's ongoing purposes.

Similarly, Paul reaffirms his reflections on the Spirit and on sustaining hope by referring to believers: "we wait eagerly for the adoption as sons, the redemption of our bodies" (Rom. 8:23). As believers, we recognize that with the exhausted anticipation of waiting, we still can mourn together as we wait. However, it is the Spirit who intercedes, encourages, and reminds believers that God is always faithful to nurture their faithfulness to God's promises from "the beginning" (Hays 2005, 148). The Spirit fills the recesses of waiting and allows believers not to suffer while waiting, but to enjoy moments of spiritual waiting (Packer 1973, 211). So, the possibility exists that to hope includes a sense of presence and anticipation; as a result of understanding and enjoying the hope that Paul extends to believers to live in wait for God's future glory, we can continue to live with perseverance, joy, and resilience, while being counter-culturally patient in suffering, loss, or grief.

The history of this theological disposition's complexities is rich, and historically, theologians have at times actively provided thoughtful reflections through their theological musings, often in theological language. John Calvin, for example, posits, "the knowledge of that which God will do at the last day (eternally in the future) will enable us to endure adversity and suffering patiently" (Calvin 1559, 320). Furthermore, Augustine suggests that the desire of God, which fulfills God's promises, will move those who desire to grow in love, faith, and humility (Augustine 1998, 242). Thus, in effect, Paul tied the human experience into a much grander narrative: while suffering is time-bound, the glory of God has eternal significance in the context of redemption

Suppose Christians work to understand and buy into Paul's reflections. In that case, they can live with confidence, pursue spiritual maturity, and hold onto a hope that can sustain them, regardless of the circumstances they find themselves in. Living in orientation to God's glory develops a life of faithful waiting, redeemed suffering, and hope despite earthly contexts.

Healing in Kingdom Perspective

The coming kingdom promises justice and joy, but it also promises to heal in ways that are deep and transformative to the human soul. Throughout both the Old and New Testaments, God is portrayed as the healer of the broken-hearted, the comforter of those who mourn, the restorer of that which is lost (Ps. 34:18; Isa. 61:1-3; Matt. 5:4). Disappointment, sadness, and anxiety are normal reactions in a sinful world, but from the perspective of the kingdom, they can also be reframed as invitations to trust in God's redeeming plan of order and purpose (France 2007, 142). Healing begins with surrendering our personal pain and unmet expectations to God, recognizing that God's thinking and purpose are beyond our understanding (Rom. 8:28).

Augustine of Hippo emphasized that when suffering is encased within God's order, it becomes a vehicle for spiritual maturity and humility (Augustine 1998, 57). Gregory of Nyssa similarly emphasized that tribulations provide transformative experiences that create Jesus-followers into sharers of God's eternal joy (Gregory 1993, 45). Therefore, the kingdom does not offer mere relief from sorrow; instead, it offers the opportunity to live our lives more purposefully in line with God's will.

Contemporary theologians affirm this eternal truth. Henri Nouwen described healing as relational, suggesting that God enters into human suffering personally, sustaining hope and the capacity to love even in the midst of sorrow (Nouwen 1992, 78). Similarly, Dallas Willard described suffering as a means of spiritual formation that fosters resilience and a character aligned with kingdom values (Willard 1998, 103). John Stott also emphasized that freedom from anxiety comes when our personal desire is quickly aligned with God's justice, leaving the ultimate restoration to God (Stott 1994, 122).

In practice, healing in the kingdom becomes a vehicle by which we seek healing, restoration, and redemption through prayer, contemplation, and the encouragement of one another. We are called to demonstrate mercy, forgiveness, and patience, and to offer and be part of God's restorative presence (Matt. 5:7; Col. 3:12-14). We seek a holistic approach that involves the heart, mind, and collaboration with the community, allowing one's present brokenness to fuel the hope and anticipation of God's promised future restoration. Living with hope in light of God's coming reign transforms our sorrow into resilience, our despair into trust, and our loss into deeper communion with the Creator (Wright 1996, 201). Healing in the kingdom is both now and not yet, encouraging Jesus-followers to take a step and welcome the fullness of God's restorative work today, while looking forward to its eventual completion.

Healing from Disappointment and Loss

In the coming kingdom, God provides healing to those who are hurt by disappointment and loss. Throughout scripture, God declares His care for the brokenhearted and the downtrodden (Ps. 34:18; Matt. 5:4). Disappointment is often located at the intersection of human expectations and divine purposes, and while the intention of the kingdom reframing of suffering places expectation on God's wisdom and grace, it also points toward suffering as an opportunity to not only trust in God's ultimate plan but to accept our vulnerability and give it to God in prayer (Isa. 61:1–3).

The early church fathers interpreted suffering as part of the divine order, a central teaching of Augustine. Augustine emphasized God's grace working toward restoration, growth, and renewal, not only from his own human failings but from the failings of humanity (Augustine 1998, 57). Gregory of Nyssa contributed to this theological legacy by describing suffering as part of a transformative process, where trials serve as experiences that lead the believer toward maturity in participating in the eternal joy characteristic of God's kingdom (Gregory 1993, 45).

Modern theologians have also taken up this theme. For example, Henri Nouwen emphasized that God encounters human suffering in the form of a relationship, allowing the individual in mourning to enter a relationship of intimacy with God, who transforms grief into new hope and capacity to love (Nouwen 1992, 78). Furthermore, Dallas Willard framed suffering as a possibility for a formation process, whereby a stronger relationship with a context of dependence on God produces greater resilience and stronger character traits of the values of God's kingdom (Willard 1998, 103).

From a practice perspective, healing requires a combination of intra-reflection and communal (social) engagement where God calls forth restoration within a community of relationships and acts of service, modeled from the suffering of Christ, who was continually living and acting out of compassion (John 14:27). By living out forgiveness, gratitude, and patience, for example, believers create these spiritual spaces, where brokenness is acknowledged, yet believers experience a continuous sense of God's sustained presence in their lives (Packer 1973, 215).

A kingdom view of healing shifts the focus from instant relief to living in a coming future hope. A kingdom understanding is meant to help believers live in the space of temporality, acknowledging that loss is only temporary and is part of God's promise of comfort, restoration, and renewed joy in the coming kingdom (Wright 1996, 201). Living in this anticipation allows believers to engage faithfully in what is right now, with current petty difficulties and the fullness of glory (believing in the goodness of God), so that believers enter now into the transformative opportunity—God's healing kingdom.

Freedom from Anxiety about Justice

Distinctly unique struggles exist between the hope of justice humans yearn for and the truth of a world gone wrong, which can lead to anxiety. We witness oppression, abuse, and inequity; it is understandable to struggle against despair or powerlessness. The kingdom of God embodies justice as the ultimate reality, resting on God's sovereign activity (Ps. 37:9–11; Rom. 12:19). Instead of taking a different approach, we are invited to trust that God will make all things right at the right time. This type of trust and disposition does not encourage passivity; it calls for an active faith and spirit of anticipation, patience, hope, and obedience (France 2001, 201).

Augustine of Hippo teaches that human justice is always flawed, but God's eternal justice is perfect and inexorable (Augustine 1998, 120). Likewise, Gregory of Nyssa discusses the aspect of divine justice by witnessing and processing through a spiritual lens that looks beyond temporal reductionism to see what God eternally intends (Gregory 1993, 67). Contemporary theologians hold the same view: N. T. Wright contends that Christ's resurrection represents God's kingdom and that ultimate justice is secured, even if not immediate (Wright 1996, 245). Henri Nouwen states that if we relinquish the burden of controlling outcomes, we can be at peace, as the believer finds peace defined by God, not by human-based or grounded activity (Nouwen 1992, 88).

In practice, if we trust that freedom from judgmental disposition includes anxiety about justice, we can actively work to be prayed up, identified, and act as a neighbor through the lens of the good news of Jesus and reconciliation and mercy in the world. We can also hope we would practice cultivation of compassionate and engaged discipleship, practice alignment of our actions with the values established by God's kingdom, where we act justly, love mercy, and walk humbly (Micah 6:8), not to disregard or ignore the suffering of this and the deprived world, but to prepare ourselves against despair. When we develop a certain depth of hope and faith, we rest on specific promises that are secure, even in the face of experiential injustice in the world. The evangelical believer stands resolute, apprehending all the elements that occur in the world, believing that God's restorative plan within the tension is being executed and that we can at times enjoy peace despite injustice (Willard 1998, 89).

God's Restoration as Ultimate Remedy for Brokenness

Brokenness, whether relational, emotional, or spiritual, is a natural part of the fallenness of this world. The kingdom of God offers the promise of not just restoration and repair, but complete restoration and renewal. In fact, Scripture emphasizes a complete restoration that encompasses our inner life, our relationships, and our communities, as seen in Isa. 61:1–4 and Joel 2:25–26. Restoration and healing are not merely ideas or concepts, but rather realities to be experienced in God's presence, grace, and transformational power (Ps. 147:3; 2 Cor. 5:17).

In the early church, church fathers like Augustine of Hippo recognized the fullness of God's restorative work, which embraced both moral and spiritual transformation. God transforms God's people into the likeness of Christ (Augustine 1998, 140). Gregory of Nyssa emphasized that the process of restoration is progressive, transforming those who are broken into individuals who are mature and whole (Gregory 1993, 89). Bonhoeffer reminded us that restoration is a relational process; through the body of Christ, we become participants in God's work of reconciliation, accompanied by acts of forgiveness, encouragement, and healing (Bonhoeffer 1959, 112).

Contemporary thinkers emphasize that genuine restoration requires hope, patience, and trust. Henri Nouwen has succinctly captured this transformation in restoration—restoration is an encounter with God as love. This encounter changes our identity and enables new relationships (Nouwen 1992, 117). Dallas Willard discusses restoration as something we experience; the kingdom "orders" our daily choices, habits, and interactions, offering a new way to live—a life of integrity and spiritual vitality in all our human experiences (Willard 1998, 101).

Practically, believers participate in God's restorative work via prayer, spiritual disciplines, and expressions of mercy. God's kingdom invites us to shift our focus away from problem-solving to a perspective of continuing life-long renewal, where pain and suffering can become a pathway to greater growth and deeper intimacy with the Creator (Stott 1994, 144). Living in the light of restoration creates space for resilience and joy, with a sense of hope for a preferred future. Ultimately, restoration allows the faithful to expect the fullness of the ultimate renewal that will come in Christ. In this way, brokenness is not the end; it is the beginning of our experiencing God's redeeming and healing power in the kingdom.

Love Shaped by the Coming Kingdom

Love will not only be an emotional response in the kingdom to come but a tangible demonstration of God's reign in relationships with others. Scripture regularly interprets the kingdom as a place where God's priorities change our loves and direct our love towards others in terms of compassion, generosity, and forgiveness. Jesus' teaching to love your neighbor (Matt. 22:37–40) reveals that to love in the kingdom way is both relational and transformative, requiring us to be involved in the well-being of others. To love in a kingdom way means to continue to do the good with respect to God's values instead of doing the good according to human-based (self-centered) criteria of convenience or worthiness (France 2007, 152).

Generosity is the result of the overflowing nature of God's kingdom and proximate evidence of this future reign. Isaiah demonstrates God's blessings upon the earth in a prophecy of a restored kingdom marked by God's justice and mercy (Isa. 9:6–7). Whenever believers are generous in giving, both freely and sacrificially, they participate in God's generosity and embody the kingdom at this time (Bauckham 2006, 78). Generosity as kingdom love involves selfless action, rather than a transactional calculation. Generosity values the community and, tangibly, embodies the love of God towards a broken and unlovable world. Nouwen (1992, 44) points out that generosity born from the Spirit involves action but is also an invitation to participate in the abundance of God's life on behalf of others. Every day giving then becomes a preview of the fulfillment of what comes in the kingdom to come.

Forgiveness is equally a part of kingdom love. Christ instructs us to forgive others just as we have been forgiven (Matt. 18:21–22). Kingdom ethics think and act differently from the human propensity towards vengeance and pride. Forgiveness is a model of God's radical inclusiveness in the reign of God, and it also models the ongoing reconciliation with God and others. Godly love is not solely occurring through the work of a human agent; rather, Godly love is of the Spirit (Packer 1973, 210). A love prompted by the Spirit leads to forgiveness and recovering an identity beyond our human moral failures, which are rooted in our relationships with others.

John Chrysostom expressed repeatedly in his homilies that love is concerned for the other practically or tangibly, and humility is cultivated through this love (Chrysostom 2000, 134). Therefore, loving is not a special calling to Christians before the age to come, but one that is foundational to the Christian life. Living redemptively in relation to one's capacity to love by giving generously and forgiving others is participation in God's grand vision, and believers provide a glimpse of the sweet and upside-down values of the coming kingdom.

Loving Others with Kingdom Priorities

In the Kingdom of God, love is not measured by cultural convenience or social duty, but by the measures of Christ's coming reign (Matt. 22:36–40; John 13:34–35). Love in the kingdom puts others first, focuses on the well-being of those on the margins, and shows God's nature of self-giving love. In contrast to human love, which can be conditional, selective, and reactive, love in the kingdom includes all people from our own proactive, sacrificial, intentional continuum (Wright 1996, 202).

Jesus embodies love in the kingdom by reaching out to the rich young ruler, the Samaritan woman, and the tax collectors in ways that subvert entirely social conventions (France 2007, 310). Augustine of Hippo notes that properly ordered love, or divine love, is guided by the affections of believers to ensure that love of neighbor follows love of God (Augustine 1998, 172). John Chrysostom reminds believers that the practical expressions of love, such as visiting the sick or feeding the hungry, embody the priorities of God's love and become tangible signs of the kingdom in our midst (Chrysostom 1992, 88).

Love in the kingdom also upends cultural norms, elevating the last, empowering the weak, and favoring reconciliation over rancor. Believers embody the ideals of God by practicing a love that is not merely emotional, but obedient, humble, and guided by the living Spirit of God (Packer 1973, 215). This love fosters unity and points to a realization of the Kingdom of God, which is already promised in Holy Scripture, providing a window into the communal reality of God's pleased purpose for the world.

In practical terms, love in the kingdom involves applying the spiritual discipline of discernment to daily decision-making. Each minute choice regarding how believers treat family, neighbors, and strangers is an opportunity to express love as God understands it, in light of the priority of justice, mercy, and compassion. Thus, believers participate in God's redeeming and transforming work, growing communities where care, reconciliation, and flourishing mark the actual gospel call (Nouwen 1992, 104). In continuity, love in the kingdom reflects divine character, and it is simultaneously a transformative force in the relationships of this day and generation, inviting others toward the renewing hope of God's coming Kingdom.

Generosity as a Foretaste of God's Abundance

Kingdom generosity represents the upside-down economy of God's reign—where giving is an act of trust in God's provision, rather than trust in a lack of scarcity (Luke 6:38; 2 Cor. 9:6–8). As believers share resources, time, and talents, they anticipate the abundant life promised to them in the coming kingdom and the economy of God's redemption. Richard Bauckham notes that generosity in the kingdom is relational and covenantal, subsuming human stewardship within God's eternal economy (Bauckham 2006, 225).

Augustine illustrates that only charity (genuine generosity) comes out of love, and the realization that God is sovereign over all of creation (Augustine 1998, 178). John Calvin reminds us that giving is not only a moral duty; it is also the expression and means of gratitude and dependence on God, who has provided us with both material and spiritual blessings in abundance (Calvin 2008, 411). By being generous, believers "perform" God's abundance, provide hope to those whom the world forgets or has rejected, and foster a shared attention and trust that God sustains life beyond our immediate reality (Nouwen 1992, 108).

Generosity is transformational for both the giver and the receiver. To be generous entails a radical shift in priorities from self-interested love to kingdom love, and it opens up opportunities for fellowship, reconciliation, and mutual flourishing among God's beloved. In Jesus' parables of the widow's mite and the multiplication of the loaves and fishes, Jesus reminds us that God takes our faithful acts of giving and can multiply them into even greater abundance than we could have ever imagined (France 2007, 331). In the fundamental act of giving, we embody God's abundant provisions and showcase to the world what a generous, gospel-shaped kingdom of God would look like.

In practice, kingdom generosity requires intentionality and reflection. Generosity is prayerfully considering God's provision, sacrificially committing oneself, and trusting God courageously in the face of the unknown. Giving can become an authentic taste of the eternal banquet, and a preview of the fullness of joy, healing, and love that the reign of God will fulfill (Packer 1973, 220).

Forgiveness as Kingdom Practice

Forgiveness is central to kingdom life, reflecting God's mercy and the reversal of worldly expectations (Matt. 18:21–22; Col. 3:13). Kingdom forgiveness is proactive, extended even when undeserved, and embodies the reconciliation that God envisions for creation. N. T. Wright argues that forgiveness reveals the power of God's reign, transforming relational brokenness into channels of grace and restoration (Wright 1996, 267).

Augustine teaches that forgiveness mirrors divine mercy, requiring humility and the renunciation of self-righteousness (Augustine 1998, 184). John Chrysostom emphasizes the practical dimension of forgiveness: it is enacted through words, deeds, and intentional choices to release resentment and pursue reconciliation (Chrysostom 1992, 92). Forgiveness is thus both spiritual and practical, reshaping relationships, communities, and the believer's inner life.

Kingdom forgiveness subverts human logic: the weak are lifted, enemies are reconciled, and those wronged become instruments of divine grace. Dietrich Bonhoeffer notes that forgiveness entails costly discipleship, demanding courage and trust in God's justice rather than human vindication (Bonhoeffer 1959, 115). By forgiving, believers participate in the redemptive work of Christ, demonstrating the reality of the kingdom in the present.

Practically, forgiveness involves prayer, reflection, and intentional engagement with those who have caused harm. It transforms attitudes of bitterness into opportunities for healing and restores broken trust wherever possible. Forgiveness is a spiritual discipline that cultivates peace, joy, and relational health, aligning believers with the values of God's reign (Nouwen 1992, 112). By embracing forgiveness, the faithful enact kingdom priorities, witnessing to God's upside-down values of mercy, love, and reconciliation in a world often defined by retaliation.

Theological Reflections

Theological reflection on the coming kingdom not only provides context for understanding God's promises but also offers direction for the believer's life. As we examine the theological work of Brueggemann, Wright, and Stott, we can see how texts shape hope, ethical possibilities, and relational discipleship. Walter Brueggemann emphasizes the importance of hope to the faith of the people of God, particularly as it is revealed in Old Testament prophecy and narrative (Brueggemann 1994, 45). Brueggemann describes hope as a communal hope that creates the possibility of orientation in the lives of the faithful even in the midst of hardship. For Brueggemann, lament and praise become common acts of trust and an investment in God's future for the community, helping the community re-embody the kingdom of God and live in anticipation of fulfilled promises, even as they suffer through the current realities of the present. This hope is upside-down in that it motivates compassion — a movement toward the good and justice — by demonstrating the values of God's coming kingdom.

N. T. Wright's perspectives are shaped by the backdrop of the "already/not yet" kingdom. Although the coming kingdom has broken forth in Jesus' resurrection, the full picture of restoration has not yet been fully realized (Wright 1996, 125). Wright examines the way in which we live in a tension-filled present, where believers live in part of the kingdom now, with the knowledge that God will ultimately fulfill His purpose. This tension prompts the believer to live faithfully in the world, as we see the actions of the reign of God in merciful deeds, acts of healing, and acts of love. Wright goes on to explain that the act of discipleship encompasses both personal formation and engagement in God's redeeming work within our society.

John Stott continues to consider kingdom values through the implications for daily living, as shaped by biblical teaching (Stott 1994, 87). Stott draws heavily from the Sermon on the Mount in describing earthly kingdom values such as humility, mercy, and being a peacemaker, and how these kingdom values move into relational, moral, and vocational settings. Stott gives texture to this process of formation between theology and devotion, explaining that the flow of ethical living is a natural outworking of being close to God and obeying His divine will.

Together, these theological influences provide a multidimensional vision: hope anchors the believer, "already/not yet" informs action, and ethical reflection guides daily living. When we connect scholarly work to a practical sense of living, it invites believers to participate by living joyfully, healing positively, and loving as both an anticipatory and a relational expression of God's coming kingdom.

Brueggemann on Hope and God's Future

Walter Brueggemann notes that hope is critical to understanding the coming kingdom; as he discusses it, hope encompasses both theological and practical orientations. Hope is not naive optimism, but an enduring expectation rooted in God's faithfulness that has been operative through all of Israel's history (Brueggemann 1994 45). Brueggemann understands the Old Testament promises of restoration—including Isaiah 9:6–7—as more than simply historical expectations, but as a way for God's people to make sense of their present struggles. By firmly situating believers within God's ongoing story of restoration, hope turns suffering into a space for God to act and reimagines human imagination toward God's anticipated reversal of injustice.

Hope is, then, inherently communal. In fact, Brueggemann (1994, 112) reads the psalms, which often lament pain and oppression, as psalms that gather communities together in the expectation of trusting in God, even in the midst of suffering. Moreover, the psalms also represent communal examples of fidelity, commitment, resilience, mutual encouragement, and practical forms of obedience, all of which prepare God's people for the upside-down kingdom. This expectation influences how lives are lived in the everyday; it shapes and motivates believers to seek justice, mercy, and love, which will bring forth a glimpse of the fullness of God's reign.

In addition, Brueggemann also differentiates between expectations and hopeful transformation. It requires aligning human activity with God's promises in a way that fosters faithful expectations, suggesting that living the Kingdom can occur even in small acts of faithfulness. In many ways, hope combines both a theological understanding and an ethical engagement, as it is oriented toward helping believers develop a spiritual stance of vigilance, social engagement, and personal piety (Brueggemann 1994 89).

Walter Brueggemann offers tremendous hope by connecting the biblical story with pastoral reflection. He wants Christians to know that living in hope cannot be divorced from living in ways that reflect the Kingdom today. He has first offered Christians a way of bridging God's promises and the activity of faith in our contemporary life together. His vision and perspective, as expressed in the faith of joy, love, and healing that comes from acknowledging God's faithfulness in the midst of anticipatory waiting, help us see that hope is never a passive experience but an active one. The hope encourages our faithful obedience, inspires courage in us, and sustains perseverance as we faithfully await the Kingdom of God.

Wright on the Already/Not Yet Kingdom

N.T. Wright's understanding of the "already/not yet" kingdom enables us to appreciate God's reign as now inaugurated in Christ, yet also shortly to be fully completed (Wright 1996 125). The "already/not yet" framework helps us to mediate the tension of living in light of experiencing God's power now, while waiting for its ultimate fulfillment in the future. The "already" aspect illustrates that the kingdom has been inaugurated through the life, death, and resurrection of Jesus: strategically confronting sin, death, and evil. While signs of God's reign in believers and communities (healing, reconciliation, restoration) are, indeed, visible in the world (Wright 2006 78), the "not yet" acknowledges that fullness of that promise is still to come. While Christians experience some aspect of that kingdom, they still await the fulfillment of God's promises, when creation will be revived, justice will have triumphed, and God will be glorified (Wright 1996 230). Living in these dualities enables all Christians to actively engage in God's mission, which keeps them focused on the justice, mercy, and evangelism of their community while remaining hopeful in the midst of present suffering. Wright emphasizes that living in this tension is not about eliminating the world, but rather about taking on ethical responsibility to act in the world according to the values of the kingdom, thereby opening up our lives to be a foretaste of the kingdom that is coming.

There is ample evidence of this tension-filled existence in Scripture. Paul is particularly conscious of the present groaning of creation and believers, while anticipating a promised and eternal redemption in his letters, and none more clearly than in Romans 8:18–25. Wright notes from these letters that in God's redemption story, hope and expectation energize faithful living in the present, which, albeit incomplete, will emerge as communities giving witness to the realities of God's kingdom, despite a yet-to-be-completed consummation (Wright 2006 112). The faithful community embodies the reversal of worldly values of the kingdom—humility, generosity, and love—while placing their trust in God's ultimate reestablishment of order and renewal of all creation.

Wright's perspective synthesizes exegesis, historical theology, and applied discipleship to offer a vision that is both academically sound and spiritually nostalgic. Embracing the already/not yet kingdom enables Christians to live confidently in hope, participate in God's mission, and lead lives of ethical integrity and spiritual authenticity that reflect the values of the eternal kingdom of God yet to come.

Stott on Kingdom Ethics and Daily Living

John Stott's reflections on kingdom ethics provide practical insights from biblical data for engaging in daily living, revealing that God's reign intentionally intends for allegiance to kingdom values to influence every human activity (Stott 1994, 87). Stott is influenced by the Sermon on the Mount, underscoring how the kingdom calls individuals to a life of integrity, humility, mercy, and peacemaking, directing believers through the ongoing acts of worship and social and community responsibilities. Stott's work has an epicenter, a fusion of theology and ethical action. Knowing God must inform matching action.

Stott observes that the ethical life of the Christian cannot be disconnected from spiritual formation. Choosing to obey God's commands, acting on the character of the fruit of the Spirit, and recognizing the needs of others in all contexts reflects authentic discipleship (Stott 1994, 102). In a life governed by these principles of ethical behavior, prayer, worship, scriptural reading, and the study of Scripture are essential, serving as the basis for ethical behavior. Therefore, Stott argues, Christians are called to embody the values of the kingdom of God in all these contexts, including the various domains of family, work, and broader society (Stott 1994 109). When Christians live these values, it serves as a visible reality of God's kingdom in the world today.

Stott also emphasizes the importance of the relational characteristic of kingdom ethics, which fosters neighborly love, reconciliation, and peacemaking that reflect God's own character as an expression of kingdom values, as encapsulated in a contrasting view of the upside-down kingdom. Living according to these standards, believers participate in God's restorative work of justice, mercy, and community well-being (Stott 1994 115), and in doing so, acts of ethical choice represent both acts of devotion to God and public testimony of God's reign.

Notably, Stott incorporates his highly developed biblicism with pastoral care and responsiveness. He demystifies complex theological structures into comprehensible and actionable insights. His emphasis on practical ethics highlights that living faithfully in the kingdom addresses more than a conceptual ideal, indeed. However, it requires engagement with ongoing commitments that involve daily actions shaping our attitudes, decisions, and relationships. Ultimately, Stott's work offers believers a viable way of life that consistently demonstrates God's kingdom values, including joy, healing, and love, serving as a living sign of God's present and future reign.

Living Kingdom Values Today

Living out kingdom values today means embracing the ethical, relational, and spiritual practices that Jesus lived and taught. The values of God's upside-down kingdom upend human priorities, inviting God's people to pursue justice, mercy, and faithfulness even if human measures of success look different (Micah 6:8). Justice is not legalism but the covenantal concern of God for the marginalized; mercy tempers justice, offering care and restoration instead of merely condemnation (Augustine 1998, 102).

Faithfulness upholds these practices—faithfulness finds every day's decisions grounded in God's character and promises.

From this grounding, service flows freely. Jesus' actions send the message that you do not serve simply as a good deed or a method to gain recognition. Serve by humbly practicing community expectant of the gift of God's reward, and knowing that obedience is worship (Chrysostom 1986, 210). Even amid our suffering or waiting, joy can come from an act of obedience. Paul assures believers that their present sufferings are temporary in light of the glory that is to be revealed. Faithfulness, being known for your witness, persevering in love, and remembering to pray, all have a part in God's restorative work (Romans 8:18–25; Nouwen 1992, 47).

Kingdom living will re-imagine relationships. Healing from past sins in an effort to move forward requires time and trust to reconcile. All of this leads to healing and growth, which strengthens the communal bonds of people (Bonaventure 1975, 52).

Radical love and inclusion in a community of faith invite all people to draw near to God, who shows no strict favor to any one culture or group. Hospitality, generosity, and forgiveness—each of which is ascribed significance to God's grace—become invitations to God's work in the world, and they become visible signs of the kingdom to the world, both present and transformative when they become habits in the community (Bauckham 2006, 88).

Prayer is the breath of kingdom living. Prayer connects the embodied heart of believers to their engagement with the will of God, with the movement of God's kingdom, and with His reign, ushering in the hope and promise of a life oriented away from oppression (Packer 1973, 215). People living in a kingdom-oriented manner are always reflected in practical, relational, and different yet interconnected manifestations of personal devotion, ethical action, and communal care.

Living kingdom values today happens through the holistic engagement of heart, mind, and hands. Justice, mercy, and faithfulness shape our moral decisions; humble service, radical love, and hospitality shape community; and prayer sustains our hope and joy. Living kingdom values means that as Christians embody these values, they are a foretaste of the coming kingdom, which aims to transform our world in the ultimate act of God's reversal and reign of peace, healing, and love (Wright 1996, 432).

Embodying Justice, Mercy, and Faithfulness

A believer's lifestyle that reflects the kingdom of God is characterized by living justly, mercifully, and faithfully, thereby demonstrating God's reign. What is evident in the Scriptures is the inescapable connection between divine justice and mercy. Micah 6:8 captures God calling God's people to do justly, to love mercy, and to walk humbly with your God. The tension between human proclivity toward self-interest and the kingdom's call for a life of sacrificial justice compels a believer to embody God's nature in their day-to-day (Augustine 1998, 102).

According to Augustine of Hippo, Christians should remember that justice is a category rooted in God's order. As such, human aspirations toward righteousness are made efficacious only through humbleness and dependence on the grace of God (Augustine 1998, 114). Likewise, mercy is not optional, as it is only reflective of God's own heart of compassion. Bonaventure pointed out that love, significant in its expression of mercy, mediates God's divine presence. This character of love reshapes our relationships and communities (Bonaventure 1975, 52).

Faithfulness is the glue that binds justice and mercy together. Faithfulness relates to fidelity to God's commands and to consistently engaging in courageous ways. John Chrysostom notes that faithfulness to a regimen of minor acts of good, such as daily honesty, patience, and service, creates ripples of kingdom affectation (Chrysostom 1986, 210). To practically embody faithfulness means advocating for the marginalized, acting as an ally for the oppressed, and responding to injustice with courageous compassion.

Living justly, mercifully, and faithfully also embodies a witness to God's upside-down values in a world saturated by power, greed, and indifferent hearts. In doing so, Christians participate in God's restorative work, embodying the ethical priorities of the kingdom, thereby exposing small glimpses of the coming reign (Bauckham 2006, 88).

Kingdom living, then, is characterized by a relational, ethical, and spiritual nature. Justice without mercy will inevitably be harsh; mercy without justice can lead to permissiveness; faithfulness ensures that both will be sustained over time. Believers should be encouraged to know that when they consistently enact all three of these dimensions, they glorify God and create communities defined by hope, love, and righteousness.

Serving Others in Expectation of God's Reward

Service to others is at the heart of kingdom living, while the reason someone offers service affects its spiritual significance. Service in God's upside-down kingdom is non-transitional; it emanates from a person engaged with the divine agenda, rather than seeking affirmation (Matthew 6:1–4). When believers are called to be like Christ, who washed the feet of His disciples, they are emulating humble love in service (Chrysostom 1986, 118). Service acknowledges the dignity of everyone as made in God's image; acts of service are, in a way, acts of God (Augustine 1998, 95).

To expect God's reward is not to think that the believer will act out of self-interest, but instead that they are trusting God recognizes their faithfulness and returns it, albeit often in mysterious ways that are not apparent to the human eye. John Calvin points out that God's reward strengthens perseverance by reminding believers that their work in the

Lord is never in vain (Calvin 1559, 423). This viewpoint imbues even the most mundane acts of service—such as feeding the hungry, comforting the bereaved, and mentoring the young—with spiritual significance, giving eternal purpose and meaning to one's life.

Faithfully serving others in expectation of a reward also promotes humility. Dietrich Bonhoeffer notes that service based on costly grace guards against pride and self-glory, while aligning the servant's will with God (Bonhoeffer 1959, 88). Service also challenges cultural standards, where recognition often determines whether something is considered a success, rather than embracing the call to accept obscurity, patience, and constancy in serving. When one serves in expectation of God's reward, joy can endure through struggle; the promise of God's reward offers a motivation that strengthens endurance and builds hope (Nouwen 1992, 52).

Furthermore, this service enables humans to thrive together. When Christians serve with an eye to kingdom-mindedness, they reflect God's justice and mercy, and ultimately make visible the hope of His reign (Psalm 37:11; Micah 6:8). Prayer grounds and undergirds this service, bringing believers' hearts to God's purposes, making them contemplative in when, how, and to whom they should serve (Packer 1973, 215).

Serving others in the hope of receiving a reward from God is a spiritual discipline that combines humility, love, and hope. It transforms ordinary acts into encounters with the divine, feeds joy, and exhibits the upside-down values of God's kingdom. By serving faithfully and consistently, believers witness the kingdom reign of God, representing God's grace and justice in tangible ways that extend and illustrate eternal realities (Wright 1996, 432).

Joyful Witness in Suffering and Waiting

To be a joyful witness within a time of suffering and waiting entails a keen dependence on God's sustaining presence. God's kingdom often comes against human expectations, as believers endure trials and opposition, or simply live in unfulfilled longing. However, Scripture reminds Christians to rejoice in every circumstance, knowing that God is always working redemptively (Romans 8:18–25). Paul himself models this exclamation of faith in his letters, encouraging believers to endure suffering with hope, framing trials as opportunities to experience faith and testify to God's faithfulness (Wright 1996, 412).

Joy amidst suffering is not naïve optimism, but is a Spirit-empowered openness to God's presence. John Chrysostom reminds readers of the excellent example of the faithful, who could be living poems of hope by becoming a picture of Christ's sustaining grace (Chrysostom 1986, 234). Likewise, Augustine insists that joy is an inner state, not one driven by worldly circumstances, and that we should ground our hope in God's promises rather than in physical or temporal relief (Augustine 1998, 101).

Waiting—for deliverance, for healing, for the reality of God's kingdom—forces spiritual maturity. Henri Nouwen describes it as a time of pre-refinery, the place where the heart discovers patience, compassion, and trusting in God's timing (Nouwen 1992, 63). By waiting in faith, Christians model what it looks like to behold the upside-down values of God's reign—trust, hope, and love—that have defined history, even when people who have long expected to experience God's intervention through hardship face hardship instead.

Further, the act of joyful witness also bears significance for the community. When Christians witness to a life of trusting God as the Spirit leads them through their suffering, their witness encourages others to trust God's providence for their lives and sustains a "taste of the kingdom." This, of course, aligns with Dallas Willard's claim that ordinary faithfulness exhibited through steadfastness is meant to be transformed into sustained demonstrations of God's reign (Willard 1998, 78).

A joyful witness in suffering and waiting embodies the nature inherent in Christ's transformative kingdom. By remaining faithful and hopeful and following the Spirit's prompting, Christians embody a countercultural joy as a proclamation of God's ultimate victory—a joy that invites others to partake of hope and anticipates the justice, healing, and love of the future reign of God (Packer 1973, 215).

Healing Through Patience and Trust

Healing from a kingdom perspective often occurs slowly, requiring patience and confidence in God's process and timing. In the Bible, it refers to both what God does privately (hidden hearts) and how God relates to others, often with gentleness and wisdom (Ps. 147:3; Isa. 40:31). In this case, patience is not passive waiting but rather an active reliance on God's way of restoring a person, fully acknowledging God's sovereignty over their circumstances and the process of transformation in a person (Wright 1996, 378).

The first church fathers highlighted trust once again, stating how healing and direction were inseparable (Pope Gregory 1863). Augustine of Hippo acknowledged that God's grace often worked through trials or seasons of waiting to teach believers how to depend on God rather than their own understanding (Augustine 1998, 214). Similarly, John Chrysostom taught that a person is considered worthy even while undergoing punishment and experiencing delay, allowing them to learn to be vigilant and humble through their suffering (Chrysostom 1986, 112). The trial became an opportunity for God to form their character, and their hope remains intact.

Waiting for healing is a practice of patience. However, it is also a time of discernment, which Origen illustrates by showing that a person is led by the Spirit patiently through a slow process of reflection, prayer, and surrender, allowing, in time, alignment and fulfillment with God's will (Origen 1996, 87). Thus, we can see that healing, technically speaking, is not simply the result of being restored, whether physical or emotional; it is about reconciliation with God, others, and oneself. Brennan Manning also highlighted the vulnerability a person feels while waiting. During this waiting period, their heart is open, providing an opportunity to build divine intimacy. This intimacy cultivates trust, which in turn builds a foundation for enduring joy (Manning 1992, 49).

Remember also that when we trust God and go through a period of slow healing, it allows space for the Spirit to refine our perspective on even our priorities, helping us reorder them and objectively recognize the difference between kingdom values and immediate gratification (Willard 1998, 132). It has been proposed that trust holds the opportunity to transform a person's pain into growth. Our suffering becomes the tutor of resilience, fostering empathetic growth that engages us in witnessing God's invisible yet faithful character in this undeserving world.

Healing is a journey of patience and trust with God. In these spaces, we embody the paradox of the upside-down kingdom: strength in surrender, peace in waiting, and love in dependence on the Divine (Packer 1973, 201). As believers learn to be patient and trusting in the transformative healing process, they not only experience restoration for themselves but also reflect God's restorative nature to a world longing for hope and wholeness (James 1:4).

Loving Radical Inclusion and Compassion

The Kingdom of God beckons followers to embrace a love that transcends social, cultural, and personal boundaries. Radical inclusion is the defining characteristic of Jesus' ministry, as exemplified by his encounters with tax collectors, lepers, and the outcasts of society, which demonstrate God's love (Luke 15:1–7; John 4:1–42). These encounters teach us that God's love is lavishly given, even to those society has deemed unworthy. Henri Nouwen emphasizes that "true compassion... involves... entering into the life-world of the other human being... being involved in their suffering" and representing God's closeness and concern (Nouwen 1992, 65).

The early Church Fathers also teach about the transformative power of compassion when given through inclusion. Augustine of Hippo provides theological guidance by teaching "that love actively seeks: there is no place for idle love" because, as God's grace flows to humanity, believers too must "love everyone in the world and be equally concerned for each person regardless of personal worthiness" (Augustine 1998, 201). John Chrysostom emphasizes this with his description of love for the outcast as the "ultimate visible testimony that God's final order is breaking into our present world" (Chrysostom 1992, 88). This radical compassion is not merely emotional; it is a shedding of expectations that results in a deliberate commitment to physical acts of service, justice, and reconciliation, seeking to reflect the holistic character of Christ.

The biblical understanding of inclusive love establishes its theological foundation on the affirmation of every person, regardless of context or ideological perception, as image bearers of God (imago Dei). Gregory of Nyssa reminds believers "that it is in seeing God in others that we are called to action—an action of caring beyond mere care for others!" (Gregory of Nyssa 1995, 134). Whether personally or socially, this orientation creates an avenue of transforming the lives of others and thus enabling community flourishing, as the church becomes a space for living out God's restorative and inclusive purposes in tangible ways.

Contemporary scholarship emphasizes the necessity of intentional and participatory effort within God's kingdom. Chester continues by suggesting that radical inclusion is generally not enough. As such, we must first unlearn the prejudices developed through our families, communities, and churches (Chester 2010, 73). Willard states, "Knowing about compassion must… set a baseline for us" within God's kingdom, one that is patient, gentle, and marks our endurance, producing a witness through us in God's way, leading others to faith (Willard 1998, 157).

In Christian practice, radical inclusive love within the community implies going to the margins, speaking the truth humbly, forgiving radically, and embodying the upside-down values of the kingdom for those outside. Such love expresses God's heart (Matt. 25:35–40) while changing their world and revealing God's love breaking into reality. God's heart for humanity, marked by radical inclusion and compassion, impels followers of Jesus to take transformative action in the Restoration and Reconciliation mission that God provides to us.

Practicing Kingdom Hospitality

Welcoming others expresses the values of God's kingdom tangibly, as faithful people extend care beyond their own comfort or social convention. In the Gospels, Jesus exemplifies this openness by embracing the marginalized and the outcast (Luke 19:1–10; Matt. 25:35–40). Such welcome is more than providing food or shelter; it embodies a kingdom ethos that recognizes the intrinsic dignity in every individual as an image bearer of God (Gen. 1:27).

Both early Fathers of the Church and medieval theologians demonstrated that this practice is a multifaceted and integral part of Christian discipleship. Augustine of Hippo taught that the welcome of a stranger imitates God's gracious welcome to all humanity, making it an act of moral and spiritual formation (Augustine 1998, 112). Similarly, John Chrysostom asserted that opening one's home and heart to others is not simply a social courtesy, but rather an extension of divine love (Chrysostom 1992, 76). These early insights illustrate that welcoming others stands at the intersection of ethical obedience and relational care, as well as theology and practice.

Medieval theologians expanded this notion beyond social ethics into a discussion of Christian discipline. Thomas Aquinas claimed that providing welcome and assistance is a moral obligation grounded in charity, as part of God's providence in creation (Aquinas 1947, II-II, 26). Toward a more spiritual dimension, Bonaventure rooted generosity toward others in a personal experience of holiness and communal flourishing (Bonaventure 1975, 88).

Today, the practice remains a vital spiritual discipline for transformation. Brennan Manning emphasized that true welcome is rooted in vulnerability and presence, an invitation into safe spaces where God's love is shown tangibly (Manning 1990, 45). Tim Chester explains that such openness is countercultural: the Christian witness of inclusion becomes a foretaste of God's coming kingdom (Chester 2010, 81). As a sign of God's reign, it is profoundly transformative in its effect on both giver and receiver.

Kingdom-shaped welcome involves patience, humility, and a listening heart, reflecting God's patient and merciful disposition (1 Pet. 4:9). God welcomes us; we welcome others. Believers who live this way exemplify the upside-down values of the kingdom in everyday life. Whether through sharing a meal, offering a listening ear, or sheltering the vulnerable, extending such care embodies the tangible love of God, embracing individuals in a community of joy, healing, and belonging.

Prayer as Participation in God's Coming Reign

Prayer is not simply a spiritual exercise but participation in the active and continuous reign of God. When Jesus teaches the disciples to pray, "Your kingdom come, Your will be done, on earth as it is in heaven" (Matt. 6:10), He invites them to enter into God's redemptive purposes. This act is relational and missional, linking human experience and divine intention (Packer 1973, 215). It is a spiritual practice in which believers discern, receive, and take part in the coming reign of God.

The Patristic tradition emphasizes this relational dimension. Augustine of Hippo notes that communion with God nurtures humility and forms reliance on divine grace, while also shaping the believer's inner life (Augustine 1998, 124). Origen describes this engagement as a way to experience fellowship with God, assuring that those who pray faithfully are led toward justice, mercy, and love (Origen 1994, 67). These early insights reveal prayer as a formative force, shaping both inward character and outward activity.

Medieval theologians expanded on this foundation. Thomas Aquinas taught that petitioning God is not merely a human activity but a means of participating in God's providential ordering of creation. For him, true prayer rightly orders relationships and intentions, aligning human will with divine wisdom (Aquinas 1947, II-II, 83). Bonaventure linked contemplation to this discipline, showing how consistent engagement cultivates union with the Spirit and nurtures action (Bonaventure 1975, 92).

Contemporary theologians also stress its transformative power. Dallas Willard explains that authentic prayer is not a passive recitation but a Spirit-led vision that enables believers to perceive reality from God's perspective, cultivating agency, awareness, and obedience to heaven's values (Willard 1998, 141). Henri Nouwen emphasizes the importance of attentive presence before God, through which believers discern invitations to love, forgive, and heal, recognizing that they are participating in the kingdom (Nouwen 1992, 56).

Prayer, therefore, should never be viewed as a passive petition. It is participatory engagement with God's purposes. Through this practice, believers encounter and witness divine justice, mercy, and restoration in tangible ways. It also forms communities centered on God's priorities. As Paul writes, "the Spirit Himself makes intercession for us with groanings which cannot be uttered" (Rom. 8:26–27), assuring us that in such engagement, believers live as agents of the upside-down kingdom while awaiting the fullness of God's future.

Walking in Daily Life with Eyes Fixed on the Kingdom

To walk in daily life with our eyes on God's kingdom is to embrace a practical way of living faith, hope, and love through spiritual attentiveness. It is to have one's life directed intentionally, knowing that in every mundane moment, one can choose to embrace and embody kingdom values. As Jesus instructed, "Seek first the kingdom of God and His righteousness, and all these things shall be added to you" (Matt. 6:33). This is not a passive pursuit; instead, it requires an intentionality of thoughts, actions, and decisions being aligned with the priorities of God's reign (Wright 1996, 214).

The early Church Fathers discussed how spiritual vision influences our ethical behavior. John Chrysostom emphasized that Christ followers should maintain their vigilance in daily actions, and small actions guided by the Holy Spirit are used to fulfill God's redemption in the world (Chrysostom 1986, 57). Augustine taught that being attentive to God in ordinary routines can bring about inner transformation and authentic bearing witness to God's love and justice (Augustine 1998, 102).

Medieval thinkers embraced this ethic of attentiveness. As a Scholastic, Thomas Aquinas framed habitual conformity with God's will in ordinary, quotidian practices as a means to support virtue and cultivate life in the soul for the benefits of eternal life (Aquinas 1947, II-II, 123). Bonaventure also emphasized attentiveness to the sacred, suggesting that all activities directed toward one in union with God, even daily mundane acts, can be elevated as praise and action for others (Bonaventure 1975, 77).

Modern theologians continue to extend the notion of spiritual vision and attentiveness to our built world and lives through a practical spirituality. Dallas Willard asserts that Kingdom living transforms work, relationships, and leisure, rendering them arenas of obedience and love (Willard 1998, 112). Henri Nouwen reminds us that attentiveness to God's presence in our daily lives leads to compassion, patience, and humility, and prepares us to give witness to the upside-down values of the Kingdom (Nouwen 1992, 61).

To walk with our eyes toward the kingdom is therefore an integrated way of life. Everything that we choose, say, and do becomes a reflection of eternal purpose. It brings the "already" and "not yet" of God's reign into reality in our lives, turning ordinary experiences and actions into sacred opportunities. When we seek God's kingdom in our daily lives, we present ourselves as faithful ambassadors of God by living lives of hope, justice, mercy, and love, while anticipating the fulfillment of God's promises (Col. 3:17; Prov. 3:5–6).

Chapter 10

Living as People of the Great Surprise

The Reversal in Daily Life

To follow Christ means to live with countercultural values. The world values different things: power, self-aggrandizement, and immediacy; yet, Scripture elevates humility, servanthood, and obedience. Each of these attitudes is indicative of God's kingdom and culture (Matt 5:3–12; Phil 2:3–8). Christians are to live counter to the disorder of these worldly values, displaying an upside-down ethic that models the priorities and character of God (Wright 2006, 78). In doing so, they offer a countercultural witness to others, introducing them to the transforming power of Christ.

Believers in God's kingdom are called to humility, gentleness, and servanthood as normative behavior. Augustine of Hippo notes that true greatness is not being socially recognized, but in proximity to God's will and toward others (Augustine 1998, 212). John Chrysostom concurs on this point, urging believers to cultivate meekness and compassion as signs of human maturity, and to imitate the person of Christ, both in word and deed (Chrysostom 1986, 145). This may be illustrated by others' rights or the unfairness of a situation, extending forgiveness when a situation justly demands accountability, or assuming the role that aligns with God, which is often obscured by the world, all of which indicate the character of God to the watching world.

Being compelled primarily by obedience, not convenience, as a form of kingdom living is another theme. Obedience is not easy and incorporates discernment, discipline, and sacrifice, but requires an intensity and devotion to God, and for God's purposes (Deut 5:32–33; John 14:15). Dietrich Bonhoeffer puts it this way: "Costly grace is the incarnation of God. It means the cross; it means the condescension of God." Being a disciple requires costly grace and the disposition to follow Christ when it contravenes one's comfort or social expectations (Bonhoeffer 1959, 89). When Christians consistently act relationally in accordance with God's will from a posture of Scripture, rather than from self-interest and expediency, they build their resiliency to choose to act from a kingdom perspective and play a role in God's ongoing redemptive story every day.

The upside-downness of worldly values creates a life in which the postures of kingdom living are humility, service, and faithful obedience. The countercultural lifestyle is not only ethical, but it is also a tangible demonstration of God's kingdom presence on earth. Every day, Christians make choices that may reflect God's tendency to transform the world, and how others can experience a Kingdom life in God's space and time.

Living Contrary to Worldly Values

To follow Jesus is to embrace a lifestyle that is inherently counter-cultural and runs counter to our society's norms, expectations, and values. While success in the world is often defined by wealth, power, fame, and self-promotion, God's kingdom is instead typified by humility, obedience, and sacrificial love (Matt. 5:3–12; Luke 14:11). Jesus' model of discipleship and proclamation of God's kingdom constantly fractures our social contracts of accepted and anticipated behavior. In fact, Jesus consistently rescues us from the reality that greatness is defined by superiority, dominance, and power, and instead opens our eyes to see that greatness lies in service, and in giving our wills and lives over to the ultimate love and cause of God (Wright 1996, 142). Living morally and ethically counter to that which our society holds as ethical and morally good is not a contrarian thought, behavior, or practice; it is the ordinary act of embodying the principles of the kingdom of God to which one is connected and accountable.

Humility is the starting point of this reversal. Augustine of Hippo argues that in our pride, we hinder and ruin our communion with God. In contrast, humility opens the believer to God's grace and purposes of alignment (Augustine 1998, 67). We do not orient our lives from a humble posture seeking recognition or reward, and we are not top-down models of humility either. We aim to, through a godly humility, distinguish who we are as individuals and misfits, while representing Jesus' meekness and servanthood that we aspire to emulate. For example, John Chrysostom, a prominent prelate, emphasizes that in God's kingdom, we possess actual authority through gentleness to those whom society often forgets and deems insignificant, rather than through coercion or self-legitimization (Chrysostom 1986, 115). These two considerations, humility and authority, run counter to the constructs of what our culture values, which can privilege assertive behavior and self-gratification or fulfillment.

Obedience, however inconvenient, is also one of those practices, but by nature, allows believers to exhibit a counter-cultural following. The imperative to obey God's commands includes our obedience to our obedience that is self-disciplined, takes discernment, and sometimes risks the state of being or the power of our convenience (Deut. 5:32–33; John 14:15). In costly discipleship, Dietrich Bonhoeffer calls this a "costly discipleship" that creates a considerable fracture between Jesus' ways and the world's perception of what is good (Bonhoeffer 1959, 89). God's ways are good, but not often convenient or easy. Believing in God's ways, though inconvenient, fosters spiritual growth and resilience and is a powerful witness to the gospel and a transformed life and heart.

Bringing these ideas together, we regard Deleuze's theory of the "world without the world" as practical because it describes how we navigate a culture that does not offer us whole value systems (Deleuze 1990, 92). The life of faith is always counter to the world. Valuing humility, service, and obedience as a daily commitment to Jesus through ordinary choices affirms God's upside-down kingdom through our lived lives to the present culture and world. The correct value in confronting society's ways is an instance of demonstrating the presence of God's reign and rule in the way we choose to align our actions with the eternality of God's values, establishing a living testimony of our transformed lives.

Humility, Gentleness, and Servanthood as Norms

Living in God's kingdom consistently fosters humility, gentleness, and servanthood as normative virtues, in tension with the assertive self-interest that characterizes much of the world's culture. The image of greatness presented by Jesus in the Gospels demonstrates that greatness in God's eyes is inextricably linked to service and meekness (Matt. 20:26–28; Mark 10:43–45). Humility is not simply a personal quality, but a relational stance that expresses dependence on God while regarding others as more important than oneself. As Augustine points out, it is pride that prevents the soul from presently understanding the truth of God (Augustine 1998, 67). In contrast, humility opens the heart to receive God's grace, wisdom, and guidance.

Gentleness complements humility as it embodies how someone who lives in God's kingdom interacts with others. John Chrysostom writes how gentleness tempers authority with compassion, mirroring Christ's own patience and love for disciples and enemies alike (Chrysostom 1986, 130). Gentleness is a purposeful stance that engages others in a way that fosters peace, and a heart disposition of meekness will nurture relationships in all areas. While gentleness is not passive, it is a countenance that values meek humility in engaging others with the gospel and represents a countercultural disposition where competition and self-promotion are absent from the essence of worldly life.

Servanthood is the outward manifestation of humility and gentleness to act on intrinsic dispositions. Paul encourages believers to live as servants who "bear one another's burdens" and "serve," and fulfill God's law through love (Gal. 6:2; Matt. 25:40). As Dietrich Bonhoeffer writes, the life of a disciple includes realizing that service is costly and includes everything in service to God (Bonhoeffer 1959, 89). Service functions both in moral formation and in ordinary public witness to the transformative power of God's kingdom through actions that may seem insignificant, yet nonetheless sustain a life of love, meekness, service, and patience.

When disciples (believers) embody the disposition of humility, gentleness, and service, they hold an ethic that counter-culturally shapes character, both individually and in community. Dispositions of humility, gentleness, and service, in Christ, provide normative, not optional, virtues for active followers of Jesus that weave together in a mutual acknowledgment of the countercultural, upside-down priorities of God's kingdom. We even see, through N. T. Wright, that the life of Christ provides patterns that ordinary believers can engage in every day to illustrate the love of God and the actions of justice of God, transcending shallow categories, while engaging feelings that allow space for God's own kingdom (Wright 1996, 142). To live out experiences, dispositions, faculties, and skills of Christian virtue, acts, and deeds related to others can shape relationships and communities, along with the views of the public and societal categories, that reflect God's reign and kingdom in ordinary ways.

Choosing Obedience Over Convenience

Obedience to God is a key aspect of life in the kingdom, often involving choosing God's will over comfort, the approval of others, or immediate pleasure. The biblical story demonstrates that God's ways are often contrary to what people most want or prefer. He invites His followers to do what is right even when it is inconvenient for them (Deut. 5:32–33; Luke 9:23–24). Obedience is not merely a way of following the rules or laws, but an expression of a relational trust in God that regards His wisdom and goodness as higher than one's own discernment. John Calvin reflects on this concept of obedience, pointing out that faithful obedience is "an act of a mind changed by grace," which reveals faith being acted upon (Calvin 1559, 210).

Holy Scripture highlights the struggle between convenience and faithfulness to the covenant. Jesus' invitation to "deny yourself, and take up your cross" (Luke 9:23) is a compelling example of the kind of daily suffering and surrender required of a disciple. In Matthew 19, the rich young ruler is another example of the allure of convenience, comfort, wealth, and social status that hinders pursuing obedience. Jonathan Edwards contends that true devotion is not to be equated with outward conformity to rules, but with aligned hearts and wills, even at the expense of worldly benefits (Edwards 1746, 112).

Obedience over convenience can be demonstrated in several mundane choices, such as integrity over expediency in our professional environments, compassion over neutrality in our conversations and relationships, or generosity over acquisition in financial stewardship. Dietrich Bonhoeffer classifies this kind of obedience as "costly discipleship" as faithfulness will require "stepping out" of — and sometimes risk everything in — the comfort of the familiar (Bonhoeffer 1959, 102). These acts of obedience are the practical expression of the upside-down logic of the kingdom of God, fostering less through more for both character and community.

When obedience is expressed in this manner and the experience becomes a habit of obedience, it matures into spiritual maturity and resilience. When an individual becomes convinced that the will of God is more reliable than their own stated preference, they experience a new rhythm of faithfulness that is counter-cultural, patterned similarly to covenantal patterns in Scripture (Deut. 7:9; Rom. 12:1–2). N. T. Wright suggests that disciplined, active choices of obedience—though small and subtle—bring about an environment of opportunity for character and witness as they manifest the reign of God's kingdom in ordinary lives (Wright 1996, 145)

The choice of obedience that prioritizes commitment and sacrifice over comfortable convenience is a weighty and significant allegiance and witness: God's work in the world is far more worthy than any personal satisfaction that comforts an individual. In this act of allegiance, believers become signposts of the kingdom of God—and counter-cultural witnesses—as they resist, yet reveal, the integrity, fidelity, and love of God's surprising reign.

Embracing Christ's Example

Following Christ is key to living as a disciple in the upside-down kingdom of God. The life of Jesus embodies how humility, obedience, and love should integrate in all aspects of human life (Matt. 11:29; Phil. 2:5–8). To follow Christ means to engage the heart and the hands, soaking up His character, and embodying that character through concrete actions. Disciples walk in Christ's way in three ways: by placing themselves in Christ's teaching, seeking to imitate His ethical emphases, and allowing the Spirit of God to guide them in making decisions in their day-to-day lives (France 2007, 88).

The way of the cross, which is the focus of Jesus' mission, informs the practical gestures of ordinary life. Following Jesus requires self-emptying, a readiness to carry burdens, and sacrificial love (Matt. 16:24; Luke 14:27). John Chrysostom emphasizes that discipleship is participative and communal, inviting believers to embody Christ's service and compassion for those around them (Chrysostom 1986, 54). Gregory of Nyssa suggests that the maturation of the spirit occurs through close observance of Christ, which is connected to obedience and meditation (Gregory 1995, 77). When believers follow the way of the cross, they reorder their priorities to focus on God's kingdom rather than the fleeting expectations of worldly success.

As disciples of Christ, living in word and deed means designing our ordinary lives as sacred spaces. It means that simple, functional acts, such as forgiveness, mercy, justice, or humble service, evoke the presence of Christ and the essence of the kingdom of God (Col. 3:12–14). Dietrich Bonhoeffer asserts that this imitation is not an option; it is costly and often unwelcoming, requiring Christians to endure with courage, perseverance, and faithfulness in the face of hardship (Bonhoeffer 1959, 98). N. T. Wright explains that discipleship, emanating from the imitation of Jesus and the cross, brings together the "already" and "not yet" of the kingdom of God, embodying the reality of God's reign in ordinary life (Wright 1996, 147).

Following the example of Christ, personal formation and communal witness join. By walking in his footsteps, taking up his cross, and imitating his life, Christians develop character and behaviors that lift the innocent and upside-down values of God's kingdom, reshaping ordinary life into ways to extend grace, service, and discipleship.

God's Surprising Way

Walking in the Footsteps of Jesus

Following Jesus is more than admiring Him; it is pursuing His character, priorities, and mission intentionally. Again and again, the Gospels illustrate that the life of Jesus was defined by humility, compassion, and submission to the Father (Phil. 2:5–8; Matt. 11:29). Disciples of Jesus are invited to absorb these qualities so they can rely upon His example in wonders throughout their daily decisions, relationships, and vocation (France 2007, 88).

The ministry of Jesus illustrates the paradox of kingdom living: greatness through servanthood, power through humility, and authority through compassion (Matt. 20:26–28). According to John Chrysostom, discipleship is not merely adherence to a list of sayings and practices, but involves concrete expressions of Christ's priorities, including advocacy for the poor, care for the needy, a willingness to serve others, and love (Chrysostom 1986, 54). Therefore, walking in His shoes involves both moral formation and involvement within God's redemptive work.

The call to follow Jesus involves a countercultural lifestyle. In a culture that glorifies self-interest, achievement, and entitlement, the way of Jesus involves self-denial, continued patience, and loving persistence (Luke 14:27). According to Gregory of Nyssa, imitation entails spiritual growth. Imitation involves both reflection on the life of Christ and also living out in practice the conduct of Christ (Gregory of Nyssa 1995, 77). Imitation in the life of Jesus does not mean mechanically mimicking behaviors but rather living in relational response with attentiveness, discernment, and prayer.

Many examples in daily life offer ample opportunities for walking in His shoes. Everyday actions—offering forgiveness, listening to others with sympathetic understanding, giving generously, or advocating for justice—are concrete expressions of the embodiment of Jesus' presence.

Theologically, Dietrich Bonhoeffer would describe obedience to Christ as a costly form of discipleship. In this case, to walk in His shoes means living in His presence with the understanding that community and a relationship with the Father require sacrifice, social ostracism, and a firm commitment to the truth (Bonhoeffer 1959, 98).

Faithful following of Jesus shapes character and community. This means that aligning one's life to His example, and not necessarily only His words, allows the believer to become an embodiment of the upside-down values of God's kingdom. From this model, the ordinary is reframed as spaces where the preference of God becomes an arena for mission, grace, service, and witness. When we walk in His shoes, following in His footsteps, it is an invitation to a mode of life that is contemplative, relational, and transformational. The tangible presence of God can be seen in daily life (Wright 1996, 147).

Following the Way of the Cross in Ordinary Life

Following the way of the cross is a fundamental call to discipleship, yet it is often dismissed as merely representative, symbolic, or abstract. Scripture connects discipleship and bearing one's cross in the identity of the disciple, reflecting a life of self-denial, humility, and obedience (Matt. 16:24; Luke 9:23). This daily practice calls believers to live their lives in the exaltation of God's values over personal comfort or gain, creating ruptures to the countercultural ethics of the kingdom. These moments of choosing the way of the cross reveal not only the common and potential ordinary aspects of life in the upside-down kingdom of God.

Dietrich Bonhoeffer asserts that the cross is not merely a theological concept discussed as a pattern of thought, but a lived experience that requires participation (Bonhoeffer 1959, 98). According to Bonhoeffer, following Jesus involves costly grace, which requires courage to act faithfully in spaces that may be opposed to or completely miss the priorities of Christ. John Chrysostom notes a similar direction toward complete transformative obedience, in which Christians must embody these perspectives through actual acts of care, justice, and service shaped by Christ's way of sacrificial love (Chrysostom 1986, 54).

The posture of the cross influences interactions in everyday life and our decision-making. Whether it is in the home as a family, at the workplace, in the community, or in everyday life, believers are called to embody the same polite humility and sense of selflessness that Jesus demonstrated. Gregory of Nyssa suggests that the practice of dying to oneself in ordinary ways extends transformational understanding and the life of faith within others (Gregory of Nyssa 1995, 77). In Colossians 3:12, 14, Paul encourages the community to "put on" compassion, kindness, humility, gentleness, and patience, demonstrating that living these virtues is part of bearing the cross itself.

Following the way of the cross in ordinary life brings together spiritual formation with witness in literally visible ways. It recognizes that the way of the cross is not simply in the moments of public ministry or extraordinary sacrifices among vibrant church communities, but is equally present in the mundane—the simple act of listening and ordinary acts of service. The cross is framed by every choice, priority, role, and relationship that helps shape these dispositions, character, and the hinge of God's kingdom in the world around us.

Imitating Christ in Word and Action

Imitating Christ in both words and actions is the cornerstone of authentic discipleship. Paul encourages believers to "imitate God, therefore, in everything" (Eph. 5:1–2), demonstrating that the life of a Christian is both an inner transformation and an external expression. Our words, gestures, and selections in life must bear evidence of a character like God—one that is honest, loving, and merciful. To help communities cultivate trust in

God's kingdom, our speech must express divine wisdom. This is a principle that the apostle Paul elaborates further, asking, "Let your conversation be always full of grace, seasoned with salt, so that you may know how to answer everyone" (Col. 4:6).

Following Christ in communities extends beyond words to acts of service, compassion, and advocacy. The ministry of Jesus always had explicit teaching, but it was anchored in action—he healed the sick, fed the hungry, and embraced the marginalized (Matt. 9:35; Luke 7:22). N.T. Wright articulates this very clearly. He argues that embodying Christ's life, as he lived it in action, is essential for kingdom living. Doing so means that our ethical and relational behavior represents the gospel; it does not leave the abstract realities of God's kingdom in the abstract, but instead experiences the concrete and witnesses the visible kingdom that is within our midst (Wright 1996, 147). Acts of daily mercy and justice are not simply admirable, but they become sacramental expressions and indeed embodied expressions of God's nature with and before others.

Early Christian history also provides one more helpful model of imitating Christ. John Chrysostom described Christians as recipients of God's loving life and as ordained "living epistles" in their embodied existence, serving as a testimony to Christ's love through both word and deed (Chrysostom 1986, 102). Gregory of Nyssa observed similar trajectories of growth in the Christian life: when our contemplation of Christ leads to action to serve the loving life of Christ, it connects contemplation with our ordinary lives (Gregory of Nyssa 1995, 77). Henri Nouwen recognizes that ordinary life, when we give ourselves over to God, is indeed our sacred life. Our ordinary lives, when opened up, become enhanced to experience Christ in the world around us. Upon ordinary tasks, such as listening to someone, comforting, or forgiving, we indeed carry the life of Christ in the world (Nouwen 1992, 56).

To imitate Christ is to be intentional, stable, and to rely on the Spirit for help. Our words and actions need to align, unified in bearing witness to

God's kingdom. When we think, speak, serve, even sacrifice, and, most importantly, are obedient, we represent the visible, upside-down values of God's kingdom and testify to an embodiment of the life of Christ.

Joy in Everyday Discipleship

In the Christian life, joy is not simply an occasional emotional high, but a consistent and steady fruit that comes from living into the values of God's kingdom. Jesus continually associates joy with obedience and faithful discipleship (John 15:10–11), and abiding in Christ's commandments brings about abiding in His joy. This joy is transformative, converting ordinary routines and relationships into sacred encounters and spiritual growth (France 2007, 212).

A calling of daily discipleship asks believers to attend to the sacred in all the ordinary things they do. Henri Nouwen writes, "To be able to see God in small and simple things (cooking, cleaning, caring for our children), [provides an opportunity for] taking our ordinary lives and turning them into an experience of devotion, joy, and even happiness" (Nouwen 1992, 37). The regular rhythm of prayers, Scripture reading, and small gestures of kindness cultivates a spiritual attentiveness that fills the ordinary moments of life with significance and joy. Joy is then less about the circumstances and more about participation in God's work in the world.

The apostle Paul also emphasizes this in Philippians 4:4, writing, "Rejoice in the Lord always." The example of Paul's life, marked by suffering and hardship, shows that joy is rooted in faithfulness, not comfort. Dietrich Bonhoeffer reminds us that it is costly grace that allows us to live in true joy, as it calls us beyond ourselves to God's mission (Bonhoeffer 1959, 114). This joy is not a flimsy one; it remains even when circumstances are difficult, because it is rooted in the unchanging and faithful character of God, not in earthly circumstances.

Further, joy in everyday discipleship is the joy of community. Acts of service, encouragement, and burden-bearing (Galatians 6:2) surround and provide spaces for the real presence of God to be expressed and flourish in our relationships (Stott 1994, 79). When we understand our ordinary lived experiences as a stage for living out the kingdom, joy is both personal and communal, as it reflects the upside-down values of God's reign

Joy in everyday discipleship is ultimately a slowly cultivated practice of gratitude, attentiveness, and obedience, where the ordinary details of life are transformed into ongoing encounters with God. It helps us recognize God's presence in both ordinary and extraordinary moments. In our ongoing rhythms of service, prayer, and care for others, we embody the joy of the kingdom of God and reveal God's surprising ways in our daily, ordinary lives.

Finding Delight in Service

Christian joy is closely tied to faithful service. The Bible consistently links joy to obedience to God's commands, often in the context of acts of love and service to others. Jesus teaches in Matthew 25:35–40 that when we serve "the least of these," we are, in fact, serving Christ, and seeing ordinary care for people be endowed with dignity and kingdom orientation. Thus, joy is not merely a feeling but a spiritual stance formed and nurtured by active involvement in God's work.

C.S. Lewis teaches that delight in service flows from the heart being rightly aligned with the will of God; when we serve out of joy rather than obligation, our work is infused with spiritual energy, offering both personal joy and communal flourishing (Lewis 1960, 102). Moreover, John Stott articulates that disciples are called to service, not just to fulfill a duty, but to rejoice in that service, understanding service to be engagement with God's redemptive work (Stott 1994, 78). Paul's exhortation in Romans 12:11 to "be joyful in hope, patient in affliction, faithful in prayer" mirrors this teaching, in that persevering in service to others creates lasting joy.

Average rhythms of life—feeding the hungry, caring for the sorrowing, mentoring or coming alongside the young—will evoke joy in the attempt to serve others. Henri Nouwen observed that acknowledging the sacredness of our daily interactions with the world enables us to share responsibility and turn ordinary activity into joyful experiences of devotion (Nouwen 1992, 41). Even simple expressions, like listening well or interjecting encouragement, provide evidence of God's character and improve the satisfaction of the servant present, who is therein acting from love, as joyful servants.

Service helps learners inhabit the upside-down values of God's kingdom while carrying the countermeasures of our culture that encourage and promote self-interest. Bonhoeffer asserts that costly grace necessitates Christians to transcend comfort and engage in sacrifice, as sacrificial service is the foundation of genuine joy in life (Bonhoeffer 1959, 112). Joy comes from the act of service as part of God's mission, and it will be demonstrated that fulfillment of life occurs in giving rather than receiving.

Emphasizing service as the root of joy will cultivate joy, resilience, and energy, thereby facilitating spiritual transformation in disciples. By following daily acts of obedience, the rhythms of life, formed by love, establish a pattern of life that represents the kingdom of God, allowing God's presence to move into the ordinary and render sacred the space and relationships encountered.

Experiencing God's Presence in Daily Routines

To encounter God's presence in everyday life is fundamental to joyful discipleship. The kingdom of God is not solely visible in special occasions or moments of spiritual ecstasy, but the kingdom unfolds in the ordinary rhythm of life. The ministry of Jesus offers a powerful example of such integration: through meals, teaching, healing, and incidental encounters, the holy invaded the ordinary (France 2007, 189). When believers become aware of God's presence in everyday activities—whether preparing a meal, commuting to work, or fulfilling their vocation—they practice the ongoing reign and work of God in the world.

Henri Nouwen notes that awareness of God's presence often requires intentionality and attentiveness. Attention and prayer can transfigure ordinary activities into sacramental moments, through gratitude and reflection (Nouwen 1992, 42). For instance, actively listening to a friend or paying careful attention to a task is transformed into an act of obedience and love. As faith is integrated into daily life, awareness of God's ongoing companionship develops, and discipleship enters new dimensions of spiritual formation.

The apostle Paul illustrates this in 1 Corinthians 10:31, when he encourages believers to do everything for the glory of God. By examining daily activities as potential means of honoring God, discipleship expands to become a way of being rather than a compartmentalized experience. Dietrich Bonhoeffer argues that present faithfulness in ordinary obligations may provide a valuable expression of what "costly" discipleship entails. He offers this as the Christian through their combination of ordinary external acts—in imitation of Christ (Bonhoeffer 1959, 102). There is a natural disposition toward joyful expectancy when believers envision God as present in their daily choices, which bring both temporal and eternal significance.

Further, awareness of God's presence also increases resiliency. Attentiveness to God provides the basis for patience, gratitude, and trust, contributing to the believer's spiritual stability in challenging situations (Stott 1994, 85). This awareness enriches community life in both the public and private domains of the church, as believers lean into and model attentiveness and care in the ordinary, thereby establishing space for other relational bonds that express God's love.

In other words, being aware of God's presence in daily routines allows life to remain a dynamic and continual encounter with the divine. Throughout the ordinary, the believer shapes spirituality in a manner that cultivates attentiveness, spiritual joy, and a kingdom presence in the world. These ordinary tasks, responsibilities, and relationships provide opportunities for an embodied Christ presence, revealing God's kingdom in often-ignored, yet also extraordinary, moments of life.

Nouwen on the Ordinary as Sacred Space

Henri Nouwen argues that the ordinary places of life—our homes, workplaces, and neighborhoods—can become sacred spaces where God's presence can be realized. Nouwen's reflections offer insight into the nature of the Christian life; it consists of more than thrilling, mysterious moments of revelation. Instead, it involves the mundane aspects of daily life, where the divine acts in unnoticeable ways and interferes with human experience (Nouwen 1992, 38). The ordinary becomes sacred space when believers practice attentiveness, hospitality, and spirituality, and recognize God at work in all things, even in the seemingly trivial aspects of existence.

This aligns with Paul's call in Romans 12:1–2, where believers are encouraged to offer their bodies as living sacrifices and to transform their minds. Ordinary actions or behaviors, such as preparing a meal, offering words of encouragement, or living with integrity in one's own life, become worship or spiritual expression when activity is infused with intent and love. In contemporary terms, Nouwen's insights resonate with the philosophy that holiness is not limited exclusively to sacred spaces, but rather exists wherever ordinary believers engage with the rhythms of daily life with attentiveness to God.

Additionally, Nouwen refers to the ordinary as a preparation for spiritual formation. The mundane and repetition—the boring—become a way of discipline, developing patience and humility (Nouwen 1992, 45). These virtues are necessary for participating in God's kingdom, which is often contrary to expectations of power, honor, and success (France 2007, 201). Finding God's presence in the ordinary cultivates a rhythm of prayer, reflection, and relational attention that enables the believer to fully embody the values of the upside-down kingdom.

Crucially, this ordinary, common disposition also informs the communal nature of group life. Nouwen emphasizes that ordinary encounters with others—such as sharing meals, engaging in attentive listening, or performing small acts of caring—become a sacred expression of God's love. In the process of sanctifying the ordinary, disciples can bear witness to God's action, showing that the reality of God's kingdom is found not only in exceptional events but also in the small and ordinary, where we practice our faith.

All of this stresses that Nouwen respects the paradigm shift he calls the ordinary: sacred space is not somewhere far away or impossible to access; it is actually woven into ordinary life. If believers accept the ordinary as sacred, they are always aware of God's presence (nearness), and their ordinary actions become open conduits of God's grace, love, and the reality of the kingdom.

Healing Through Kingdom Living

The kingdom of God not only offers hope and joy but also a deep sense of restoration for broken lives. The healing experienced from a kingdom perspective encompasses emotional, relational, and spiritual aspects, indicating God's restoration of creation and humanity to their rightful place. The Scriptures depict God as the ultimate restorer and healer who can fix what is broken, restore what is severed, and renew what is weary (Ps. 147:3; Isa. 61:1). Healing is not just the removal of pain, but the presence of God's grace as we journey through life (Wright 1996, 312).

Living in the kingdom invites believers to heal and restore brokenness, as that is part of God's restorative plan. When human beings embody God's forgiveness, mercy, and reconciliation, they become a means of healing in the places where they dwell. John Chrysostom emphasizes the pastoral dimension of caring for one another in relationships, which entails practicing gentleness and compassion in our interactions with others, acknowledging that the health of the community depends on the active expression of God's kingdom (Chrysostom 1986, 102). Augustine of Hippo reminds us that healing is tied to alignment with God's will, and when the soul is aligned with God, it is at peace—and this peace reflects the healing of the soul (Augustine 1998, 134).

Practicing kingdom living will also involve addressing internal brokenness, such as resentment, envy, and pride. The Apostle Paul urges believers to clothe themselves in the fruit of compassion, kindness, humility, and patience, calling them to live lives naturally mitigated from the damage that sin and conflict cause (Col. 3:12–13). Henri Nouwen states that "healing happens when we live our ordinary lives with sacred attention," whereby ordinary actions such as prayer, service, and reflection allow the presence of God to dwell in the ordinary (Nouwen 1992, 47).

Healing in kingdom living is a holistic, dynamic process that incorporates personal transformation, relational restoration, and communal flourishing. When embodied in kingdom living, believers are part of the renewal of hearts and community, illustrating the truth that the gospel is not only a salvific message but also a practical way of living a life grounded in wholeness, peace, and reconciliation. Furthermore, when lived out, the church becomes a prophecy of God's healing presence, inviting others to receive the healing wholeness that comes from a life lived upside-down in the kingdom.

Restoring Broken Relationships

Healing and restoration are essential aspects of the kingdom of God, which reflects the reconciliation brought about by Christ on the cross. Throughout Scripture, we see that reconciliation is a vital concept. For example, Jesus teaches that when reconciliation is needed, a disciple should first restore their relationship with the person and then offer their gifts to God (Matt. 5:23–24). This demonstrates Jesus' belief that worship and spiritual health were contingent on being reconciled. Disturbed relationships, whether with family, friends, or community, disturb our connection with one another, as well as our understanding of the kingdom of God in daily life (France 2007, 215).

Healing relationships begins with humility and a willingness to self-examine. Augustine of Hippo notes that acknowledging personal fault and dependence on God's grace is fundamental for reconciliation (Augustine 1998, 112). By confessing wrongs and seeking forgiveness, the believer participates in God's great work of healing all humanity who have reconciliation in Christ. Likewise, John Chrysostom suggests that reconciliation is a continuous practice of love which requires patience, conversation, and empathy to rebuild trust and harmony (Chrysostom 1986, 58)

Additionally, we find forgiveness to be a crucial factor. Forgiveness is not just about one's own relief, but is a kingdom act that reflects God's own forgiveness to us (Col. 3:13). When a believer forgives another, she relinquishes the power of resentment. She creates a place for reconciling the relationship while displaying the upside-down values of the kingdom—humility and mercy take the place of pride, revenge, and resentment. There are practical ways to make steps toward healing through honest communication, accountability, and shared spiritual practices.

Once again, restored relationships shine a light on the transformative work of God. They demonstrate for all that God's reign is no longer just considered spiritual, but a relational experience where relationships are forever changed. As all our relationships are restored, the community experiences the active presence of living in the kingdom of God, demonstrating that the gospel is ultimately restorative.

So, to heal broken relationships requires intention, grace, and perseverance. Through humility, seeking forgiveness, exercising grace and mercy, we advance the kingdom of God in our relational spheres, engaging in the mission of restoration and reconciliation that reminds the world of Christ in the world.

Freedom from Comparison and Envy

To live in God's kingdom means a radical reorientation of the heart, especially when it comes to viewing ourselves and loving others. Comparison and envy are real, human struggles that can rob us of our joy, undermine our values, and hurt our communities. The Bible regularly encourages believers to cultivate a spirit of contentment within God's provision and calling, teaching that each person's gifts and opportunities are divinely appointed by God (1 Cor. 12:4–7; Gal. 6:4–5). Freedom is only possible when our hearts are freed from the tyranny of comparison and the corrosive effects of envy.

Living in the kingdom of God reframes our perspective on others. Rather than determining our worth based on accomplishments, possessions, or attention, believers are invited to take joy in others' flourishing as the overflowing expression of God's grace (Rom. 12:15). C. S. Lewis argues that God's grace reorients desire, transforming what would have been envy into legitimate admiration rooted in love and encouragement (Lewis 1960, 79), and forming a genuine community in which we celebrate one another's triumphs and serve alongside each other, rather than competing from a place of scarcity.

Spiritual practices help anchor us in this freedom. Daily prayer, reflection on scripture, and the act of gratitude turn our hearts to trust God's sovereignty in our lives, knowing we each move in a designed and directed way (Packer 1973, 215). Likewise, Augustine of Hippo notes that envy is born from a misordered desire, and only a turned heart toward God can reorder those affections and give us peace (Augustine 1998, 122). When we direct ourselves toward God's calling and purpose, we find contentment in our unique contributions and resist the pull of envy and competition for what belongs to us alone.

Moreover, freedom from comparison also enhances our emotional and relational well-being. Henri Nouwen argues that envy leads to isolation, while gratitude and joy within a community build connection and intimacy (Nouwen 1992, 54). By living the kingdom values of humility, patience, and encouragement, we embody the upside-down ways of God, living in a counter-cultural freedom and wholeness.

Freedom from comparison and envy is an integral part of the kingdom of God. It is a means of changing perspective, building community, and understanding God's heart. The believer who chooses to embrace this freedom is a witness to the upside-down kingdom, a means of God's grace, and an encouragement, bringing joy and peace into our everyday lives.

Healing Wounds Through Forgiveness and Patience

Living in the kingdom of God is fundamentally about restoration, reconciliation, grace, and the slow, yet powerful, action of God in the hearts of people. The practices of forgiveness and patience facilitate the healing of individual and communal wounds. Jesus, during his earthly ministry, was extremely clear about the centrality of forgiveness and patience when he said, "Be kind to one another, tender-hearted, forgiving one another as Christ has forgiven you" (Eph. 4:32). When believers extend forgiveness to one another, they are joining God in a restorative work, repairing broken relationships, and creating spaces for peace in our daily life.

The orientation of the heart in forgiveness does not excuse hurt or dismiss justice; instead, it redirects the heart away from bitterness, vengeance, and resentment. John Calvin affirms that true faith produces a posture of letting go of unnecessary grudges because ultimately, God is the only judge (Calvin 1559, 412). Patience will serve believers well because, like forgiveness, it creates space for growth, repentance, and the unfolding of God's slow and redemptive purposes. Augustine reminds us that our human hearts are often delicate, and although it may seem undesirable at times, God has a purpose for extended periods; we need patience to reflect God's patience and encourage long-term reconciliation (Augustine 1998, 223).

The practices of forgiveness and patience also lead to personal and emotional healing. Henri Nouwen writes, "Holding on to our resentment and anger distorts and blocks the spiritual life that leads to intimacy with God and others" (Nouwen 1992, 88). In practicing patience, believers need time for the development of relationships, formative and healing time, and trust to be restored over time. The need for patience is especially true in communities where acts of transgression are prevalent; patience can impact our immediate reaction. We hold ourselves accountable to offer patience and grace in all our relationships, allowing them to flourish.

Forgiveness and patience are both active, not passive, responses to our life experiences shaped by the kingdom of God. Dietrich Bonhoeffer reminds us that costly grace usually requires us to endure pain with love and steadfastness, like Christ on the cross (Bonhoeffer 1959, 101). When believers practice forgiveness and patience with one another, it is an embodiment of God's upside-down ways. In other words, the kingdom is not perishable, but present in our everyday living.

The healing that takes place through both forgiveness and patience is revolutionary. Each interacts with and confronts the ruptured world around us by restoring relationships, helping to heal emotional disorders, and serving as a witness to God's kingdom in everyday contexts. The believer is simply an instrument of God's grace when they embrace such practices and live a reflection of Christ's reconciling love, embodying the lasting imprint of God's restorative work.

Love as the Defining Mark

Love stands as the distinctive feature of kingdom living; it is a mark of our actions and our character. Within the Gospels, Jesus cites love as the defining characteristic that distinguishes the citizen of God's kingdom, holding greater weight than simple rites or authentic social belonging (Matt. 22:37–40). When believers reach out in care and concern, even to those whom society tolerates, confronts, or dismisses, believers are called to an act of radical love—leaving comfortable boundaries to advance the radical love seen in Christ himself. This love embodied the outcast, healed the broken, and forgave the undeserving (France 2007, 156).

Kingdom love can be expressed with acts of generosity and compassion for others. By opening our resources, time, and attention, we embody God's abundant, grace-filled presence in an otherwise stark and burdensome world. Tim Chester notes that acts of serving others, in ways that demonstrate God's priorities, build community and offer glimpses of God's kingdom in everyday life (Chester 2010, 82). Generosity must not be thought of as just giving away goods or as being materialistic. However, it can also include emotional or affirmational support, or being selflessly attentive to another's concerns, as evidence of God's desire for humanity to flourish. Compassion observes distress before anything else, but acts beyond mere empathy because it beckons a response to alleviate suffering and to re-establish the dignity of the afflicted.

The call made by Paul to "bear one another's burdens" (Gal. 6:2) builds on this relational component of love. To bear another's burdens is not a vague suggestion; ultimately, it is the responsibility of the church—the body of Christ. When a person or a community assumes a relational practice of bearing one another's burden, they place themselves within a sense of mutual accountability; we need each other. John Stott notes that practicing this loving action of shared suffering builds the church's community space with humility, patience, and maturity reflective of Christ, and provides the church with resilience in community (Stott 1994, 128). By doing this, believers participate in God's reconciling work; they embrace models of the life of God's kingdom that turn upside down worldly models of individual selfishness, pride, and isolation

However, love as the defining mark is transformative. It is made visible in its consistently costly, action-oriented, and countercultural approach to recognizing God, not just in the ordinary, but in the most extraordinary life contexts. Christians demonstrate love for neighbor, and engaging in acts of generosity and caring for one another by bearing burdens can include a radical life of the upside-down priorities of God's kingdom as its ultimate testimony to the gospel, shaping communities that are expressive of God's grace, God's justice, and God's mercy. Living within the confines of an intentional, give-and-take relational love is a form of alignment between human life and God's purposes, proclaiming the ultimate witness of God's kingdom as a foretaste of God's fullness.

Loving Neighbors Beyond Comfort Zones

The teachings of Jesus consistently overturn the cultural understanding of love by requiring His followers to love those beyond their own circle. In the Parable of the Good Samaritan (Luke 10:25–37), He asks believers to act lovingly toward people across cultural, social, and even personal lines. Kingdom love cannot be limited by what is convenient or familiar, or to what one prefers. Kingdom love seeks out the good of the other, regardless of whether it costs them something or makes them uncomfortable (France 2007, 213). This radical love ethic challenges our tendency to prefer loving people who are like us and exclude others. It instead reflects God's inclusive heart.

To demonstrate love in its entirety beyond the comfort zone requires intentionality and courage. It means seeing people the way God sees them, knowing they are made in God's image—with inherent dignity—and acting toward them in ways that reflect God's grace. John Chrysostom has pointed out the same for Christian love; it is an active love that is sacrificial and initiatory in nature. Kingdom love addresses the needs of the marginalized, the hurting, and the socially ostracized, making the presence of the kingdom of God visible through concrete acts (Chrysostom 1986, 72).

This kind of love is also relational—love extends beyond goodwill feelings to tangible expressions, such as visiting the lonely and bringing them comfort, helping the needy, or advocating for justice. When believers step out to cross social, racial, and economic boundaries, they enact God's reconciling work (establishing glimpses of God's restorative, transformative power) in today's fractured world. Augustine of Hippo noted that this outside love is also an act of humility and dependence on God; love for those beyond the familiar circle fosters trust in God's provision and grace, or as Augustine states, "all human relationships are rooted in grace" (Augustine 1998, 55).

This love is crucial to the narrative of Christ, for time and again, Christ's own life and ministry put the outsider, the sinner, or the vulnerable person at the forefront of the crowd. Living loving others is indeed countercultural and goes against the very fabric of many of our societal norms, where people are excluded, judged, and ignored. In giving love toward one another, believers canonize the upside-down values of God's kingdom and testify to God's transformative work within us (in our hearts) and within our neighborhoods and communities. This kind of love blesses others, often while simultaneously enhancing the spiritual formation of the giver of love. It shapes character for mature discipleship, builds empathy in us even when we hold a different perspective, and enlarges our souls and our capacity for God's presence.

Loving neighbors beyond our comfort zones is living out what it means to embody the kingdom: it is radical kingdom love, kingdom love that reaches down below itself, or in some cases, even risks bits of ourselves for the other, kingdom love that transforms lives in ways human efforts could never.

Practicing Generosity and Compassion

Generosity and compassion are essential marks of the kingdom of God, demonstrating God's character and the ethical implications of discipleship. Throughout Scripture, believers are called to live with open hands and open hearts, caring for the poor, the dispossessed, and the suffering and marginalized (Colossians 3:12–14). To practice generosity and compassion is not merely an optional act of kindness. Still, those who strive to live a kingdom life express God's love in embodied forms (Packer 1973, 214). Through generosity, Christians participate cooperatively in God's work of restoration by offering their resources, their time, and their attention to the needs of others.

Compassion, the active outworking of empathy, requires engagement rather than mere sympathy or concern for the suffering of others. Indeed, the mercy ministry to those in pain and sorrow, as found in the encounters of Jesus—from the lepers to the grieving—portrays love that wades into human shame and pain without reservations (France 2007, 412). Therefore, while believers extend compassion in mentoring others, they embody the heart of God in broken systems, challenging indifference, and building relational bridges where disillusionment and need predominates. The earliest church exemplifies this practice through a community of shared space and sacrificial giving, indicating that generosity is both a spiritual discipline and a communal need (Bruce 1990, 87).

Generosity, as a practice, also transforms the giver. Loosening attachment to things and personal comfort promotes trust in God's provision through relationship and dependence on God, thereby developing greater humility of spirit. Bonhoeffer observed such practices in developing a life of costly grace, where discipleship calls for one to learn to love and care for others, even at one's own expense (Bonhoeffer 1959, 76). The outward display of compassionate action and generous living promotes social transformation, built on the premise of solidarity and hope, and provides a visible demonstration of God's kingdom in the everyday realities of living.

Generosity and compassion are dependent on and shape one another. Generosity without compassion is limited to something remaining transactional; compassion without generosity may be charitable, but it is also limited. Generosity and compassion together provide a living representation of holistic kingdom ethics, where the pursuit of the heart is congruous with the work of the hand, and both are necessary. Believers live and demonstrate the ethics of the kingdom of God by imitating Christ, who gave himself entirely for the sake of all humanity, through the maturity of stewardship. Jesus teaches that the kingdom comes through a witness of loving, yet action (Chester 2010, 145).

Through the incorporation of practices of generosity and compassion, Christians become conduits of God's love and witness to the surrounding world a transformational kingdom, particularly in a world dominated by self-interest and forms of sacrifice and care. This practice promotes spiritual maturity and growth, fosters faith, and reveals the transformative power of God when we live in submission to His kingdom.

God's Surprising Way

Paul's Call to Bear One Another's Burdens

The notion of carrying each other's burdens is a profound idea that embodies being in community as Christians in the relational and ethical sense of God's kingdom. Paul states, "Bear one another's burdens, and so fulfill the law of Christ" (Gal. 6:2), which places caring for one another at the heart of discipleship. Carrying the burdens of others is not just a practical idea, but is actually a theological mandate: it expresses the love of Christ and nurtures the body of believers. When we carry the burdens of others—emotionally, spiritually, or physically—we demonstrate both the church's interrelatedness and God's interest in human flourishing (Packer 1973, 218).

To carry the burdens of others means that we need a posture of empathy, patience, and humility. Paul's language implies that carrying the burdens of others means we must actively participate in the trials and challenges of others rather than only passively sympathizing. Practically, this could involve seeking counsel, providing resources, or simply being there to walk alongside those who suffer. This kind of emotion is reflective of the ministry of Jesus, who fully entered into the world of human pain, addressing mourning, sickness, and the sinner (France 2007, 423). In modeling the love of Christ, believers participate in God's work of redemption, embodying a visible ethic of the kingdom through tangible relationships.

Carrying the burdens of others offers an opportunity for spiritual growth, benefiting both the giver and the receiver of the burden. For the carrier, this creates humility, selflessness, and reliance on God's strength, acknowledging that we are not able to bear the weight of another's struggles alone (Chester 2010, 158). For the burdened, this can provide tangible care and emotional support, as well as a recognition of God's love through fellow believers. Paul reiterates that the Christian life is not individualistic, but communal, and that faith resides in the context of mutual responsibility, where each person contributes to the ability of the whole body of Christ to flourish.

Moreover, carrying one another's burdens provides a dynamic counter against envy, pride, and isolation, as recognizing the values of the kingdom are upside down. The life of the church does not forget that spiritual maturity is not reflected solely through being pious, but in significant ways through our capacity to share in the trials and joys of others. In this action, Christians become real-life emblems of the gospel, imparting love that transcends personal interest, reflecting the very essence of the sacrificial love of Christ (Bruce 1990, 89).

Carrying each other's burdens is a command that holds a blessing, as it fosters a community that reflects the heart of God. It is through these acts of shared suffering and care that the church enacts the Kingdom of God in the journey of everyday life, obeying Christ's law with love and presence among His people.

Biblical Anchors

The believer's existence is anchored and oriented by the biblical vision of God's kingdom. This vision provides lasting, stable anchors in a context of reversal of worldly values. A key component of this vision is the Great Commandment, where Jesus teaches us to "You shall love the Lord your God with all your heart, with all your soul, and with all your mind" and then adds "You shall love your neighbor as yourself" (Matt. 22:37–40). These two commands, together, convey the ethical and relational heart of the kingdom of God, emphasizing that love for God and love for others are inextricably linked. This dual focus challenges the believer to hold together devotion and action, and develop relationships that reflect God's love of covenant (France 2007, 321).

Jesus' parables also offer insight into what life in the kingdom looks like. The Gospels tell parables, such as the Good Samaritan, the Lost Sheep, and the Worker in the Vineyard, to subvert our human expectations of ethics. Each parable reveals the heart of God, which cares for the lost, calls for radical generosity, and emphasizes mercy over rule-following (Bauckham 2006, 189). Parables are more than a lesson in morality; they serve as an intentional invitation into the reign of God as it unfolds within our lives, in stories that reveal the values and priorities of God's kingdom in a concrete and relatable way.

The early church provides both a historic and practical example of how to live out these biblical anchors. Acts 2:42–47 describes people who devoted themselves to teaching, fellowship, breaking bread with one another in prayer, being generous, having all things in common, and being concerned and devoted to one another. In the early church, we begin to see a reversal of worldly norms: wealth was uniformly shared, social boundaries were crossed, and communal responsibility took precedence over individual interest (Bruce 1990, 67). Their life together demonstrates how to embody the teachings of Christ, and now provides contemporary Christians with both inspiration and an example for living out kingdom values in today's world.

Being anchored in scripture reminds the believer that the gospel is not just theoretical, but is a life of relationships and action. As the Great Commandment, parables, and early church teachings embody, scripture serves as a guide to living life that embodies both love, justice, and mercy. Together, these biblical anchors also re-anchor the believer in God's vision, which is the foundation upon which joy, healing, and love flourish fully in everyday life.

The Great Commandment: Love God and Neighbor

Central to Jesus' ethical teaching is the Great Commandment, which succinctly expresses the whole meaning of God's law: "You shall love the Lord your God with all your heart, with all your soul, and with all your mind. This is the first and great commandment. Moreover, the second is like it; You shall love your neighbor as yourself" (Matt. 22:37–40). This commandment serves as both a theological foundation and a practical reference point for the Christian life. Loving God with heart, soul, and mind expresses a total devotion of one's total being—the whole of one's being emotionally, spiritually, and intellectually—the lordship of God, because God is the ultimate source of life, joy, and meaning (France 2007, 321).

Loving one's neighbor involves a commitment to God in a communal, human relationship. Love is not a feeling; it is a discipline of action, particularly with those on the margins, oppressed, and neglected. Jesus' teaching radically changes the notion of obedience to the law from ritual to relational fidelity, where mercy, justice, and compassion are the natural consequences of loving God (Bauckham 2006, 189). Therefore, the vertical relationship and horizontal action reinforce the idea of worship in relationship, as the love of God cannot be practiced without the love of your neighbor.

The Great Commandment articulates the wholeness of this kingdom life. Augustine of Hippo notes that a soul ordered by right loves achieves peace, since God and neighbor are inextricably linked objects of the human heart's orientation (Augustine 1998, 45). Love becomes the motive and measure of life disciplines, moral choices, ethical priorities, and communal life engagements to take part in God's upside-down kingdom. In this humility, acts of service and relational fidelity transform the horizontal spaces of life into a life of the kingdom that opposes injustice, pride, and exploitation within itself.

This teaching challenges the living out of these through daily reflection and disciplined practice. Acts of service, reconciliation, generosity, and presence in the lives of others are specific practices of this dual love. The Great Commandment grounds the believer in an outward life directed towards the heart of God as well as the flourishing of those around them in their environments and communities, implicating one another in the rhythm of love and compassion that begins to reveal what it is to live and take part in God's work through Jesus Christ. It is therefore a guide that is timeless, practical, and transformative, illustrating the manner of character not only in the individual believer but also in the believer's community.

Jesus' Parables on Kingdom Living

The parables of Jesus offer insight into the character of God's kingdom and, more specifically, the values that govern life in the kingdom. Jesus does not offer abstract moral lessons but tells vivid, relatable stories to describe spiritual realities and calls hearers to see God's reality to live with faith and obedience. By doing this, he often challenged the hearer's preconceived ideas, demonstrating the upside-down nature of life in the kingdom of God (France 2007, 254).

For example, the Parable of the Good Samaritan (Luke 10:25–37) challenges the concept of neighbor, demonstrating how love transcends social, ethnic, and religious boundaries. Kingdom living calls for tangible compassion, with no place for prejudice, where mercy supersedes convenience. Likewise, the Parable of the Workers in the Vineyard (Matt. 20:1–16) demonstrates God's generosity and grace, flipping human expectations of fairness and merit. Kingdom practitioners understand that living in God's kingdom is relational in its economy of reward rather than a transaction based on actions and efforts (Bauckham 2006, 198).

Parables also point to the importance of attentiveness and readiness. The Parable of the Ten Virgins (Matt. 25:1–13) emphasizes the importance of vigilance and preparedness for God's unfolding kingdom. Kingdom communities live with an eternal perspective and open themselves to God's unfolding reign, which informs their daily decision-making. The Parable of the Mustard Seed (Matt. 13:31–32) illustrates the transformative and expansive nature of the kingdom of God, showing how the seemingly small act of faithfulness participates in God's great purposes for the future, growing both subtly and powerfully.

The style of teaching through parables inherently invites contemplation and personal appropriation. As the listener hears the story, it is the content of the narrative that invites the listener to see themselves in the story, to examine their assumptions, and ultimately guide their hearts back to the homing device of kingdom values. Gregory of Nyssa notes that the narrative style itself activates the listener's spiritual perception, allowing divine truth to permeate ordinary thought and life (Gregory of Nyssa 1995, 112).

The parables of Jesus teach a life of humility, mercy, and faithful obedience. They reveal a kingdom living characterized by love, grace, and justice, calling disciples to live in ways that reflect God's overturning and transforming kingdom in the everyday rhythms of life. While kingdom living requires a present sacrificial practice, it also anticipates hopeful expectation informed by engaged hearts and faithful hope.

The Early Church as a Model of Upside-Down Living

The early church serves as a tangible example of living in God's kingdom rather than the ways of society. From the very beginning, the initial followers of Christ displayed a radical commitment to love, generosity, and life together that completely overturned the conventional social and economic norms of the broader culture. In the Book of Acts, faithful believers are portrayed as loving and caring for the downtrodden, sharing their possessions, and practicing communal living, prioritizing the common good over individual gain (Acts 2:42–47). This represents the reversal of cultural values and the implications of living further into the gospel by embodying it in daily life (Bruce 1990, 78).

Second, early Christians modeled humility and servanthood in positions of leadership. Leaders, such as the apostles, did not exercise Christ-like authority over the community through domination or privilege but through servanthood, teaching, and self-sacrificing love (Chrysostom 1986, 45). The example of servant leadership challenged hierarchical norms of power and invited others to organize around care and accountability. This ethical practice occurred within the wider social context, where early Christians cared for widows, orphans, and the sick, thereby reintroducing the notion that the disposition of mercy and justice mattered more than status or wealth.

Third, the early church incorporated spiritual formation into the practical expression of communal life. Underpinning community life was the physical rhythms of prayer, teaching, and fellowship, all of which were grounded in a profound devotion to God (Augustine 1998, 112). That is, the newly formed Christians integrated worship, focusing on it amidst the everyday tasks of life. They demonstrated how one's faith can shape one's entire life pattern based on the values of the kingdom. They looked forward to the fullness of God's reign and demonstrated that it was possible to live upside down and contrary to everyday life; the implications of those behaviors were lived-out realities, not simple abstract concepts.

Fourth, the community life pattern also offered a counter-spiritual narrative to the cultural normality of the day. Through radical generosity, ethical integrity, and faithful adherence to the mission of God, the early church presented a credible alternative to the surrounding society's values of success, power, and self-interest. Gregory of Nyssa writes, "A community that emphasizes these specific principles has created a visible reflection of God's transforming presence on earth" (Gregory of Nyssa 1995, 178).

The early church lived upside-down by assimilating faith, ethics, and communal life into their practice of faith. They demonstrated that God's kingdom is most clearly manifested when believers abound in humility, servanthood, and sacrificial love. The early church provides both a model for contemporary discipleship and a present distilled down view of the coming reign of God.

Theological Reflections

The experience of life as a disciple within God's upside-down kingdom is elaborated and sharpened by the theological writings of significant Christian writers. Dietrich Bonhoeffer emphasizes that following Jesus comes at a cost, which discipleship must embrace by focusing on intentional abandon, moral courage, and participation in God's mission (Bonhoeffer 1959, 78). Bonhoeffer describes "costly grace," often directing Christians beyond nominal belief to authenticity, marked by obedience and costly love. Bonhoeffer's thinking on discipleship emphasizes a tension of comfort in the world and high expectations of God's community. These expectations of belonging lead Christians to realize that discipleship includes themselves and their community in daily change.

From a distinctly New Testament background, N.T. Wright emphasizes discipleship through the "already/not yet" of the kingdom (Wright 1996, 214). Wright understands the reign of God is realized in Christ, yet to be fulfilled. This logic helps believers understand their vocation: that they belong to God's kingdom now, and therefore, are called to embody justice, mercy, and reconciliation in everyday life, while also anticipating the restoration of all creation. The kingdom is both the "now" of obedience and the "not yet" of fulfillment.

J.I. Packer helps us connect joy and obedience (Packer 1973, 215). Packer believes that obedient living is transformative, leading to joy in God and character reform. Joy comes easily when your daily living choices, relationships, and ways of being are aligned with God's will, therefore living into kingdom values. Packer reminds us that discipleship encompasses a relationship in which joy in God can accompany moral living and spiritual formation.

Lastly, John Calvin, from the Reformed theological legacy, emphasizes that we are all called to live faithfully every day (Calvin 1559, 322). Faithfulness does not hinge solely on faith practices or spiritual formations, but extends to work, family, and civic engagement. Calvin notably reformulates vocation in ways that attest to the biblical truth that God's kingdom intrudes into all life and our daily structures, where holiness is incarnate in our ordinary lives.

All of theology gives us a helpful picture of discipleship. Bonhoeffer will challenge cost, Wright contextualizes the action of Christ, Packer speaks to joy leading to obedient living, and Calvin speaks to faithful living every day. With the integration of these writings from highly regarded Christians, we are well-supported in enacting and living God's upside-down ways in the world. Even when the cost may dissuade us, we can faithfully and joyfully act and embody kingdom ways in both sacred and ordinary life.

Bonhoeffer on Discipleship and Costly Grace

Dietrich Bonhoeffer's writing on discipleship presents a radical vision of what it means to follow Christ, one that rejects shallow expressions of faith and cultural capitulation. As he lays out in *The Cost of Discipleship*, Bonhoeffer distinguishes between "cheap grace"—a minimum-commitment, nominal faith—and "costly grace," which consists of surrender, radical obedience, and indifference to the moral cost (Bonhoeffer 1959, 45). For Bonhoeffer, discipleship is inseparable from the lifework, suffering, and example of Jesus. Christians are called to actively participate in God's reign, to accept the risk of ethical self-denial, and to serve others at their own personal cost.

A central aspect of Bonhoeffer's thinking is that grace is never without costs. While God's forgiveness is granted without merit, it always invites a response in the form of obedience. Obedience is not legalism; obedience is relational, conveying trust and love within a community, along with fidelity to the one who leads faith into a community of mission. In everyday life, examples include mercy over self-interest, the risk of confronting unjust practices, or humble service without recognition. Bonhoeffer draws attention to the concrete elements of discipleship; faith extends to being lived out both inside and outside worship services on Sunday mornings, grounding the legwork of kingdom life in the rhythms of everyday life

Bonhoeffer is also attentive to the communal aspects of costly grace. Participating in the life of each other's church is costly grace lived out in the communal life of the church. This is exemplified in the communal life of believers, characterized by relationships marked by love, humility, and service, even to a sacrificial extent. Bonhoeffer's communal ethic alludes to the biblical pattern of shared life, generosity, and care for the marginalized (Acts 2:44-47).

Bonhoeffer is calling contemporary followers of Jesus into a radical, transformative vision of living for Christ that, in many ways, rejects cultural complicity and a "passive" and empty religious life. Discipleship is, in his assessment, intensely personal and inherently collective, and there is no discipleship without a living obedience to the example of Christ. Discipleship reorients ordinary daily life to literally be the venue where God's surprising kingdom is revealed. Bonhoeffer aims to reframe the choices of daily life as vectors of grace, witness, and moral courage. In costly grace, there is possibility and a more authentic negotiating of God's call on our lives, faithful living in community, and embodying the upside-down values of the kingdom in every aspect of life.

Wright on the Kingdom Now

Scholar N. T. Wright's work on the kingdom of God emphasizes both its present and future aspects, highlighting the tension that theologians often refer to as the "already/not yet" tension (Wright 1996, 89). Wright contends that Jesus inaugurated the kingdom through his life, teaching, miracles, and most significantly, the resurrection, as embodied evidence of God's power breaking into history. Believers in Christ are welcome to participate now, in everyday experience, in God's kingdom and reign, and the consummation to come.

For Wright, the kingdom is no mere abstract spiritual reality; rather, it is a physical reality that has the capacity to change and transform the world. It can be seen in acts of justice, mercy, reconciliation, and in worship, which reflect God's intentions and purposes in creation. Wright claims that Christians are called to embody these values in their own lives, in their domestic lives, their work lives, and in their community lives, through their choices and how they inhabit their organizations and relationships, and embody Christ's values and priorities. The moral dimension of the kingdom is inseparable from the social, because faithful living necessitates personal holiness and a living engagement in the world as it reaches for shalom, consistent with Jesus' call to love one's neighbor and serve the marginalized (Matt. 25:31–46).

Wright emphasizes a second point, which is the role of the Spirit who empowers Christians to live as those displaced—to live as kingdom citizens, in the present. Through the Spirit, believers are empowered to withstand the patterns of the world, pursue justice, and seek relational peace. The present reality of the kingdom prompts Christians to view everyday life as a holy space where God's reign intersects with tangible and physical realities (Wright 2006, 121). Even in mundane, invisible acts of obedience and compassion, the very values of God's upside-down reign find root, and seeds are sown for future hope.

Wright goes on to add that anticipating the consummation that is characteristic of the kingdom shapes present actions. Christians live with a forward-looking faith that looks at every situation with the confidence that God will renew all of creation; God will ultimately bring justice to the world. This final vision is what inspires future courage to endure trials, ethical courage, and agency and care for others—the value of God's reign lived out in word and deed. Living out the values of the kingdom in everyday life positions believers to be witnesses to God's surprising, transformative, and unexpected work, becoming agents who embody hope, justice, and love, even in a broken world, for the present.

Wright proposes a theology of the kingdom that calls Christians to integrate a response to the kingdom now, in anticipation of its future hope, and to live ethically, courageously, and responsively to the unfolding activity of God's will. The present is evident in every act of obedience to the Spirit, as well as in community and relationships where Christians interpret and discern the reign of God.

Packer on Joy and Obedience

J.I. Packer emphasizes that true Christian joy is closely tied to obedience to God. Joy is more than just an emotion based on circumstances; it is a deep and lasting joy rooted in knowing and experiencing God's presence (Packer 1973, 215). Obedience is not just an obligation; it is how believers participate in God's life, aligning their will to his, and enjoying the experience of faithful living.

Packer argues that the act of obedience functions as a maker of spiritual formation, shaping both the heart and mind to be more like God's character. When believers follow God's commands, they can live in harmony with God's grace, even in the face of trials, and find stability and perspective in an often chaotic world. Joy is the byproduct of this faithful alignment, both a fruit of obedience and a reflection of God's work (Packer

1973, 220). This also means that everyday events, whether at work, in the family, or in the community, become avenues of spiritual delight, and everyday acts take on a sacred character.

Theological reflection reminds us that obedience is better understood as a relational concept, rather than a transactional one. Packer draws on biblical narratives to argue that God delights in his people's willing response to his will (John 14:15). This relational act of obedience moves believers toward intimacy with God. Joy is not simply an experience of contentment but participation in the expanding purposes of God. Spiritual life, therefore, will be ethical, service-oriented, and marked by moral courage, all grounded in the confident knowledge of God's sustaining love and promises (Rom. 12:1–2).

Moreover, Packer moves from obedience to hope, noting that continual faithfulness prepares believers for future glory. Tuning one's life to the Word of God is a spiritual discipline that deepens resilience, moral character, and a joy that transcends worldly circumstance. Such a vision importantly recognizes that the absence of difficulty does not determine joy, but by the presence of God in the life of each believer, discovered in acts of faith, service, and love.

Packer presents a bigger vision of Christian life, in which joy and obedience are intertwined. By following God's commands, believers enter into a transforming reality of a flourishing life. Obedience leads to joy, and joy leads to more obedience, drawing believers into the life of God, which is an expression of the purposes of God's kingdom in our daily lives.

Calvin on Living Faithfully in Daily Life

John Calvin's theology emphasizes the importance of faith for the enjoyment of every dimension of daily life. In Calvin's view, it is the Christian's vocation to engage creation actively in ways that acknowledge God's control and serve His Word (Calvin 1559, 112). Faith means to live well, to live ethically, and to live consistently in making progress toward living as God would have us live

Calvin asserts that no segment of a Christian's life is exempt from God's rule, which lends significance to ordinary work and service to God. Work, home, and community service are not secular activities that one engages in apart from their spiritual life; instead, they are opportunities to give God glory and tangibly represent His kingdom (Calvin 1559, 118). This perspective affords a sense of vocation, where every activity has some part in God's redeeming plan.

At the heart of Calvin's teaching is the notion of obedience and humility. To live faithfully means recognizing our human limitations and trusting God's grace to provide the strength and insight necessary for moral discernment and endurance (Calvin 1559, 122). Through Christ's grace and the work of the Spirit, faithful Christians are marked by integrity, perseverance, and consistency, as reflected in the way they embody the ethical values of the kingdom in their ordinary lives.

Calvin stresses that faithfulness includes communal accountability. Christians are called to live in ways that reflect well on the community, living justly, mercifully, and stewarding their lives in a way that pleases God (Matt. 22:37–40). When Christians engage with others as faithful members of the community, this displays God's love in tangible ways that connect the believer's devotion and social responsibility. In this, obedience and service become cyclical and mutually dependent; faithful living encourages spiritual growth, and spiritual growth, in turn, informs faithful living

Calvin develops a view of Christianity in which devotion is deeply embedded in daily living. Faith is a real, lived experience that consists of actions of service, ethical decisions, and constant obedience, producing a life filled with coherence, moral courage, and joy in God's providential care. Faithful living causes the believer to be involved in God's kingdom activity, demonstrating that the ordinary experiences of life shaped by God's grace become a stage for God's artistry and glory.

Practicing the Great Surprise Today

To live as a participant in God's astounding kingdom requires intentionality with our day-to-day lives. God's "great surprise," in His upside-down ways, invites us to embody values that are frequently at odds with societal norms, demonstrating love, joy, and healing in our ordinary lives. This journey begins through intentional choices rooted in everyday life that establish both character and testimony. Every interaction with family, coworkers, and even strangers can become a canvas for us to paint the ethics of the kingdom (Chester 2010, 45; Wright 1996, 312).

The day-to-day life choices we make that reflect the kingdom can range from minor, simple actions to significantly larger gut decisions. The practice of humility, patience in the face of trials, and generosity to those in need are tangible ways we can illustrate God's surprise by reversing worldly priorities. When we consciously choose obedience over convenience, compassion over indifference, and service over selfishness, we are pursuing the radical ethic of Christ in real time (Bonhoeffer 1959, 102; Packer 1973, 198). Even regular routines, when done—such as preparing meals, answering emails, and mentoring a coworker—can serve a spiritual purpose, transforming the ordinary into a sacred opportunity.

Community also plays a vital role in experiencing and practicing the great surprise. We are not called to embody the values of the kingdom within ourselves, but rather, we can do this in relationships with those who mirror God's love. Shared life offers communal encouragement and accountability—spaces where collectively, love, joy, and healing are cultivated (Nouwen 1992, 77). The church, small groups, and friendships intentionally structured for this purpose become like a laboratory for experimenting with, recalibrating, and celebrating the principles of the kingdom.

Additionally, embodying God's upside-down ways will require courage and creativity. In work, family, and neighborhood scenarios, we meet the cultural norms of society with a spirit of patience, grace, and unwavering commitment to justice and mercy (Wright 2006, 145). All the ways we follow through on a choice to serve, uphold ethical norms, or make principled speech can assert the reality of a kingdom that surprises and transforms.

Lastly, engaging in the great surprise is a lifelong journey. It involves devotion, reflection, and action, and it generates lives infused with hope, faith, and ultimate love. When lives lived in practical alignment with God's kingdom values are viewed in ordinary moments, they demonstrate the extraordinary reality of God's transformative ways in tangible and everyday ways.

Daily Choices that Reflect the Kingdom

The reality of kingdom living is realized in the everyday decisions that we make in life. While theological truths and spiritual beliefs are important, it is through habitual choices that the upside-down ways of God become visible. The call upon believers is to align every action, word, and thought with the values of Christ's kingdom, making the point that God's reign is absolute and in action in human experience (Chester 2010, 51; Wright 1996, 315).

Little acts of obedience and kindness are most clearly a display of the reality of God's kingdom on earth. Choosing patience in the face of frustration, speaking a word of encouragement to a tired colleague, and extending hospitality to a stranger are tangible examples of how love, mercy, and justice are embodied in ordinary, daily settings. These choices shape who we are, strengthen our faith, and create practices of discipleship that form nations, families, and cultures over time (Bonhoeffer 1959, 108; Nouwen 1992, 81). Living in the reality of the kingdom of God, or living upside-down, is to live in the ordinary parts of life.

The intentional action of reflecting God's values and priorities over society's values and priorities requires discernment and courage. Christians are intentional; we must not be influenced by consumerism, self-centeredness, and cultural conformity, but instead embrace a countercultural ethic of humility, generosity, and integrity (Packer 1973, 221; Wright 2006, 150). These decisions often involve ethical tension, yet prayer and the Holy Spirit guide us in making wise and faithful daily choices in life.

Also, daily choices stretch beyond the personal to relational engagement. A kingdom that reflects living invites accountability, seeks reconciliation, and works for justice, which points others toward the reality of the reign of God. Whether in our family patterns, our workplace, or our civic responsibilities, the life of the believer becomes a natural witness that demonstrates the transformational quality of God's upside-down wisdom (Chester 2010, 63; Wright 1996, 318).

Choices for the kingdom demonstrate a life of intention, joy, and spiritual integrity. These choices prove that the great surprise of God's reign is not abstract, but concrete, and it calls all followers of Jesus to be involved in practicing and bringing kingdom values into earthly expression. When we consistently choose love, service, and obedience, we shape the present and future reality of God's kingdom.

Community as a Laboratory for Love, Joy, and Healing

The Christian life is never meant to be lived in isolation. Scripture consistently emphasizes the relational nature of God's kingdom, where the church functions as both a spiritual family and a laboratory for practicing kingdom values (Chester 2010, 77; Nouwen 1992, 95). Within the community of believers, love, joy, and healing are not abstract ideals but lived realities, tested, refined, and made visible through human interaction.

Love within the community provides the primary context in which Christ's teachings are applied. The call to bear one another's burdens (Gal. 6:2) is not theoretical; it requires practical engagement, empathy, and sacrificial care. Through shared struggles, encouragement, and mutual accountability, believers cultivate a culture of care that reflects God's character and fosters spiritual growth (Bonhoeffer 1959, 112; Augustine 1998, 134). Even disagreements, when approached with humility and patience, become opportunities for teaching, reconciliation, and deepening trust.

Joy in the Christian community is similarly experiential. It is nurtured through shared worship, celebration, and service, where the presence of God is experienced collectively. The early church exemplified this dynamic: believers met together daily, shared possessions, and rejoiced in both the trials and victories of their members (Acts 2:42–47). Such shared life demonstrates that joy is not merely an internal sentiment but a communal expression of God's kingdom at work in human relationships (Chester 2010, 79; Wright 1996, 330).

Healing, both emotional and spiritual, is another key outcome of a Christ-centered community. Through confession, encouragement, and the practice of forgiveness, wounds inflicted by sin, envy, or broken relationships find restoration (Matt. 18:15–17). Spiritual disciplines—prayer, guidance, and teaching—are interwoven with relational care, creating an environment where individuals experience God's restorative power tangibly (Nouwen 1992, 97; Bonhoeffer 1959, 115).

In this "laboratory," the believer learns to integrate faith with action, demonstrating that God's upside-down kingdom is relational, transformative, and communal. By engaging intentionally in the practices of love, joy, and healing within the community, believers participate actively in God's work, embodying the present reality of His reign and preparing for its ultimate fulfillment.

Witnessing God's Upside-Down Ways in Work, Family, and Neighborhood

Being a follower of Christ entails living out the values of God's kingdom in every context, forming an "upside-down" dynamic that is in stark contrast to how the world works (Wright 2006, 142; Packer 1973, 180). Work, family, and neighborhood become the vehicles through which kingdom characteristics—such as humility, service, justice, and compassion—take shape into tangible activities, thereby transforming everyday experiences and activities into opportunities for spiritual growth.

In the workplace, a follower of Christ is challenged to be known for integrity, generosity, and excellence—not for the sake of self-promotion, but for the sake of God (Col. 3:23–24). This upside-down approach can manifest as prioritizing fairness over competition, serving one's colleagues sacrificially, or practicing patience and grace in the midst of pressure and conflict (Stott 1994, 85; Calvin 1559, 290). Every decision, favorable or not, is a display that God's values are more important than a worldly notion of success.

Family life is also a powerful place for a follower of Christ to embody the kingdom. The love, forgiveness, and sacrificial service in the family embody Christ's relationship with the church (Eph. 5:21–33). Parents, siblings, and married partners model patience and reconciliation, demonstrating to children and family what it means to live in the upside-down way of God's kingdom (Augustine 1998, 210; Bonhoeffer 1959, 120). Even in familial conflict, choosing humility and mercy over pride and bitterness has a distinct impact on changing the trajectory of responses and demonstrating the transformative power of the gospel.

Neighborhoods and communities provide examples of how one can live differently. Kindness, justice, ministry to the marginalized, and faithfully loving your neighbor display the fundamental nature of God's kingdom (Luke 10:25–37). In this case, acts of mercy, generosity, and being a good neighbor reflect ways of being that are distinct from a way of living rooted in self-interest, fear, or apathy (Chester 2010, 88; Nouwen 1992, 103).

Living an upside-down life is not contingent on grand gestures. Living out the upside-down way is more about incremental and ordinary ways of living faithfully. Through work, family, and neighborhood, a follower of Christ has tangible opportunities to display the kingdom, showing that qualities of living—such as humility, service, and sacrificial love—inform ways of being that involve radical faith lived out in the midst of everyday life.

Living with Hope, Faith, and Persistent Love

In Christian discipleship, believers are called to a way of life characterized by a steadfast hope, unwavering faith, and persistent love, which expresses the reality of God's kingdom breaking into daily life (Wright 2008, 67; Packer 1973, 210). These qualities are not abstract ideals but lived principles that must inform one's choices, relationships, and responses to the good and the bad.

Hope holds the believer in the tension of the "already and not yet" of the kingdom of God (Rom. 8:18–25). Hope energizes Christians to endure hardships with the firm knowledge that while the present may hold struggles, the hardships will not last, and God's promises stand (Nouwen 1992, 45). Hope is both anticipatory and practical and propels all action that advances justice, mercy, and reconciliation in the here and now (Brueggemann 1994, 112). Hope is the lens through which ordinary experiences take on eternal importance.

Faith is closely tied with hope in one's relationship with God and requires believing in God's character and divine provision. There are numerous opportunities in daily life to practice faith as one lives in obedience, patience, or relies on God rather than human strength (Heb. 11:1–3). Faith becomes experienced when someone chooses what is right, compassionate, and courageous even when the outcome is unknown (Bonhoeffer 1959, 89; Augustine 1998, 205). In doing so, believers demonstrate that the kingdom of God is real, as evidenced in their transformed life patterns and behaviors.

Persistent love—agape—roots hope and faith in real experience. Love can bear or endure beyond seasonality and circumstances, forgiving wrongs and reconciling divided lives, and carrying the burdens of others (1 Cor. 13:4–7; Col. 3:12–14). Love shapes interactions in families, communities, workplaces, and even with strangers, demonstrating that God's upside-down kingdom is at work within the norms of individual human relationships (Chester 2010, 95; Nouwen 1996, 102).

Ultimately, the hope, faith, and persistent love embodied in one's life are a holistic response to the considerable surprise of God's breaking into ordinary life, His kingdom. Living these virtues enables Christians to become living witnesses of the reign of God and invite others into that ongoing journey, as they catch a glimpse of God's nearness through the actual presence of His people and return to good order, inviting others to the redemptive purpose of God in the world.

References/Bibliography

À Kempis, Thomas. 1425. *The Imitation of Christ*. Translated by Aloysius Croft. New York: Image Books, 1997.

Aquinas, Thomas. 1274. *Summa Theologica*. Translated by Fathers of the English Dominican Province. Westminster, MD: Christian Classics, 1981.

Aquinas, Thomas. 1947. *Summa Theologica*. Translated by Fathers of the English Dominican Province. New York: Benziger Brothers.

Augustine of Hippo. 1991. *The City of God*. Translated by Henry Bettenson. London: Penguin.

Augustine of Hippo. 1998. *Confessions*. Translated by Henry Chadwick. Oxford: Oxford University Press.

Bauckham, Richard. 1996. *Jesus and the God of Israel*. Grand Rapids: Eerdmans.

Bauckham, Richard. 2006. *Jesus and the Eyewitnesses: The Gospels as Eyewitness Testimony*. Grand Rapids: Eerdmans.

Billings, J. Todd. 2011. *Union with Christ: Reframing Theology and Ministry for the Church*. Grand Rapids, MI: Baker Academic.

Bonhoeffer, Dietrich. 1959. *Life Together*. Translated by John W. Doberstein. New York: Harper & Row.

Bonhoeffer, Dietrich. 1959. *The Cost of Discipleship*. New York: Macmillan.

Bonhoeffer, Dietrich. 1995. *The Cost of Discipleship*. New York: Touchstone.

Bonhoeffer, Dietrich. 2009. *Letters and Papers from Prison*. Edited by Eberhard Bethge. Minneapolis: Fortress Press.

Bonaventure. 1268. *Commentary on the Sentences*. Florence: Quaracchi Press.

Bonaventure. 1975. *Journey of the Mind to God*. Translated by Philotheus Boehner. Hyde Park, NY: New City Press.

Brueggemann, Walter. 1994. *The Message of the Psalms: A Theological Commentary*. Minneapolis: Augsburg Fortress.

Brueggemann, Walter. 1994. *Theology of the Old Testament: Testimony, Dispute, Advocacy*. Minneapolis: Fortress Press.

Bruce, F. F. 1988. *The New Testament Documents: Are They Reliable?* Downers Grove, IL: InterVarsity Press.

Bruce, F. F. 1990. *The Book of Acts*. Grand Rapids: Eerdmans.

Calvin, John. 1559. *Institutes of the Christian Religion*. Translated by Henry Beveridge. Peabody, MA: Hendrickson.

Carson, D. A. 1991. *The Gospel According to John*. Grand Rapids, MI: Eerdmans.

Chester, Tim. 2010. *A Meal with Jesus: Discovering Grace, Community, and Mission around the Table*. Wheaton, IL: Crossway.

Chrysostom, John. c. 347–407. *Homilies on Various Texts*. Translated by J. W. S. Kennedy. London: SPCK, 202.

Chrysostom, John. 1986. *Homilies on 2 Corinthians*. Translated by Robert C. Hill. Crestwood, NY: St. Vladimir's Seminary Press.

Chrysostom, John. 1986. *Homilies on Matthew*. In *Nicene and Post-Nicene Fathers*, First Series, Vol. 10, edited by Philip Schaff. Peabody, MA: Hendrickson.

Chrysostom, John. 1992. *Homilies on the Gospel of John*. Edited by W. R. W. Stephens. Downers Grove, IL: InterVarsity Press.

Edwards, Jonathan. 1746. *The Religious Affections*. Boston: T. & J. Fleet.

France, R. T. 2007. *The Gospel of John*. Grand Rapids: Eerdmans.

France, R. T. 2007. *The Gospel of Matthew*. Grand Rapids: Eerdmans

Gregory of Nyssa. 1993. *On the Soul and the Resurrection*. Translated by Abraham J. Malherbe. Washington, DC: Catholic University of America Press.

Gregory of Nyssa. 1995. *The Life of Moses*. Translated by Abraham J. Malherbe and Everett Ferguson. New York: Paulist Press

Hauerwas, Stanley. 2001. *With the Grain of the Universe: The Church's Witness and Natural Theology*. Notre Dame, IN: University of Notre Dame Press.

Holy Bible. 1982. *New King James Version*. Nashville: Thomas Nelson.

Irenaeus. 1997. *Against Heresies*. Translated by Dominic J. Unger. New York: Paulist Press.

Kuyper, Abraham. 1898. *Lectures on Calvinism*. Grand Rapids, MI: Eerdmans.

Lewis, C. S. 1943. *Mere Christianity*. New York: Macmillan.

Lewis, C. S. 1960. *The Four Loves*. London: Geoffrey Bles.

Luther, Martin. 1520. *The Theology of the Cross*. Wittenberg: Johann Rhau-Grunenberg.

Luther, Martin. 1957. *Lectures on Romans*. Translated by Wilhelm Pauck. Philadelphia: Fortress Press.

Luther, Martin. 1960. *The Freedom of a Christian*. Philadelphia: Muhlenberg Press.

Manning, Brennan. 1990. *The Ragamuffin Gospel*. Nashville: Thomas Nelson.

Manning, Brennan. 1992. *Abba's Child: The Cry of the Heart for Intimate Belonging*. Nashville: Thomas Nelson.

Manning, Brennan. 1993. *The Signature of Jesus: The Call to a Life of Radical Love*. New York: HarperCollins

Moo, Douglas J. 1996. *The Letters to the Colossians and Philemon*. Grand Rapids: Eerdmans.

Nouwen, Henri. 1992. *Life of the Beloved: Spiritual Living in a Secular World*. New York: Crossroad.

Nouwen, Henri. 1994. *The Return of the Prodigal Son: A Story of Homecoming*. New York: Image Books.

Nouwen, Henri. 1996. *Life of the Beloved*. New York: Crossroad.

Origen. 1996. *On First Principles*. Translated by G. W. Butterworth. Washington, DC: Catholic University of America Press.

Origen. 1999. *Commentary on 2 Corinthians*. Translated by Ronald E. Heine. Washington, DC: Catholic University of America Press.

Owen, John. 1968. *The Mortification of Sin in Believers*. Edinburgh: Banner of Truth.

Owen, John. 1980. *The Works of John Owen, Vol. 7*. Edinburgh: Banner of Truth.

Packer, J. I. 1973. *Knowing God*. Downers Grove, IL: InterVarsity Press.

Paul. In the Holy Bible, Colossians 3:12–14; Romans 8:18–25.

Stott, John. 1986. *The Cross of Christ*. Downers Grove, IL: InterVarsity Press.

Stott, John. 1994. *The Message of the Sermon on the Mount*. Downers Grove, IL: InterVarsity Press.

Torrell, Jean-Pierre. 2005. *Saint Thomas Aquinas: The Person and His Work*. Washington, DC: Catholic University of America Press.

Willard, Dallas. 1998. *The Divine Conspiracy: Rediscovering Our Hidden Life in God*. San Francisco: HarperSanFrancisco.

Willard, Dallas. 1998. *The Spirit of the Disciplines: Understanding How God Changes Lives*. San Francisco: HarperSanFrancisco.

Wright, N. T. 1996. *Jesus and the Victory of God*. Minneapolis: Fortress Press.

Wright, N. T. 2006. *Simply Jesus: A New Vision of Who He Was, What He Did, and Why He Matters*. New York: HarperOne.

Wright, N. T. 2008. *Surprised by Hope*. New York: HarperOne.

www.ingramcontent.com/pod-product-compliance
Lightning Source LLC
LaVergne TN
LVHW011926070526
838202LV00054B/4507